Turbo Pascal®
Programmer's Library

Turbo Pascal®
Programmer's Library

Kris Jamsa
and
Steven Nameroff

Osborne **McGraw-Hill**
Berkeley, California

Osborne **McGraw-Hill**
2600 Tenth Street
Berkeley, California 94710
U.S.A.

For information on translations and book distributors outside of the U.S.A., please write to Osborne **McGraw-Hill** at the above address.

A complete list of trademarks appears on page 485.

Turbo Pascal® Programmer's Library

 234567890 DODO 89876

ISBN 0-07-881238-0

Jon Erickson, Acquisitions Editor
Lorraine Aochi, Technical Editor
Herbert Schildt, Technical Reviewer
Fran Haselsteiner, Project Editor

Contents

Preface

Pascal was developed in 1971 by Niklaus Wirth in response to a growing need for a structured, modular, strongly typed, and systematic programming language. Wirth, who had previously developed the languages Algol and PL/1, understood the importance of providing a programming language that would encourage structured programming, aid program development, and facilitate the learning of advanced programming concepts, such as pointers, records, and dynamic variables.

Since that time, Pascal has become the accepted standard for teaching data structures and programming concepts at many universities. As graduates leave the academic arena, they take Pascal to the rest of the world. Thanks to Borland's Turbo Pascal, Pascal is likely to become the most widely used microcomputer programming language over the next several years. In fact, the Turbo Pascal environment has become so popular that most programming language developers will have no choice but to migrate to the interactive programming environment that it provides. In addition, Turbo Pascal will have a significant impact on the ISO Pascal standard. Pascal compilers at all levels—from microcomputer to mainframe—will begin to look more like Turbo Pascal, with interactive program development and a powerful collection of built-in library routines. In the years to come, businesses and organizations will view the skills of a programmer with a strong background in Pascal—especially Turbo Pascal—as a valuable asset.

Library Routines

Maintaining a library of routines is one of the best ways to enhance the productivity of programmers. Programmers often spend time creating routines already existing in other applications. If you work in a programming shop, keeping suitable routines in a library will increase the productivity of all programmers in the organization for several reasons. First, duplication of effort is minimized since every programmer has access to the routines in the library. Second, programming skills are improved through exposure to "good" code: examining another programmer's code provides an important opportunity to learn and to exchange ideas. Finally, standardization of code, documentation, and error checking is possible because the source code is available for examination. If you are a hobbyist, placing your routines into a library will improve your diskette organization.

This text provides an extensive library of routines for the Turbo Pascal programming environment. Each routine was developed to simplify its integration into your applications programs. The library meets the needs of both the novice and the most seasoned Turbo Pascal programmers. The novice can create useful programs within minutes simply by invoking the routines in this text. The veteran Pascal programmer will find unlimited programming capabilities via the ROM-BIOS and DOS services, the interrupt-handling routines, and the wild-card file manipulation provided. In addition, all programmers will benefit from the presentation of the routines in Borland's Turbo Toolbox and Graphix Toolbox. No matter what your background is, the routines presented in this text provide the most powerful library of Pascal routines ever offered in a text or diskette package.

Development Philosophy

We had two basic goals in developing the routines in this text. The first was to provide the most useful collection of Pascal programming tools ever offered. In a programmer community as large as Turbo Pascal's, the needs of the programmers are diverse, making our goal difficult to meet. By the end of this text, you will see that the vast number of routines presented in each chapter have indeed covered a wide range of user needs.

The second and more important goal was to illustrate good programming practices. Thus, prior to the development of the first routine, we identified the attributes of "good" programs and developed a standard that each routine had to meet before it could be included in the text. These attributes and standards are

- Consistent usage
- Complete documentation
- Structured code
- Thorough error detection and correction
- Restriction of side effects.

As you examine the routines, you should immediately note the consistent documentation format used throughout the text. Uppercase letters denote variable identifiers, type identifiers, and constants specific to the routines. If you have to examine large quantities of code, you will appreciate the extra effort made to ensure consistency among the routines.

In addition, each routine supports the structured programming concepts. The use of **goto**s and global variables has been restricted, which decreases the possibility of errors from side effects while increasing the ability to modify each routine. Error detection is performed in all I/O routines to ensure consistent results. If you have not yet developed a programming standard, the routines provided in the following chapters illustrate good programming habits.

Chapter Contents

This text assumes that you are familiar with, or are in the process of learning, Turbo Pascal. It is not intended to be tutorial on Turbo Pascal.

- **Chapter 1** provides a language overview and Pascal syntax charts, each accompanied by programming examples. Take time to examine these charts. Each contains information critical to understanding the programming language completely.

- **Chapter 2** completes the Turbo library of mathematical, transcendental, and radix-conversion routines. The chapter presents functions that provide decimal-to-binary, -to-octal, -to-hexadecimal, and -to-anybase conversions, as well as the complete set of trigonometric functions.

- **Chapter 3** introduces arrays and the development of generic routines, which can be applied to arrays of the type integer or real. Bit masking and the Pascal implementation of sets are also introduced.

- **Chapter 4** focuses on sorting and searching. The routines support arrays of type integer, real, or string. Several sorting and searching algorithms are presented, each accompanied by detailed descriptions and illustrations.

- **Chapter 5** provides the most complete set of string-manipulation routines available for any programming language. The chapter examines routines that provide complete substring manipulation, with or without regard to the case of the characters in the string. These routines lay the foundation for the file- and pipe-manipulation routines presented in later chapters.

- **Chapter 6** presents pointers and their use in creating dynamic data structures, such as linked lists and binary trees.

- **Chapter 7** provides a set of procedures for program-controlled input and output. Since I/O is always one of the most demanding programming considerations, the savings in development time provided by this chapter will make this text one of the most useful programming tools available to Pascal programmers.

- **Chapter 8** expands upon the I/O routines presented in Chapter 7 to produce several menu- and screen-driven I/O routines. Each routine uses typed constants to increase the number of applications that they can support. Using arrow keys to simplify user I/O is also illustrated.

- **Chapter 9** provides routines that allow program control of the ROM-BIOS and DOS services. Among these are routines that control the video display, create and manipulate directories, and support wild-card file manipulation.

- **Chapter 10** uses the routines developed in the preceding chapters to produce several file-manipulation routines. The chapter presents procedures similar to the utilities provided in the DOS and UNIX environments that support file manipulation based upon wild-card characters.

- **Chapter 11** illustrates the pipe and shows how Turbo Pascal programs can be modified to support redirection of input and output.

- **Chapter 12** presents Borland's Turbo Toolbox. Each programming tool provided in the package—Turbo-ISAM, Turbo-SORT, and GINST—is examined in detail. A sample database program that uses the tools presented in previous chapters and the Turbo Toolbox is included.

- **Chapter 13** introduces Borland's Graphix Toolbox. The chapter offers several programming examples that illustrate the use of the toolbox routines in graphics and applications programs. In addition, the calling sequence and types required for each routine in the Graphix Toolbox are provided.

- **Chapter 14** contains several routines that are grouped under the title "Miscellaneous Turbo Procedures." Among these are routines that manipulate the keyboard buffer, illustrate synchronization of the video retrace in applications that directly access the video display memory, and access the IBM PC ports.

- **Appendix A** provides the calling sequence and types required for the built-in Turbo Pascal functions and procedures.

- **Appendix B** presents the ASCII codes for characters.

Diskette Package

There are thousands of lines of code in this book. All the routines are provided in their entirety, so you may type them at your computer as you need them. A diskette package is also available. This diskette package includes all of the routines presented in this text plus a collection of over 30 additional programs and routines.

The diskette package includes a complete driver for the file-manipulation routines presented in Chapter 10 and several additional graphics, interrupt handling, mathematical, file-manipulation, and utility functions. A hardbound manual that presents the calling sequence of each routine and additional insight into Turbo Pascal, DOS, and the ROM-BIOS is also included.

Complete source code for all of the routines is provided on a 5 1/4-inch floppy disk in MS-DOS format for $59.95 plus $4.00 shipping and handling. Write to:

Kris Jamsa Software, Inc.
Box 26031
Las Vegas, Nevada 89126

—Kris Jamsa
Steven Nameroff

Please send me the Turbo Pascal Programmer's Library on disk. My payment of $63.95 ($59.95 plus $4 for shipping and handling) is enclosed.

_____ check

_____ money order

Name _____

Address _____

City _____ State _____ ZIP _____

Kris Jamsa Software, Inc.   Box 26031   Las Vegas, Nevada 89126

C H A P T E R

1

Uniquely Turbo Pascal

This chapter will serve as a quick reference guide for you while you examine the routines in this book. The chapter first illustrates several key concepts, unique to Turbo Pascal, that have been used in the routines throughout the text. The chapter then presents the syntax charts that show correct syntax in Turbo Pascal. Don't worry if you are not familiar with syntax charts. By the end of this chapter, you should appreciate the level of information that they provide and the simplicity of their interpretation.

Typed Constants

In Turbo Pascal, you can define typed constants. You can use these constants later as parameters to procedures and functions, in the same manner as you use variables passed by values. To define a *typed constant*, you must specify the name and type of the constant at declaration, as shown here:

```
const
  Number_Of_Students: integer = 255;
  Number_Of_Classes : byte = 25;
  School_Name       : string[4] = 'UNLV';
```

Typed constants are particularly useful with structured types. For example, consider the following definitions:

```
type
  MENU_REC = record
    NUM_CHOICES : integer;
    MENU_WIDTH  : integer;
    CHOICES     : array [1..14] of char;
    DESCRIPTIONS: array [1..14] of STRING79;
    TITLE       : STRING79;
    PROMPT      : STRING79;
  end;
const
  GRADES_MAIN_MENU : MENU_REC = (
    NUM_CHOICES  : 5;
    MENU_WIDTH   : 50;
    CHOICES      : '1234E            ';
    DESCRIPTIONS : ('Add a student to the master list',
                    'Delete a student from the master list',
                    'Print grade report',
                    'Exit program','','','','','','','','','');
    TITLE        : 'Student Grade Program';
    PROMPT       : 'Enter choice or use arrow key and hit <ENTER>')
```

Given these definitions, if you have a routine called *Display—Menu* that expects records of type **MENU—REC**, Turbo allows you to pass it the typed constant **Main—Menu**. If you later need to display a different menu, you can define a typed constant of type **MENU— REC**, which contains the appropriate fields. The routines presented in Chapter 8 make extensive use of typed constants.

Logical Devices

Turbo Pascal simplifies input and output to devices by allowing programs to treat them as text files. For example, if you need to write to the printer, a channel to the device is created by **Assign** as follows:

```
Assign (FILE_POINTER, 'Lst:');
Rewrite (FILE_POINTER);
```

You can use the file pointer created by **Assign** in the same fashion as text file pointers. The following list summarizes Turbo Pascal's predefined logical devices:

Aux: Auxiliary device—input or output
Con: Console device—input or output
Kbd: Keyboard device—input only
Lst: List device, normally the printer—output only
Trm: Terminal device—input or output
Usr: User device—input or output

The auxiliary device, **Aux:**, is associated with the first communications port on the IBM PC and PC compatibles. Data can be read from or written to this device. The console device, **Con:**, provides buffered input from the keyboard, which allows you to edit a line of text. You can use **Con:** for both input and output. Data written to **Con:** is sent to the terminal display.

The keyboard device, **Kbd:**, allows input directly from the keyboard. Unlike input from **Con:** or **Trm:**, the data read from **Kbd:** is not echoed to the screen. You can use **Kbd:** for passwords and other applications in which the data input by the user should not be displayed on the screen. The list device, **Lst:**, allows you to write information to the printer. DOS also supports the device name **Prn:** for output to the printer.

The terminal device, **Trm:**, can be used for input and output. Unlike input from **Con:**, the data input from **Trm:** is not buffered. Each character input from **Trm:** is echoed to the screen. Data written to **Trm:** is displayed on the user's terminal. The user device, **Usr:**, is used to obtain data from user-written I/O drivers.

The routines presented in the remainder of this section illustrate the use of these logical devices.

Compiler Directives

The routines presented throughout this book make extensive use of the following compiler directives.

B   Default Logical I/O Device Selection. This directive specifies whether the logical device **Con:** (designated by **B+**) or **Trm:** (designated by **B−**) will be used for input/output throughout the entire program. The default value is **B+**.

C Control Character Interpretation Active/Inactive. This directive specifies whether the I/O routines will interpret control characters throughout the entire program. When active (designated by **C+**), control characters will be interpreted, which will slow screen output. The default value is **C+**.

D Device Status Checks Active/Inactive (DOS only). This directive specifies whether I/O to a device should be performed on a character-by-character basis with device status checks performed with each I/O (**D+**), or by buffering the data and performing the I/O without testing the device status.

F Number of Open Files (DOS only). This directive specifies the maximum number of open files that the program can have active at one time. The default setting is **F16**. This directive depends on the file **CONFIG.SYS**, which is used at startup to configure the operating system. Ensure that CONFIG.SYS contains the statement

```
FILES=n
```

where the value n is the number of files that you wish to have open at one time.

G Input File Buffer Size (DOS only). This directive allows redirection of input via the pipe or redirection operators, which are discussed in Chapter 11. The default is **G0**, which directs I/O to the logical device selected with the **B** compiler directive. A value greater than 0 causes redirection of input with the buffer size specified.

I I/O Error Handling Active/Inactive. This directive specifies who is responsible for performing I/O error checking. The default is **I+**, which causes Turbo Pascal to include code for error checking. When inactive (**I−**), the program must provide I/O error detection. (See the section on I/O error checking that follows next in this chapter.)

I Include File Directive. This directive causes Turbo to include other Turbo Pascal source files into the program for compilation. (See the section on include files that follows later in this chapter.)

K Stack Checking Active/Inactive. This directive specifies whether Turbo Pascal will test the stack space prior to subroutine calls. This ensures adequate room for local variables. The default is **K+**, which causes the test for space. Unless your application requires very high speed, do not turn stack space checking off.

P Output Buffer Size (DOS only). This directive is similar to the **G** compiler directive in that it allows redirection of output through the pipe or redirection operators, which are discussed in Chapter 11. The default value is **P0**, which assigns output to the device selected by the **B** compiler directive. A value greater than 0 will result in redirection of output with the specified buffer size.

R Index Range Check Active/Inactive. This directive specifies whether Turbo Pascal will include code to test index operations to ensure that they remain within the defined bounds. The default value is **R−**, which turns range checking off. This in turn increases the speed of the application. It is a good habit to enable range checking during the development cycle of a program.

U User Interrupt Checking Active/Inactive. This directive specifies whether a user will be able to terminate the execution of a program at any point by pressing CTRL-C. The default value is **U−**, which allows users to terminate programs. If you develop interactive programs, you will probably want to disable the user's ability to terminate programs in this manner with **U+**.

V Strict Type Checking of String Parameters Active/Inactive. This directive specifies whether the types of strings passed as variable parameters to subroutines must match exactly. The default is **V+**, which states that types must be identical. A compiler error will occur if a string defined as type **string[20]** is passed as a variable parameter to a routine that expects a string of type **string[25]**.

I/O Error Checking

By default, Turbo Pascal provides error checking after each I/O operation. If an error occurs, Turbo Pascal will display an error message and the program will terminate. Rather than allowing programs to terminate in this manner, you will often find it useful to trap and handle I/O errors within a program. The compiler directive {**$I±**} turns I/O error checking on and off. The default setting is error checking on {**$I+**}.

To trap I/O errors, a program must disable error checking with the {**$I−**} directive, perform the I/O, and test the status of the operation. The status of an I/O operation is determined through the built-in function **IOResult**. If an error occurs, **IOResult** will return the error number associated with the error. If the I/O operation is successful, **IOResult** will return the value 0. The following code segment traps I/O errors during the reset of the file specified by the first command-line parameter:

```
{$I-}                    {turn off error checking}
Assign (FILE_POINTER, ParamStr(1));
Reset (FILE_POINTER);
{$I+}                    {turn on error checking}

STATUS := IOResult;

if (STATUS = 0) then
  writeln ('File successfully opened')
else
  writeln ('File does not exist');
```

If the program uses the value of **IOResult** more than once, the result must first be placed into a variable by the expression

```
STATUS := IOResult;
```

since each call to **IOResult** resets the return value to 0.

In addition to trapping I/O errors, the process specified in the code segment just given is used to trap errors that occur within the procedures **ChDir**, **GetDir**, **MkDir**, and **RmDir**. Here is an example of error trapping with **ChDir**:

```
{$I-}               {turn off error checking}
Chdir (ParamStr(1));
{$I+}               {turn on error checking}

STATUS := IOResult;
```

The routines provided in the remainder of the text make extensive use of I/O error checking.

Include Files

Several advanced routines in this book utilize the {$I FILENAME} compiler directive to include Pascal source files. These source files are called *include files*. For standardization, the routines presented in each chapter are grouped into files with the extension .TOL. For example, the string routines presented in Chapter 5 are assumed to be in the file STRINGS.TOL. (All tools in the diskette package provided by the authors of this book follow this standard to simplify integration of the routines into your applications.)

Include files provide several advantages to Turbo Pascal programs. First, including the same files within a series of programs ensures that the routines are used consistently throughout applications. Second, include files limit the number of routines that programmers have to examine to a manageable number. This second advantage removes much of the clutter from a source file.

Efficient Use of Overlays

One restriction of Turbo Pascal programs is that data sizes and code sizes are restricted to 64K each. To compensate for this limitation, Turbo Pascal supports overlays, which trade speed for increased size. Before you examine methods to increase execution speed of programs that use overlays, here is an in-depth look at overlays.

Turbo Pascal programs restrict the code size of an application to 64K; but if you have developed a large database program, for example, the code may exceed 64K, as shown here:

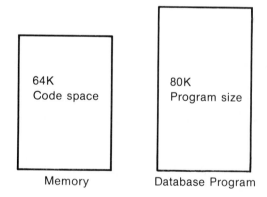

One restriction of Turbo Pascal programs is that data sizes and code

Overlays allow programs to substitute routines in designated sections of the 64K memory area that contains the code. If the database program that you developed consists of four sections (such as **Add**, **Delete**, **List**, and **Modify**), overlays allow a program to bring the code for each section into memory as required. When the segment of code that performs a **Modify** is in the program's memory, the code for adding, listing, and deleting resides on disk, as shown here:

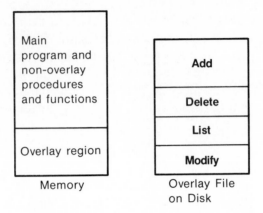

Memory   Overlay File
                on Disk

Overlays are created in programs by the keyword **Overlay**. The following code skeleton would place the four procedures (**Add**, **Delete**, **List**, and **Modify**) into an overlay:

```
program DataBase;

{types and constant declarations}

overlay procedure Add;

overlay procedure Delete;

overlay procedure List;

overlay procedure Modify;

{variable declarations}

begin
  {code for main program}
end.
```

Defining the procedures in this manner causes all four to be placed into the same overlay. If you were to **list** your directory, you would see a second file with the same name as the source file, except that it would have the extension .000. This file would contain the overlays. If each procedure is large, you may need to create four distinct overlays by separating each overlay procedure with a non-overlay procedure, as shown here.

```
program DataBase;

{types and constant declarations}

overlay procedure Add;              {overlay group 000}

procedure Clear_Screen;

overlay procedure Delete;           {overlay group 001}

procedure Clear_to_EOL ;

overlay procedure List ;            {overlay group 002}

procedure Set_Cursor (ROW, COLUMN);

overlay procedure Modify ;          {overlay group 003}

{variable declarations}

begin
   {code for main program}
end.
```

The overlay region within the program will always equal the size of the largest overlay.

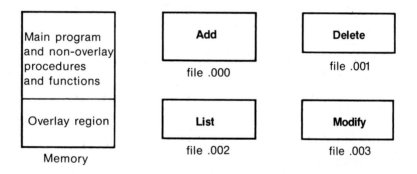

If your programs are small, overlays are not a concern. However, if you must use overlays, understanding how the actual processing occurs will help you to use them in a way that is not obvious to the user. Each time that a program references an overlay procedure, the memory management routines test to see if the routine is in memory. If it is, the routine is executed; if it is not, the memory management routines will load the routine into memory from disk. Therefore, each reference to an overlay procedure requires additional processing, which results in slower execution. The time required to load the routine from a floppy disk can be so great that the user must stop and wait.

To limit the impact of overload delays, you should place your overlays at logical separations in the code, such as in menu areas. In addition, you can decrease the load time by using a RAM disk to store the overlay files. A *RAM disk* is a software-controlled area set aside by the operating system in memory. The RAM disk acts just like another disk: if you have a computer with two floppy disks, installing a RAM disk will give you a third drive (C:). Since the RAM disk resides in memory, its speed is not restricted by mechanical parts, as is the case with disk drives. Therefore, access to files in the RAM disk will occur almost as fast as normal memory references. If you place your overlay files into a RAM disk, users will probably never know that the programs are using overlays.

You can install a RAM disk by specifying a device driver in the file CONFIG.SYS. Each time the system boots, the operating system will install the RAM drive. Software drivers for RAM drives are readily available.

After you have installed the RAM drive, you simply copy the overlay files to it. Since the RAM disk acts like a standard disk, it will respond to any DOS command. Remember that the RAM disk is contained in memory, and it is therefore lost when the system reboots or power is lost.

Within the Turbo Pascal programs that use overlays, you must inform the memory management routines that the overlays exist in the RAM disk, instead of the default directory. The built-in function **OvrPath** performs this function. You can invoke the routine with a standard DOS path:

```
begin
  OvrPath ('C:');    {drive C is the RAM drive}

  {remainder of code}
end.
```

There are a few restrictions in the way you can use overlays. First, the number of overlay groups cannot exceed 99. As shown earlier, an overlay group is created by separating overlay procedures with non-overlay procedures. Second, because overlays within the same group share the same memory space, they cannot reside in memory simultaneously. This means that overlay procedures in the same group cannot call each other. Finally, overlay procedures cannot be recursive—either directly or indirectly. A *directly recursive procedure* is a procedure that calls itself. An *indirectly recursive procedure* is a procedure that calls another procedure that, in turn, calls the first procedure. If you work around these restrictions, you should find overlays to be a very convenient tool.

Syntax Charts

Before you examine the syntax charts, here are some terms that you must learn:

- An *expression* is a symbol or series of symbols that express a mathematical operation. The following are valid expressions in Turbo Pascal:

```
TOTAL_SCORE / NUM_STUDENTS

TOTAL_SCORE


SCORE < AVERAGE
```

- An *identifier* is a unique name that identifies an object. An example of an identifier is a variable name.

- A *literal* is a constant value. In the syntax charts given later in this chapter, literals are normally the reserved words and punctuation marks that appear in Pascal.

Read syntax charts from left to right, in the direction of the arrows that connect the symbols. Since syntax charts are composed of symbols, you can usually understand the syntax charts of a language, even though you may have never programmed in that language. Many experienced computer scientists use syntax charts, rather than trying to memorize the syntax for constructs they may not use on a daily basis. Unfortunately, most people are never properly introduced to syntax charts. After you understand the flow of a syntax chart, it becomes a useful tool. The symbols in Table 1-1 are used in Pascal syntax charts.

Table 1-1. Symbols Used in Syntax Charts

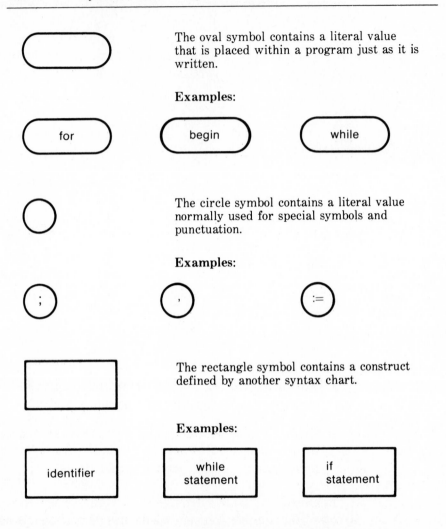

The oval symbol contains a literal value that is placed within a program just as it is written.

Examples:

The circle symbol contains a literal value normally used for special symbols and punctuation.

Examples:

The rectangle symbol contains a construct defined by another syntax chart.

Examples:

Consider the following example:

file of STUDENT—RECORD

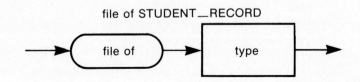

If you start with the first item in the syntax chart and follow the direction of the arrows, the syntax chart shows the following:

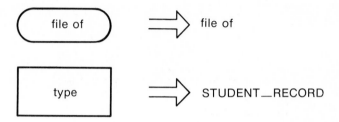

The first symbols in Table 1-1 are straightforward: the oval and circle are used in syntax charts to denote literals. You simply use the value that they contain. The rectangle informs you that the item it contains is defined in terms of another syntax chart. For example, consider the following **while** loop:

```
while i < 10 do
   begin
     writeln (i);
     i := i + 1;
   end;
```

Here is the syntax chart for the **while** statement:

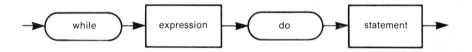

As shown earlier, the literals **while** and **do** are straightforward. The expression in the sample **while** loop is **i < 10**, and the statement is the compound statement

```
begin
   writeln (i);
   i := i + 1;
end;
```

A *compound statement* is one or more statements enclosed by a **begin** and **end**, as shown in the syntax chart that follows.

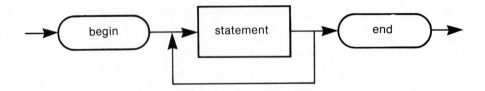

If the syntax chart contains more than one possible path, as shown here, you must determine the desired path and continue to follow the direction of the arrows:

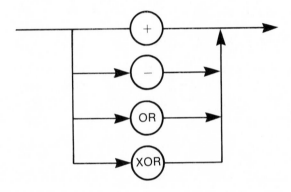

Syntax charts are only meant to be used as a guide to the correct syntax of a language. If you have never worked with syntax charts, you may find them intimidating at first. If you try to compare the various constructs presented in this text (the **while**, **if-then-else**, and **repeat** statements, for example) to their syntax-chart representations, you should begin to recognize the flow of the charts. If you don't understand a particular chart, first try implementing the construct in Turbo Pascal and then compare your implementation to the chart. It is important that you become familiar with syntax charts, since their popularity is continuing to grow each day. The following syntax charts illustrate the syntax associated with Turbo Pascal. Programming examples follow most of the syntax charts.

Actual Parameter

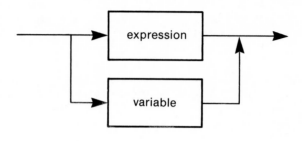

Examples

```
SCORES
3 * SCORE[1]
```

Adding Operator

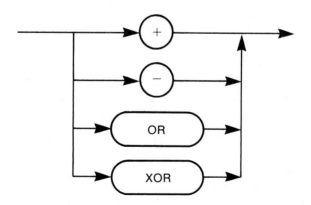

Array Constant

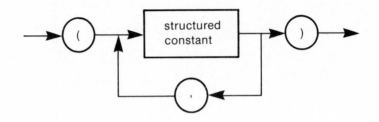

Example

```
const

MONTHS : array[1..12]  of string20 =
   ('January', 'February', 'March', 'April', 'May', 'June',
    'July', 'August', 'September', 'October', 'November',
'December');
```

Array Type

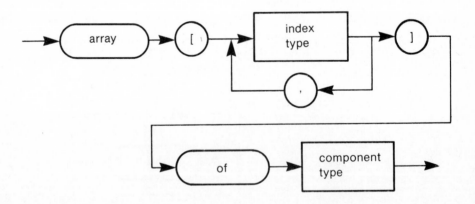

Example

```
array [1..NUM_STUDENTS] of STUDENT_RECORDS
```

Array Variable

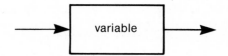

Assignment Statement

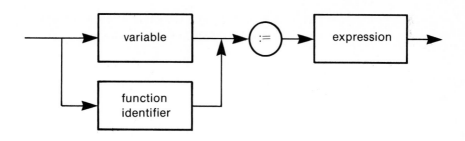

Examples

```
SUM := 0;
AVERAGE_VALUE := SUM / NUM_STUDENTS;
```

Base Type

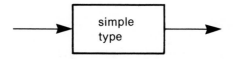

Block

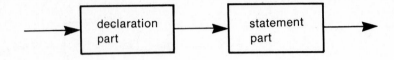

Example

```
var
  I  : integer;
  SUM: real;
begin
  SUM := 0;

  for I := 1 to NUM_STUDENTS do
    SUM := SUM + TEST_SCORES[i];

  Average_Value := SUM / NUM_STUDENTS;
end;
```

Case Element

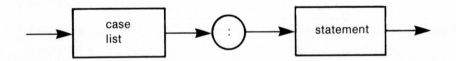

Example

```
255: Writeln ('File not found');
```

Case Label

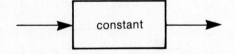

Case Label List

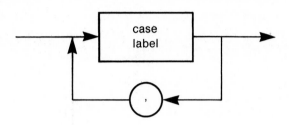

Case List

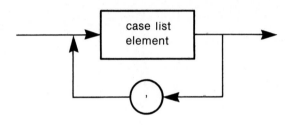

Case List Element

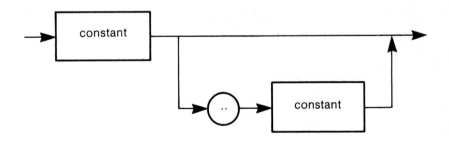

Examples

```
1
1..5
```

Case Statement

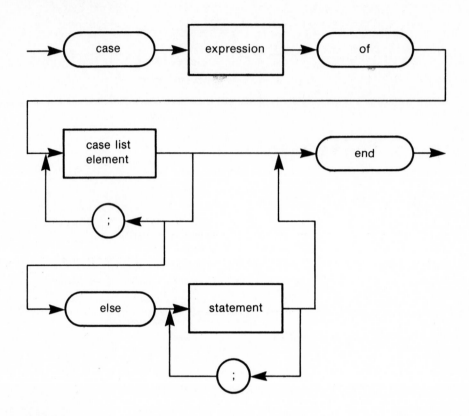

Example

```
case Choice of
  1: Enter_Data (GRADES);
  2: Display_Data (GRADES);
  3: Print_Data (GRADES);
  4: DONE := true;
end;
```

Comment

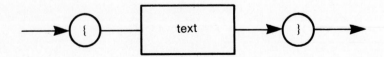

Examples

```
{ single-line comment }

{ comments can span
  several lines }
```

Complemented Factor

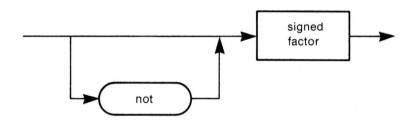

Example

```
not Eof
```

Component Type

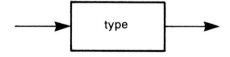

Component Variable

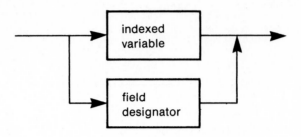

Compound Statement

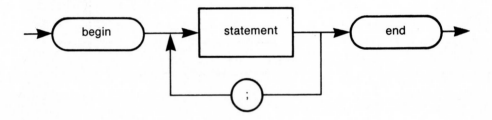

Example

```
begin
  Writeln (I);
  I := I + 1;
end;
```

Conditional Statement

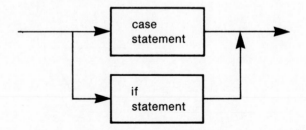

Constant

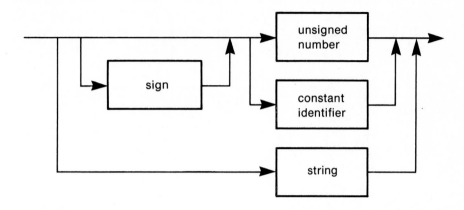

Examples

```
+45
'A constant string'
```

Constant Definition

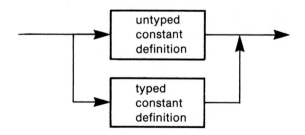

Constant Definition Part

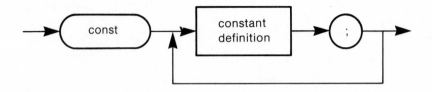

Examples

```
const
  NUM_STUDENTS = 255;

const
  NUM_CLASSES = 25;
  NUM_TEACHERS = 15;
```

Constant Identifier

Control Character

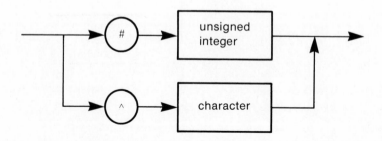

Examples

```
const
  BELL   = ^G;
  BELL_2 = #7;
```

Control Variable

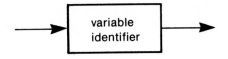

Declaration Part

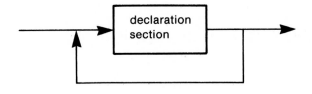

Declaration Section

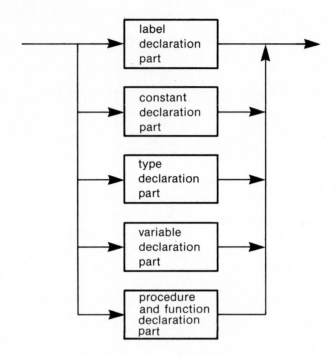

Example

```
label
  FATAL_ERROR;

const
  NUM_SCORES = 255;

type
  TEST_RESULTS = array[1..NUM_SCORES] of integer;

var
  GLOBAL_VARIABLE: integer;  {declared here makes it global}

procedure Get_Scores (var SCORES: STUDENT_ARRAY);
begin
  {code for Get_Scores}
end;
```

Digit

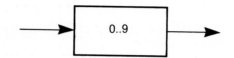

Digit Sequence

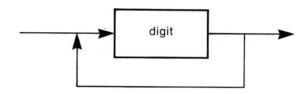

Empty Statement

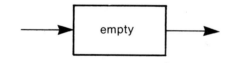

Example

```
repeat {empty statement} until KeyPressed;
```

Entire Variable

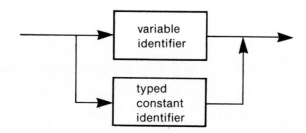

Expression

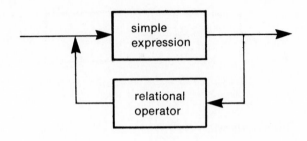

Examples

4 - 3

SCORE > AVERAGE

Factor

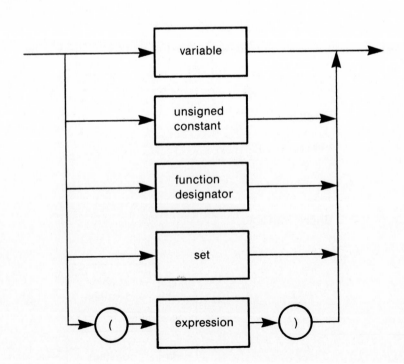

Field Designator

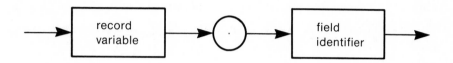

Example

```
STUDENT.NAME
```

Field List

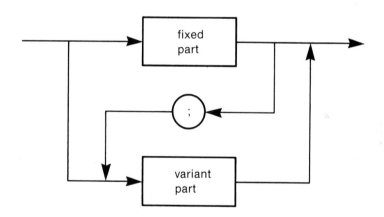

Example

```
NAME : STRING79;
GRADE,
AGE  : integer;
case PARENTS_MARITAL_STATUS: MARITAL_STATUS of
  MARRIED      : (HOME_PHONE: PHONE);
  DIVORCED     : (FATHERS_PHONE,
                  MOTHERS_PHONE: PHONE);
  SINGLE_PARENT: (HOME_PHONE: PHONE);
```

Field Identifier

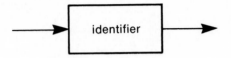

File Identifier

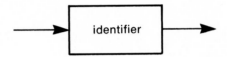

File Identifier List

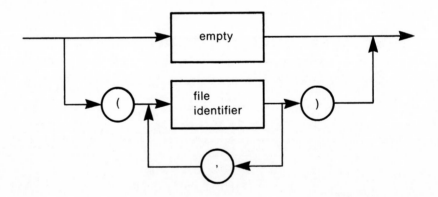

Example

```
(input, output)
```

File Type

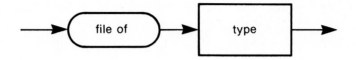

Example

```
file of STUDENT_RECORDS;
```

Final Value

Fixed Part

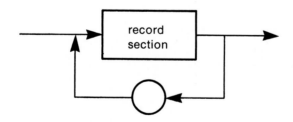

For List

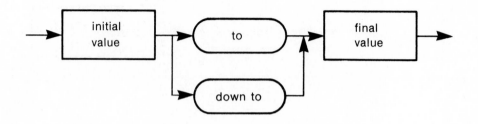

For Statement

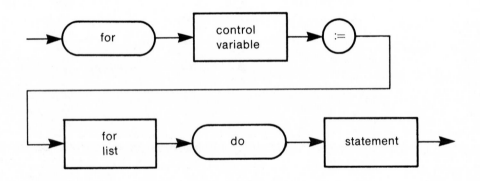

Examples

```
for I := 1 to 100 do
  Writeln (STUDENT[I].NAME);

for I := NUM_STUDENTS downto 1 do
  Writeln (STUDENT[I].SCORE);
```

Formal Parameter Section

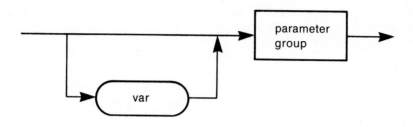

Examples

```
var DAY, MONTH, YEAR: integer;
FILENAME, STUDENT_NAME: STRING79;
```

Function Declaration

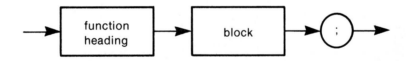

Example

```
function Average_Score (TEST_SCORES: SCORES): real;
var
  I  : integer;
  SUM: real;
begin
  SUM := 0;

  for I := to NUM_STUDENTS do
    SUM := SUM + TEST_SCORE[I];

  Average_Score := SUM / NUM_STUDENTS;
end;
```

Function Designator

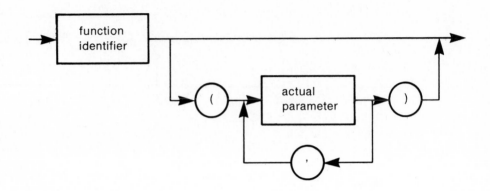

Examples

```
Average_Score (TEST)
Sum_Numbers (1, 2, 3)
```

Function Heading

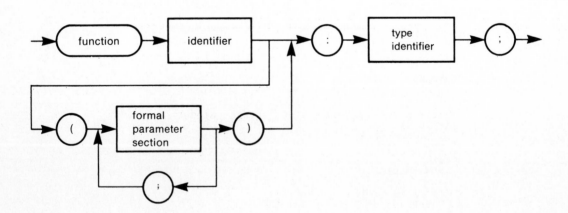

Examples

```
function Average_Score (TEST_SCORES: SCORES): real;
function KeyPressed: boolean;
```

Function Identifier

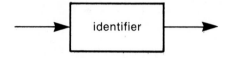

Goto Statement

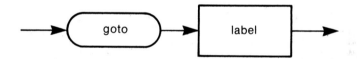

Example

```
goto FATAL_ERROR;
```

Hex Digit

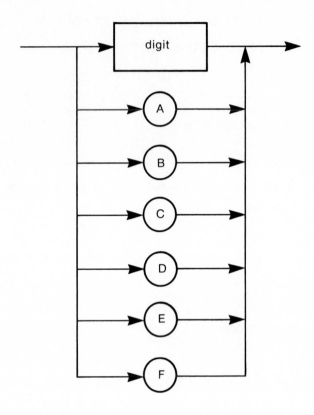

Hex Digit Sequence

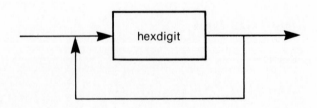

Examples

F F
A F

Identifier

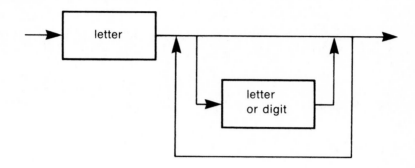

Examples

```
NAME
TEST123
NUMBER_OF_SCORES
```

Identifier List

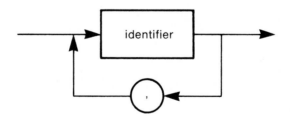

Example

```
NAME, TEST123, NUMBER_OF_SCORES
```

If Statement

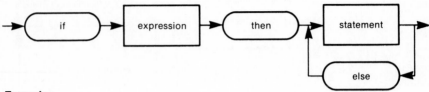

Examples

```
if (Fatal_Error) then
  Exit(3);

if (FATAL_ERROR) then
  Exit(2)
else
  Count_Blessings (NEW_FILE);

if (ERROR = 1) then
  Writeln ('File not found')
else if (ERROR = 2) then
  Writeln ('Invalid Operation Requested')
else
  Writeln ('Unknown error');
```

Index Type

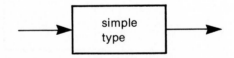

Indexed Variable

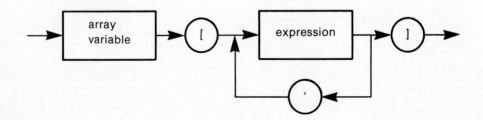

Examples

```
TEST_SCORES[100]
TEST_SCORES[NUM_STUDENTS-3]
TIC_TAC_TOE [3, 2]
```

Initial Value

Inline List Element

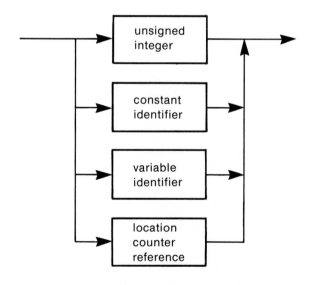

Inline Statement

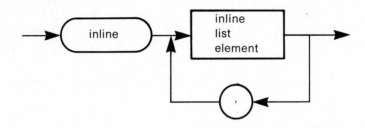

Example

```
inline ($50/$53/$51/$52/$56/$57/$1E/$06/$FB);
```

Label

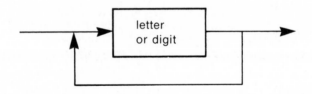

Example

```
FATAL_ERROR:
```

Label Declaration Part

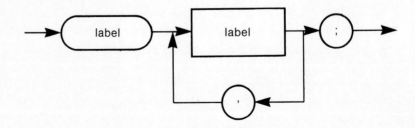

Examples

```
label
  FATAL_ERROR;

label
  FATAL_ERROR, ALMOST_FATAL_ERROR;
```

Letter

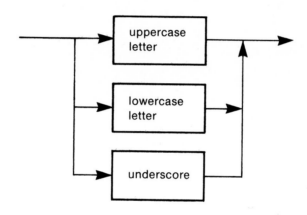

Letter or Digit

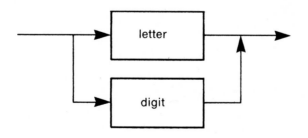

Location Counter Reference

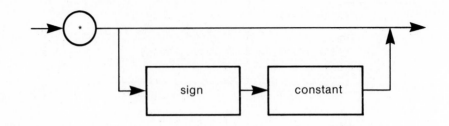

Examples

```
*

*+3
```

Lowercase Letter

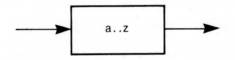

Multiplying Operator

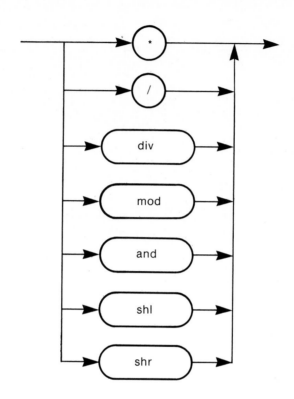

Parameter Group

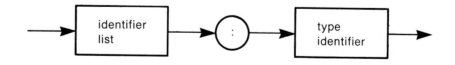

Example

```
DAY, HOUR, MINUTE: integer
```

Pointer Type

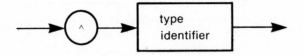

Example

```
STUDENT = record
  NAME     : STRING79;
  GRADE    : integer;
  NEXT_PTR: ^STUDENT;
end;
```

Pointer Variable

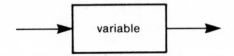

Procedure and Function Declaration Part

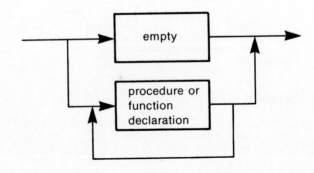

Procedure Declaration

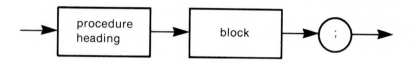

Example

```
procedure Clear_Screen;
begin
  Writeln (Chr(27), '[H', Chr(27), '[J');
end;
```

Procedure Heading

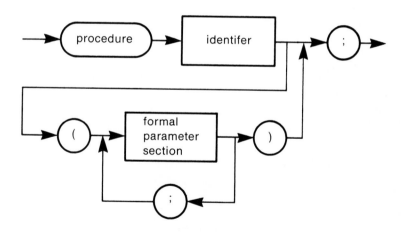

Examples

```
procedure Clear_Screen;

procedure Display_File (FILE_NAME: STRING79;
                        DISPLAY_PAGE: integer);
```

Procedure or Function Declaration

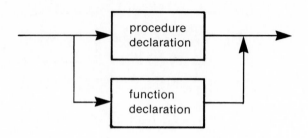

Procedure Statement

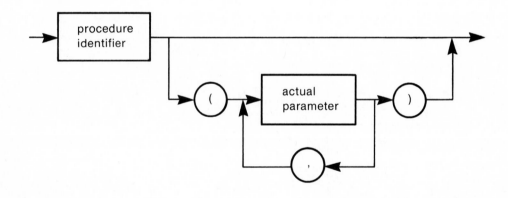

Examples

```
Clear_Screen;
Display_File ('DATA.DAT', 3);
```

Program

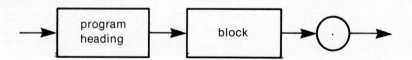

Example

```
program Display_Message ;

begin
  writeln ('Message to display');
end.


{ no program heading }

begin
  writeln ('Message to display');
end.

program More_Complex ;

const
  NUM_STUDENTS = 255;

type
  STUDENT_ARRAY = array [1..NUM_STUDENTS] of integer;

procedure Get_Scores (var SCORES: STUDENT_ARRAY);
begin
  {code for Get_Scores}
end;

function Average_Score (SCORES: STUDENT_ARRAY): real;
begin
  {code for Average_Score}
end;

var
  TEST_SCORES: STUDENT_ARRAY;

begin
  Get_Scores (TEST_SCORES);
  writeln ('The average score is ', Average_Score (TEST_SCORES));
end.
```

Program Heading

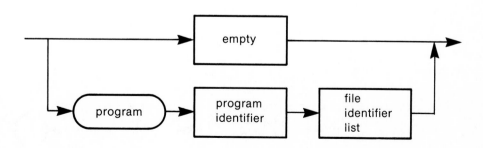

Examples

```
{ no heading is valid }
program Program_Name ;
program Program_Name (input, output);
```

Program Identifier

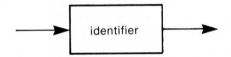

Record Constant

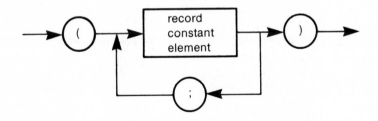

Record Constant Element

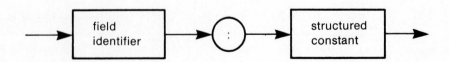

Record Section

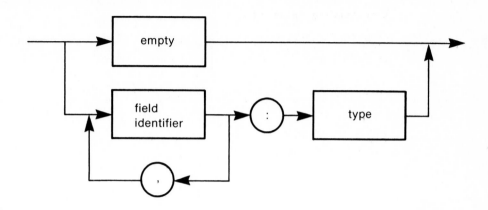

Examples

```
TEST_SCORE: integer;

TEST_SCORE,
STUDENT_ID: integer;
```

Record Type

Example

```
record
  NAME   : STRING79;
  GRADE  : integer;
  PASSING: boolean;
end
```

Record Variable

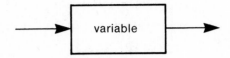

Record Variable List

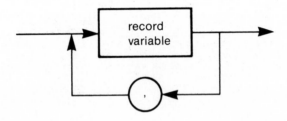

Referenced Variable

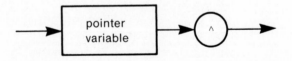

Relational Operator

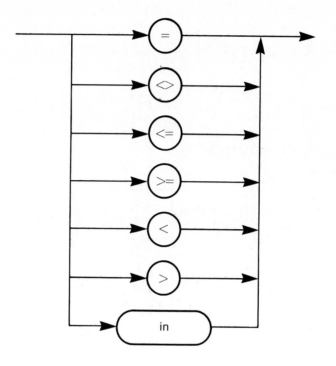

Repeat Statement

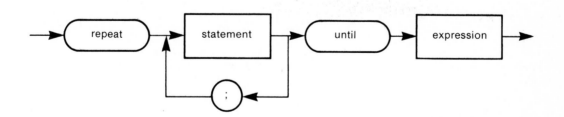

Examples

```
repeat until KeyPressed;

repeat
  writeln (I);
  I := I + 1;
until I > 100;
```

Repetitive Statement

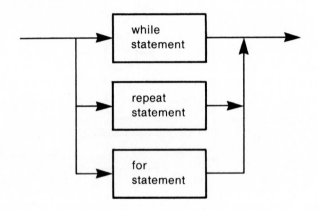

Result Type

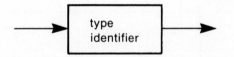

Scalar Type

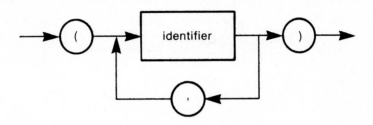

Example

```
(Pascal, C, Modula, Ada, FORTRAN)
```

Scale Factor

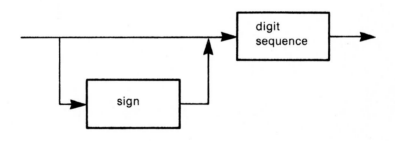

Example

```
+4
```

Set

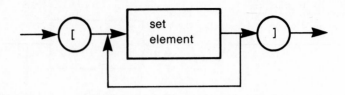

Examples

```
[1..255]
['a'..'z']
```

Set Constant

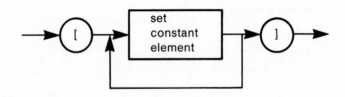

Example

```
[1..33]
```

Set Constant Element

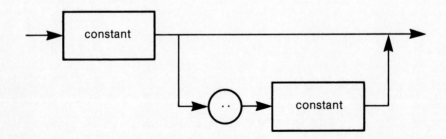

Examples

```
1
1..10
```

Set Element

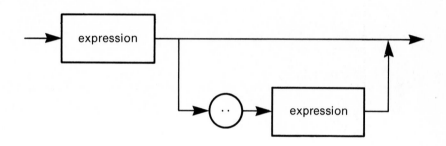

Set Type

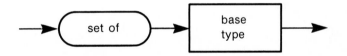

Example

```
set of DAYS
```

Sign

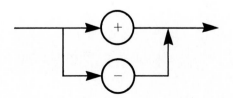

Signed Factor

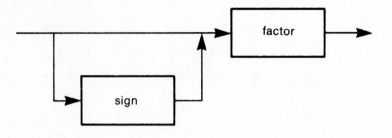

Simple Expression

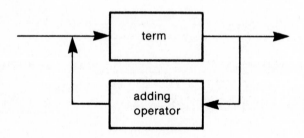

Simple Statement

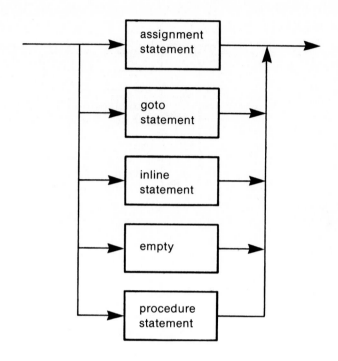

Examples

```
SUM := 0;
goto FATAL_ERROR;
```

Simple Type

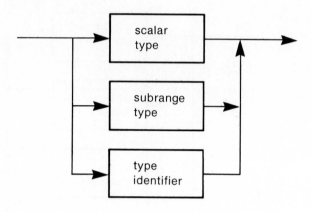

Statement

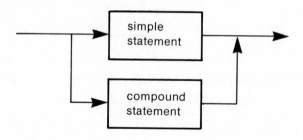

Statement Part

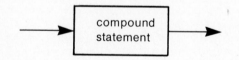

Example

```
begin
  SUM := 0;

  for I := 1 to NUM_SCORES do
    SUM := SUM + TEST_SCORE[I];
end;
```

String

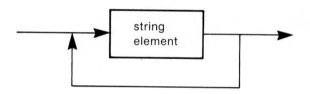

String Element

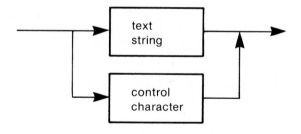

String Type

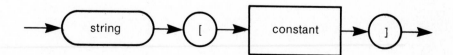

Examples

```
string [79]

string [MAX_STRING]
```

Structured Constant

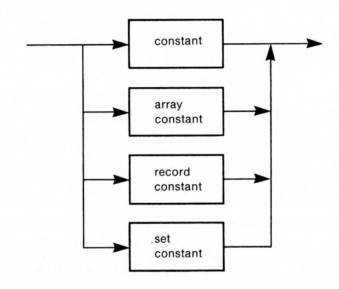

Structured Constant Definition

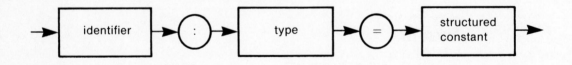

Structured Statement

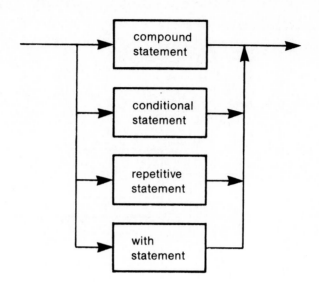

Structured Type

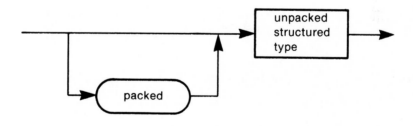

Subrange Type

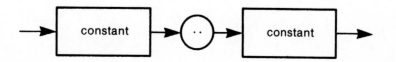

Examples

```
1..5
MONDAY..FRIDAY
```

Tag Field

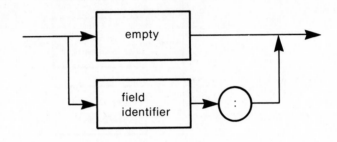

Term

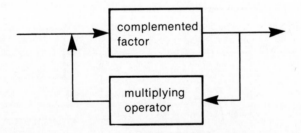

Text String

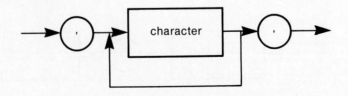

Example

```
'This is a text string'
```

Type

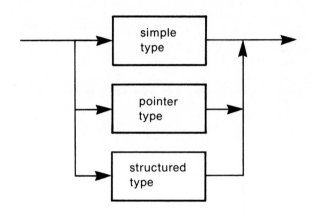

Type Definition

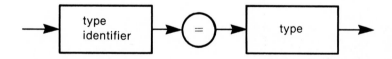

Example

```
STUDENT_BODY = array [1..NUM_STUDENTS] of STUDENT_RECORDS;
```

Type Definition Part

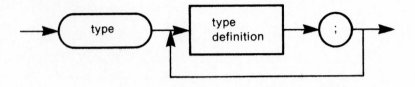

Example

```
type
  TEST_SCORE = array [1..NUM_STUDENTS] of integer;

type
  TEST_SCORE = array [1..NUM_STUDENTS] of integer;
  GRADES     = array [1..NUM_STUDENTS] of char;
```

Type Identifier

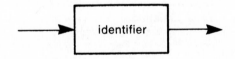

Typed Constant Identifier

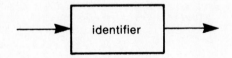

Unpacked Structure Type

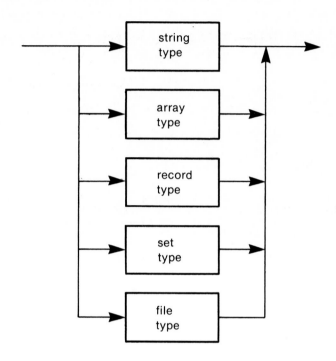

Unsigned Constant

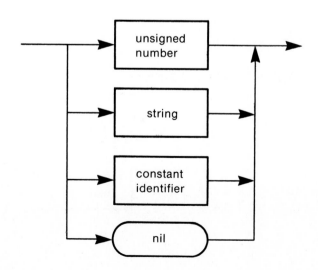

Examples

```
$FF
```

```
'A string constant'
```

Unsigned Integer

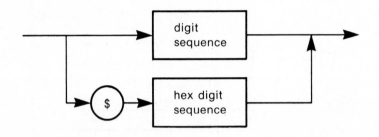

Examples

```
324
```

```
$FFF
```

Unsigned Number

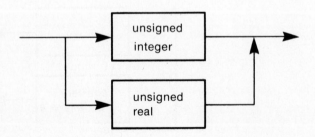

Unsigned Real

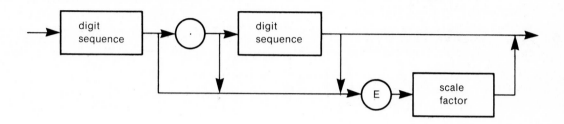

Examples

```
343.4
4.3E4
2.3E-4
```

Untyped Constant Declaration

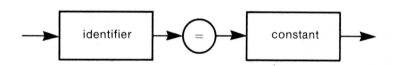

Example

```
NUM_STUDENTS = 255
```

Uppercase Letter

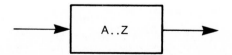

Variable

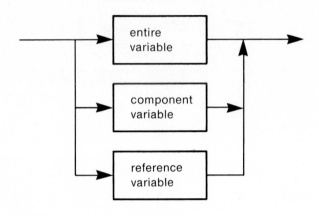

Variable Declaration

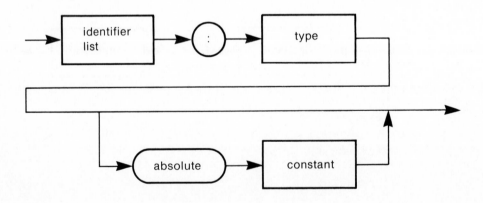

Examples

```
HIGH, LOW, AVERAGE: real;
COMMAND_LINE: array [0.127] of byte absolute Cseg:$80;
```

Variable Declaration Part

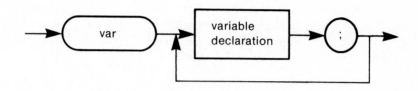

Examples

```
var
  SCORES: TEST_SCORES;

var
  NAME   : STRING79;
  SCORES : TEST_SCORES;
```

Variable Identifier

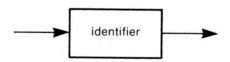

Variant

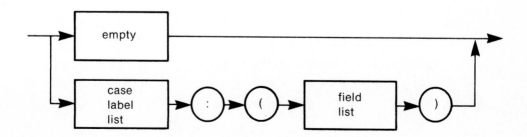

Variant Part

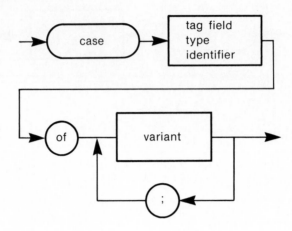

While Statement

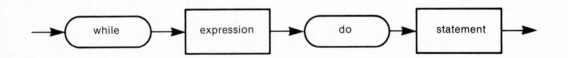

Example

```
while (not Eof) do
  begin
    Readln (INPUT_STRING);
    Writeln (INPUT_STRING);
  end;
```

With Statement

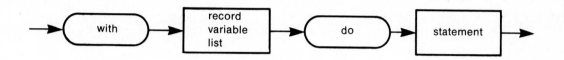

Example

```
with STUDENT_RECORD do
  begin
    Writeln (NAME, GRADE, AVERAGE);
  end;
```

C H A P T E R

2

Mathematical Routines

Although Turbo Pascal includes many mathematical functions in its standard package, it is still incomplete. This chapter provides some trigonometric and exponential functions that are not found in Turbo, as well as a set of routines for base conversion.

Trigonometry and Exponentiation

The astute student who works with trigonometry and exponentiation soon realizes that the various functions are closely related. Thus, even though Turbo Pascal provides a minimal set of mathematical functions, the missing ones can be determined by combining the functions provided. An example of this is the tangent function, **Tan(ANGLE)**, which, although not found in the Turbo package, can be computed with **Sin(ANGLE)/Cos(ANGLE)**.

The inverse trigonometric functions are a little more complicated. Turbo Pascal provides the standard function **Arctan**, but does not include the functions *Arc—Sine* or *Arc—Cosine*, which must be derived. (The inverse functions are defined so that if $y = \sin(x)$, $x = \arcsin(y)$ or $\arcsin(\sin(y)) = y$.) Suppose that the arcsine of a number X is the angle Θ (theta). You can form a right triangle if you know that

$$\sin(\Theta) = \frac{\text{opposite leg}}{\text{hypotenuse}}$$

Since X is also $X/1$, the partial triangle is

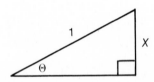

You can compute the length of the missing leg by using the Pythagorean theorem. The complete triangle is shown here:

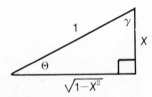

With the same triangle,

$$\tan(\Theta) \quad \frac{\text{opposite leg}}{\text{adjacent leg}} = \frac{X}{\sqrt{1-X^2}}$$

These facts are all combined to derive arcsin (X):

$$\begin{aligned}\text{arcsin } (X) &= \Theta \\ &= \arctan \ (\tan \ (\Theta)) \\ &= \arctan\left(\frac{X/}{\sqrt{1-X^2}}\right)\end{aligned}$$

The arccos function comes from the angle γ (gamma) in the complete triangle shown earlier:

$$\begin{aligned}\text{arccos } (X) &= \gamma \\ &= \arctan \ (\tan \ (\gamma)) \\ &= \arctan \frac{(\ \sqrt{(1-X^2)})}{X}\end{aligned}$$

Here are the *Arc—Sine* and *Arc—Cosine* routines:

```
function Arc_Sine (NUMBER: real): real;
{
DESCRIPTION:
    This routine computes the Arcsine of a number.

VALUE RETURNED:
    The Arcsine of the number in radians

PARAMETERS:
    NUMBER (in) - number to compute Arcsine of

SAMPLE CALL:
    ANGLE := Arc_Sine (0.707);

NOTES:
    Numbers that are greater than 1 or less than -1 will
produce a run-time error.

-------------------------------------------------------------}

  begin

{compute Arcsine based on Arctangent}
    Arc_Sine := ArcTan (NUMBER/SQRT(1-NUMBER*NUMBER));
    end;
```

```
function Arc_Cosine (NUMBER: real): real;
{
DESCRIPTION:
    This routine computes the Arccosine of a number.
```

```
VALUE RETURNED:
    The Arccosine of the number in radians

PARAMETERS:
    NUMBER (in) - number to compute Arccosine of

SAMPLE CALL:
    ANGLE := Arc_Cosine (0.707);

NOTES:
    Numbers that are greater than 1 or less than -1 will
produce a run-time error.

----------------------------------------------------------}

  begin

{compute Arccosine based on Arctangent}
    Arc_Cosine := ArcTan (SQRT(1-NUMBER*NUMBER)/NUMBER);
  end;
```

Pascal is one of the few languages that do not have direct implementations of exponentiation. However, you can derive exponentiation from logarithms and the **Exp**, or antilogarithm, function. Based on the two mathematical relationships

$$Z = e^{\ln(Z)}$$

$$\ln(Y^X) = X \cdot \ln(Y)$$

this equation can be derived as shown here:

$$Y^X = e^{\ln(Y^X)}$$

$$= e^{\,X \cdot \ln(Y)}$$

In Pascal, you can write the equation as

```
Power := Exp(X * Ln(Y));
```

by using the *Power* function provided later. (Two other functions presented here, *Log10* and *Factorial*, will not be derived in this text.) Also included is the function *Is—Prime*: it determines if a number is prime by attempting integer division on all numbers less than or equal to the square root of the tested number.

```
function Power (NUMBER, EXPONENT: real): real;
{
DESCRIPTION:
    This routine takes a number to a power (exponentiation).

VALUE RETURNED:
    The power of the number

PARAMETERS:
    NUMBER (in) - the base number
    EXPONENT (in) - the power desired

SAMPLE CALL:
    CUBED := Power (NUMBER, 3.0);

NOTES:
    Power := NUMBER**EXPONENT;

-----------------------------------------------------------}

  begin

{compute power using logarithms}
    Power := Exp(EXPONENT * Ln(NUMBER));
  end;
```

```
function Log10 (NUMBER: real): real;
{
DESCRIPTION:
    This function computes the base 10 logarithm of a number.

VALUE RETURNED:
    The logarithm of the number

PARAMETERS:
    NUMBER (in) - the number to take the log of

SAMPLE CALL:
    I := Log10 (100);     (would return 2)

NOTES:
    Numbers less than or equal to 0 will give a run-time error.

----------------------------------------------------------}

  begin

{compute the base 10 log based on the natural log}
    Log10 := Ln(NUMBER)/Ln(10.0);
  end;
```

```
function Factorial (NUMBER: integer): real;
{
DESCRIPTION:
    This function computes the factorial of a number.

VALUE RETURNED:
    The factorial of the number

PARAMETERS:
    NUMBER (in) - the number to take the factorial of

SAMPLE CALL:
    I := Factorial (5);     (would return 120)

NOTES:              •
    Numbers less than 1 will return 1.
    Numbers greater than 33 will give a run-time error.
    Factorial = N(N-1)(N-2)(N-3)...(3)(2)(1)
    Although Factorials are always integers, a real number
stores numbers higher than 32767 (Factorial(8) would be the
highest integer allowed).

------------------------------------------------------------}

  var
    FACT: real;                 {temporary factorial}
    I   : integer;              {counter for loop}

  begin
    FACT := 1;

{loop through each number with a multiplying accumulator}
    for I := 2 to NUMBER do
      FACT := FACT * I;
    Factorial := FACT;
  end;
```

```
function Is_Prime (NUMBER: integer): boolean;
{
DESCRIPTION:
    This function determines if a number is prime.

VALUE RETURNED:
    A flag that is true if the number is prime

PARAMETERS:
    NUMBER (in) - the number in question

SAMPLE CALL:
    B := Is_Prime (5);     (would return true)

------------------------------------------------------------}

  var
    PRIME: boolean;             {temporary variable}
    TEST : integer;             {counter for loop}
```

```
begin
  PRIME := true;
  TEST := 2;

{loop through each number until not prime or the square
root is reached}
  while PRIME and (TEST <= Int(Sqrt (NUMBER))) do
    if NUMBER mod TEST = 0 then
      PRIME := false
    else
      TEST := TEST + 1;

  Is_Prime := PRIME;
end;
```

Base Conversion

A number in some other base (binary, octal, hexadecimal, or another *foreign* or nondecimal base) cannot be manipulated internally in high-order languages like Turbo Pascal. However, some applications require output in a foreign base. The rest of the routines in this chapter are designed to support base conversion to and from decimal.

Numbers in foreign bases are almost always better represented internally in string variables, rather than in integer or real variables. Bases larger than 10 must be in strings, because they can contain characters as numbers (A=10, B=11, C=12, and so on). Due to byte size, a numeric variable cannot hold a number in a base smaller than 10 when it is entered as if it were in base 10. For example, the number 100 in base 2 is 1100100(2), which will not fit into an integer variable if it is not recognized as a binary number. Therefore, the subroutines in this chapter accept only string variables for numbers in other bases. They require the type

```
type
  STRING79 = string[79];
```

This will be explained in detail in Chapter 5.

The algorithm for converting a number in a foreign base to a base 10 or decimal number is fairly straightforward. First you must realize that a decimal number is based on powers of 10; for example,

$$4274.23(10) = 4 \times 10^3 + 2 \times 10^2 + 7 \times 10^1 + 4 \times 10^0 + 2 \times 10^{-1} + 3 \times 10^{-2}$$

In the same manner, numbers in other bases are based on powers of their respective bases, as shown here:

Octal: $4274.23(8) = 4{\times}8^3 + 2{\times}8^2 + 7{\times}8^1 + 4{\times}8^0 + 2{\times}8^{-1} + 3{\times}8^{-2}$

Hexadecimal: $4274.23(16) = 4{\times}16^3 + 2{\times}16^2 + 7{\times}16^1 + 4{\times}16^0 + 2{\times}16^{-1} + 3{\times}16^{-2}$

Thus, converting from a foreign base to base 10 is simply adding up the right side of equations like those just shown. The steps to convert the base 8 (octal) example are

$$\begin{aligned} 4274.23(8) &= 4{\times}512 + 2{\times}64 + 7{\times}8 + 4{\times}1 + 2{\times}0.125 + 3{\times}0.015625 \\ &= 2048 + 128 + 56 + 4 + 0.25 + 0.046875 \\ &= 2236.296875 \end{aligned}$$

However, some real numbers in odd bases do not directly convert to base 10, and some round-off error may occur, as shown in this example:

$$\begin{aligned} 102.1(3) &= 1{\times}3^2 + 2{\times}3^0 + 1{\times}3^{-1} \\ &= 9 + 2 + 0.3333333\ldots \\ &= 11.33333333\ldots \end{aligned}$$

The procedure *Anybase_to_Decimal* uses this algorithm. It returns an error if an invalid number is entered. For example, 76 is a valid base 8 number, but it is not valid in base 7. The fundamental rule is that numbers in a given base, N, can range from 0 to $N-1$. The base input for this function can be as high as 36, since Z=35.

```
function Basechar_to_Integer (CHARACTER: char): integer;
{
DESCRIPTION:
    This function converts a character in a large base to
an integer.

VALUE RETURNED:
    The integer equivalent of the character

PARAMETERS:
    CHARACTER (in) - the character of interest

SAMPLE CALL:
    I := Basechar_to_Integer ('A');     (would return 10)
```

NOTES:
    This function is primarily for internal use by
Anybase_to_Digital.

```
------------------------------------------------------------}

  begin

{if the character is a digit, do a normal ASCIIZ conversion}
    if CHARACTER <= '9' then
       Basechar_to_Integer := Ord(CHARACTER) - Ord('0')

{if the character is a letter, convert such that A=10, B=11, etc.}
    else
       Basechar_to_Integer := Ord(UpCase(CHARACTER)) - Ord('A') + 10;
  end;
```

```
Procedure Anybase_to_Decimal (FOREIGN: STRING79;
                                  BASE: integer;
                          var DECIMAL: real;
                          var BASE_ERROR: boolean);
{
DESCRIPTION:
    This procedure converts an number in a foreign base to a
decimal number.

PARAMETERS:
    FOREIGN (in) - the number of interest
    BASE (in) - the base of the number
    DECIMAL (out) - the decimal equivalent
    BASE_ERROR (out) - return status (true if error occurred)

TYPES REQUIRED:
    STRING79 - used for all strings

LIBRARY ROUTINES USED:
    Power - takes a number to a power (exponentiation)
    Basechar_to_Integer - converts a character to its
integer equivalent

SAMPLE CALL:
    Anybase_to_Decimal ('4274.23', 8, NUM, ERROR);
                        (would return 2236.296875)

------------------------------------------------------------}

  var
    I,                          {counter for loop}
    DIGIT,                      {decimal digit}
    EXPONENT,                   {current exponent}
    DECIMAL_POINT: integer;     {location of the decimal point}
    TEMPNUM      : STRING79;    {temporary input value}

  begin
    TEMPNUM := FOREIGN;
```

```
{determine the size of the input number}
    DECIMAL_POINT := Pos ('.', FOREIGN);
    if DECIMAL_POINT = 0 then
      EXPONENT := Length (TEMPNUM) - 1
    else
      begin
        EXPONENT := DECIMAL_POINT - 2;

{eliminate the decimal point}
        TEMPNUM := Copy (TEMPNUM, 1, DECIMAL_POINT-1) +
                   Copy (TEMPNUM, DECIMAL_POINT+1, Length(TEMPNUM));
      end;

    DECIMAL := 0;

    BASE_ERROR := false;

{loop through all characters}
    for I := 1 to Length (TEMPNUM) do
      begin

{determine the integer equivalent of the current character}
        DIGIT := Basechar_to_Integer (TEMPNUM[I]);
        if (DIGIT < 0) or (DIGIT >= BASE) then
          BASE_ERROR := true;

{accumulate the decimal sum}
        DECIMAL := DECIMAL + DIGIT * Power (BASE, EXPONENT);
        EXPONENT := EXPONENT - 1;

      end;
  end;
```

Converting a decimal number to another base essentially reverses the algorithm for converting a foreign-base number to decimal (as discussed earlier). The decimal number must be rewritten into combinations of the foreign base's powers. You can do this most easily by a process of repeated subtraction. For example, consider converting the decimal number 1223 to base 16 (hexadecimal). The number 16^3 is 4096, which is too large, so you must start with 16^2, or 256. Start by subtracting 256 from 1223 until the difference is less than 256:

$$1223 - 256 = 967$$
$$967 - 256 = 711$$
$$711 - 256 = 455$$
$$455 - 256 = 199$$

This gives you the equation

$$1223 = 4{\times}256 + 199$$

Once the number is less than 16^2, go on to 16^1, as shown here:

$$199 - 16 = 183$$
$$183 - 16 = 167$$
$$167 - 16 = 151$$
$$151 - 16 = 135$$
$$135 - 16 = 119$$
$$119 - 16 = 103$$
$$103 - 16 = 87$$
$$87 - 16 = 71$$
$$71 - 16 = 55$$
$$55 - 16 = 39$$
$$39 - 16 = 23$$
$$23 - 16 = 7$$

This gives you the equation

$$1223 = 4{\times}256 + 12{\times}16 + 7$$

Finally, you can determine the answer:

$$1223 = 4{\times}16^2 + 12{\times}16^1 + 7{\times}16^0$$
$$= 4C7(16)$$

Base 10 numbers with decimal points continue with powers of the foreign base less than 0 in the same manner. As with *Anybase_ to_Decimal*, this conversion may not be exact, so the result is computed accurately only to six decimal places.

In the function *Decimal_to_Anybase*, no error status is required. The final procedure in this chapter, *Anybase_to_Anybase*, calls the other two functions in sequence. *Anybase_to_Anybase* will return an error if the *Anybase_to_Decimal* conversion was unsuccessful.

```
function Integer_to_Basechar (NUMBER: integer): char;
{
DESCRIPTION:
    This function converts an integer to a character for bases
larger than ten.

VALUE RETURNED:
    The character equivalent of the integer

PARAMETERS:
    NUMBER (in) - the integer of interest
```

```
SAMPLE CALL:
    CH := Integer_to_Basechar (10);     (would return 'A')

NOTES:
    This function is primarily for interal use by
Decimal_to_Anybase.

-----------------------------------------------------------}

  begin
    if NUMBER <= 9 then
      Integer_to_Basechar := Chr(NUMBER + Ord('0'))
    else
      Integer_to_Basechar := Chr(NUMBER - 10 + Ord('A'));
  end;
```

```
function Decimal_to_Anybase (DECIMAL: real;
                             BASE: integer): STRING79;
{
DESCRIPTION:
    This function converts a decimal number to a number in a
foreign base.

VALUE RETURNED:
    A string containing the foreign-base equivalent

PARAMETERS:
    DECIMAL (in) - the number of interest
    BASE (in) - the base of the number to be computed

TYPES REQUIRED:
    STRING79 - used for all strings

LIBRARY ROUTINES USED:
    Power - takes a number to a power (exponentiation)
    Integer_to_Basechar - converts a number to its
character equivalent

SAMPLE CALL:
    NUM := Decimal_to_Anybase (1223, 16);
                             (would return '4C7')

-----------------------------------------------------------}

  var
    COUNT,                        {running counter of current digit}
    EXPONENT: integer;            {current exponent}
    TEMPNUM : STRING79;           {temporary final value}

  begin

{determine starting exponent}
```

```
{if number is less than 1, start at -1 to include 0's}
    if DECIMAL < 1.0 then
      begin
        TEMPNUM := '0.';
        EXPONENT := -1;
      end

{if number is greater than 1, starting exponent is one less
than the exponent that is greater than the starting number}
    else
      begin
        TEMPNUM := '';
        EXPONENT := 0;
        while Power (BASE, EXPONENT) <= DECIMAL do
          EXPONENT := EXPONENT + 1;
        EXPONENT := EXPONENT - 1;
      end;

{loop until number is close enough}
    while DECIMAL > 0.0000001 do
      begin

{count the number of times the power is subtracted from the
starting number}
        COUNT := 0;
        while DECIMAL >= Power (BASE, EXPONENT) - 0.0000001 do
          begin
            DECIMAL := DECIMAL - Power (BASE, EXPONENT);
            COUNT := COUNT + 1;
          end;

{concatenate the digit to the string}
        TEMPNUM := TEMPNUM + Integer_to_Basechar (COUNT);
        if EXPONENT = 0 then
          TEMPNUM := TEMPNUM + '.';

{go to the next digit}
        EXPONENT := EXPONENT - 1;
      end;

    Decimal_to_Anybase := TEMPNUM;
  end;
```

```
Procedure Anybase_to_Anybase (FIRSTNUM: STRING79;
                 FIRSTBASE, SECONDBASE: integer;
                          var SECONDNUM: STRING79;
                          var BASE_ERROR: boolean);
{
DESCRIPTION:
    This procedure converts an number in a foreign base to a
number in another foreign base.
```

```
PARAMETERS:
    FIRSTNUM (in) - the number of interest
    FIRSTBASE (in) - the base of the known number
    SECONDBASE (in) - the base of the unknown number
    SECONDNUM (out) - the new number in the other base
    BASE_ERROR (out) - return status (true if error occurred)

TYPES REQUIRED:
    STRING79 - used for all strings

LIBRARY ROUTINES USED:
    Anybase_to_Decimal - converts a foreign-base number to decimal
    Decimal_to_Anybase - converts a decimal number to a foreign base

SAMPLE CALL:
    Anybase_to_Anybase ('4274', 8, 16, NUM, ERROR);
                            (would return '8BC.')

----------------------------------------------------------}


  var
    DECIMAL: real;              {temporary decimal number}

  begin

{convert the foreign-base number to decimal}
    Anybase_to_Decimal (FIRSTNUM, FIRSTBASE, DECIMAL, BASE_ERROR);

{if the conversion was successful, convert the decimal number
to the new foreign-base number}
    if not BASE_ERROR then
      SECONDNUM := Decimal_to_Anybase (DECIMAL, SECONDBASE);
  end;
```

3

Array Manipulation

When Pascal programmers discuss data structures, many of them immediately talk about linked lists and binary trees. Pascal does provide a wealth of programming tools via dynamic data structures. Nevertheless, arrays remain an essential (and often underused) data structure. This chapter presents several characteristics of generic array manipulation routines.

A major goal when developing any programming routine is to keep the code as generic as possible. Generic routines minimize both duplication of effort and the amount of coding and testing when modifications are required. Although most programmers are proficient with array manipulation, many fail to develop routines that are truly generic.

Array manipulation routines should not restrict the range of index values. You can accomplish this by not only passing the array to each routine, but also the lower and upper bounds, as shown in the following:

```
Sum (POSITIVE, 1, 10);
```

Each routine can determine the number of elements in the array as follows:

```
NUM_ELEMENTS := Abs(UPPER_BOUND - LOWER_BOUND) + 1;
```

Most programs that manipulate arrays use only one type of array. Routines can be designed that take advantage of this characteristic, which increases their generic nature. Each array manipulation routine in this chapter is based on the following types:

ARRAY—ELEMENT
ARRAY—TYPE

Therefore, if a routine needs to total an array containing, for example, 100 values of type **real**, the following types must be declared:

```
ARRAY_ELEMENT = real;
ARRAY_TYPE = array [1..100] of ARRAY_ELEMENT;
```

If a different program manipulates integer values, you can simply change the type declarations to

```
ARRAY_ELEMENT = integer;
ARRAY_TYPE = array [1..100] of ARRAY_ELEMENT;
```

Several of the following statistical routines appear to perform trivial tasks. Developing each routine as an individual function, however, increases the readability and reusability of the code.

```
function Minimum_Value (VALUES: ARRAY_TYPE;
     LOWER_BOUND, UPPER_BOUND: integer): ARRAY_ELEMENT;
{
DESCRIPTION:
    This routine examines an array of values and
    returns the minimum value found.
```

```
PARAMETERS:
    VALUES (in) - the array of values to examine
    LOWER_BOUND (in) - the lowest array index
    UPPER_BOUND (in) - the highest array index

VALUE RETURNED:
    the minimum value in the array

TYPES REQUIRED:
    ARRAY_TYPE must be defined as an array of ARRAY_ELEMENT
    ARRAY_ELEMENT must be defined as the type of the elements in
                  the array provided

SAMPLE CALL:
    MIN := Minimum_Value (VALUES, 1, 10);

-----------------------------------------------------------}

  var
    INDEX: integer;
    CURRENT_MINIMUM: ARRAY_ELEMENT;

  begin
    CURRENT_MINIMUM := VALUES [LOWER_BOUND];

    for INDEX := LOWER_BOUND + 1 to UPPER_BOUND do
      if (VALUES[INDEX] < CURRENT_MINIMUM) then
        CURRENT_MINIMUM := VALUES [INDEX];

    Minimum_Value := CURRENT_MINIMUM;
  end;
```

```
function Maximum_Value (VALUES: ARRAY_TYPE;
    LOWER_BOUND, UPPER_BOUND: integer): ARRAY_ELEMENT;
{
DESCRIPTION:
    This routine examines an array of values and
    returns the maximum value found.

PARAMETERS:
    VALUES (in) - array of values to examine
    LOWER_BOUND (in) - the lowest array index
    UPPER_BOUND (in) - the highest array index

VALUE RETURNED:
    the maximum value in the array

TYPES REQUIRED:
    ARRAY_TYPE must be defined as an array of ARRAY_ELEMENT
    ARRAY_ELEMENT must be defined as the type of the elements in
                  the array provided

SAMPLE CALL:
    MAX := Maximum_Value (VALUES, 1, 10);

-----------------------------------------------------------}
```

```
var
  INDEX: integer;
  CURRENT_MAXIMUM: ARRAY_ELEMENT;

begin
  CURRENT_MAXIMUM := VALUES [LOWER_BOUND];

  for INDEX := LOWER_BOUND + 1 to UPPER_BOUND do
    if (VALUES[INDEX] > CURRENT_MAXIMUM) then
      CURRENT_MAXIMUM := VALUES [INDEX];

  Maximum_Value := CURRENT_MAXIMUM;
end;
```

```
function Sum_Values (VALUES: ARRAY_TYPE;
  LOWER_BOUND, UPPER_BOUND: integer): ARRAY_ELEMENT;
{
DESCRIPTION:
    This routine returns the sum of the values contained in
    the array VALUES.

PARAMETERS:
    VALUES (in) - the array of values to sum
    LOWER_BOUND (in) - the lowest array index
    UPPER_BOUND (in) - the highest array index

VALUE RETURNED:
    the sum of the values in the array

TYPES REQUIRED:
    ARRAY_TYPE must be defined as an array of ARRAY_ELEMENT
    ARRAY_ELEMENT must be defined as the type of the elements in
                  the array provided

SAMPLE CALL:
    SUM := Sum_Values (VALUES, 1, 10);

-----------------------------------------------------------}

  var
    INDEX: integer;
    SUM: ARRAY_ELEMENT;

  begin
    SUM := 0;

    for INDEX := LOWER_BOUND to UPPER_BOUND do
      SUM := SUM + VALUES [INDEX];

    Sum_Values := SUM;
  end;
```

```
function Average_Value (VALUES: ARRAY_TYPE;
    LOWER_BOUND, UPPER_BOUND: integer): real;
{
DESCRIPTION:
    This routine returns the average value contained in the
    array VALUES.

PARAMETERS:
    VALUES (in) - array of values to return the average of
    LOWER_BOUND (in) - the lowest array index
    UPPER_BOUND (in) - the highest array index

VALUE RETURNED:
    the average value in the array

TYPES REQUIRED:
    ARRAY_TYPE must be defined as an array of the type provided

LIBRARY ROUTINES USED:
    Sum_Values - returns the sum of the values contained in an array
                 of type ARRAY_TYPE

SAMPLE CALL:
    AVE := Average_Value (VALUES, 1, 10);

------------------------------------------------------------}

  begin
    Average_Value := Sum_Values(VALUES, LOWER_BOUND, UPPER_BOUND) /
                     Abs(UPPER_BOUND - LOWER_BOUND + 1);
  end;
```

```
function Ascending_Order (VALUES: ARRAY_TYPE;
     LOWER_BOUND, UPPER_BOUND: integer): boolean;
{
DESCRIPTION:
    This routine examines an array of values and
    returns TRUE if the values are in ascending
    (lowest to highest) order, or FALSE otherwise.

PARAMETERS:
    VALUES (in) - the array of values to examine
    LOWER_BOUND (in) - the lowest array index
    UPPER_BOUND (in) - the highest array index
VALUE RETURNED:
    TRUE if values are ascending
    FALSE otherwise

TYPES REQUIRED:
    ARRAY_TYPE must be defined as an array of the type provided

SAMPLE CALL:
    if (Ascending_Order (VALUES, 1, 10)) then

------------------------------------------------------------}
```

```
    var
      INDEX          : integer;
      CORRECT_ORDER : boolean;

    begin
      INDEX := LOWER_BOUND;
      CORRECT_ORDER := True;

      while ((INDEX <= UPPER_BOUND -1) and CORRECT_ORDER) do
        if (VALUES [INDEX] >= VALUES [INDEX + 1]) then
          CORRECT_ORDER := False
        else
          INDEX := INDEX + 1;

      Ascending_Order := CORRECT_ORDER;
    end;
```

```
procedure  Median (VALUES: ARRAY_TYPE;
 LOWER_BOUND, UPPER_BOUND: integer;
        var MEDIAN_VALUE: real;
             var STATUS: byte);
{
DESCRIPTION:
    This routine examines an array of values and returns
    the median.  If the values are not in ascending order
    ERROR is returned.

PARAMETERS:
    VALUES (in) - array of values to return the median of
    LOWER_BOUND (in) - the lowest array index
    UPPER_BOUND (in) - the highest array index
    MEDIAN_VALUE (out) - the median of the values in the array
    STATUS (out) - the success status of the routine

TYPES REQUIRED:
    ARRAY_ELEMENT must be defined as the type of the elements
                    in the array provided
    ARRAY_TYPE must be defined as an array of the type provided

LIBRARY ROUTINES USED:
    Ascending_Order - returns True if the values in the array are
                    in ascending order, otherwise Fals

SAMPLE CALL:
    Median (VALUES, 1, 10, MEDIAN_VALUE, STATUS);

--------------------------------------------------------}

  Const
    ERROR = 0;
    NO_ERROR = 1;

  var
    NUM_ELEMENTS: integer;

  begin
    NUM_ELEMENTS := Abs(UPPER_BOUND - LOWER_BOUND) + 1;
```

```
    if (not Ascending_Order(VALUES, LOWER_BOUND, UPPER_BOUND)) then
      STATUS := ERROR
    else
      begin
        if (NUM_ELEMENTS mod 2 = 1) then
          MEDIAN_VALUE := VALUES [(LOWER_BOUND + NUM_ELEMENTS div 2)]
        else
          MEDIAN_VALUE := (VALUES [(LOWER_BOUND + NUM_ELEMENTS div 2)] +
                           VALUES [(UPPER_BOUND - NUM_ELEMENTS div 2)]) / 2.0;
        STATUS := NO_ERROR;
      end;
end;
```

```
  procedure Get_Mode (VALUES: ARRAY_TYPE;
                LOWER_BOUND,
                UPPER_BOUND: integer;
                  var MODE: ARRAY_ELEMENT;
                  var STATUS: byte);
  {
  DESCRIPTION:
      This routine examines an array of values and returns the
      modal value.  If the values are not in ascending order
      the value ERROR is returned.  If more than one modal value
      exists the status DUPLICATE_MODES is returned and the
      first mode is used.

  PARAMETERS:
      VALUES (in) - the array of values to examine for the modal value
      MODE (out) - the modal value
      LOWER_BOUND (in) - the lowest array index
      UPPER_BOUND (in) - the highest array index
      STATUS (out) - the success status of the routine

  TYPES REQUIRED:
      ARRAY_TYPE must be defined as an array of the type provided

  SAMPLE CALL:
      Get_Mode (VALUES, 1, 10, MODE, STATUS);

  NOTES:
      Status values returned:
          ERROR - values were not in ascending order
          NO_ERROR - successful operation
          DUPLICATE_MODES - more than one modal value existed

  ------------------------------------------------------------}

    const
      ERROR = 0;
      NO_ERROR = 1;
      DUPLICATE_MODES = 2;

    var
      MAX_VALUE,
      CURRENT_VALUE    : ARRAY_ELEMENT;
      CURRENT_COUNT,
      MAX_COUNT, INDEX : integer;
```

```
begin
  MAX_COUNT := -1;
  INDEX   := LOWER_BOUND;
  STATUS := NO_ERROR;

  if (not Ascending_Order (VALUES, LOWER_BOUND, UPPER_BOUND)) then
    STATUS := ERROR
  else
    begin
      while ((INDEX <= UPPER_BOUND) and (STATUS = NO_ERROR)) do
        begin
          CURRENT_VALUE := VALUES[INDEX];
          CURRENT_COUNT := 0;

          while ((VALUES[INDEX] = CURRENT_VALUE) and
                 (INDEX <= UPPER_BOUND)) do
            begin
              CURRENT_COUNT := CURRENT_COUNT + 1;
              INDEX := INDEX + 1;
            end;

          if (CURRENT_COUNT = MAX_COUNT) then
            STATUS := DUPLICATE_MODES

          else if (CURRENT_COUNT > MAX_COUNT) then
              begin
                MAX_COUNT := CURRENT_COUNT;
                MAX_VALUE := CURRENT_VALUE;
              end;
        end;
    end;
  MODE := MAX_VALUE;
end;
```

Variance and Standard Deviation

Two of the most widely used statistical tools are *variance* and *standard deviation*. Statisticians use them to analyze the *expected value*, or average, of a population. If, for example, 100 different programs are run on two different computers, an expected value representing how much faster the first computer is in comparison to the second can be computed. Statisticians can use either the standard deviation or the variance to determine the accuracy of the expected value by describing the average deviation from the sample mean. The variance is computed by using the equation

$$V = \frac{1}{N} \sum_{i=1}^{N} (D_i - M)^2$$

The standard deviation is the square root of the variance:

$$std = \sqrt{\frac{V*N}{N-1}}$$

In both equations, N is the number of elements in the sample, D is an element in the sample data, and M is the sample's mean.

The standard deviation is the more important of the two values because its result is more understandable. In the example just given, if computer 1 averages 3 seconds faster than computer 2, possible values would be as follows:

Expected value:	3 seconds
Variance:	4 (seconds)^2
Standard deviation:	2 seconds

When the variance is calculated, the difference of each element and the mean is squared to produce only positive numbers; otherwise, the sum would always be 0 by default.

Here are the routines for determining variance and standard deviation:

```
function Variance (VALUES: ARRAY_TYPE;
 LOWER_BOUND, UPPER_BOUND: integer): real;
{
DESCRIPTION:
    This routine returns the variance of the values contained
    within the array VALUES.

PARAMETERS:
    VALUES (in) - the array of values to return the variance of
    LOWER_BOUND (in) - the lowest array index
    UPPER_BOUND (in) - the highest array index

VALUE RETURNED:
    the variance of the array

TYPES REQUIRED:
    ARRAY_TYPE must be defined as an array of the type provided

LIBRARY ROUTINES USED:
    Average_Value - returns the average value in an array of type
                    ARRAY_TYPE

SAMPLE CALL:
    VARC := Variance (VALUES, 1, 10);

-------------------------------------------------------------}
```

```
var
  INDEX  : integer;
  SUM,
  AVERAGE: real;

begin
  SUM := 0;

  AVERAGE := Average_Value (VALUES, LOWER_BOUND, UPPER_BOUND);

  for INDEX := LOWER_BOUND to UPPER_BOUND do
    SUM := SUM + Sqr(VALUES [INDEX] - AVERAGE);

  Variance := SUM / Abs(UPPER_BOUND - LOWER_BOUND +1);
end;
```

```
function Standard_Deviation (VALUES: ARRAY_TYPE;
            LOWER_BOUND, UPPER_BOUND: integer): real;
{
DESCRIPTION:
    This routine returns the standard deviation of
    the values contained in the array VALUES.

PARAMETERS:
    VALUES (in) - the array of values to return the standard deviation of
    LOWER_BOUND (in) - the lowest array index
    UPPER_BOUND (in) - the highest array index

VALUE RETURNED:
    the standard deviation of the values contained in the array

TYPES REQUIRED:
    ARRAY_TYPE must be defined as an array of the type provided

LIBRARY ROUTINES USED:
    Variance - returns the variance of the values contained in
               an array of ARRAY_TYPE

SAMPLE CALL:
    S_Dev := Standard_Deviation (VALUES, 1, 10);

----------------------------------------------------------}

  var
  NUM_ELEMENTS: integer;
  VARC        : real;         {variance of the values}

  begin
      VARC := Variance (VALUES, LOWER_BOUND, UPPER_BOUND);

      NUM_ELEMENTS := Abs(UPPER_BOUND - LOWER_BOUND) + 1;

      Standard_Deviation := Sqrt((VARC * NUM_ELEMENTS) / (NUM_ELEMENTS - 1));
  end;
```

Least Squares Fit

The *least squares fit* is one of the simplest methods of determining the linear equation that will best fit a collection of sample data values. For example, given the following distribution of values,

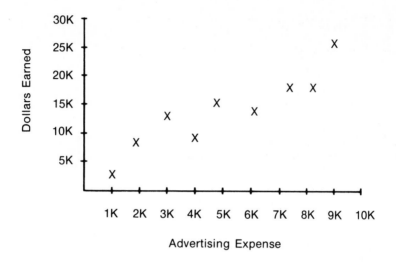

the least squares algorithm provides the linear equation that best fits the data, as shown here:

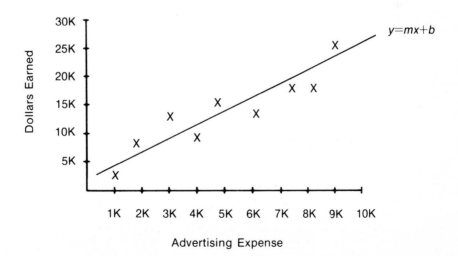

The line shown is called the *line of best fit*. However, it is important to note that the routine will produce a linear equation that describes any set of data points—despite its nonlinearity.

Linear equations are expressed in slope-intercept format. The procedure **Least_Square** returns the slope and the Y-intercept of the line that best fits the data:

```
procedure Least_Square (X, Y: ARRAY_TYPE;
    LOWER_BOUND, UPPER_BOUND: integer;
        var SLOPE, INTERCEPT: real);
{
DESCRIPTION:
    This routine uses a Least Square algorithm to
    estimate the slope and intercept for a given
    set of X and Y values.

PARAMETERS:
    X (in) - array of X values
    Y (in) - array of Y values
    LOWER_BOUND (in) - lowest array index
    UPPER_BOUND (in) - highest array index
    SLOPE (out) - slope of the X and Y values
    INTERCEPT (out) - the intercept of the X and Y values

TYPES REQUIRED:
    ARRAY_ELEMENT must be defined as the type of the elements
                    in the array provided
    ARRAY_TYPE must be defined as an array of the type provided

SAMPLE CALL:
    Least_Square (XVALUES, YVALUES, 1, 10, SLOPE, INTR);

------------------------------------------------------------}

    var
      INDEX, NUM_ELEMENTS               : integer;
      XSUM, YSUM, XSQUARED_SUM, XY_SUM: real;

    begin
      XSUM := 0.0;            {sum of the x values}
      YSUM := 0.0;            {sum of the y values}
      XSQUARED_SUM := 0.0; {sum of the x values squared}
      XY_SUM := 0.0;          {sum of x[i] * y[i]}

{compute the sums}
      for INDEX := LOWER_BOUND to UPPER_BOUND do
        begin
          XSUM := XSUM + X[INDEX];
          YSUM := YSUM + Y[INDEX];
          XSQUARED_SUM := XSQUARED_SUM + (X[INDEX] * X[INDEX]);
          XY_SUM := XY_SUM + (X[INDEX] * Y[INDEX]);
        end;

      NUM_ELEMENTS := Abs(UPPER_BOUND - LOWER_BOUND) + 1;
      SLOPE := ((XSUM * YSUM) - (NUM_ELEMENTS * XY_SUM)) /
               ((XSUM * XSUM) - (NUM_ELEMENTS * XSQUARED_SUM));

      INTERCEPT := (YSUM - (SLOPE * XSUM)) / NUM_ELEMENTS;
    end;
```

Statisticians use *residuals* to determine the "goodness of fit" of the linear equation. A residual is the distance of each value from the line of best fit. For example, the difference between the actual value of Y and the approximated $\hat{Y}$ is a residual, as shown by this equation:

$$\text{RESIDUAL} := Y - \hat{Y};$$

The sum of the residuals for the entire array can determine the validity of the linear equation. For example, if the data is linear, as shown here,

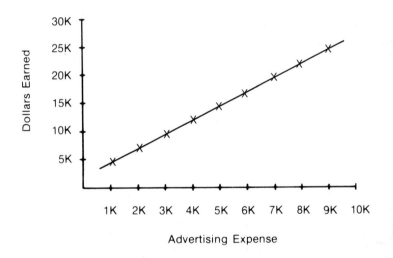

the sum of the residuals will be 0. As the line less approximates the data, the sum will be greater.

Each of the routines introduced so far can support many applications. However, they are limited because they require knowledge of the data type. Because Pascal interprets values of type **integer** differently from values of type **real**, the routines had to recognize the array's type.

However, an application that moves or copies a set of values to a different location can perform the manipulation in a context-free manner. For example, to copy ten integer values to a different array, the routine does not need to examine the actual values. Instead, the routine only needs to know the number of bytes to copy. If you later need to move values of type **real**, you tell the routine the number of bytes to move. Use the built-in Turbo Pascal function **Sizeof** to provide the size of an object in bytes, as shown here:

```
program Sizeof_Test (input, output);
  var
    X : array [1..10] of integer;
  begin

    writeln ('X requires ', Sizeof (X), ' bytes');

  end.
```

The next procedure illustrates the ideal generic array manipulation routine. It defines the local type **ARRAY_TYPE** for the source and destination arrays. Imagine that the local variables **SOURCE** and **DESTINATION** overlay the arrays passed by the calling routine. The routine assigns these variables to the actual memory locations of the passed arrays. If the calling routine passes the arrays **ARRAY1** and **ARRAY2**, **SOURCE** and **DESTINATION** will reference the following:

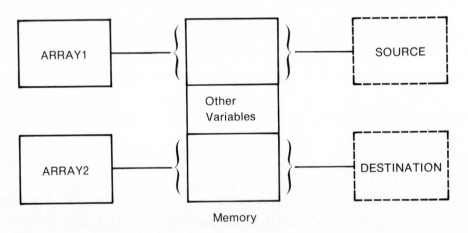

Memory

When the routine copies the byte referenced by **SOURCE[I]** to **DESTINATION[I]**, the byte referenced by **ARRAY1[I]** is assigned to **ARRAY2[I]**.

There are a few applications that cannot be easily implemented with generic routines. Nevertheless, if you break your routines into smaller, more generic procedures, the applications will be much easier to write, test, and modify. The following routine provides the generalized procedure for copying arrays:

```
procedure Array_Copy (var SOURCE_ARRAY, DESTINATION_ARRAY;
                          ARRAY_SIZE: integer);
{
DESCRIPTION:
    This routine copies the contents of SOURCE_ARRAY
    to DESTINATION_ARRAY.

PARAMETERS:
    SOURCE_ARRAY (in) - the array of values to copy
    DESTINATION_ARRAY (out) - the array to copy the values into
    ARRAY_SIZE (in) - number of bytes in the source array

SAMPLE CALL:
    Array_Copy (VALUES, SAVE_VALUES, Sizeof (VALUES));

NOTES:
    This procedure will work for arrays of any type.  It is
    essential therefore that you provide an accurate number
    of bytes for the size of the source array.

    --------------------------------------------------------}

type
  ARRAY_TYPE  = array [1..MaxInt] of byte;
var
  SOURCE      : ARRAY_TYPE absolute SOURCE_ARRAY;
  DESTINATION: ARRAY_TYPE absolute DESTINATION_ARRAY;
  INDEX       : integer;
begin
  for INDEX := 1 to ARRAY_SIZE do
    DESTINATION [INDEX] := SOURCE [INDEX];
end;
```

Bit Masking

Most Pascal programmers must decide whether to use arrays or dynamic data structures when they program. Inherent in most programming applications is the trade-off between time and space. Normally, routines that use arrays run faster than those using dynamic data structures, because of the overhead associated with memory allocation. To minimize the amount of space required, many applications use *bit masking*, which assigns a unique value to each bit in an array of values.

Consider the following example: The students at a college in the Midwest must purchase new activity cards. The current enrollment is 16,000, and each student has a unique identification number that ranges from 0 to 15,999. The Dean of Students has requested that you provide a sorted listing of the ID numbers of the students who have already purchased the new cards. There are several ways to produce the sorted listing. First, an array dimensioned from 0 to 15,999 can be used as follows:

```
STUDENT_BODY = array [0..15999] of integer;
```

Each element in the array can then be assigned the value 0 or 1, based on whether or not a student has purchased an activity card.

A second method is to create a dynamic list of the students who have purchased the cards. One way to organize this is in a binary tree, as shown here:

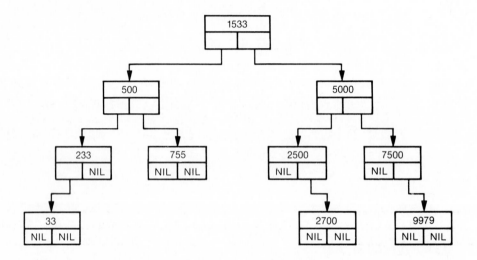

The third method is to use a bit mask. Remember that a bit mask assigns a unique value to each bit in a word, which is generally two bytes. In so doing, a bit mask allows a single word to represent several values. In Turbo Pascal, a variable of type **integer** uses 16 bits. Therefore, if each bit is used, a single integer can represent 16 students, as shown here:

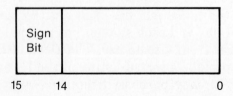

In this example, if you consider the students with identification numbers from 0 to 15, the bits are used as follows:

Bit 0 = Student 0
Bit 1 = Student 1
Bit 2 = Student 2
Bit 3 = Student 3
.
.
.
Bit 15 = Student 15

A zero value in a specific bit means that the student has not purchased the card. For example, the bit combination

0000000000000101

indicates that only students 0 and 2 have purchased the card.

More than 16 students must be represented in this example; this can be done by simply defining an array and using each bit in the same fashion. Since each integer value can represent 16 students, the array size has decreased to 1000:

16,000 div 16 = 1000

You can now define each student by a word-and-bit combination; for example,

Student 1   = Word   0 Bit 1
Student 10   = Word   0 Bit 10
Student 17   = Word   1 Bit 1
Student 32   = Word   2 Bit 0
Student 15999 = Word   999 Bit 15

The value for the word is calculated as

```
WORD := ID_NUMBER div 16;
```

and the value for the bit is computed as

```
BIT := ID_NUMBER mod 16;
```

When a student purchases an activity card, the student's identification number is placed in the file **ACTIVITY.DAT**. To produce the sorted listing for the Dean, you must read each ID number from the file and assign the value 1 to the word-and-bit position that corresponds to the student. For example, if the identification number were 84, you would assign the value 1 to word 5, bit 4:

$$84 \text{ div } 16 = 5$$
$$84 \text{ mod } 16 = 4$$

After you read the entire file, search the array, word-by-word and bit-by-bit, for the value 1. The student identification numbers that correspond to the word-and-bit combination are output to produce the sorted list.

The easiest way to manipulate bits in Pascal is to use sets. When you define a set, Pascal represents each member with a bit. Consider the following declarations:

```
BITS = 0..15;

WORDS = set of BITS;

STUDENT_BODY = array [0..999] of WORDS;
```

Since you are using sets, you must use the set operators + (intersect) and **in**. For example, to add a student to the list, you would use

```
WORD := ID_NUMBER div 16;

BIT := ID_NUMBER mod 16;

BIT_MAP [WORD] := BIT_MAP [WORD] + [BIT];
```

To determine if a student had purchased a card, you would use

```
if (BIT in BIT_MAP[WORD]) then
```

The following program opens the file **ACTIVITY.DAT** and reads the ID numbers. The bits in the mask are initially set to 0. ID numbers are read one at a time and the corresponding student is updated in the bit mask. After the file has been read, the program searches through the bit mask and outputs the identification numbers of all students who have purchased the card.

```
Program Bit_Mapping (input, output);

Const
  WORD_SIZE = 16;                    {number of bits in a word}
  MAX_WORDS = 999;                   {array size required}
  MSB = 15;

Type

  BITS = set of 0..MSB;              {number of bits in a word}
  MAP = array [0..MAX_WORDS] of BITS; {the bit map}

  FILE_IDENTIFIER = string[20];      {input file name}

{------------------------------------------------------------------------}
{                            Initialize_Bit_Map                          }
{------------------------------------------------------------------------}

procedure Initialize_Bit_Map (var BIT_MAP: MAP);
  var
    WORD: integer;

  begin

{set the bits in each word of the bit map to zero}
    for WORD := 0 to MAX_WORDS do
      BIT_MAP[WORD] := [];           {empty set}

  end;

{------------------------------------------------------------------------}
{                           Write_Sorted_Values                         }
{------------------------------------------------------------------------}

procedure Write_Sorted_Values (BIT_MAP: MAP);
  var
    WORD,             {word in the map we are examining}
    BIT : integer;    {bit position within the word}

  begin

{for each word, bit position, see if the bit has been set and if so}
{print the value which corresponds}

    for WORD := 0 to MAX_WORDS do
      for BIT := 0 to WORD_SIZE -1 do
        if (BIT in BIT_MAP [WORD]) then
          writeln (WORD_SIZE * WORD + BIT);
  end;

{------------------------------------------------------------------------}
{                       Map_Unsorted_Values_From_File                   }
{------------------------------------------------------------------------}

procedure Map_Unsorted_Values_From_File (FILE_NAME: FILE_IDENTIFIER;
                                         var BIT_MAP: MAP);
  var
    VALUE       : integer;   {value read from the input file to be}
                             {mapped into the bit map}
    INPUT_FILE  : text;      {file pointer to the input file}
```

```
    WORD_POSITION,                    {values are mapped based on word and bit}
                                      {position. word_position is the is the bit}
                                      {map index to the word which contains the}
                                      {bit which specifies the actual value}
    BIT_POSITION: integer;            {an N bit word is capable of mapping N}
                                      {values.  bit_position contains the bit}
                                      {within the word which represents the}
                                      {value that has been input}

  begin

    Assign (INPUT_FILE, FILE_NAME);   {open the input file}
    Reset (INPUT_FILE);

{read the values contained in the file specified until and end of file}
{is found and place them into the map}
    while (not eof(INPUT_FILE))
      begin
        Readln (INPUT_FILE, VALUE);              {place the next value in the map}
        WORD_POSITION := VALUE div WORD_SIZE;    {Example: 15 div 16 = 0 }
        BIT_POSITION  := VALUE mod WORD_SIZE;    {         15 mod 16 = 15}
                                                 {    says word 0, bit 15}
{place the value into the map}
        BIT_MAP [WORD_POSITION] := BIT_MAP [WORD_POSITION] + [BIT_POSITION];
      end;

    close (INPUT_FILE);
  end;

{-------------------------------------------------------------------------}
{                          Main Program                                   }
{-------------------------------------------------------------------------}

  var
    BIT_MAP : MAP;    {array of words where each combination of (word, bit
                       position) maps to a unique value.  for example,
                              MAP (word 0, bit 1) = 1
                              MAP (word 0, bit 2) = 2
                                        :
                              MAP (word 1, bit 0) = 16}

  begin

    Initialize_Bit_Map (BIT_MAP);  {start with a new map}

    Map_Unsorted_Values_from_file ('x.dat', BIT_MAP);

    Write_Sorted_Values (BIT_MAP);

  end.
```

Remember that the compromise between time and speed will always exist. There are many applications, such as the program you have just studied, that use bit masking to minimize the amount of space they consume.

C H A P T E R

4

Searching and Sorting

Most applications that use arrays search for specific values or require the values to be in either ascending or descending order. Searching and sorting are important parts of most computer applications. Selecting the correct algorithm for sorting and searching applications can have a significant impact upon the execution time of your programs. Computer scientists have thoroughly researched the characteristics of sorting and searching algorithms. They find that several algorithms will execute much faster than others, because fewer iterations are required in order to sort an array or to locate a specific value.

This chapter introduces searching—using the sequential and binary searches—and sorting—using the bubble, selection, Shell, and quick sorts. As in Chapter 3, the routines are generic. Each routine will support arrays of type **integer** and **real**, as well as user-defined strings. The type of array is defined by **ARRAY—TYPE**, and the sorting order (either ascending or descending) is a parameter to each routine.

Searching

Many programming applications require table lookup for specific values. For example, assume the following arrays contain employee information:

Index	EMPLOYEE		ID NUMBER		SALARY
0	Boy		1111		30000
1	Burnham		2222		45000
2	Byrd		3700		38000
3	Davis		4201		25000
4	Eubank		5001		60000
5	Grant		5500		35000
6	Jones		6200		45000
7	Kempf		7777		50000
8	Rosaschi		8001		55000
9	Watson		8372		32000

If management wants to access Jones's salary, a program can search the array **EMPLOYEE** sequentially until the name is found. It can then locate the salary associated with the index value that points to Jones. In this case, index 6 points to a salary of $45,000.

The Sequential Search

The *sequential search* is the simplest searching algorithm. Values are stored as elements in the array. Each time a value must be found, the sequential search starts with the first element in the array and examines the elements one after another until either the value is found or the elements are exhausted. In the example of the employee information array given earlier, the search would first test the element Boy and then examine successive values of the array until it found the element Jones. The following routine implements the sequential search:

```
procedure Sequential_Search (VALUES: ARRAY_TYPE;
            LOWER_BOUND, UPPER_BOUND: integer;
                    DESIRED_VALUE: ARRAY_ELEMENT;
                     var LOCATION: integer;
                        var FOUND: boolean);
{
DESCRIPTION:
    This routine searches the array VALUES for the value
    contained in the variable DESIRED_VALUE.  If the value
    is found the variable FOUND is set to true and LOCATION
    is the index to the value.  If the value is not found,
    FOUND is set to false.

PARAMETERS:
    VALUES (in) - the array of values to search
    LOWER_BOUND (in) - the lowest element in the search range
    UPPER_BOUND (in) - the highest element in the search range
    DESIRED_VALUE (in) - the value to search for
    LOCATION (out) - the element of the array to compare to DESIRED_VALUE
    FOUND (out) - true if the desired value is found; otherwise, false

TYPES REQUIRED:
    ARRAY_TYPE - the type of the array
    ARRAY_ELEMENT - the element type of the array

SAMPLE CALL:
    Sequential_Search (VALUES, 1, 10, 15, LOCATION, FOUND);

----------------------------------------------------------}

  begin
    FOUND := false;

    LOCATION := LOWER_BOUND;

{examine successive values until the desired value is found
 or each element in the array has been examined}
    while ((LOCATION <= UPPER_BOUND) and (not FOUND)) do
      if (VALUES[LOCATION] = DESIRED_VALUE) then
        FOUND := true
      else
        LOCATION := LOCATION + 1;
  end;
```

The Binary Search

In the previous application, the sequential search successfully found the desired information; however, you can reduce the number of iterations required to find the data by using a different searching algorithm, such as the *binary search*. To perform a binary search, the array must be in ascending order.

The binary search is one of the quickest searching algorithms used by programmers. Unlike the sequential search, which examines successive elements of the array, the binary search reduces the number of elements that must be examined by a factor of two with each iteration until the desired record is found. If you use the sequential search to search the employee information for Jones's salary, the process requires seven iterations. The binary search requires only four iterations, which reduces the execution time. The decrease in execution time becomes more important as array sizes increase.

The first iteration of the binary search examines the entire array. Using the employee information example, imagine that the variables **LOW** and **HIGH** are assigned the values 0 and 9. The variable **MID—INDEX** is the middle element in the search range. **VALUES[MID—INDEX]** contains the value that you will compare to **DESIRED—VALUE**. To calculate **MID—INDEX**, you use

```
MID_INDEX := (HIGH + LOW) div 2;
```

Since **div** performs integer division, **MID—INDEX** is assigned the value 4, as follows.

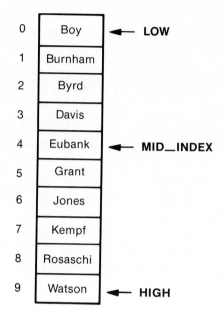

If the value contained in **VALUES[MID_INDEX]** equals the desired value, the search is completed by setting a variable called **FOUND** to true.

If the value contained in **VALUES[MID_INDEX]** is greater than the desired value, the algorithm modifies the search range, because the value indicates that there is no reason to search past that point for the desired value. For example, imagine that the array contains the following information.

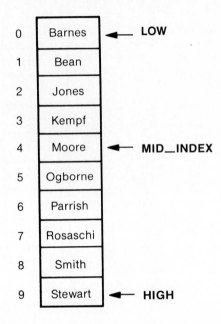

Since you are searching for Jones, there is no reason to search above **VALUES[MID—INDEX]** for the name. The search then modifies the value of **HIGH** as follows:

```
HIGH := MID_INDEX - 1;
```

In effect, this creates a new range of names to examine. The value of **MID—INDEX** is also modified:

```
MID_INDEX := (HIGH + LOW) div 2;
```

The new range of names then contains

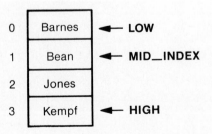

Similarly, if the initial array contains

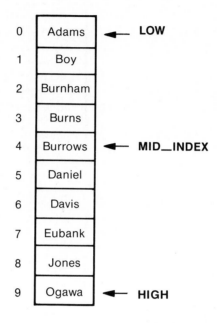

and you are searching for Jones, there is no need to search below
VALUES[MID_INDEX] for the name. The search modifies the
value contained in **LOW** by the statement

```
LOW := MID_INDEX + 1;
```

which produces this new range:

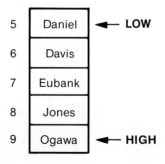

The algorithm recomputes **MID—INDEX** to yield

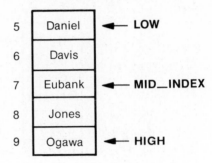

After the desired value is found, the variable **FOUND** terminates the search; however, in case the value is not found, a secondary test is required. For example, if the array contains

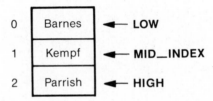

and the desired value is Jones, the first iteration will modify **HIGH** and **MID—INDEX** as follows:

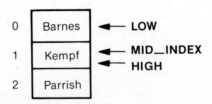

The second iteration produces

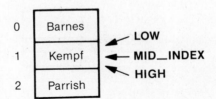

The third iteration illustrates the error that will occur if the algorithm does not perform the secondary test that prevents the array boundaries from being overrun:

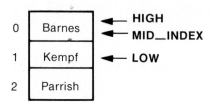

If the desired value is not found, the algorithm will attempt to access invalid subscripts, which results in an error. The complete test necessary to prevent this error becomes

```
while ((not FOUND) and (HIGH >= LOW)) do
```

If the desired value is not found, the variable **FOUND** remains false and should be examined by the calling routine.

The following routine implements the complete binary search:

```
procedure Binary_Search (VALUES:  ARRAY_TYPE;
                LOW, HIGH: integer;
            DESIRED_VALUE: ARRAY_ELEMENT;
            var MID_INDEX: integer;
                var FOUND: boolean);
{
DESCRIPTION:
    This routine searches the array VALUES for the value
    contained in the variable DESIRED_VALUE.  If the value
    is found the variable FOUND is set to true and the value
    in MID_INDEX is the index to the value.  If the value is not
    found, FOUND is set to false.

PARAMETERS:
    VALUES (in) - the array of values to search
    LOW (in) - the lowest element in the search range
    HIGH (in) - the highest element in the search range
    DESIRED_VALUE (in) - the value to search for
    MID_INDEX (out) - the element of the array to compare to DESIRED_VALUE
    FOUND (out) - true if the desired value is found; otherwise, false

TYPES REQUIRED:
    ARRAY_TYPE - must be defined to the type of the array
    ARRAY_ELEMENT - must be defined to the element type of the
                    array

SAMPLE CALL:
    Binary_Search (VALUES, 1, 10, 15, LOCATION, FOUND);

-----------------------------------------------------------}
```

```
   begin
     FOUND := false;    { assume the value is not present }

     MID_INDEX := (HIGH + LOW) div 2;

     while ((not FOUND) and (HIGH >= LOW)) do
       begin
         if (VALUES[MID_INDEX] = DESIRED_VALUE) then
             FOUND := true

{define the new search ranges}
         else if (VALUES[MID_INDEX] > DESIRED_VALUE) then
           HIGH := MID_INDEX - 1
         else
           LOW := MID_INDEX + 1;

{compute the index to the next value to examine}
         MID_INDEX := (HIGH + LOW) div 2;
       end;
   end;
```

Sorting

Many programming applications require that data be processed in either *ascending* (lowest to highest) or *descending* (highest to lowest) order. In such instances, you must use a sorting algorithm to place the data in order. The sorting algorithms introduced here are the bubble sort, the selection sort, the Shell sort, and the quick sort.

All of the array manipulation routines in Chapter 3 were based upon the type **ARRAY_TYPE**. Consequently, duplicate routines for arrays of different types did not have to be developed. Remember, if you develop two routines to sort data in ascending and descending order, your programming efforts have been needlessly duplicated. To avoid duplicate routines, the sorting algorithms in this chapter let you specify the desired order (ascending or descending) as a parameter. Each sorting routine invokes this routine to exchange values:

```
procedure Exchange_Values (var A, B: ARRAY_ELEMENT);
{
DESCRIPTION:
    This routine exchanges the values contained in the
    variables A and B.

PARAMETERS:
    A, B (in/out): the values to be exchanged

TYPES REQUIRED:
    ARRAY_ELEMENT - the element type of the array

SAMPLE CALL:
    Exchange_Values (VALUES[I], VALUES[J]);

-----------------------------------------------------------}
```

```
var
  TEMP: ARRAY_ELEMENT;   { temporary storage for the exchange }

begin

{exchange the values}
    TEMP := A;
    A  := B;
    B  := TEMP;

  end;
```

The Bubble Sort

The *bubble sort* is a popular sorting algorithm because of its simplicity. It is so named because, with each iteration, a value moves almost like a bubble to the top of the array. Because the bubble sort compares adjacent elements, the number of iterations it requires makes it inefficient for large arrays. If your array contains more than 30 elements, you should use either the Shell sort or the quick sort.

For example, imagine that the array **VALUES** contains

0	44
1	33
2	55
3	22
4	11

The first iteration of the bubble sort for ascending order will perform four evaluations:

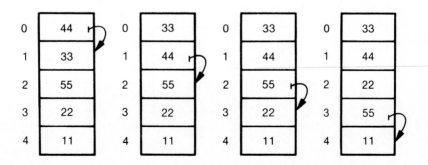

Since the largest value in the array is in the correct location after the first iteration, the algorithm examines only the first four elements on the second iteration:

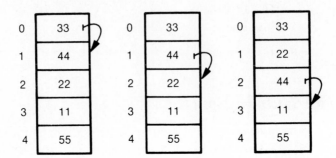

In the third iteration, only three elements are examined:

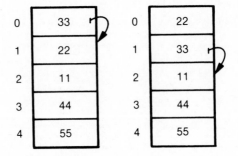

The final iteration ensures that the first two array elements are in the correct order:

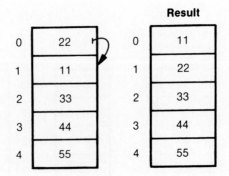

The following routine implements the bubble sort:

```
procedure Bubble_Sort (var VALUES: ARRAY_TYPE;
        LOWER_BOUND, UPPER_BOUND: integer;
                  IS_ASCENDING: boolean);
{
DESCRIPTION:
    This routine sorts the contents of the array VALUES via
    the bubble sort algorithm.

PARAMETERS:
    VALUES (in/out) - the array of values to sort
    LOWER_BOUND (in) - the lowest index value
    UPPER_BOUND (in) - the highest index value
    IS_ASCENDING (in) - true if ascending order is desired

TYPES REQUIRED:
    ARRAY_TYPE - the type of the array to be sorted

LIBRARY ROUTINES USED:
    Exchange_Values - exchanges the values of two variables

SAMPLE CALL:
    Bubble_Sort (VALUES, 1, 10, true);

-------------------------------------------------------}

  var
    I, J : integer;    { array indices }

  begin
    for J := UPPER_BOUND downto LOWER_BOUND + 1 do
        for I := LOWER_BOUND to J - 1 do
           if ((VALUES[I] > VALUES[J]) and (IS_ASCENDING)) then
             Exchange_Values (VALUES[I], VALUES[J])
           else if ((VALUES[I] < VALUES[J]) and (not IS_ASCENDING)) then
             Exchange_Values (VALUES[I], VALUES[J]);
    end;
```

The Selection Sort

The *selection sort* is another simple sorting algorithm. Although most institutions teach the bubble sort, many programmers find that the selection sort is easier to understand and to use without losing efficiency.

In the selection sort, elements are sorted by selecting the maximum or minimum value (depending on ascending or descending order) with each iteration.

Assume that the following array is sorted in ascending order.

0	44
1	33
2	55
3	22
4	11

The first iteration selects the minimum value and places it in the first element. To accomplish this iteration the sort first selects 1 as the **CURRENT** index. The sort then compares elements in the array to **VALUES[CURRENT]**. If one of the values is greater, the two values are exchanged.

The first iteration selects the minimum value as follows:

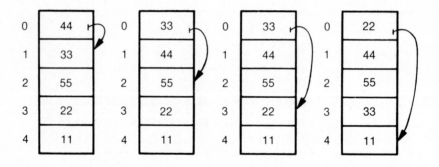

The second iteration places the second smallest value in element 2:

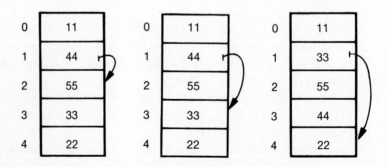

The third iteration selects the third smallest value:

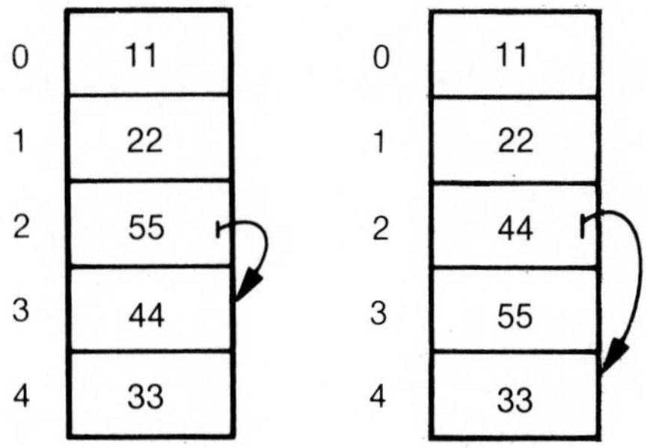

The fourth iteration results in the sorted array:

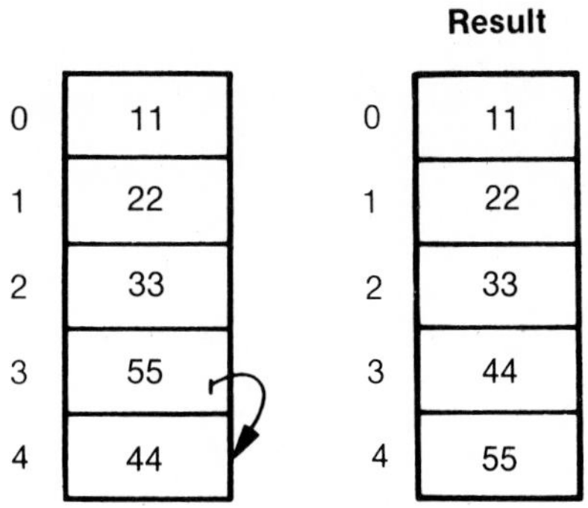

Result

Here is the routine for the selection sort:

```
procedure Select_Sort (var VALUES: ARRAY_TYPE;
         LOWER_BOUND, UPPER_BOUND: integer;
                    IS_ASCENDING: boolean);
{
DESCRIPTION:
    This routine sorts the contents of the array VALUES via
    the select sort.

PARAMETERS:
    VALUES (in/out) - the array of values to sort
    LOWER_BOUND (in) - the lowest index value
    UPPER_BOUND (in) - the highest index value
    IS_ASCENDING (in) - true if ascending order is desired

TYPES REQUIRED:
    ARRAY_TYPE - the type of the array

LIBRARY ROUTINES USED:
    Exchange_Values - exchanges the values of two variables

SAMPLE CALL:
    Select_Sort (VALUES, 1, 10, true);

-----------------------------------------------------------}
```

```
var
   I, J   : integer;  { indices into the array }
   CURRENT: integer;  { the current index }

begin
   for I := LOWER_BOUND to UPPER_BOUND - 1 do
      begin
         CURRENT := I;

{select the minimum or maximum value remaining and place it in
 the current index}
         for J := I + 1 to UPPER_BOUND do
            if ((VALUES[J] > VALUES[CURRENT]) and (IS_ASCENDING)) then
               Exchange_Values (VALUES[J], VALUES[CURRENT])
            else if ((VALUES[J] < VALUES[CURRENT]) and (not IS_ASCENDING)) then
               Exchange_Values (VALUES[J], VALUES[CURRENT]);
      end;
   end;
```

The Shell Sort

The *Shell sort* was developed by Donald Shell to overcome the bubble sort's inefficiency with large arrays. The Shell sort differs from the bubble sort because it compares elements that are spaced farther apart before comparing adjacent elements. This removes much of the array's disorder in early iterations.

The Shell sort uses a variable called **GAP** that is initially set to the value of one-half of the number of elements in the array. The value of **GAP** specifies the distance between each pair of comparison elements in the array. For example, in

0	1011
1	1088
2	1022
3	1077
4	1033
5	1066
6	1044
7	1055

the elements compared will initially be separated by a gap of 4. **GAP** is assigned a value of 4. The first iteration of the array compares all of the elements separated by this distance. The process is repeated until no exchanges occur with a gap of 4:

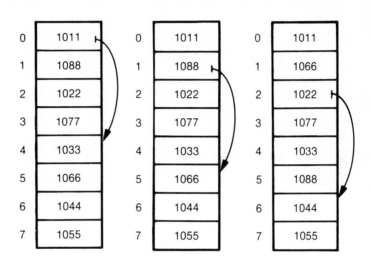

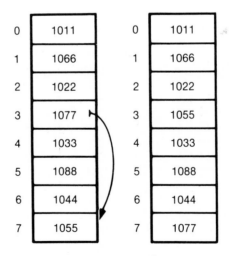

When no more exchanges can occur with a gap of 4, the algorithm modifies **GAP** to **GAP div 2**. The elements separated by a gap of 2 are then compared until no exchanges occur.

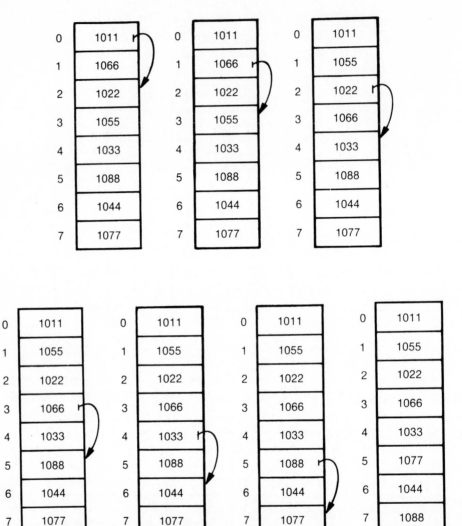

When no more exchanges can occur with a gap of 2, **GAP** is again modified to **GAP div 2**, and the process is continued with a gap of 1. When no exchanges occur with a gap of 1, **GAP** is assigned the value of **GAP div 2**. In this case, integer division assigns **GAP** the value of 0, which is the ending condition.

No exchanges

0	1011
1	1022
2	1033
3	1044
4	1055
5	1066
6	1077
7	1088

The following routine implements the Shell sort:

```
procedure Shell_Sort (var VALUES: ARRAY_TYPE;
       LOWER_BOUND, UPPER_BOUND: integer;
                   IS_ASCENDING: boolean);
{
DESCRIPTION:
    This routine sorts the contents of the array VALUES via
    the Shell sort.

PARAMETERS:
    VALUES (in/out) - the array of values to sort
    LOWER_BOUND (in) - the lowest index value
    UPPER_BOUND (in) - the highest index value
    IS_ASCENDING (in) - true if ascending order is desired

TYPES REQUIRED:
    ARRAY_TYPE - the type of the array

LIBRARY ROUTINES USED:
    Exchange_Values - exchanges the values of two variables

SAMPLE CALL:
    Shell_Sort (VALUES, 1, 10, true);

----------------------------------------------------------}

  var
    I, GAP             : integer;
    EXCHANGE_OCCURRED : boolean;   { true if an exchange occurred }
                                   { with the current gap }

  begin
    GAP := Abs((UPPER_BOUND - LOWER_BOUND) + 1) div 2 ;

    repeat
      repeat
```

```
{keep sorting the array with the current gap until no exchanges
  occur}
        EXCHANGE_OCCURRED := false;
        for i := LOWER_BOUND to UPPER_BOUND - GAP do
          if ((VALUES[I] > VALUES[I + GAP]) and (IS_ASCENDING)) then
            begin
              Exchange_Values (VALUES[I], VALUES[I + GAP]);
              EXCHANGE_OCCURRED := true;
            end
          else if ((VALUES[I] < VALUES[I + GAP]) and (not IS_ASCENDING)) then
            begin
              Exchange_Values (VALUES[I], VALUES[I + GAP]);
              EXCHANGE_OCCURRED := true;
            end;
      until (not EXCHANGE_OCCURRED);
      GAP := GAP div 2:
{when GAP is equal to 0 the sort is completed}
    until (GAP = 0);
  end;
```

The Quick Sort

Although the efficiency of the Shell sort increases as the number of elements in the array increases, it too has limitations. The *quick sort,* which is a recursive sorting algorithm, increases the speed of the sort as the number of elements in the array approaches 150 to 200 elements. In fact, the quick sort is one of the fastest array-sorting algorithms in use today.

The quick sort sorts data by breaking a list of values into a series of smaller lists. For example, if the array

START	0	60
	1	20
	2	10
	3	30
	4	40
	5	50
	6	80
	7	70
END_LIST	8	0

is passed to the quick sort routine, the algorithm will select the value contained in **VALUES[(START+END—LIST) div 2]**—in this case, **VALUES[4]**—as the list separator. Any values in the list that are less than or equal to the list separator are placed in one list, and the values that are greater than the list separator are placed into a second list, as shown here:

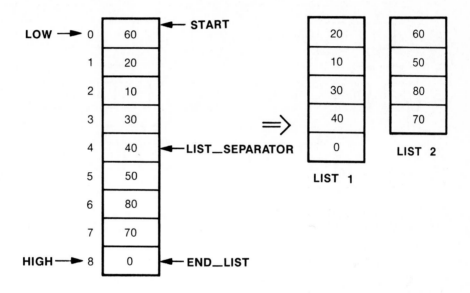

The same process is carried out on each sublist, or range, until each contains only one element. At that point, the array will be sorted.

Figure 4-1 illustrates the sequence in which the sublists are constructed. The sort splits the list into two parts: the smaller items are placed in the left-hand list, and the larger items into the right-hand list. The process is repeated until there is only one item in each list and the items are sorted from left to right.

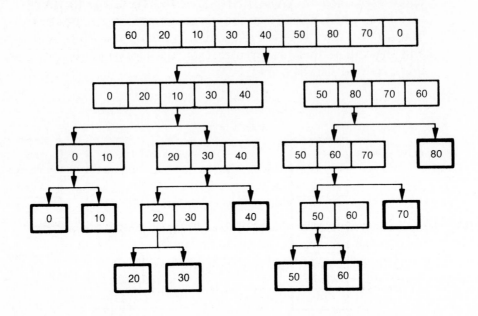

Figure 4-1. *Sequence of sublist construction using a quick sort*

As another example, imagine that the array

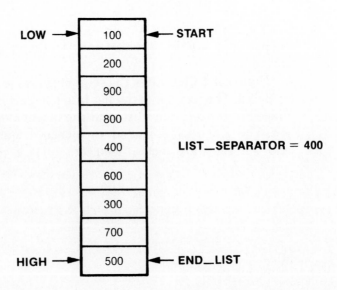

is passed to the quick sort routine to be sorted in ascending order. It is first divided into two lists. The variable **LOW** is assigned to the first element in the list. The variable **HIGH** is assigned to the last element in the list. The variable **LOW** is then incremented until **VALUES[LOW]** contains a value that is greater than or equal to the **LIST‗SEPARATOR**. (For descending order, the value must be less than the **LIST‗SEPARATOR**.)

```
while (VALUES[LOW] < LIST_SEPARATOR) do
  LOW := LOW + 1;
```

When **VALUES[LOW]** contains a value that is greater than or equal to the value contained in **LIST‗SEPARATOR**, the **while** loop terminates. As shown here, the value in **HIGH** is decremented until **VALUES[HIGH]** contains a value that is less than or equal to **LIST‗ SEPARATOR**:

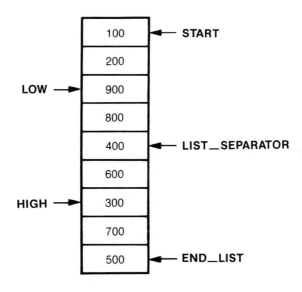

When the value contained in **VALUES[HIGH]** is less than or equal to the value contained in **LIST‗SEPARATOR**, the **while** loop terminates and the values contained in **LOW** and **HIGH** are compared. If the value in **LOW** is less than the value in **HIGH**, the values are exchanged; otherwise, the value in **LOW** is incremented:

```
if (LOW < HIGH) then
  Exchange_Values (VALUES[LOW], VALUES[HIGH])
else
  LOW := LOW + 1;
```

This process is repeated until **LOW** is greater than **HIGH**.

Once the value in **LOW** is greater than the value in **HIGH**, you have two lists. The first contains the elements from **START** to **HIGH**, and the second contains the elements from **LOW** to **END—LIST**:

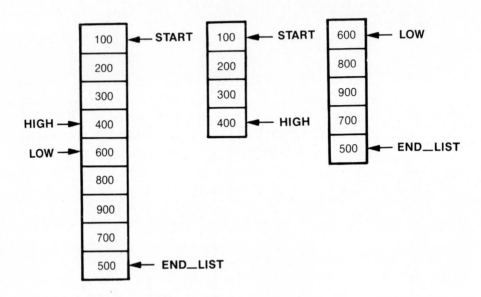

Each list then is passed recursively to the routine, and each is also subdivided into lists. This process will continue until each list contains only one element.

The following routine implements the quick sort:

```
procedure Quick_Sort (var VALUES: ARRAY_TYPE;
                          START, END_LIST: integer;
                             IS_ASCENDING: boolean);
                          {
DESCRIPTION:
     This routine sorts the contents of the array VALUES via
     the quick sort algorithm.

PARAMETERS:
     VALUES (in-out) - the array of values to sort
     START (in) - the first element in the list
     END_LIST (in) - the last element in the list
     IS_ASCENDING (in) - true if ascending order is desired

TYPES REQUIRED:
     ARRAY_TYPE - must be defined to the type of the array
```

```
LIBRARY ROUTINES USED:
    Exchange_Values - exchanges the values of two variables

SAMPLE CALL:
    Quick_Sort (VALUES, 1, 10, true);

    ------------------------------------------------------------}

  var
    LOW, HIGH      : integer;
    LIST_SEPARATOR: ARRAY_ELEMENT;

  begin
    LOW := START;
    HIGH := END_LIST;
    LIST_SEPARATOR := VALUES[(START+END_LIST) div 2];

{make the two sublists}
    repeat
      begin
        if (IS_ASCENDING) then
          begin
            while (VALUES[LOW] < LIST_SEPARATOR) do
              LOW := LOW + 1;

            while (VALUES[HIGH] >= LIST_SEPARATOR) do
              HIGH := HIGH - 1;
          end
        else
          begin
            while (VALUES[LOW] > LIST_SEPARATOR) do
              LOW := LOW + 1;

            while (VALUES[HIGH] <= LIST_SEPARATOR) do
              HIGH := HIGH - 1;
            end;

          if (LOW < HIGH) then
            Exchange_Values (VALUES[LOW], VALUES[HIGH])
          else
              LOW := LOW + 1;
        end;
      until (LOW > HIGH);

    {recursively sort the lower list}
        if (START < HIGH) then
          Quick_Sort (VALUES, START, HIGH, IS_ASCENDING);

    {recursively sort the higher list}
        if (LOW < END_LIST) then
          Quick_Sort (VALUES, LOW, END_LIST, IS_ASCENDING);
      end;
```

Selecting the proper sorting algorithm has a definite impact on the execution time of your routines. Compilers that provide a sorting routine usually use the quick sort. If you experiment with each routine, using arrays of 30, 300, and 3000 elements, you should find that the execution time of each routine is almost the same for 30 elements; that the bubble sort is much slower than the other sorts for 300 elements; and that the quick sort is much faster than the others for an array of 3000 elements. However, you will also find that the recursive nature of the quick sort makes it slower for smaller lists.

Each sorting routine has attributes that make it more efficient for a specific application. You will find that you can increase the speed of your sorts by examining the number of elements in the array and invoking the sort that is best suited for the application.

5

String Manipulation

Although the type **string** is not found in standard Pascal, it is an integral part of any high-order programming language and is included in Turbo Pascal. In Turbo Pascal, characters are normally stored in strings. This chapter provides several helpful functions and subroutines for string manipulation that are not standard for Turbo Pascal.

String Types

Type compatibility is always important for generic string-manipulation routines. The best way to deal with this problem is to define a "standard" string type. This chapter will use the type

```
STRING79 = string[79];
```

The maximum limit of 79 characters is used because it is one character less than the total screen width. You should be especially cautious when using the eightieth column because when you enter a character from that column, the cursor is placed on the next line of the screen. You should also be careful when making an entry on the twenty-fifth line of the screen, because the entire screen will then scroll up. You should avoid this at all costs (for reasons that will become more evident in Chapter 7).

The first two procedures presented here convert strings to uppercase and to lowercase, respectively. Turbo Pascal provides the standard function **UpCase**, which converts a single character to uppercase. Thus, the procedure *Str—to—Uppercase* is a simple loop; however, it is used extensively in the routines that need to perform searches that ignore case. Both routines ignore nonalphabetic characters.

```
procedure Str_to_Uppercase (var STR: STRING79);
{
DESCRIPTION:
    This routine converts a string to uppercase letters.

PARAMETERS:
    STR (in/out) - string to be converted

TYPES REQUIRED:
    STRING79 - used for all strings

SAMPLE CALL:
    Str_to_Uppercase (NAME_STRING);

NOTES:
    Nonalphabetic characters are not affected by this call.

------------------------------------------------------------}

    var
      I:  integer;                        {counter for loops}

    begin

{call UpCase for each character in the string}
        for I := 1 to Length (STR) do
            STR[I] := UpCase (STR[I]);

    end;
```

```
procedure Str_to_Lowercase (var STR: STRING79);
{
DESCRIPTION:
    This routine converts a string to lowercase letters.

PARAMETERS:
    STR (in/out) - string to be converted

TYPES REQUIRED:
    STRING79 - used for all strings

SAMPLE CALL:
    Str_to_Lowercase (NAME_STRING);

NOTES:
    Nonalphabetic characters are not affected by this call.

-------------------------------------------------------------}

  var
    I:    integer;                    {counter for loops}

  begin

{loop through each character in the string}
    for I := 1 to Length (STR) do

{if the character is uppercase, make it lowercase}
      if (STR[I] >= 'A') and (STR[I] <= 'Z') then
        STR[I] := Chr(Ord(STR[I]) + 32)
    end;
```

Finding Substrings

The next set of procedures finds characters or substrings within other strings. Turbo Pascal provides the procedure **Pos**, which finds the first occurrence of an object string within a target string. In many cases, however, you need a routine that does the same thing while ignoring the case of a character. The procedure *Next—Pos* finds the next occurrence of the target string. You can then use an option to make it ignore the case of the string. The last parameter to *Next—Pos* is the Boolean **IGNORE—CASE**, which will convert local copies of both strings to uppercase when true, enabling the routine to find all occurrences regardless of case.

As an example, suppose the string **NAMESTRING** contains the value

```
NAMESTRING := 'St. Stevens, Justin';
```

The call

```
POSITION := Pos('st', NAMESTRING);
```

would return 16, the first occurrence of "st" in **NAMESTRING**. If you want to ignore the case and find "st" in the first position, you must call *Next—Pos*, finding the first occurrence by placing a 0 as the third parameter:

```
POSITION := Next_Pos ('st', NAMESTRING, 0, true);
```

This call would place a 1 in **POSITION**. If the final parameter were changed to false, the function would return 16, as shown earlier.

The third parameter in *Next—Pos* moves along the target string to find later occurrences. The call

```
POSITION := Next_Pos ('st', NAMESTRING, 2, true);
```

would return 5, which is the next occurrence of "st" after the second character of the target string. Thus, the loop

```
POSITION := Next_Pos ('st', NAMESTRING, 0, true);
while POSITION > 0 do
  begin
    {display position number, or other code here}
    POSITION := Next_Pos ('st', NAMESTRING, POSITION, true);
  end;
```

could be used to find all three occurrences of the substring.

If you only want to find the last occurrence of one string in another, you can use the function *Right—Pos*. The final routine in this section, *Str—Count*, uses the loop just given to find the number of occurrences of a substring within a string.

```
function Next_Pos (OBJECT, TARGET: STRING79;
                   LAST_POS: integer;
                   IGNORE_CASE: boolean): integer;
{
DESCRIPTION:
    This function scans the string TARGET to find the next occurrence
of the OBJECT within the TARGET.
```

VALUE RETURNED:
    The location of the next occurrence of the object within the
target, or 0 if not found

PARAMETERS:
    OBJECT (in) - substring to search for
    TARGET (in) - the string being searched
    LAST_POS (in) - the last position of object within target
    IGNORE_CASE (in) - flag to note case differences

TYPES REQUIRED:
    STRING79 - used for all strings

LIBRARY ROUTINES USED:
    Str_to_Uppercase - converts a string to uppercase letters

SAMPLE CALL:
    I := Next_Pos ('t', 'Test two', 4, true);   (would return 6)

NOTES:
    The LAST_POS does not have to be a valid position -- this
routine will just not look at that position or anywhere to the
left of it.

    --}

```
  var
    NPOS,                         {temporary next position}
    I, J  : integer;              {counters for loops}
    SAME_SO_FAR: boolean;         {check for each character}

  begin

{if case is to be ignored, convert the local copies of the
strings to uppercase}
    if IGNORE_CASE then
      begin
        Str_to_Uppercase (TARGET);
        Str_to_Uppercase (OBJECT);
      end;

{value can never be -1, so set temporary variable to -1 and loop until
 it changes}
    NPOS := -1;



{start at position to the right of the last one}
    I := LAST_POS + 1;

    while NPOS < 0 do

{if you have checked the entire target, the object is not there}
      if I > (Length (TARGET) - Length (OBJECT) + 1) then
        NPOS := 0
      else
        begin
```

```
{check each character in the object against the target}
        J := 1;
        SAME_SO_FAR := true;
        while SAME_SO_FAR and (J <= Length (OBJECT)) do

{if the same so far, check the next character}
            if TARGET[I+J-1] = OBJECT[J] then
            J := J + 1
            else
                SAME_SO_FAR := false;

{if each character matched, the position has been found}
            if SAME_SO_FAR then
                NPOS := I

{if there was a difference, move target pointer one character
 to the right}
            else
                I := I + 1;
        end;

    Next_Pos := NPOS;
  end;
```

```
function Right_Pos (OBJECT, TARGET: STRING79;
                        IGNORE_CASE: boolean): integer;
{
DESCRIPTION:
    This function scans the string TARGET to find the last occurrence
of the OBJECT within the TARGET.  It serves as a complement to the
Turbo Pascal function Pos.

VALUE RETURNED:
    The location of the rightmost occurrence of the object within the
 target, or 0 if not found

PARAMETERS:
    OBJECT (in) - substring to search for
    TARGET (in) - the string being searched
    IGNORE_CASE (in) - flag to note case differences

TYPES REQUIRED:
    STRING79 - used for all strings

LIBRARY ROUTINES USED:
    Str_to_Uppercase - converts a string to uppercase letters

SAMPLE CALL:
    I := Right_Pos ('T', 'Test two', true);    (would return 6)

----------------------------------------------------------------}

  var
    RPOS,                                   {temporary right position}
    I, J   : integer;                       {counters for loops}
    SAME_SO_FAR: boolean;                   {check for each character}
```

```
    begin

{if case is to be ignored, convert the local copies of the
strings to uppercase}
    if IGNORE_CASE then
      begin
        Str_to_Uppercase (TARGET);
        Str_to_Uppercase (OBJECT);
      end;

    RPOS := 0;

{start at rightmost place where the object could fit}
    I := Length (TARGET) - Length (OBJECT) + 1;

{if you have checked the entire target, the object is not there}
    while (RPOS = 0) and (I >= 1) do
      begin

{check each character in the object against the target}


        J := 1;
        SAME_SO_FAR := true;
        while SAME_SO_FAR and (J <= Length (OBJECT)) do

{if the same so far, check the next character}
          if TARGET[I+J] = OBJECT[J] then
            J := J + 1
          else
            SAME_SO_FAR := false;

{if each character matched, the position has been found}
          if SAME_SO_FAR then
            RPOS := I

{if there was a difference, move target pointer one character
 to the left}
          else
            I := I - 1;
      end;

    Right_Pos := RPOS;
  end;
```

```
function Str_Count (OBJECT, TARGET: STRING79;
                    IGNORE_CASE: boolean): integer;
{
DESCRIPTION:
    This function scans the string TARGET to find the number of
occurrences of the OBJECT within the TARGET.

VALUE RETURNED:
    The total number of occurrences of the object within the target
```

```
PARAMETERS:
    OBJECT (in) - substring to search for
    TARGET (in) - the string being searched
    IGNORE_CASE (in) - flag to note case differences

TYPES REQUIRED:
    STRING79 - used for all strings

LIBRARY ROUTINES USED:
    Next_Pos - finds the next occurrence of object within target

SAMPLE CALL:
    I := Str_Count ('t', 'Test two', false);    (would return 2)

------------------------------------------------------------}

  var
    COUNT,                          {temporary total count}
    NPOS : integer;                 {temporary next position}

  begin
    COUNT := 0;
    NPOS := 0;

    repeat

{look for the next position of object within target}
      NPOS := Next_Pos (OBJECT, TARGET, NPOS, IGNORE_CASE);

{if the object was found, increment the counter}
      if NPOS > 0 then
        COUNT := COUNT + 1;

{repeat until the next position doesn't exist}
    until NPOS = 0;
    Str_Count := COUNT;
  end;
```

Replacing Substrings

After you have found all substrings in a target string, you are ready to replace those substrings if you wish. The procedures *Str_Replace_First* and *Str_Replace_All* work the same as a typical "replace" or "substitute" command in an editor. *Str_Replace_First* calls *Next_Pos* to find a substring, and if the substring is found, replaces it with another string. The **IGNORE_CASE** flag is included and is simply passed on to *Next_Pos*.

Str_Replace_All replaces all occurrences of a given substring with a substitute string. The call to *Next_Pos* in the find loop discussed in the last section circumvents any recursion problems. For example, suppose a string **SENTENCE** is assigned to the following sentences:

```
SENTENCE := 'John runs fast.  Joe runs fast, too.';
```

If you wanted to replace all occurrences of "fast" with "very fast," you could try to do it with this loop:

```
SUCCESS := true;
while SUCCESS do
   Str_Replace_First (SENTENCE, 'fast', 'very fast',
                      false, SUCCESS);
```

The first iteration would change the sentence to

```
'John runs very fast.  Joe runs fast, too.'
```

However, the second iteration would find the first "fast" again since it is a substring of the new replacement string. The sentence would then read

```
'John runs very very fast.  Joe runs fast, too.'
```

This means that the loop will be completed only by a run-time error. The call

```
Str_Replace_All (SENTENCE, 'fast', 'very fast', false, NUM);
```

would make the two substitutions that you desired, with no infinite loop.

Another useful routine is *First—Difference*, which determines where a difference occurs between two strings. If the two strings differ in length, the function returns a number that is one more than the length of the smaller string.

You can use the last routine in this chapter, *Reverse—Substring*, to reverse the order of the characters in all or part of a string.

```
procedure Str_Replace_First (var TARGET: STRING79;
                   OLDSUBSTR, NEWSUBSTR: STRING79;
                            IGNORE_CASE: boolean;
                     var OLDSUBSTR_FOUND: boolean);
```

```
    {
    DESCRIPTION:
        This function scans the string TARGET to replace an old string
    with a new one.

    PARAMETERS:
        TARGET (in/out) - the string being changed
        OLDSUBSTR (in) - the undesired substring
        NEWSUBSTR (in) - the substring to be inserted
        IGNORE_CASE (in) - flag to note case differences
        OLDSUBSTR_FOUND (out) - flag to note successful replacement

    LIBRARY ROUTINES USED:
        Next_Pos - finds the next occurrence of object within target

    TYPES REQUIRED:
        STRING79 - used for all strings

    SAMPLE CALL:
        I := Str_Replace_First ('Test two', 't', 's', true, FOUND);
                                        (would become 'sest two')


    ------------------------------------------------------------}


      var
        NPOS : integer;                    {temporary next position}

      begin

    {look for the first position of object within target}
        NPOS := Next_Pos (OLDSUBSTR, TARGET, 0, IGNORE_CASE);

    {if the object was found, replace the string}
        if NPOS > 0 then
          begin
            Delete (TARGET, NPOS, Length(OLDSUBSTR));
            Insert (NEWSUBSTR, TARGET, NPOS);
            OLDSUBSTR_FOUND := true;
          end

    {if the object was not found, return an error}
        else
          OLDSUBSTR_FOUND := false;
      end;
```

```
    procedure Str_Replace_All (var TARGET: STRING79;
                 OLDSUBSTR, NEWSUBSTR: STRING79;
                          IGNORE_CASE: boolean;
                 var NUM_SUBSTITUTIONS: integer);
    {
    DESCRIPTION:
        This function scans the string TARGET to replace an old string
    with a new one.

    PARAMETERS:
        TARGET (in/out) - the string being changed
        OLDSUBSTR (in) - the undesired substring
        NEWSUBSTR (in) - the substring to be inserted
        IGNORE_CASE (in) - flag to note case differences
        NUM_SUBSTITUTIONS (out) - number of replacements made
```

```
    TYPES REQUIRED:
        STRING79 - used for all strings

    LIBRARY ROUTINES USED:
        Next_Pos - finds the next occurrence of object within target

    SAMPLE CALL:
        I := Str_Replace_All ('Test two', 't', 's', false);
                                        (would become 'Tess swo')

    -----------------------------------------------------------}

      var
        NPOS : integer;                    {temporary next position}

      begin
        NUM_SUBSTITUTIONS := 0;
        NPOS := 0;
        repeat

{look for the next position of object within target}
        NPOS := Next_Pos (OLDSUBSTR, TARGET, NPOS, IGNORE_CASE);

{if the object was found, replace the string}
        if NPOS > 0 then
          begin
            Delete (TARGET, NPOS, Length(OLDSUBSTR));
            Insert (NEWSUBSTR, TARGET, NPOS);

{move the pointer to past the new string to avoid replacing part of
the new one}
            NPOS := NPOS + Length(NEWSUBSTR);
            NUM_SUBSTITUTIONS := NUM_SUBSTITUTIONS + 1;
          end;

{repeat until the next position doesn't exist}
        until NPOS = 0;


      end;
```

```
function First_Difference (STRING1, STRING2: STRING79;
                                  IGNORE_CASE: boolean): integer;
{
DESCRIPTION:
    This function determines the first character where a difference
occurs between two strings.

VALUE RETURNED:
    The location of the first difference, or 0 if no difference

PARAMETERS:
    STRING1 (in) - first string to be compared
    STRING2 (in) - second string to be compared
    IGNORE_CASE (in) - flag to note case differences

TYPES REQUIRED:
    STRING79 - used for all strings

LIBRARY ROUTINES USED:
    Str_to_Uppercase - converts a string to uppercase letters
```

```
SAMPLE CALL:
    I := First_Difference ('Test1', 'TesT', true);     (would return 5)

NOTES:
    If one string is a different length than the other, the
strings are considered to be different at one more than the length
of the smaller string.

----------------------------------------------------------}

  var
    DIFF,                            {temporary first difference}
    I     : integer;                 {counter for loop}

  begin

{if case is to be ignored, convert the local copies of the
strings to uppercase}
    if IGNORE_CASE then
      begin
        Str_to_Uppercase (STRING1);
        Str_to_Uppercase (STRING2);
      end;

    I := 1;

{value can never be -1, so set temporary variable to -1 and loop until
 it changes}
    DIFF := -1;
    while DIFF < 0 do

{if you've hit the end of both strings at the same time, the
 strings are the same}
      if (I > Length (STRING1)) and (I > Length (STRING2)) then
        DIFF := 0

{if you've hit the end of only one string, the first difference is
 one more than the length of the smaller string}
      else if (I > Length (STRING1)) or (I > Length (STRING2)) then
        DIFF := I

{if a difference is found, set the temporary variable}
      else if STRING1[I] <> STRING2[I] then
        DIFF := I

{otherwise, check the next two characters in the strings}
      else
        I := I + 1;

    First_Difference := DIFF;
  end;
```

```
procedure Reverse_Substring (var STR: STRING79;
                    START_POS, END_POS: integer);
{
DESCRIPTION:
    This routine reverse a part of a string.
```

```
PARAMETERS:
    STR (in/out) - string to be output
    START_POS (in) - first character to reverse
    END_POS (in) - last character to reverse

TYPES REQUIRED:
    STRING79 - used for all strings

SAMPLE CALL:
    Reverse_Substring (PALINDROME, 1, Length (PALINDROME));

-----------------------------------------------------------}

  var
    TEMPCH: char;                      {temporary variable}

  begin

{exchange characters until the pointers match or cross}
    while START_POS < END_POS do
      begin
        TEMPCH          := STR[START_POS];
        STR[START_POS] := STR[END_POS];
        STR[END_POS]   := TEMPCH;
        START_POS       := START_POS + 1;
        END_POS         := END_POS - 1;
      end;
  end;
```

C H A P T E R

6

Pointers and Dynamic Data Structures

Arrays enable programmers to manipulate data sets with relative ease. However, when these data sets get extremely large, operations like searching and sorting take much longer. Another problem occurs when the size of a data set is either unknown or constantly changing, because you must then dimension the arrays to the highest possible limit, which allocates a lot of memory. This chapter solves both of these problems by developing data structures that are always ordered and making these structures dynamic, so that memory is allocated only as necessary.

Using pointer types solves the size problem; using linked lists and binary trees solves the ordering problem. You can solve these problems independently of each other. Lists using pointer types do not have to be in any order. Linked lists and binary trees can be implemented by using arrays of records (with integer pointers to indices). But when you are dealing with large amounts of data, both problems often arise, so both are handled with dynamic data structures.

Stacks

The simplest dynamic data structure is the *stack*. Stacks are used primarily by operating systems and high-level language drivers. A stack is *dynamic*—it grows and shrinks as required. Think of the stack as being similar to a stack of cafeteria trays. Trays are placed on the stack from the top; the top tray is taken off the stack by a customer going through the line. This scenario is called the *last-in, first-out model:* the last tray placed on the stack is the first taken off.

To increase the generic nature of the stacks, you must define the type **ENTRY_TYPE**. This may be any type—from a simple type to a record structure. The actual stack type definition is as follows:

```
type
  STACK_PTR = ^STACK;
  STACK = record
    ENTRY: ENTRY_TYPE;              {the entry on the stack}
    NEXT : STACK_PTR;              {pointer to the next record}
  end;
```

The pointer **NEXT** is what links the records together. Since all stack operations take place at the top of the stack, you only need to keep track of the top pointer, which is passed as a parameter.

Here is a sample set of stack operations. Suppose a stack is used to keep track of what part of a code is being executed. Every time that a procedure calls another, the name of the new procedure is placed on the stack. When the procedure is complete, the name is taken off the stack. During program execution, a sample stack might contain the following:

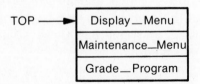

Imagine that when a certain procedure, *Display—Menu*, calls another procedure, *Put—String*, you can use the procedure *Stack—Push* to place the routine name on the stack. Here, the name is added and the TOP pointer is moved up:

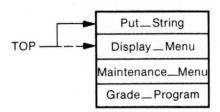

When *Put—String* is finished, a call to *Stack—Pop* would take the name off the stack. If a run-time error occurred, you could use *Stack—Pop* to "dump" the procedure names so that you could determine where the error occurred. *Stack—Pop* retrieves the entry name, moves the TOP pointer down, and deletes the unwanted record, as shown here:

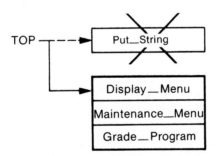

Here are the *Stack—Push* and *Stack—Pop* routines:

```
procedure Stack_Push (var TOP: STACK_PTR;
                     NEW_ENTRY: ENTRY_TYPE);
{
DESCRIPTION:
    This routine pushes an entry onto a stack.

PARAMETERS:
    TOP (in/out) - the pointer to the top of the stack
    NEW_KEY (in) - the entry to push onto the stack

TYPES REQUIRED:
    ENTRY_TYPE - the type of the keyed information stored
```

```
        OTHER_TYPE - the type of all non-ordered information
        STACK_PTR - the stack data structure

SAMPLE CALL:
    Stack_Push (STACK, 45);

------------------------------------------------------------}


    var
       TEMP_TOP: STACK_PTR;          {temporary record}

    begin

{create a new record}
    New(TEMP_TOP);

{fill the new record with the entry information}
    TEMP_TOP^.ENTRY := NEW_ENTRY;

{link the new record to the top of the stack}
    TEMP_TOP^.NEXT := TOP;

{set the top of the stack to the new record}
    TOP := TEMP_TOP;
  end;
```

```
procedure Stack_Pop (var TOP: STACK_PTR;
           var DESIRED_ENTRY: ENTRY_TYPE;
             var EMPTY_STACK: boolean);
{
DESCRIPTION:
    This routine pops the top record off of the stack and
returns the value of its contents.  If the stack is empty,
an error flag is set.

PARAMETERS:
    TOP (in/out) - the pointer to the top of the stack
    DESIRED_ENTRY (out) - the entry retrieved from the stack
    EMPTY_STACK (out) - error flag denoting an empty stack

TYPES REQUIRED:
    ENTRY_TYPE - the type of the keyed information stored
    OTHER_TYPE - the type of all non-ordered information
    STACK_PTR - the stack data structure

SAMPLE CALL:
    Stack_Pop (STACK, LAST_NUMBER, EMPTY);

------------------------------------------------------------}


    var
       TEMP_TOP: STACK_PTR;          {a temporary record}

    begin
```

```
{if the stack is empty, set the error flag}
    if TOP = nil then
      EMPTY_STACK := true
    else
      begin
        EMPTY_STACK := false;

{fill the desired record with the top record information}
        DESIRED_ENTRY := TOP^.ENTRY;

{remember the current stack top for later disposal}
        TEMP_TOP := TOP;

{move the top down}
        TOP := TOP^.NEXT;

{dispose of the old top record}
        Dispose (TEMP_TOP);
      end;
  end;
```

Linked Lists

Although stacks serve an important function in keeping track of data, you usually need more versatility for dynamic data applications. *Linked lists* have a structure similar to that of stacks, but they are linked together to maintain an order. Thus, you can retrieve information from the middle of a linked list by traveling through the entries in the list.

Records that define linked lists should be as generic as possible. Linked lists require that one field be the *key*, which is the field that will be ordered. You must define the type **KEY—TYPE** as any simple type (**integer, real, char,** or **string**). Keys do not have to be unique, but if two keys are duplicates, an extraction (discussed later) will find only the first record. You must define any other information that is associated with the key and stored in the list as the type **OTHER—TYPE**. This type is often a record type, so that many elements can be stored. Here is the definition of the linked-list data structure:

```
type
  LIST_PTR = ^LINK_RECORD;
  LINK_RECORD = record
    KEY: KEY_TYPE;                    {the keyed entry in the list}
    OTHER: OTHER_TYPE;               {all non-ordered information}
    NEXT : LIST_PTR;                 {pointer to the next record}
  end;
```

The pointer **NEXT** links all of the records together: when a linked list is passed as a parameter, only the pointer to the beginning of the list needs to be passed.

Displaying a set of records that have a linked-list data structure requires the use of a *traveling pointer*. This pointer starts at the list pointer, displays the current values, and then "travels" down to the next record. The code for the movement of the traveling pointer is simple and straightforward:

```
TEMP_PTR := LIST_START;                {start at the beginning}
while TEMP_PTR <> nil do                  {loop until the end}
  begin
    writeln (TEMP_PTR^.KEY, TEMP_PTR^.OTHER);      {display}
    TEMP_PTR := TEMP_PTR^.NEXT;                     {travel}
  end;
```

Use temporary variables as traveling pointers because, if you alter **LIST—START**, you will not know where each record is in the heap.

For example, consider a list of animals. This list can be linked so that the elements are always in alphabetical order, as shown here:

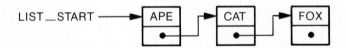

To add the element DOG to the list, you would initialize a pointer at the beginning of the list and travel until the pointer was pointing to the record that was immediately before the new one:

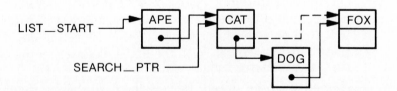

Thus, you insert a record into the list by pointing the new record to the next record, and pointing the last record to the new record. Because the list stays in alphabetical order, it never needs to be sorted. The routine *Linked—List—Insert* places a new record into the proper spot in a list.

You can only extract the top record of a stack. However, you can retrieve any record from a linked list. The routine *Linked__List__Extract* searches through the list for a given key and then returns the contents of the entire record. If the key was not found, the routine sets a flag.

Deleting a record from a linked list is similar to inserting a record. A pointer starts at the beginning of the list and searches for the key of the record to delete. Using the animal list given earlier, deleting DOG would bring the search pointer to the third record:

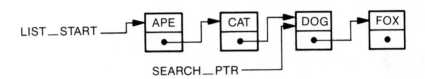

Deleting a record with *Linked__List__Delete* is done by connecting the pointer before the unwanted record to the record following it. After the record is out of the list, the record is disposed of:

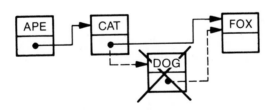

Here are the linked-list routines:

```
procedure Linked_List_Insert (var LIST_START: LIST_PTR;
                                  NEW_RECORD: LINK_RECORD);
{
DESCRIPTION:
    This routine inserts a record into a linked list, keeping
the list in ascending order.

PARAMETERS:
    LIST_START (in/out) - the pointer to the front of the list
    NEW_RECORD (in) - the record to insert into the list
```

```
TYPES REQUIRED:
    KEY_TYPE - the type of the keyed information stored
    OTHER_TYPE - the type of all non-ordered information
    LIST_PTR - the linked list data structure

SAMPLE CALL:
    Linked_List_Insert (START_PTR, NEW_REC);

NOTES:
    The LIST_START must be initialized to nil before calling
this routine for the first time.

-----------------------------------------------------------}


  var
    SEARCH_PTR,                     {the pointer used for searching}
    LAST_PTR,                       {the last record searched}
    TEMP_PTR  : LIST_PTR;           {a temporary record}
    LOCATED   : boolean;            {was the location found yet?}

  begin
  {create a new record and place the information in it}
      New(TEMP_PTR);
      TEMP_PTR^ := NEW_RECORD;
      TEMP_PTR^.NEXT := nil;

      SEARCH_PTR := LIST_START;

  {if the list is empty, make the new record the only one}
      if SEARCH_PTR = nil then
        LIST_START := TEMP_PTR
      else
        begin

  {search until just before we've gone too far, or until the
  list is exhausted}
          LOCATED := false;
          while (SEARCH_PTR <> nil) and not LOCATED do
            if SEARCH_PTR^.KEY < NEW_RECORD.KEY then
              begin
                LAST_PTR := SEARCH_PTR;
                SEARCH_PTR := SEARCH_PTR^.NEXT
              end
            else
              LOCATED := true;

  {have the new record point to the next record}
          TEMP_PTR^.NEXT := SEARCH_PTR;

  {if the new record will be the first record, set the starting
  pointer}
          if SEARCH_PTR = LIST_START then
            LIST_START := TEMP_PTR

  {otherwise, point the last record to the new record}
          else
            LAST_PTR^.NEXT := TEMP_PTR;
        end;
    end;
```

```
procedure Linked_List_Extract (LIST_START: LIST_PTR;
                               SEARCH_KEY: KEY_TYPE;
                      var EXTRACTED_RECORD: LINK_RECORD;
                               var LOCATED: boolean);
{
DESCRIPTION:
    This routine extracts a record from a linked list.  If
the keyed entry is not found an error is returned.  The
list need not be in order.

PARAMETERS:
    LIST_START (in) - the pointer to the front of the list
    SEARCH_KEY (in) - the keyed entry to search for
    EXTRACTED_RECORD (out) - the entire record found
    LOCATED (out) - the error flag (true if the record
        was found successfully)

TYPES REQUIRED:
    KEY_TYPE - the type of keyed information stored
    OTHER_TYPE - the type of all non-ordered information
    LIST_PTR - the linked list data structure

SAMPLE CALL:
    Linked_List_Extract (START_PTR, 'Joe', OLD_REC, THERE);

----------------------------------------------------------}


   var
      SEARCH_PTR: LIST_PTR;              {the pointer used for searching}

   begin

{start at the top of the list}
    SEARCH_PTR := LIST_START;

{search until the key is found, or until the list is exhausted}
    LOCATED := false;
    while (SEARCH_PTR <> nil) and not LOCATED do
      if SEARCH_PTR^.KEY <> SEARCH_KEY then
        SEARCH_PTR := SEARCH_PTR^.NEXT
      else
        LOCATED := true;

    if LOCATED then
      EXTRACTED_RECORD := SEARCH_PTR^;
    end;
```

```
procedure Linked_List_Delete (var LIST_START: LIST_PTR;
                                  OLD_KEY: KEY_TYPE;
                              var STATUS: byte);
{
DESCRIPTION:
    This routine deletes a record from a linked list.  If
the list is empty, or if the key was not found an error
is returned.  The list need not be in ascending order.
```

```
PARAMETERS:
    LIST_START (in/out) - the pointer to the front of the list
    OLD_KEY (in) - the key entry of the record to delete
    STATUS (out) - error status (0 is successful)

TYPES REQUIRED:
    KEY_TYPE - the type of the keyed information stored
    OTHER_TYPE - the type of all non-ordered information
    LIST_PTR - the linked list data structure

SAMPLE CALL:
    Linked_List_Delete (START_PTR, 'Joe', SUCCESS);

NOTES:
    See constant definitions below for error codes.

--------------------------------------------------------------}


  const                              {error codes}
    SUCCESSFUL_DELETION = 0;
    KEY_NOT_FOUND       = 1;
    LIST_EMPTY          = 2;

  var
    SEARCH_PTR,                      {the pointer used for searching}
    TEMP_PTR  : LIST_PTR;            {a temporary record}
    LOCATED   : boolean;             {was the location found yet?}

  begin

{if the list is empty, set the error flag}
    if LIST_START = nil then
      STATUS := LIST_EMPTY

{if the record to delete is the first record, move the
starting pointer}
    else if OLD_KEY = LIST_START^.KEY then
      begin
        STATUS := SUCCESSFUL_DELETION;

{use a temporary pointer to dispose of the unwanted record}
        TEMP_PTR := LIST_START;
        LIST_START := LIST_START^.NEXT;
        Dispose (TEMP_PTR);
      end

    else
      begin

{search until just before we've gone too far, or until the
list is exhausted}
        LOCATED := false;
        SEARCH_PTR := LIST_START;
        while (SEARCH_PTR^.NEXT <> nil) and not LOCATED do
          if SEARCH_PTR^.NEXT^.KEY <> OLD_KEY then
            SEARCH_PTR := SEARCH_PTR^.NEXT
          else
            LOCATED := true;

{if the key was not found, set the error flag}
        if not LOCATED then
          STATUS := KEY_NOT_FOUND
        else
```

```
            begin
               STATUS := SUCCESSFUL_DELETION;

{use a temporary pointer to dispose of the unwanted record}
               TEMP_PTR := SEARCH_PTR^.NEXT;

{close up the list}
               SEARCH_PTR^.NEXT := SEARCH_PTR^.NEXT^.NEXT;
               Dispose (TEMP_PTR);
            end;
        end;
    end;
```

Doubly Linked Lists

Using a linked list is a convenient way to display a list in some sort of order. You could easily print out animal names in alphabetical order in the linked-list example described earlier. However, problems arise when the list needs to be in reverse order. A singly linked list makes it nearly impossible to do anything in the opposite order of the list.

Doubly linked lists solve this problem. A *doubly linked list* has the same record structure as a regular linked list, except that an extra field is added: a pointer to the previous record. Thus, the list is maintained in both ascending and descending order at the same time. Here is the record structure of this type of list:

```
type
  DBL_LIST_PTR = ^DBL_LINK_RECORD;
  DBL_LINK_RECORD = record
    KEY: KEY_TYPE;              {the keyed entry in the list}
    OTHER: OTHER_TYPE;          {all non-ordered information}
    NEXT : DBL_LIST_PTR;        {pointer to the next record}
    LAST : DBL_LIST_PTR;        {pointer to the previous record}
  end;
```

Two pointers are required to maintain a doubly linked list: one pointing to the beginning of the list, and one pointing to the end. The animal-list example given earlier would be implemented by a doubly linked list as shown here:

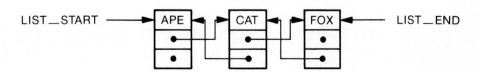

You can list the names in alphabetical order by using the same algorithm that you used for the regular linked list. However, listing them in reverse order requires a slight change:

```
TEMP_PTR := LIST_END;                          {start at the end}
while TEMP_PTR <> nil do          {loop until the beginning}
  begin
    writeln (TEMP_PTR^.KEY, TEMP_PTR^.OTHER);      {display}
    TEMP_PTR := TEMP_PTR^.LAST;                      {travel}
  end;
```

Making an insertion into a doubly linked list is also similar to the process for the regular linked list except that you must connect the reverse pointers. If you add DOG back into the animal list, the list would look like this:

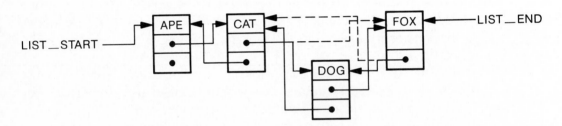

As shown later in *Doubly — Linked — List — Delete*, you must close up two pointers when making a deletion for a doubly linked list, instead of closing up one pointer as you did with a linked list.

Here are the routines for doubly linked lists:

```
procedure Doubly_Linked_List_Insert
                (var LIST_START, LIST_END: DBL_LIST_PTR;
                      NEW_RECORD: DBL_LINK_RECORD);
{
DESCRIPTION:
    This routine inserts a record into a doubly linked list,
maintaining ascending order.

PARAMETERS:
    LIST_START (in/out) - the pointer to the front of the list
    LIST_END (in/out) - the pointer to the back of the list
    NEW_RECORD (in) - the record to be inserted

TYPES REQUIRED:

    KEY_TYPE - the type of the keyed information stored
    OTHER_TYPE - the type of all non-ordered information
    DBL_LIST_PTR - the doubly linked list data structure
```

```
SAMPLE CALL:
    Doubly_Linked_List_Insert (START_PTR, END_PTR, NEW_REC);

NOTES:
    Both LIST_START and LIST_END must be initialized to nil
before calling this routine for the first time.

------------------------------------------------------------}


  var
    SEARCH_PTR,                        {the pointer used for searching}
    TEMP_PTR  : DBL_LIST_PTR;          {a temporary record}
    LOCATED   : boolean;               {was the location found yet?}

  begin

{create a new record and place the information in it}
    New(TEMP_PTR);
    TEMP_PTR^ := NEW_RECORD;
    TEMP_PTR^.NEXT := nil;
    TEMP_PTR^.LAST := nil;

    SEARCH_PTR := LIST_START;

{if the list is empty, make the new record the only one}
    if SEARCH_PTR = nil then
      begin
        LIST_START := TEMP_PTR;
        LIST_END := TEMP_PTR;
      end
    else
      begin

{search until we've gone too far, or until the
list is exhausted}
        LOCATED := false;
        while (SEARCH_PTR <> nil) and not LOCATED do
          if SEARCH_PTR^.KEY < NEW_RECORD.KEY then
            SEARCH_PTR := SEARCH_PTR^.NEXT
          else
            LOCATED := true;

{have the new record point to the current record}
        TEMP_PTR^.NEXT := SEARCH_PTR;

{if the new record will be the first record, set the starting
pointer}
        if SEARCH_PTR = LIST_START then
          begin
            LIST_START := TEMP_PTR;

            SEARCH_PTR^.LAST := TEMP_PTR;
          end

{if the new record will be the last record, set the ending
pointer}
        else if SEARCH_PTR = nil then
          begin
            TEMP_PTR^.LAST := LIST_END;
            LIST_END^.NEXT := TEMP_PTR;
            LIST_END := TEMP_PTR
          end
```

```
{if new record is in the middle, make connections in both
directions}
        else
          begin
            TEMP_PTR^.LAST := SEARCH_PTR^.LAST;
            SEARCH_PTR^.LAST^.NEXT := TEMP_PTR;
            SEARCH_PTR^.LAST := TEMP_PTR;
          end;

      end;
  end;
```

```
procedure Doubly_Linked_List_Delete (var LIST_START,
                            LIST_END: DBL_LIST_PTR;
                            OLD_KEY: KEY_TYPE;
                            var STATUS: byte);
{
DESCRIPTION:
    This routine deletes a record from a doubly linked list.
If the list is empty, or if the key is not contained in the
list, an error is returned.  The list need not be in ascending
order.

PARAMETERS:
    LIST_START (in/out) - the pointer to the front of the list
    LIST_END (in/out) - the pointer to the back of the list
    OLD_KEY (in) - the key of the record to delete
    STATUS (out) - the error status (0 is successful)

TYPES REQUIRED:
    KEY_TYPE - the type of the keyed information to be stored
    OTHER_TYPE - the type of all non-ordered information
    DBL_LIST_PTR - the doubly linked list data structure

SAMPLE CALL:
    Doubly_Linked_List_Delete (START_PTR, END_PTR, 'Smith', SUCCESS);

NOTES:
    See the constant definitions below for error codes.

---------------------------------------------------------}

  const                            {error codes}
    SUCCESSFUL_DELETION = 0;
    KEY_NOT_FOUND       = 1;
    LIST_EMPTY          = 2;

  var
    SEARCH_PTR,                    {the pointer used for searching}
    TEMP_PTR  : DBL_LIST_PTR;      {a temporary record}

  begin
{if the list is empty, set the error flag}
    if LIST_START = nil then
      STATUS := LIST_EMPTY
```

```
{if the record to delete is the first record, move the
starting pointer}
     else if OLD_KEY = LIST_START^.KEY then
        begin
           STATUS := SUCCESSFUL_DELETION;

{use a temporary pointer to dispose of the unwanted record}
           TEMP_PTR := LIST_START;
           LIST_START := LIST_START^.NEXT;
           LIST_START^.LAST := nil;
           if LIST_START = nil then
              LIST_END := nil;
           Dispose (TEMP_PTR);
        end

{if the record to delete is the last record, move the
ending pointer}
     else if OLD_KEY = LIST_END^.KEY then
        begin
           STATUS := SUCCESSFUL_DELETION;

{use a temporary pointer to dispose of the unwanted record}
           TEMP_PTR := LIST_END;
           LIST_END := LIST_END^.LAST;
           LIST_END^.NEXT := nil;
           Dispose (TEMP_PTR);
        end

        else
           begin

{search until just before we've gone too far, or until the
list is exhausted}
           SEARCH_PTR := LIST_START;
           while (SEARCH_PTR <> nil) and (SEARCH_PTR^.KEY <> OLD_KEY) do
              SEARCH_PTR := SEARCH_PTR^.NEXT;
{if the key was not found, set the error flag}
           if SEARCH_PTR = nil then
              STATUS := KEY_NOT_FOUND
           else
              begin
                 STATUS := SUCCESSFUL_DELETION;

{close up the list}
                 SEARCH_PTR^.NEXT^.LAST := SEARCH_PTR^.LAST;
                 SEARCH_PTR^.LAST^.NEXT := SEARCH_PTR^.NEXT;
                 Dispose (SEARCH_PTR);
              end;
           end;
     end;
```

Binary Trees

Linked lists and doubly linked lists solve the problems of memory allocation and sorting speed. However, searching a linked list must be done sequentially. A binary search on a linked list is just as slow as a sequential search (or slower, for a regular linked list). You use the binary tree structure to keep records in sorted order and to speed up the search process.

As with the doubly linked list, the binary tree record requires two pointers. The top record, known as the *root*, breaks off into two *branches*, the left and the right. Each data item is called a *node*. Each branch on the tree has pointers to two more branches. The record structure of the binary tree is as follows:

```
type
  TREE_PTR = ^TREE_RECORD;
  TREE_RECORD = record
    KEY: KEY_TYPE;              {the keyed entry on the tree}
    OTHER: OTHER_TYPE;          {all non-ordered information}
    LEFT : TREE_PTR;            {pointer to the left branch}
    RIGHT: TREE_PTR;            {pointer to the right branch}
  end;
```

When records are added to a binary tree, the value of the key is compared to the key of the root. If the value is less, a search pointer will go to the left branch. If the value is more, the pointer will go to the right branch. This process continues until it finds an empty branch on which to place the new record.

Using the animal-list example, suppose that the tree structure looks like this:

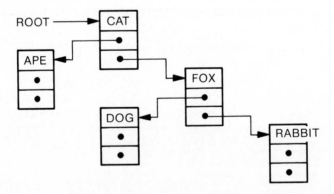

When *Binary—Tree—Insert*, which is given later, is called to add ELEPHANT to the tree, the search pointer will go right at CAT, left at FOX, and right at DOG. Since the subsequent branch is empty, ELEPHANT will be placed there, as shown here:

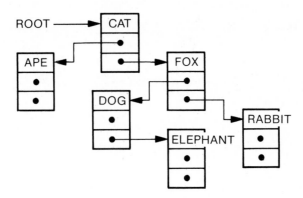

A search on a binary tree is simply the first part of an insert. The search pointer travels over the tree until it finds either the key or an empty branch. This type of search is done in *Binary__Tree__ Extract* (given later).

Listing a binary tree in sorted order is best done recursively. Since you can consider each subtree of a binary tree to be a tree itself, sorting the list simply becomes a matter of "visiting" the branches in the proper order. You can sort in ascending order by visiting the left branch, then the root, and then the right branch. Sorting in descending order would be visiting the right branch, then the root, and then the left branch.

Making a deletion on a binary tree is more complex. If a node has no branches (which is known as a *leaf*), you can remove it with no other changes. If the node has branches, you must restructure the tree so the order is maintained. Deletion then becomes a matter of moving one of the branches up, and "hanging" the other branch on the end of the one.

For example, try to delete FOX from the animal-list tree given earlier. When *Binary__Tree__Delete* is called, it first searches for the key. When it finds FOX, it takes the entire left subtree (DOG) and moves it into the branch where FOX used to be. It then travels down the right side of the new subtree until it finds an empty leaf, and then hangs the right node (RABBIT) there. The tree now looks like this:

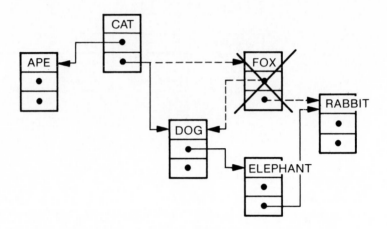

After deleting FOX, the tree looks like this:

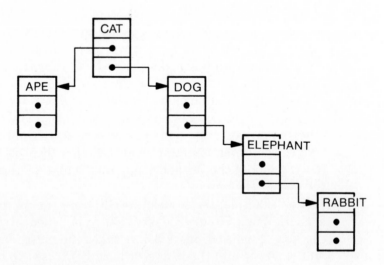

Here are the routines for the binary tree:

```
procedure Binary_Tree_Insert (var ROOT: TREE_PTR;
                                  NEW_RECORD: TREE_RECORD);
{
DESCRIPTION:
    This routine inserts a record into a binary tree, maintaining
ascending order.

PARAMETERS:
    ROOT (in/out) - the pointer to the root of the tree
    NEW_RECORD (in) - the record to add to the tree

TYPES REQUIRED:
    KEY_TYPE - the type of the keyed information stored
    OTHER_TYPE - the type of all non-ordered information
    TREE_PTR - the binary tree data structure

SAMPLE CALL:
    Binary_Tree_Insert (ROOT, 'Sam');

NOTES:
    The ROOT must be initialized to nil before calling this
routine for the first time.

-------------------------------------------------------------}
  var
    SEARCH_PTR,                    {the pointer used for searching}
    PARENT_PTR,                    {the last record searched}
    TEMP_PTR  : TREE_PTR;          {a temporary record}

  begin
    SEARCH_PTR := ROOT;

{traverse the tree until an empty branch is found}
    while SEARCH_PTR <> nil do
      begin
        PARENT_PTR := SEARCH_PTR;
        if NEW_RECORD.KEY < SEARCH_PTR^.KEY then
          SEARCH_PTR := SEARCH_PTR^.LEFT
        else
          SEARCH_PTR := SEARCH_PTR^.RIGHT;
      end;

{create a new branch and place the new record on it}
    New(TEMP_PTR);
    TEMP_PTR^ := NEW_RECORD;
    TEMP_PTR^.LEFT := nil;
    TEMP_PTR^.RIGHT := nil;

{if this is the first record, set the root}
    if SEARCH_PTR = ROOT then
      ROOT := TEMP_PTR
    else if NEW_RECORD.KEY < PARENT_PTR^.KEY then
      PARENT_PTR^.LEFT := TEMP_PTR
    else
      PARENT_PTR^.RIGHT := TEMP_PTR;

  end;
```

```
function Size_of_Binary_Tree (ROOT: TREE_PTR): integer;
{
DESCRIPTION:
    This routine determines the number of elements in
a binary tree.

VALUE RETURNED:
    The number of elements in the tree.

PARAMETERS:
    ROOT (in) - the pointer to the root of the tree

TYPES REQUIRED:
    KEY_TYPE - the type of the keyed information stored
    OTHER_TYPE - the type of all non-ordered information
    TREE_PTR - the binary tree data structure

SAMPLE CALL:
    I := Size_of_Binary_Tree (ROOT);

-------------------------------------------------------------}

  begin

{if the branch is not empty, the size of the branch is one plus
the size of each of its branches}
    if ROOT <> nil then
      Size_of_Binary_Tree := 1 + Size_of_Binary_Tree (ROOT^.LEFT)
              + Size_of_Binary_Tree (ROOT^.RIGHT)
    else
      Size_of_Binary_Tree := 0;
  end;
```

```
procedure Binary_Tree_Extract (ROOT: TREE_PTR;
                       DESIRED_KEY: KEY_TYPE;
                  var EXTRACTED_RECORD: TREE_RECORD;
                       var LOCATED: boolean);
{
DESCRIPTION:
    This extracts a record from a binary tree based on a
given key.   If the key is not found, an error flag is set.

PARAMETERS:
    ROOT (in) - the pointer to the root of the tree
    DESIRED_KEY (in) - the key of the record to search for
    EXTRACTED_RECORD (out) - the entire record found
    LOCATED (out) - flag to indicate a successful search

TYPES REQUIRED:
    KEY_TYPE - the type of the keyed information stored
    OTHER_TYPE - the type of all non-ordered information
    TREE_PTR - the binary tree data structure

SAMPLE CALL:
    Binary_Tree_Extract (ROOT, 'Sam', TREE_REC, FOUND);

-------------------------------------------------------------}
```

```
   var
     SEARCH_PTR: TREE_PTR;              {the pointer used for searching}

   begin
     SEARCH_PTR := ROOT;

{traverse the tree until the key is found or until
an empty branch is found}
     while (DESIRED_KEY <> SEARCH_PTR^.KEY) and (SEARCH_PTR <> nil) do
       if DESIRED_KEY < SEARCH_PTR^.KEY then
         SEARCH_PTR := SEARCH_PTR^.LEFT
       else
         SEARCH_PTR := SEARCH_PTR^.RIGHT;

{if the branch is empty, the key was not found}
     if SEARCH_PTR = nil then
       LOCATED := false
     else
       begin
         LOCATED := true;
         EXTRACTED_RECORD := SEARCH_PTR^;
       end;
   end;
```

```
   procedure Binary_Tree_List (ROOT: TREE_PTR);
   {
DESCRIPTION:
     This routine lists the entries of a binary tree in
ascending order.

PARAMETERS:
     ROOT (in) - the pointer to the root of the tree

TYPES REQUIRED:
     KEY_TYPE - the type of the keyed information stored
     OTHER_TYPE - the type of all non-ordered information
     TREE_PTR - the binary tree data structure

SAMPLE CALL:
     Binary_Tree_List (NAMES);

-------------------------------------------------------}


   begin

{if the branch is empty, return one level of recursion.  If
not, traverse the left side, list the node, and traverse
the right side}
     if ROOT <> nil then
       begin
         Binary_Tree_List (ROOT^.LEFT);

{display the keyed value of the current branch}
         writeln (ROOT^.KEY);

{display the non-ordered information.
***   THIS MUST BE ALTERED IF OTHER_TYPE IS A RECORD}
         writeln (' ', ROOT^.OTHER);
```

```
          Binary_Tree_List (ROOT^.RIGHT);
      end;
  end;
```

```
   procedure Binary_Tree_Delete (var ROOT: TREE_PTR;
                                 OLD_KEY: KEY_TYPE;
                                 var STATUS: byte);
   {
   DESCRIPTION:
       This routine deletes a record from a binary tree,
   maintaining its ascending order.  If the tree is empty,
   or if the key is not contained on the tree, an error
   is returned.

   PARAMETERS:
       ROOT (in/out) - the pointer to the root of the tree
       OLD_KEY (in) - the key of the record to delete from the tree
       STATUS (out) - error flag (0 is successful)

   TYPES REQUIRED:
       KEY_TYPE - the type of the keyed information stored
       OTHER_TYPE - the type of all non-ordered information
       TREE_PTR - the binary tree data structure

   SAMPLE CALL:
       Binary_Tree_Delete (ROOT, 'Sam', SUCCESS);

   NOTES:
       See the constant definitions below for the error
   codes.

   ----------------------------------------------------------}

     const                          {error codes}
       SUCCESSFUL_DELETION = 0;
       KEY_NOT_FOUND       = 1;
       TREE_EMPTY          = 2;

     var
       SEARCH_PTR,                  {the pointer used for searching}
       PARENT_PTR,                  {the last record searched}
       TEMP_PTR,                    {a temporary record}
       TEMP2_PTR : TREE_PTR;        {another temporary record}

     begin
       if ROOT = nil then
         STATUS := TREE_EMPTY
       else
         begin
           SEARCH_PTR := ROOT;

   {traverse the tree until the key is found or until
   an empty branch is found}
           while (OLD_KEY <> SEARCH_PTR^.KEY) and (SEARCH_PTR <> nil) do
             begin
               PARENT_PTR := SEARCH_PTR;
```

```
              if OLD_KEY < SEARCH_PTR^.KEY then
                 SEARCH_PTR := SEARCH_PTR^.LEFT
              else
                 SEARCH_PTR := SEARCH_PTR^.RIGHT;
           end;

{if the branch is empty, the key was not found}
           if SEARCH_PTR = nil then
              STATUS := KEY_NOT_FOUND
           else
              begin
                 STATUS := SUCCESSFUL_DELETION;

{if there is no left branch, replace the deleted
node with its right branch}
                 if SEARCH_PTR^.LEFT = nil then
                    TEMP_PTR := SEARCH_PTR^.RIGHT
                 else
                    begin
                       TEMP_PTR := SEARCH_PTR^.LEFT;
                       TEMP2_PTR := TEMP_PTR;
                       while TEMP2_PTR^.RIGHT <> nil do
                          TEMP2_PTR := TEMP2_PTR^.RIGHT;
                       TEMP2_PTR^.RIGHT := SEARCH_PTR^.RIGHT;
                    end;

{connect the parent to the new replacement}
                 if ROOT = SEARCH_PTR then
                    ROOT := TEMP_PTR
                 else if PARENT_PTR^.LEFT = SEARCH_PTR then
                    PARENT_PTR^.LEFT := TEMP_PTR
                 else
                    PARENT_PTR^.RIGHT := TEMP_PTR;
                 Dispose (SEARCH_PTR);
              end;
        end;
   end;
```

C H A P T E R

7

Input and Output

Although computers save time, space, and money, they tend to frighten most people. Too often, a computer program may be awkward to use because it has a poor user interface. A program may solve complex equations and store vast amounts of data, but unless it is easy to use, it is practically worthless.

Chapters 7 and 8 deal with the portion of a program that is often the most important portion—the user interface. This chapter provides routines for simple input from the keyboard and output to the screen. Chapter 8 builds on these routines to develop more complex input and output (I/O).

Improving a User Interface

There are two keys to making a user interface more appealing. The first is the *appearance* of the output messages. For example, items written in red tend to stand out, and blinking messages stick out almost too much. If one message looks different from the rest, it draws attention to itself. The second key is the *screen location* of the input and output. Programs in which all input and output take place at the bottom left of the screen get visually tiresome.

The effective combination of these two characteristics is called *screen management*. Screen management involves thinking of the computer monitor as a television rather than as an electric typewriter. When a program starts, the screen should clear and the user should get a picture of what will happen next. After everything on that screen is completed, the next full screen appears. For instance, suppose a program requires ten entries for computing a student's eligibility for financial aid. The names of the ten entries should appear on the screen at once. The user can then enter each number, one at a time, knowing exactly what comes next.

Turbo Pascal provides utilities not found in standard Pascal that aid in developing standard user interface routines. One of these is the **string** type, discussed in depth in the Chapter 5. The routines in this chapter use the type

```
STRING79 = string[79];
```

to standardize the parameters passed among procedures. Another nonstandard Pascal feature used heavily in these input and output routines is the **GotoXY** procedure. This subroutine allows the programmer to position the cursor anywhere on the 25 × 80 screen. In addition, the Turbo procedures **TextColor** and **TextBackground** are used to set the foreground and background colors of the I/O that follows them.

The following output routines take full advantage of both video attributes and output location. Among these, the *Put— String* routine requires not only a string for output, but also location and attribute specifications. Other output routines allow for the displaying of numbers and centered messages. The *Put—Prompt* procedure erases a line before it displays the string. The *Put—Error* routine

forces the user to acknowledge a message by pressing any key on the
console.

```
procedure Set_Video (ATTRIBUTE: integer);
{
DESCRIPTION:
    This routine sets the video attributes for future input and output.

PARAMETERS:
    ATTRIBUTE (in) - video attribute [0-7]

SAMPLE CALL:
    Set_Video (2);

NOTES:
    The attribute code, based on bits, is as follows:
        0 - normal video        1 - reverse video
        2 - bold video          3 - reverse and bold
        4 - blinking video      5 - reverse and blinking
        6 - bold and blinking   7 - reverse, bold and blinking

-----------------------------------------------------------}

    var
      BLINKING,                  {number to add for blinking}
      BOLD: integer;             {number to add for bold}

    begin

{set the blinking color based on MSB}
    BLINKING := (ATTRIBUTE and 4) * 4;        {0 or 16}

{set the reverse video colors}
    if (ATTRIBUTE and 1) = 1 then
      begin

{set the bold color based on middle bit}
        BOLD := (ATTRIBUTE and 2) * 7;        {0 or 14}
        TextColor (1 + BLINKING + BOLD);      {DARK OR WHITE}
        TextBackground (3);                   {CYAN}
      end

{set the normal video colors}
    else
      begin
        BOLD := (ATTRIBUTE and 2) * 5 div 2; {0 or 5}
        TextColor (7 + BLINKING + BOLD);      {GRAY OR RED}
        TextBackground (0);                   {DARK}
      end;
  end;
```

```
procedure Put_String (OUT_STRING: STRING79;
                LINE, COL, ATTRIB: integer);
{
```

```
DESCRIPTION:
    This routine outputs a string at a given location on the screen
    with a given video attribute.

PARAMETERS:
    OUT_STRING (in) - string to be output
    LINE (in) - screen line [1-24]
    COL (in) - screen column [1-80]
    ATTRIB (in) - video attribute [0-7]

TYPES REQUIRED:
    STRING79 - used for all strings

LIBRARY ROUTINES USED:
    Set_Video - sets the video attribute

SAMPLE CALL:
    Put_String ('This is in the lower-left corner', 24, 1, 0);

NOTES:
    See Set_Video for the code for the video attribute.

----------------------------------------------------------}

  begin

{set up the video attributes and the cursor location}
    Set_Video (ATTRIB);
    GotoXY (COL, LINE);
    write (OUT_STRING);

{reset to normal video}
    Set_Video (0);
  end;
```

```
procedure Put_Centered_String (OUT_STRING: STRING79;
                               LINE, ATTRIB: integer);
{
DESCRIPTION:
    This routine centers a string on a given line on the screen
    with a given video attribute.

PARAMETERS:
    OUT_STRING (in) - string to be output
    LINE (in) - screen line [1-24]
    ATTRIB (in) - video attribute [0-7]

TYPES REQUIRED:
    STRING79 - used for all strings

LIBRARY ROUTINES USED:
    Put_String - outputs a string at a given location

SAMPLE CALL:
    Put_Centered_String ('This is a Sample Title', 5, 3);
```

```
NOTES:
    See Set_Video for the code for the video attribute.
    Centering is done by setting the starting column to
    40 - Length/2 .

------------------------------------------------------------}

  begin

{calculate the column number and output the string}
    Put_String (OUT_STRING, LINE, 40 - Length (OUT_STRING) div 2, ATTRIB);
  end;
```

```
procedure Put_Real (NUMBER: real;
        LINE, COL, ATTRIB,
        NUM_LENGTH, NUMDEC: integer);
{
DESCRIPTION:
    This routine outputs a real number at a given location on
    the screen with a given format and video attribute.

PARAMETERS:
    NUMBER (in) - number to be output
    LINE (in) - screen line [1-24]
    COL (in) - screen column [1-80]
    ATTRIB (in) - video attribute [0-7]
    NUM_LENGTH (in) - total number of places to use (right justify) [2-80]
    NUMDEC (in) - number of decimal places [0-(NUM_LENGTH-1)]

TYPES REQUIRED:
    STRING79 - used for all strings

LIBRARY ROUTINES USED:
    Put_String - outputs a string at a given location

SAMPLE CALL:
    Put_Real (PI, 5, 10, 0, 6, 3);

NOTES:
    See Set_Video for the code for the video attribute.

------------------------------------------------------------}

  var
    TEMP_STR: STRING79;                {temporary string}

  begin

{convert the number to a string and output the string}
    Str (NUMBER:NUM_LENGTH:NUMDEC, TEMP_STR);
    Put_String (TEMP_STR, LINE, COL, ATTRIB);
  end;
```

```
procedure Put_Integer (NUMBER, LINE, COL,
                       ATTRIB, NUM_LENGTH: integer);
{
DESCRIPTION:
    This routine outputs an integer at a given location on
    the screen with a given format and video attribute.

PARAMETERS:
    NUMBER (in) - number to be output
    LINE (in) - screen line [1-24]
    COL (in) - screen column [1-80]
    ATTRIB (in) - video attribute [0-7]
    NUM_LENGTH (in) - total number of places to use (right justify) [1-80]

TYPES REQUIRED:
    STRING79 - used for all strings

LIBRARY ROUTINES USED:
    Put_String - outputs a string at a given location

SAMPLE CALL:
    Put_Integer (COUNT, 5, 10, 0, 6);

NOTES:
    See Set_Video for the code for the video attribute.

--------------------------------------------------------------}


  var
    TEMP_STR: STRING79;               {temporary string}

  begin

{convert number to a string and output the string}
    Str (NUMBER:NUM_LENGTH, TEMP_STR);
    Put_String (TEMP_STR, LINE, COL, ATTRIB);
  end;
```

```
procedure Put_Prompt (OUT_STRING: STRING79;
                      LINE, COL: integer);
{
DESCRIPTION:
    This routine outputs a string on a given line on the screen
    after erasing that line.

PARAMETERS:
    OUT_STRING (in) - string to be output
    LINE (in) - screen line [1-24]
    COL (in) - screen column [1-80]

TYPES REQUIRED:
    STRING79 - used for all strings

LIBRARY ROUTINES USED:
    Put_String - outputs a string at a given location
```

```
SAMPLE CALL:
    Put_Prompt ('Please enter your full name: ', 24, 1);

NOTES:
    Prompts are always written in bold reverse-video.

--------------------------------------------------------}

  begin

{clear to the end of the line and output the string}
    GotoXY (COL, LINE);
    ClrEol;
    Put_String (OUT_STRING, LINE, COL, 3);
  end;
```

```
procedure Put_Error (OUT_STRING: STRING79;
                     LINE, COL: integer);
{
DESCRIPTION:
    This routine outputs an error message on a given line on the screen
    and waits for the user to input any key.

PARAMETERS:
    OUT_STRING (in) - string to be output
    LINE (in) - screen line [1-24]
    COL (in) - screen column [1-80]

TYPES REQUIRED:
    STRING79 - used for all strings

LIBRARY ROUTINES USED:
    Put_String - outputs a string at a given location

SAMPLE CALL:
    Put_Error ('ERROR: no more students.  Press any key to
continue.', 24, 1);

NOTES:
    Errors are always written in reverse-bold-blinking.

------------------------------------------------------}

  var
    ANY_CHAR : char;                {character input from the user}

  begin

{Output the string and wait for a response}
    Put_String (OUT_STRING, LINE, COL, 7);
    read (kbd, ANY_CHAR);
  end;
```

Screen management for output routines is relatively simple, since output is under programmer control. However, input is more difficult. The standard procedure **Readin** puts few (if any) limitations on user input. For example, if a string field is only ten characters in length, standard Pascal will allow the user to enter many more characters, but it will accept only the first ten. This is dangerous not only because the user expects the complete entry to be stored, but also because it tends to destroy screen management. Standard Pascal also has a problem with numeric entry: if the user accidentally types in a nonnumeric character at the start of numeric input, a fatal run-time error occurs and the program halts.

The following input routines solve these problems. The *Get__ String* routine reads in a string at a certain screen location. One of the input parameters to the routine is the maximum length of the input. If a reverse-video attribute is selected, the length of the string is highlighted. If the user tries to enter more than the length of the string, the bell rings. *Get__String* also allows the user to correct the most recent value of a string by using the right-arrow key. For example, suppose the value of a string is

Borlind, Frank

To correct the spelling of the name, the user can use the right-arrow key to move over to the "i," type an **a**, and then use the right-arrow key to go to the end of the field. *Get__Integer* and *Get__Real* solve the run-time error problem by calling *Get__String* and converting the string to a number by using the Turbo procedure **Val** as shown here.

```
procedure Get_String (var IN_STRING: STRING79;
                          LINE, COL,
                     ATTRIB, STR_LENGTH: integer);
{
DESCRIPTION:
    This routine inputs a string at a given location on
    the screen with a given video attribute.

PARAMETERS:
    IN_STRING (in/out) - string to be input
    LINE (in) - screen line [1-24]
    COL (in) - screen column [1-80]
    ATTRIB (in) - video attribute [0-7]
    STR_LENGTH (in) - total number of places to use [1-80]
```

```
TYPES REQUIRED:
    STRING79 - used for all strings

LIBRARY ROUTINES USED:
    Put_String - outputs a string at a given location

SAMPLE CALL:
    Get_String (NAME, 5, 10, 2, 26);

NOTES:
    See Set_Video for the code for the video attribute.
    This routine inputs one character at a time so it can
    control the echo.
    The right arrow is used to allow the user to use a character
    from the current value of the string.
    Input is not allowed past the length given.
    The length of the string is highlighted to let user know
    how much can be entered.

    --------------------------------------------------------------}


    const
      BELL             = 7;      {ASCII bell}
      BACK_SPACE       = 8;      {ASCII backspace}
      CARRIAGE_RETURN = 13;      {ASCII carriage return}
      ESCAPE           = 27;     {ASCII escape character}
      RIGHT_ARROW      = 77;     {IBM right-arrow escape sequence}

    var
      OLDSTR : STRING79;         {original string}
      IN_CHAR: char;             {character input from terminal}
      I      : integer;          {counter for string length}

    begin

{highlight spaces past the original string up to the string length}
    OLDSTR := IN_STRING;
    Put_String (IN_STRING, LINE, COL, ATTRIB);

    for I := Length (IN_STRING) to STR_LENGTH - 1 do
      Put_String (' ', LINE, COL + I, ATTRIB);

{read in first char; if RETURN use old string}
    GotoXY (COL, LINE);
    read (kbd, IN_CHAR);
    if Ord (IN_CHAR) <> CARRIAGE_RETURN then
      IN_STRING := '';

{process characters one at a time}
    while Ord (IN_CHAR) <> CARRIAGE_RETURN do
      begin

{if backspace, remove character entered}
        if Ord (IN_CHAR) = BACK_SPACE then     {backspace}
          begin
            if Length (IN_STRING) > 0 then
              begin
                IN_STRING[0] := Chr(Length (IN_STRING) - 1);
                write (Chr(BACK_SPACE));
                write (' ');
```

```
                          write (Chr(BACK_SPACE));
                     end;
              end

     {check for arrow keys - double character with ESCAPE as first char}
              else if Ord(IN_CHAR) = ESCAPE then
                 begin
                    read (kbd, IN_CHAR);

     {if right arrow, use old string}
                    if Ord(IN_CHAR) = RIGHT_ARROW then
                       begin
                          if Length (OLDSTR) > Length (IN_STRING) then
                             begin
                                IN_STRING[0] := Chr(Length (IN_STRING) + 1);
                                IN_CHAR := OLDSTR[Ord(IN_STRING[0])];
                                IN_STRING[Ord(IN_STRING[0])] := IN_CHAR;
                                write (IN_CHAR);
                             end
                       end

     {ring bell if user tries to use the right arrow past the length
     of the string}
                    else
                       write (Chr(BELL));
                 end

     {if "normal" character, add it to the string}
              else if Length (IN_STRING) < STR_LENGTH then
                 begin
                    IN_STRING[0] := Chr(Length (IN_STRING) + 1);
                    IN_STRING[Ord(IN_STRING[0])] := IN_CHAR;
                    write (IN_CHAR);
                 end

     {otherwise, ring the bell}
              else
                 write (Chr(BELL));
              read (kbd, IN_CHAR);
           end;

     {echo the string with the right attribute}
        Put_String (IN_STRING, LINE, COL, ATTRIB);
        for I := Length (IN_STRING) to STR_LENGTH - 1 do
           Put_String (' ', LINE, COL + I, 0);

     end;
```

```
procedure Get_Real (var NUMBER: real;
           LINE, COL, ATTRIB,
           NUM_LENGTH, NUMDEC: integer);

{
```

```
DESCRIPTION:
    This routine inputs a real number at a given location on
    the screen with a given video attribute.

PARAMETERS:
    NUMBER (in/out) - real number to be input
    LINE (in) - screen line [1-24]
    COL (in) - screen column [1-80]
    ATTRIB (in) - video attribute [0-7]
    NUM_LENGTH (in) - total number of places to use [1-80]
    NUMDEC (in) - number of decimal places [0-(NUM_LENGTH-1)]

TYPES REQUIRED:
    STRING79 - used for all strings

LIBRARY ROUTINES USED:
    Put_String - outputs a string at a given location
    Get_String - inputs a string from a given location

SAMPLE CALL:
    Get_Real (GPA, 5, 10, 2, 6, 2);

NOTES:
    See Set_Video for the code for the video attribute.
    See Get_String for other information.

------------------------------------------------------------}

    const
      BELL = 7;                       {ASCII bell}

    var
      VALCODE      : integer;         {code from string conversion}
      ORIGINAL_STR,                   {original string}
      TEMP_STR     : STRING79;        {string input from terminal}
      TEMP_REAL    : real;            {attempted conversion from string}

    begin
      Str (NUMBER:NUM_LENGTH:NUMDEC, ORIGINAL_STR);

{keep trying to input until only digits are entered}
      repeat
        TEMP_STR := ORIGINAL_STR;

{get the input in string form}
        Get_String (TEMP_STR, LINE, COL, ATTRIB, NUM_LENGTH);

{remove leading blanks}
        while TEMP_STR[1] = ' ' do
          TEMP_STR := Copy (TEMP_STR, 2, Length (TEMP_STR));

{attempt to convert it to a real number}
        Val (TEMP_STR, TEMP_REAL, VALCODE);

{if conversion fails, ring the bell}
        if (VALCODE <> 0) then
          write (Chr(BELL));
      until VALCODE = 0;
```

```
{convert back to string with proper format and re-echo}
    NUMBER := TEMP_REAL;
    Str (NUMBER:NUM_LENGTH:NUMDEC, TEMP_STR);
    Put_String (TEMP_STR, LINE, COL, ATTRIB);
  end;
```

```
procedure Get_Integer (var NUMBER: integer;
                       LINE, COL,
              ATTRIB, NUM_LENGTH: integer);
{
DESCRIPTION:
    This routine inputs an integer at a given location on
    the screen with a given video attribute.

PARAMETERS:
    NUMBER (in/out) - integer to be input
    LINE (in) - screen line [1-24]
    COL (in) - screen column [1-80]
    ATTRIB (in) - video attribute [0-7]
    NUM_LENGTH (in) - total number of places to use [1-80]

TYPES REQUIRED:
    STRING79 - used for all strings

LIBRARY ROUTINES USED:
    Put_String - outputs a string at a given location
    Get_String - inputs a string from a given location

SAMPLE CALL:
    Get_Integer (SCORE, 5, 10, 2, 4);

NOTES:
    See Set_Video for the code for the video attribute.
    See Get_String for other information.

-----------------------------------------------------------}

  const
    BELL = 7;                        {ASCII bell}

  var
    VALCODE     : integer;           {code from string conversion}
    ORIGINAL_STR,                    {original string}
    TEMP_STR    : STRING79;          {string input from terminal}
    TEMP_INT    : integer;           {attempted conversion from string}

  begin
    Str (NUMBER:NUM_LENGTH, ORIGINAL_STR);

{keep trying to input until only digits are entered}
    repeat
      TEMP_STR := ORIGINAL_STR;

{get the input in string form}
      Get_String (TEMP_STR, LINE, COL, ATTRIB, NUM_LENGTH);
```

```
{remove leading blanks}
     while TEMP_STR[1] = ' ' do
        TEMP_STR := Copy (TEMP_STR, 2, Length (TEMP_STR));

{attempt to convert it to a real number}
     Val (TEMP_STR, TEMP_INT, VALCODE);

{if conversion fails, ring the bell}
        if (VALCODE <> 0) then
           write (Chr(BELL));
     until VALCODE = 0;

{convert back to string with proper format and re-echo}
     NUMBER := TEMP_INT;
     Str (NUMBER:NUM_LENGTH, TEMP_STR);
     Put_String (TEMP_STR, LINE, COL, ATTRIB);
   end;
```

Many programs that reflect good screen management require a routine that categorizes the response of a user. Here are the two category types required by the next routine:

```
RESPONSE_TYPE = (NO_RESPONSE, ARROW, KEY, RETURN);
MOVEMENT = (NONE, LEFT, RIGHT, UP, DOWN);
```

If the user enters a character from the keyboard, **RESPONSE— TYPE** becomes **KEY**. If the user types a carriage return, it becomes **RETURN**. If the user presses an arrow key, **RESPONSE— TYPE** is set to **ARROW** and the variable of type **MOVEMENT** is set to the direction of the arrow. Arrow directions on IBM-PC compatibles are translated by an escape character (ASCII 27) followed by a character like **M** or **K**. These two-character combinations are known as *escape sequences*.

The following procedure, *Get—Response*, is used extensively in Chapter 8 for user input. It returns three variables: one for the type of response, one for the arrow direction (if any), and one for the keyboard character entered (if any). Escape sequences other than the arrow keys are not allowed.

```
procedure Get_Response (var RESPONSE    : RESPONSE_TYPE;
                        var DIRECTION   : MOVEMENT;
                        var KEY_RESPONSE: char);
{
DESCRIPTION:
    This routine gets one character from the keyboard and
    categorizes it as either an arrow key, a carriage return,
    or a key.  Arrows are broken down by direction.
```

```
PARAMETERS:
    RESPONSE (out) - type of response (see type RESPONSE_TYPE)
    DIRECTION (out) - which arrow key was hit, if any
    KEY_RESPONSE (out) - key entered, if any

TYPES REQUIRED:
    RESPONSE_TYPE = (NO_RESPONSE, ARROW, KEY, RETURN) -
      used to distinguish type of response (NO_RESPONSE should
      never be returned)
    MOVEMENT = (NONE, LEFT, RIGHT, UP, DOWN) -
      used to define arrow direction

SAMPLE CALL:
    Get_Response (RTYPE, ARROW_DIR, KEY_ENTERED);

NOTES:
    Only uppercase letters are return in KEY_RESPONSE.

------------------------------------------------------------}

    const
      BELL            = 7;          {ASCII bell}
      CARRIAGE_RETURN = 13;         {ASCII carriage return}
      ESCAPE          = 27;         {ASCII escape character}
      RIGHT_ARROW     = 77;         {IBM right-arrow escape sequence}
      LEFT_ARROW      = 75;         {IBM left-arrow escape sequence}
      DOWN_ARROW      = 80;         {IBM down-arrow escape sequence}
      UP_ARROW        = 72;         {IBM up-arrow escape sequence}

    var
      IN_CHAR: char;               {temporary storage of input variable}

    begin
      RESPONSE := NO_RESPONSE;
      DIRECTION := NONE;
      KEY_RESPONSE := ' ';

{loop until a valid key is entered}

    repeat
      read (kbd, IN_CHAR);

{check for arrow keys - two character entry with ESCAPE as first char}
      if Ord(IN_CHAR) = ESCAPE then
        begin
          RESPONSE := ARROW;

{arrows are actually two-character responses}
          read (kbd, IN_CHAR);
          if Ord(IN_CHAR) = LEFT_ARROW then
            DIRECTION := LEFT
          else if Ord(IN_CHAR) = RIGHT_ARROW then
            DIRECTION := RIGHT
          else if Ord(IN_CHAR) = DOWN_ARROW then
            DIRECTION := DOWN
          else if Ord(IN_CHAR) = UP_ARROW then
            DIRECTION := UP

{bad escape sequence; ring the bell}
```

```
        else
          begin
            RESPONSE := NO_RESPONSE;
            write (Chr(BELL));
          end
    end

{check for carriage returns}
      else if Ord(IN_CHAR) = CARRIAGE_RETURN then
        RESPONSE := RETURN

{check for key entered, set to uppercase}
      else
        begin
          RESPONSE := KEY;
          KEY_RESPONSE := UpCase (IN_CHAR);
        end;
    until RESPONSE <> NO_RESPONSE;
  end;
```

Prompted Input

The next few procedures, combining several input and output routines given earlier in this chapter, are useful input tools. They first highlight the description of the input, which is located just to the left of the actual input. Then they display the prompt at a desired location. After the user enters a value, the routines will remove the highlight from the description and return the input value.

As an example, assume that the description **Student Name:** and its current value, **Joe Schmoe**, have been displayed with the *Put—String* subroutine. The procedure call

```
Get_Prompted_String (STUDENT_NAME, 1, 30, 'Student Name: ', 5, 2,
    'Please enter the full name of the student.', 24, 2);
```

would have the effects shown in Figure 7-1. The circled numbers in the figure point out each effect in the following list:

1. **Student Name:** will be displayed in red.

2. The prompt **Please enter the full name of the student.** will be displayed with a cyan background and white foreground on the bottom line of the screen, after that line has been erased.

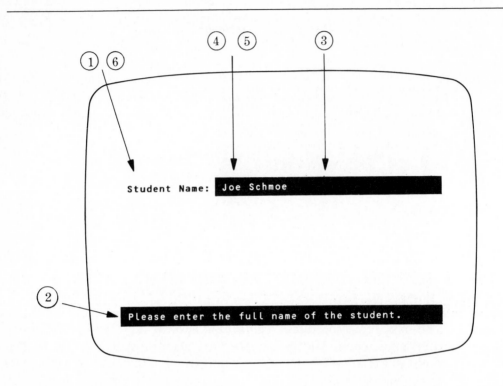

Figure 7-1. *A sample display created by* Get—Prompted—String

3. Since **Joe Schmoe** is 10 characters in length, the 20 spaces after the name will become cyan background (to show the maximum length allowed).

4. The user will enter the new name, using the right arrow to keep the old characters.

5. The string will be echoed with cyan background only for the actual string length.

6. The description **Student Name:** will be rewritten with normal video.

```
procedure Get_Prompted_String (var IN_STRING: STRING79;
                               INATTR, STR_LENGTH: integer;
                                        STRDESC: STRING79;
                               DESCLINE, DESCCOL: integer;
                                         PROMPT: STRING79;
                                 PRLINE, PRCOL: integer);
{
DESCRIPTION:
    This routine inputs a string at a given location on the screen
    with a given video attribute, which includes highlighting the
    description and displaying a prompt.

PARAMETERS:
    IN_STRING (in/out) - string to be input
    INATTR (in) - video attribute of string [0-7]
    STR_LENGTH (in) - length of string to be input [1-79]
    STRDESC (in) - string descriptor (to be highlighted)
    DESCLINE (in) - descriptor screen line [1-24]
    DESCCOL (in) - descriptor screen column [1-80]
    PROMPT (in) - prompt to ask for input
    PRLINE (in) - prompt line [1-24]
    PRCOL (in) - prompt column [1-80]

TYPES REQUIRED:
    STRING79 - used for all strings

LIBRARY ROUTINES USED:
    Put_String - outputs a string at a given screen location
    Put_Prompt - outputs a string after clearing the line
    Get_String - inputs a string at a given screen location

SAMPLE CALL:
    Get_Prompted_String (NAME, 1, 30, 'Student name: ', 10, 2,
                         'Enter student''s full name.', 24, 2);

NOTES:
    This routine was designed to save time for programs involving
    a lot of user interaction.  See each individual routine for other
    notes.

-----------------------------------------------------------}

  begin

{highlight the descriptor and display the prompt}
    Put_String (STRDESC, DESCLINE, DESCCOL, 2);
    Put_Prompt (PROMPT, PRLINE, PRCOL);

{get the input}
    Get_String (IN_STRING, DESCLINE, DESCCOL + Length (STRDESC),
                INATTR, STR_LENGTH);

{de-highlight the descriptor}
    Put_String (STRDESC, DESCLINE, DESCCOL, 0);
  end;
```

```
procedure Get_Prompted_Real (var INNUMBER: real;
                 INATTR, NUM_LENGTH, INNUMDEC: integer;
                                     STRDESC: STRING79;
                         DESCLINE, DESCCOL: integer;
                                      PROMPT: STRING79;
                           PRLINE, PRCOL: integer);
{
DESCRIPTION:
     This routine inputs a real number at a given location on the screen
     with a given video attribute, which includes highlighting the descriptor
     and displaying a prompt.

PARAMETERS:
     INNUMBER (in/out) - real number to be input
     INATTR (in) - video attribute of real number [0-7]
     NUM_LENGTH (in) - total number of places to be input [1-79]
     INNUMDEC (in) - number of decimal places in number [0-(NUM_LENGTH-1)]
     STRDESC (in) - string descriptor (to be highlighted)
     DESCLINE (in) - descriptor screen line [1-24]
     DESCCOL (in) - descriptor screen column [1-80]
     PROMPT (in) - prompt to ask for input
     PRLINE (in) - prompt line [1-24]
     PRCOL (in) - prompt column [1-80]

TYPES REQUIRED:
     STRING79 - used for all strings

LIBRARY ROUTINES USED:
     Put_String - outputs a string at a given screen location
     Put_Prompt - outputs a string after clearing the line
     Get_Real - inputs a string at a given screen location

SAMPLE CALL:
     Get_Prompted_Real (COST, 1, 30, 'Item cost: ', 10, 2,
                     'Enter the cost of item in dollars.', 24, 2);

NOTES:
     This routine was designed to save time for programs involving
     a lot of user interaction.  See each individual routine for other
     notes.
     The number location is assumed to be right after the descriptor.

----------------------------------------------------------}

     begin

{highlight the descriptor and display the prompt}
     Put_String (STRDESC, DESCLINE, DESCCOL, 2);
     Put_Prompt (PROMPT, PRLINE, PRCOL);

{get the input}
     Get_Real (INNUMBER, DESCLINE, DESCCOL + Length (STRDESC),
                        INATTR, NUM_LENGTH, INNUMDEC);

{de-highlight the descriptor}
     Put_String (STRDESC, DESCLINE, DESCCOL, 0);
     end;
```

```
procedure Get_Prompted_Integer (var INNUMBER: integer;
                            INATTR, NUM_LENGTH: integer;
                                       STRDESC: STRING79;
                            DESCLINE, DESCCOL: integer;
                                        PROMPT: STRING79;
                              PRLINE, PRCOL: integer);
{
```

DESCRIPTION:
    This routine inputs an integer at a given location on the screen
    with a given video attribute, which includes highlighting the
    descriptor and displaying a prompt.

PARAMETERS:
    INNUMBER (in/out) - integer to be input
    INATTR (in) - video attribute of number [0-7]
    NUM_LENGTH (in) - length of number to be input [1-79]
    STRDESC (in) - string descriptor (to be highlighted)
    DESCLINE (in) - descriptor screen line [1-24]
    DESCCOL (in) - descriptor screen column [1-80]
    PROMPT (in) - prompt to ask for input
    PRLINE (in) - prompt line [1-24]
    PRCOL (in) - prompt column [1-80]

TYPES REQUIRED:
    STRING79 - used for all strings

LIBRARY ROUTINES USED:
    Put_String - outputs a string at a given screen location
    Put_Prompt - outputs a string after clearing the line
    Get_Integer - inputs a string at a given screen location

SAMPLE CALL:
    Get_Prompted_Integer (AGE, 1, 30, 'Student age: ', 10, 2,
                    'Enter Student''s age.', 24, 2);

NOTES:
    This routine was designed to save time for programs involving
    a lot of user interaction. See each individual routine for other
    notes.
    The integer location is assumed to be right after the descriptor.

--}

```
  begin

{highlight the descriptor and display the prompt}
    Put_String (STRDESC, DESCLINE, DESCCOL, 2);
    Put_Prompt (PROMPT, PRLINE, PRCOL);

{get the input}
    Get_Integer (INNUMBER, DESCLINE, DESCCOL + Length (STRDESC),
                INATTR, NUM_LENGTH);

{de-highlight the descriptor}
    Put_String (STRDESC, DESCLINE, DESCCOL, 0);
  end;
```

8

Menus and Special I/O

In Chapter 7, you learned the importance of a professional and effective user interface. The routines in this chapter provide tools for I/O combinations that utilize all of the fundamental principles of screen management. These routines make extensive use of the input and output routines given in Chapter 7.

Menus

One of the most common ways of allowing a user to choose one of many options is the *menu*. Menus are better than queries, because if a menu is designed properly, it leaves no room for user error. A menu also gives users a visual display of their options, instead of forcing them to remember commands or refer to a manual.

Including a frame on all of your screens gives your application a more consistent and professional appearance. The *Display—Frame* routine puts a frame around part of the screen to make the portion inside stand out. The *Display—Menu* procedure uses the frame to center a menu on the screen automatically.

The menu record format is

```
type
  MENU_REC = record
     NUM_CHOICES : integer;
     MENU_WIDTH  : integer;
     CHOICES     : array [1..14] of char;
     DESCRIPTIONS: array [1..14] of STRING79;
     TITLE       : STRING79;
     PROMPT      : STRING79;
  end;
```

NUM—CHOICES determines the total number of options on the menu. Fourteen is the maximum number of choices allowed, for two reasons: first, any more than that tends to confuse a user; second, more than 14 options will not fit on the screen without being cramped. **MENU—WIDTH** determines the width of the frame around the menu. **CHOICES** are single characters that the user can type to select an option. These can be set automatically to the numbers **1..NUM—CHOICES,** as many menu routines are, but allowing for other characters increases readability and flexibility. For example, a sample menu for a grade program could be drawn with the following typed constant:

```
const
  GRADES_MAIN_MENU : MENU_REC = (
     NUM_CHOICES : 5;
     MENU_WIDTH  : 50;
     CHOICES     : '1234E            ';
     DESCRIPTIONS: ('Add a student to the master list',
                    'Delete a student from the master list',
                    'Add/Change the grades for a student',
                    'Print grade report',
                    'Exit program', '','','','','','','','','');
     TITLE       : 'Student Grade Program';
     PROMPT      : 'Enter choice or use arrow key and hit <ENTER>');
```

Thus, the call

```
Display_Menu (GRADES_MAIN_MENU);
```

would yield the screen shown in Figure 8-1. (If this seems confusing, follow the *Display—Menu* procedure given later.)

After the menu is displayed, the *Get—Menu—Response* subroutine gives the user two ways to choose an option. When the routine is called, a default menu choice is highlighted. The first method allows the user to use the arrow keys (up or down) to change the highlighted choice to the desired choice; the user then enters a carriage return. The other method allows the user to type the character of the required option. With the second method, the corresponding action takes place without the user entering a carriage return. This dual-method approach increases flexibility and allows the same program to satisfy two sets of user preferences.

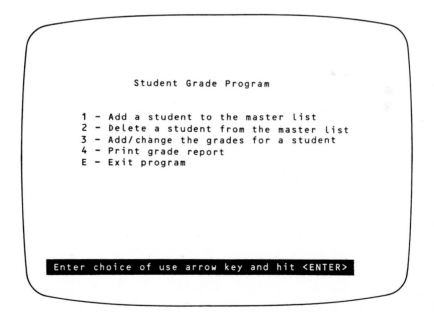

Figure 8-1. A sample call to Display—Menu

```
procedure Display_Frame (NUM_LINES,
                         NUM_COLS: integer);
{
DESCRIPTION:
    This routine displays a frame around a section of the screen.

PARAMETERS:
    NUM_LINES (in) - screen height out to the frame [1-20]
    NUM_COLS (in) - screen width out to the frame [1-73]

SAMPLE CALL:
    Display_Frame (8, 50);

NOTES:
    The frame is displayed in reverse video.
    The routine uses parts of the extra character set, found in
    the Turbo Pascal Reference manual.
    The number of lines and columns passed into this routine represent
    the size of the blank space inside the frame -- the frame itself
    included three columns on each side and two lines at the top and
    bottom.

---------------------------------------------------------------}

  var
     LEFT_COL,                  {leftmost column of the frame}
     TOP_LINE,                  {top line of the frame}
     COL, LINE: integer;        {counters for loops}

  begin

{limit the frame size to 20x73 so that
the complete frame can fit on the screen}
     if NUM_LINES > 20 then
        NUM_LINES := 20;
     if NUM_COLS > 73 then
        NUM_COLS := 73;
     Set_Video (1);

{calculate the upper-left corner of the frame including frame size}
     TOP_LINE := 12 - NUM_LINES div 2 - 3;     {subtract 3 for frame height}
     if TOP_LINE < 1 then
        TOP_LINE := 1;
     LEFT_COL := 40 - NUM_COLS div 2 - 3;      {subtract 3 for frame width}
     if LEFT_COL < 1 then
        LEFT_COL := 1;

{display the top line}
     GotoXY (LEFT_COL, TOP_LINE);
     write (' ', Chr(218));
     for COL := 1 to NUM_COLS+2 do
        write (Chr(196));
     write (Chr(191), ' ');

{display the second line}
     GotoXY (LEFT_COL, TOP_LINE+1);
     write (' ', Chr(179), ' ');
     for COL := 1 to NUM_COLS do
        write (Chr(220));
     write (' ', Chr(179), ' ');
```

```
{display each of the middle lines}
    for LINE := TOP_LINE + 2 to TOP_LINE + NUM_LINES + 2 do
      begin
        GotoXY (LEFT_COL, LINE);
        write (' ', Chr(179), ' ');
        GotoXY (LEFT_COL+NUM_COLS+3, LINE);
        writeln (' ', Chr(179), ' ');
      end;

{display the second-to-last line}
    GotoXY (LEFT_COL, TOP_LINE+NUM_LINES+3);
    write (' ', Chr(179), ' ');
    for COL := 1 to NUM_COLS do
      write (Chr(223));
    write (' ', Chr(179), ' ');

{display the last line}
    GotoXY (LEFT_COL, TOP_LINE+NUM_LINES+4);
    write (' ', Chr(192));
    for COL := 1 to NUM_COLS+2 do
      write (Chr(196));
    write (Chr(217), ' ');
    Set_Video (0);
  end;
```

```
procedure Display_Menu (MENU: MENU_REC);
{
DESCRIPTION:
    This routine displays a menu centered on the screen.

PARAMETERS:
    MENU (in) - menu to be displayed

TYPES REQUIRED:
    STRING79 - used for all strings
    MENU_REC - menu information record

LIBRARY ROUTINES USED:
    Display_Frame - displays a frame on the screen
    Put_String - outputs a string at a given location on the screen
    Put_Centered_String - centers a string on a line on the screen

SAMPLE CALL:
    Display_Menu (MAIN_MENU);

NOTES:
    The frame is displayed and centered automatically.
    All choices, descriptions, the title, and the prompt are all
    displayed automatically in a location determined by the routine.
    Menu is single-spaced for 8 or more choices.

-------------------------------------------------------------}

  var
    LEFT_COL,                   {leftmost column of the frame}
    TOP_LINE,                   {top line of the frame}
    SPACING,                    {spacing between choices - 1 or 2}
    I       : integer;          {counter for loops}
```

```
  begin
    ClrScr;
    with MENU do
      begin

{determine the menu location and the spacing between choices}
        if NUM_CHOICES > 7 then
          SPACING := 1
        else
          SPACING := 2;
        TOP_LINE := 10 - (NUM_CHOICES*SPACING) div 2 -
                   (2-SPACING) * NUM_CHOICES mod 2;
        LEFT_COL := 41 - MENU_WIDTH div 2;

{display the frame and title}
        Display_Frame (NUM_CHOICES*SPACING + 3, MENU_WIDTH);
        Put_Centered_String (TITLE, TOP_LINE+1, 2);

{display the choices and descriptions}
        for I := 1 to NUM_CHOICES do
          begin
            Put_String (CHOICES[I], TOP_LINE + I*SPACING + 2, LEFT_COL+2, 2);
            Put_String ('- ' + DESCRIPTIONS[I], TOP_LINE + I*SPACING + 2,
                        LEFT_COL + 4, 0);
          end;

{display the prompt}
        Put_Prompt (PROMPT, TOP_LINE + NUM_CHOICES*SPACING + 7,
                    LEFT_COL - 3);
      end;
  end;
```

```
procedure Get_Menu_Response (MENU: MENU_REC;
                var USERS_CHOICE: char);
{
DESCRIPTION:
    This routine gets a menu choice from the user, either by
    manually typing a character or by using the arrow keys and
    pressing RETURN.

PARAMETERS:
    MENU (in) - menu already displayed
    USERS_CHOICE (in/out) - choice selected by user

TYPES REQUIRED:
    STRING79 - used for all strings
    MENU_REC - menu information record
    RESPONSE_TYPE - type of input (from Get_Response)
    MOVEMENT - direction of arrow key input (from Get_Response)

LIBRARY ROUTINES USED:
    Get_Response - gets a response from the user
    Put_String - outputs a string at a given location on the screen

SAMPLE CALL:
    Get_Menu_Response (MAIN_MENU, RESPONSE);
```

```
NOTES:
    This routine assumes the menu has already been displayed by
    Display_Menu.
    Arrow keys change the highlighted description.
    This routine will not return until a valid response is made.

----------------------------------------------------------}

    var
       CURRENT_CHOICE,             {choice selected and highlighted}
       SPACING,                    {spacing between choices}
       FIRST_LINE,                 {top line of menu}
       DESC_COL,                   {column of first desc. char}
       I       : integer;          {counter for loops}
       RESP    : RESPONSE_TYPE;    {keyboard response - see Get_Response}
       DIR     : MOVEMENT;         {arrow key response}
       FOUND   : boolean;          {flag for choice search}

    begin
      with MENU do
        begin

{determine the current (highlighted) choice}
          CURRENT_CHOICE := NUM_CHOICES;
          for I := 1 to NUM_CHOICES do
            if USERS_CHOICE = CHOICES[I] then
              CURRENT_CHOICE := I;

{recalculate menu positions and spacing}
          if NUM_CHOICES > 7 then
            SPACING := 1
          else
            SPACING := 2;
          FIRST_LINE := 12 - (NUM_CHOICES*SPACING) div 2 -
                 (2-SPACING)*NUM_CHOICES mod 2;
          DESC_COL := 47 - MENU_WIDTH div 2;

{get user responses until a choice is made}
          repeat

{highlight current choice}
            Put_String (DESCRIPTIONS[CURRENT_CHOICE],
                FIRST_LINE + CURRENT_CHOICE*SPACING, DESC_COL, 1);

{get response at end of prompt}
            GotoXY (DESC_COL - 8 + Length(PROMPT),
                    FIRST_LINE + NUM_CHOICES*SPACING + 5);
            Get_Response (RESP, DIR, USERS_CHOICE);

{de-highlight current choice}
            Put_String (DESCRIPTIONS[CURRENT_CHOICE],
                FIRST_LINE + CURRENT_CHOICE*SPACING, DESC_COL, 0);
            case RESP of

{if up or down arrow - change current choice}
              ARROW: if (DIR = DOWN) and (CURRENT_CHOICE = NUM_CHOICES) then
                       CURRENT_CHOICE := 1
```

```
            else if DIR = DOWN then
                CURRENT_CHOICE := CURRENT_CHOICE + 1
            else if (DIR = UP) and (CURRENT_CHOICE = 1) then
                CURRENT_CHOICE := NUM_CHOICES
            else if DIR = UP then
                CURRENT_CHOICE := CURRENT_CHOICE - 1;

{if key entered, search for match in CHOICES array}
            KEY: begin
                FOUND := false;
                for I := 1 to NUM_CHOICES do
                    if USERS_CHOICE = CHOICES[I] then
                        begin
                            FOUND := true;
                            CURRENT_CHOICE := I;
                        end;
                    if FOUND then
                        RESP := RETURN

{if not matched, ring the bell}
                    else
                        write (Chr(7));
                end;

{if carriage return, use current choice}
            RETURN: USERS_CHOICE := CHOICES[CURRENT_CHOICE];
                end;

            until RESP = RETURN;

{re-highlight chosen choice}
            Put_String (DESCRIPTIONS[CURRENT_CHOICE],
                FIRST_LINE + CURRENT_CHOICE*SPACING, DESC_COL, 1);
        end;
    end;
```

Toggle Routines

The next set of routines are called *toggle routines*. The word *toggle* is taken from an electronic switch that is always either on or off. This definition has been extended to include a data set in which the value of a toggle variable is one and only one member of the set. This is similar to the way a rotary switch operates. When a user enters a *Get_Toggle* routine, that user can toggle among the choices by using the arrow keys.

For example, consider a program that customizes printouts. After it receives the name of the file to be printed, the program needs to know the type of print to be used: compressed, elite, pica, or expanded. A program written by a novice might force the user to type in the entire name, generating an error message every time the print type is misspelled. A better program would ask for the first character of the print type, or it would give numbers to the choices and ask the user for a number. Since these options still allow for user error, the toggle routines would force the user to make a proper choice and therefore would not return errors.

The record used by both the one-row and the one-column routines looks like this:

```
type
  TOGGLE_REC = record
    NUM_CHOICES: integer;
    STRINGS    : array [0..8] of STRING79;
    LOCATIONS  : array [0..8] of integer;
  end;
```

As in the section on menus, **NUM―CHOICES** determines the total number of options on the menu. **STRINGS** are the descriptions of the options in the toggle set. **LOCATIONS** for the one-row toggle represent the column of each first character of the descriptions. This record gives the programmer maximum flexibility for displaying the options on the screen. The 0 element in each array is for the title of the toggle. A maximum number of 8 elements was chosen because any more might become too tedious for a user to toggle through.

The print-type example given earlier requires the following typed constant:

```
const
  PRINT_TOGGLE : TOGGLE_REC = (
    NUM_CHOICES: 4;
    STRINGS    : ('PRINT TYPE:', 'Compressed', 'Elite', 'Pica',
                  'Expanded', '','','','');
    LOCATIONS  : (5, 20, 35, 43, 50, 0, 0, 0, 0));
```

The choices would be displayed on the screen across line 5 by using this code:

```
PRINT_TYPE := 3;              {set default type to Pica}
Put_1line_Toggle (PRINT_TOGGLE, 5, PRINT_TYPE);
```

The top of the screen would then look like Figure 8-2.

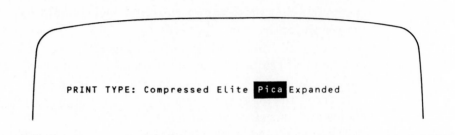

PRINT TYPE: Compressed Elite Pica Expanded

Figure 8-2. *A sample line produced by* Put—1line—Toggle

The call

```
Get_1line_Toggle (PRINT_TOGGLE, 5, PRINT_TYPE,
    'Use the arrow keys to select a print type', 24, 1);
```

would then display the prompt at the bottom left of the screen and would allow the user to change the print type by using the left- and right-arrow keys. After the desired selection is made, the user simply presses the RETURN key to continue.

```
procedure Put_1line_Toggle (TOGGLE: TOGGLE_REC;
                    LINE, CHOICE: integer);
{
DESCRIPTION:
    This routine displays a group of strings that the user can
    toggle through to pick one.  The toggle routines are
    applicable only when one and only one choice is
    needed.  All choices fit on the same line on the screen.

PARAMETERS:
    TOGGLE (in) - choices to be displayed
    LINE (in) - screen line to place choices
    CHOICE (in) - current or default choice

TYPES REQUIRED:
    TOGGLE_REC - toggle information record

LIBRARY ROUTINES USED:
    Put_String - outputs a string at a given location on the screen

SAMPLE CALL:
    Put_1line_Toggle (GRADE_TOGGLE, 10, RESPONSE);

NOTES:
    A default choice must be set by the calling routine so that it
    may be highlighted.

----------------------------------------------------------}
```

```
    var
      I: integer;                        {counter for loops}

    begin
      with TOGGLE do
        begin

{print toggle descriptor, then each choice, on same line}
          Put_String (STRINGS[0], LINE, LOCATIONS[0], 0);
          for I := 1 to NUM_CHOICES do
            Put_String (STRINGS[I], LINE, LOCATIONS[I], 0);

{highlight current or default choice}
          if (CHOICE < 1) or (CHOICE > NUM_CHOICES) then
            CHOICE := 1;
          Put_String (STRINGS[CHOICE], LINE, LOCATIONS[CHOICE], 1);
        end;
    end;
```

```
    procedure Get_1line_Toggle (     TOGGLE: TOGGLE_REC;
                                       LINE: integer;
                                  var CHOICE: integer;
                                     PROMPT: STRING79;
                              PRLINE, PRCOL: integer);
    {
    DESCRIPTION:
        This routine allows the user to choose one of a group of
        strings using the arrow and RETURN keys.

    PARAMETERS:
        TOGGLE (in) - choices already displayed
        LINE (in) - screen line where choices have been placed [1-24]
        CHOICE (in/out) - choice chosen by user
        PROMPT (in) - informative prompt for user
        PRLINE (in) - screen line of prompt [1-24]
        PRCOL (in) - screen column of first character of prompt [1-80]

    TYPES REQUIRED:
        TOGGLE_REC - toggle information record
        RESPONSE_TYPE - type of input (from Get_Response)
        MOVEMENT - direction of arrow key input (from Get_Response)
        STRING79 - used for all strings

    LIBRARY ROUTINES USED:
        Get_Response - gets a response from the user
        Put_String - outputs a string at a given location on the screen

    SAMPLE CALL:
        Get_1line_Toggle (GRADE_TOGGLE, 10, RESPONSE,
            'Use arrow keys to change grade', 24, 1);

    NOTES:
        This routine assumes the toggle choices have already been
        displayed by Put_1Line_Toggle.
        Left- and right-arrow keys change the highlighted description.
        This routine will always return a valid response.

    ----------------------------------------------------------------}
```

```
    var
       RESP : RESPONSE_TYPE;      {keyboard response - see Get_Response}
       DIR  : MOVEMENT;           {direction of arrow key hit}
       KEYCH: char;               {character entered by user}

    begin
       Put_Prompt (PROMPT, PRLINE, PRCOL);
       with TOGGLE do
         begin

  {highlight the toggle descriptor and the current choice}
          Put_String (STRINGS[0], LINE, LOCATIONS[0], 2);
          if (CHOICE < 1) or (CHOICE > NUM_CHOICES) then
          CHOICE := 1;
          Put_String (STRINGS[CHOICE], LINE, LOCATIONS[CHOICE], 1);
          RESP := NO_RESPONSE;

{get user responses until a carriage return is entered}
          while RESP <> RETURN do
            begin
              Get_Response (RESP, DIR, KEYCH);
              case RESP of
                ARROW :

{left arrow - move left with wraparound}
                  if DIR = LEFT then
                    begin
                      Put_String (STRINGS[CHOICE], LINE, LOCATIONS[CHOICE], 0);
                      if CHOICE = 1 then
                        CHOICE := NUM_CHOICES
                      else
                        CHOICE := CHOICE - 1;
                      Put_String (STRINGS[CHOICE], LINE, LOCATIONS[CHOICE], 1);
                    end

{right arrow - move right with wraparound}
                  else if DIR = RIGHT then
                    begin
                      Put_String (STRINGS[CHOICE], LINE, LOCATIONS[CHOICE], 0);
                      if CHOICE = NUM_CHOICES then
                        CHOICE := 1
                      else
                        CHOICE := CHOICE + 1;
                      Put_String (STRINGS[CHOICE], LINE, LOCATIONS[CHOICE], 1);
                    end

{all other keys are invalid - ring bell}
                  else
                    write (Chr(7));
                KEY:  write (Chr(7));
                RETURN: ;
              end;
            end; {while}
          Put_String (STRINGS[0], LINE, LOCATIONS[0], 0);
        end;
    end;
```

If you wish to use less screen space, the one-column toggle routines place the title and toggle choices on separate rows with the first column lined up. Many programs that require a mouse use this type of routine. For example, a painting program could use this record to determine the shape of an object to be drawn:

```
const
   SHAPE_TOGGLE : TOGGLE_REC = (
      NUM_CHOICES: 6;
      STRINGS    : ('OBJECT SHAPE:', 'Square', 'Circle', 'Oval',
                    'Rectangle', 'Line','General polygon','','');
      LOCATIONS  : (1, 2, 3, 4, 5, 6, 7, 0, 0));
```

The **LOCATIONS** for the one-column toggle represent the line numbers on which the strings will be displayed. These numbers are usually sequential. The *Put—1col—Toggle* routine displays the options. The call

```
Get_1col_Toggle (SHAPE_TOGGLE, 3, OBJECT_SHAPE,
   'Use the arrow keys to select a shape',22,2);
```

produces the screen shown in Figure 8-3. The user must use the up- and down-arrow keys to make a selection.

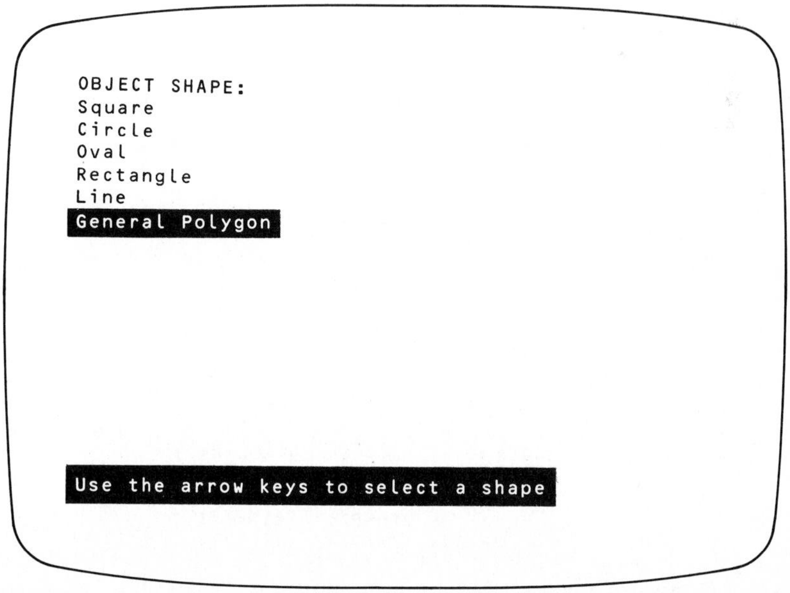

Figure 8-3. *A sample screen produced by* Get—1col—Toggle

```
procedure Put_1col_Toggle (TOGGLE: TOGGLE_REC;
                      COL, CHOICE: integer);
{
DESCRIPTION:
    This routine displays a group of strings that the user can
    toggle through to pick one.  The toggle routines are
    applicable only when one and only one choice is
    needed.  Choices are displayed in column fashion.

PARAMETERS:
    TOGGLE (in) - choices to be displayed
    COL (in) - screen column to place choices
    CHOICE (in) - current or default choice

TYPES REQUIRED:
    TOGGLE_REC - toggle information record

LIBRARY ROUTINES USED:
    Put_String - outputs a string at a given location on the screen

SAMPLE CALL:
    Put_1Col_Toggle (GRADE_TOGGLE, 5, RESPONSE);

NOTES:
    A default choice must be set by the calling routine so that it
    may be highlighted.

-----------------------------------------------------------}

  var
    I: integer;                    {counter for loops}

  begin
    with TOGGLE do
      begin

{print toggle descriptor, then each choice, in same column}
        Put_String (STRINGS[0], LOCATIONS[0], COL, 0);
        for I := 1 to NUM_CHOICES do
          Put_String (STRINGS[I], LOCATIONS[I], COL, 0);

{highlight current or default choice}
        if (CHOICE < 1) or (CHOICE > NUM_CHOICES) then
          CHOICE := 1;
        Put_String (STRINGS[CHOICE], LOCATIONS[CHOICE], COL, 1);
      end;
  end;
```

```
procedure Get_1col_Toggle (    TOGGLE: TOGGLE_REC;
                               COL: integer;
                           var CHOICE: integer;
                               PROMPT: STRING79;
                           PRLINE, PRCOL: integer);
{
DESCRIPTION:
    This routine allows the user to choose one of a group of
    strings using the arrow and RETURN keys.
```

```
PARAMETERS:
    TOGGLE (in) - choices already displayed
    COL (in) - screen column where choices have been placed [1-80]
    CHOICE (in/out) - choice chosen by user
    PROMPT (in) - informative prompt for user
    PRLINE (in) - screen line of prompt [1-24]
    PRCOL (in) - screen column of first character of prompt [1-80]

TYPES REQUIRED:
    TOGGLE_REC - toggle information record
    RESPONSE_TYPE - type of input (from Get_Response)
    MOVEMENT - direction of arrow key input (from Get_Response)
    STRING79 - used for all strings

LIBRARY ROUTINES USED:
    Get_Response - gets a response from the user
    Put_String - outputs a string at a given location on the screen

SAMPLE CALL:
    Get_1col_Toggle (GRADE_TOGGLE, 5, RESPONSE,
            'Use up and down arrow keys to change grade', 24, 1);

NOTES:
    This routine assumes the toggle choices have already been
    displayed by Put_1col_Toggle.
    Up and down arrow keys change the highlighted description.
    This routine will always return a valid response.

-----------------------------------------------------------}

  var
    RESP : RESPONSE_TYPE;         {keyboard response - see Get_Response}
    DIR  : MOVEMENT;              {direction of arrow key hit}
    KEYCH: char;                  {character entered by user}

  begin
    Put_Prompt (PROMPT, PRLINE, PRCOL);
    with TOGGLE do
      begin

{highlight the toggle descriptor and the current choice}
        Put_String (STRINGS[0], LOCATIONS[0], COL, 2);
        if (CHOICE < 1) or (CHOICE > NUM_CHOICES) then
          CHOICE := 1;
        Put_String (STRINGS[CHOICE], LOCATIONS[CHOICE], COL, 1);
        RESP := NO_RESPONSE;

{get user responses until a carriage return is entered}
        while RESP <> RETURN do
          begin
            Get_Response (RESP, DIR, KEYCH);
            case RESP of
              ARROW:

{up arrow - move up with wraparound}
                if DIR = UP then
                  begin
                    Put_String (STRINGS[CHOICE], LOCATIONS[CHOICE], COL, 0);
                    if CHOICE = 1 then
                      CHOICE := NUM_CHOICES
                    else
                      CHOICE := CHOICE - 1;
                    Put_String (STRINGS[CHOICE], LOCATIONS[CHOICE], COL, 1);
                  end
```

```
{down arrow - move down with wraparound}
                  else if DIR = DOWN then
                    begin
                      Put_String (STRINGS[CHOICE], LOCATIONS[CHOICE], COL, 0);
                      if CHOICE = NUM_CHOICES then
                        CHOICE := 1
                      else
                        CHOICE := CHOICE + 1;
                      Put_String (STRINGS[CHOICE], LOCATIONS[CHOICE], COL, 1);
                    end

{all other keys are invalid - ring bell}
                  else
                    write (Chr(7));
                KEY:    write (Chr(7));
                RETURN: ;
              end;
            end; {while}
          Put_String (STRINGS[0], LOCATIONS[0], COL, 0);
        end;
    end;
```

When the options of a toggle set are large strings and the column toggle is undesirable, the two-line toggle routines should be used. These routines act just like the one-line toggle, except that the locations are split between two lines. Pressing the right-arrow key from the rightmost choice on the first line highlights the leftmost choice on the second line. The up- and down-arrow keys are disabled.

The record structure for two-line toggles is the same as that for the other toggle routines. However, a drop in the location number indicates that the rest of the choices fall on the next line.

The two-line toggle routines require the use of a simple function called *Which—Line*. This function returns the line number of a given choice. Using *Which—Line* eliminates the requirement of including the same *if-then* statement many times in the same routine.

```
function Which_Line (LINE, CHOICE, SPLIT: integer): integer;
  begin
    if CHOICE <= SPLIT then
      Which_Line := LINE
    else
      Which_Line := LINE + 1;
  end;
```

A good example of the two-line toggle set is a list of regions in the United States. Although there are only seven regions, their names are too large to fit completely on one line. The following is a typed

Figure 8-4. *A sample record produced by* Put__2line__Toggle

constant that demonstrates this:

```
const
   REGION_TOGGLE: TOGGLE_REC = (
      NUM_CHOICES: 7;
      STRINGS    : ('MAJOR REGION:', 'New England', 'Atlantic Coastal',
                    'North Central', 'South Central', 'Rocky Mountain',
                    'Pacific Coastal', 'Alaska/Hawaii', '');
      LOCATIONS  : (1, 20, 40, 60, 2, 20, 40, 60, 0));
```

If you assume that the first choice is the default, using a call to
Put__2line__Toggle would place this record on line 3, as shown in
Figure 8-4.

If as a user you wanted to set the region to "Rocky Mountain," you
would press the right-arrow key four times. Each time, the highlighted choice would move right. When it reached the last option on
the top line (North Central), the next right arrow would go to the
first option on the second line (South Central), and finally to Rocky
Mountain. Pressing RETURN would complete the entry.

```
procedure Put_2line_Toggle (TOGGLE: TOGGLE_REC;
                     LINE, CHOICE: integer);
{
DESCRIPTION:
   This routine displays a group of strings that the user can
   toggle through to pick one.  The toggle routines are
   applicable only when one and only one choice is
   needed.  Choices require two lines to fit on the screen.
```

```
PARAMETERS:
    TOGGLE (in) - choices to be displayed
    LINE (in) - screen line to place choices
    CHOICE (in) - current or default choice

TYPES REQUIRED:
    TOGGLE_REC - toggle information record

LIBRARY ROUTINES USED:
    Which_Line - determines which of two lines the choice is on
    Put_String - outputs a string at a given location on the screen

SAMPLE CALL:
    Put_2line_Toggle (GRADE_TOGGLE, 10, RESPONSE);

NOTES:
    A default choice must be set by the calling routine so that it
    may be highlighted.

------------------------------------------------------------}

  var
    SPLIT_NUM,                  {the last choice on the first line}
    I: integer;                 {counter for loops}

  begin
    with TOGGLE do
      begin

{determine the last choice on the first line}
        for I := 1 to NUM_CHOICES-1 do
          if LOCATIONS[I+1] < LOCATIONS[I] then
            SPLIT_NUM := I;

{print toggle descriptor, then each choice, on the two lines}
        Put_String (STRINGS[0], LINE, LOCATIONS[0], 0);
        for I := 1 to NUM_CHOICES do
          Put_String (STRINGS[I], Which_Line (LINE, I, SPLIT_NUM),
                      LOCATIONS[I], 0);

{highlight current or default choice}
        if (CHOICE < 1) or (CHOICE > NUM_CHOICES) then
          CHOICE := 1;
        Put_String (STRINGS[CHOICE], Which_Line (LINE, CHOICE, SPLIT_NUM),
            LOCATIONS[CHOICE], 1);
      end;
  end;
```

```
procedure Get_2line_Toggle (     TOGGLE: TOGGLE_REC;
                                   LINE: integer;
                             var CHOICE: integer;
                                 PROMPT: STRING79;
                         PRLINE, PRCOL: integer);
{
DESCRIPTION:
    This routine allows the user to choose one of a group of
    strings using the arrow and RETURN keys.
```

```
PARAMETERS:
    TOGGLE (in) - choices already displayed
    LINE (in) - screen line where choices have been placed [1-24]
    CHOICE (in/out) - choice chosen by user
    PROMPT (in) - informative prompt for user
    PRLINE (in) - screen line of prompt [1-24]
    PRCOL (in) - screen column of first character of prompt [1-80]

TYPES REQUIRED:
    TOGGLE_REC - toggle information record
    RESPONSE_TYPE - type of input (from Get_Response)
    MOVEMENT - direction of arrow key input (from Get_Response)
    STRING79 - used for all strings

LIBRARY ROUTINES USED:
    Which_Line - determines which of two lines the choice is on
    Get_Response - gets a response from the user
    Put_String - outputs a string at a given location on the screen

SAMPLE CALL:
    Get_2line_Toggle (GRADE_TOGGLE, 5, RESPONSE,
            'Use left and right arrow keys to change grade', 24, 1);

NOTES:
    This routine assumes the toggle choices have already been
    displayed by Put_2line_Toggle.
    Up and down arrow keys change the highlighted description.
    This routine will always return a valid response.

    -----------------------------------------------------------}

    var
      RESP : RESPONSE_TYPE;       {keyboard response - see Get_Response}
      DIR  : MOVEMENT;            {direction of arrow key hit}
      KEYCH: char;                {character entered by user}
      SPLIT_NUM,                  {the last choice on the first line}
      I     : integer;            {counter for loop}
    begin
      Put_Prompt (PROMPT, PRLINE, PRCOL);
      with TOGGLE do
        begin

{determine the last choice on the first line}
          for I := 1 to NUM_CHOICES-1 do
            if LOCATIONS[I+1] < LOCATIONS[I] then
              SPLIT_NUM := I;

{highlight the toggle descriptor and the current choice}
          Put_String (STRINGS[0], LINE, LOCATIONS[0], 2);
          if (CHOICE < 1) or (CHOICE > NUM_CHOICES) then
            CHOICE := 1;
          Put_String (STRINGS[CHOICE], Which_Line (LINE, CHOICE, SPLIT_NUM),
                                          LOCATIONS[CHOICE], 1);
          RESP := NO_RESPONSE;

{get user responses until a carriage return is entered}
          while RESP <> RETURN do
            begin
              Get_Response (RESP, DIR, KEYCH);
              case RESP of
                ARROW:
```

```
{left arrow - move left with wraparound}
                    if DIR = LEFT then
                       begin
                          Put_String (STRINGS[CHOICE], Which_Line (LINE, CHOICE,
                                   SPLIT_NUM), LOCATIONS[CHOICE], 0);
                          if CHOICE = 1 then
                             CHOICE := NUM_CHOICES
                          else
                             CHOICE := CHOICE - 1;
                          Put_String (STRINGS[CHOICE], Which_Line (LINE, CHOICE,
                                   SPLIT_NUM), LOCATIONS[CHOICE], 1);
                       end

{right arrow - move right with wraparound}
                    else if DIR = RIGHT then
                       begin
                          Put_String (STRINGS[CHOICE], Which_Line (LINE, CHOICE,
                                   SPLIT_NUM), LOCATIONS[CHOICE], 0);
                          if CHOICE = NUM_CHOICES then
                             CHOICE := 1
                          else
                             CHOICE := CHOICE + 1;
                          Put_String (STRINGS[CHOICE], Which_Line (LINE, CHOICE,
                                   SPLIT_NUM), LOCATIONS[CHOICE], 1);
                       end

{all other keys are invalid - ring bell}
                    else
                       write (Chr(7));
                 KEY:  write (Chr(7));
                 RETURN: ;
              end;
           end; {while}
           Put_String (STRINGS[0], LINE, LOCATIONS[0], 0);
        end;
     end;
```

Data Entry

When the user needs to enter a few numbers, the *Put—Real* and *Put—Prompted—Real* procedures given in Chapter 7 provide adequate capabilities. However, when an entire table of data values needs to be displayed or updated, a more sophisticated set of routines is required.

The *Put—Data—Values* and *Get—Data—Values* procedures are designed for this type of application. Both require a two-dimensional array that could be defined as follows:

```
type
   DATA_ARRAY = array [1..20, 1..10] of real;
```

The size of the array can depend on the application. The only requirement for these routines is that the array must be of type **real**.

Suppose you are keeping track of a set of test scores. (Chapter 10 will give file routines to store these scores in a file and to enter them into the data array.) The scores can be displayed with the call to *Put_Data_Values*.

```
Put_Data_Values (TEST_SCORES, 15, 5, 4, 1, 6, 5);
```

This call defines a table that is 15 rows by 5 columns. The number will be displayed in *xx.x* format (as a percentage), and the upper-left corner will be the sixth line, fifth column. An example of this display is shown in Figure 8-5.

91.5	87.0	72.1	99.9	21.2
92.3	89.1	74.2	95.4	34.5
71.2	68.5	53.6	75.2	9.2
88.0	84.2	69.3	90.1	20.3
64.3	61.7	46.8	72.3	0.1
98.6	95.2	80.3	99.8	40.5
71.7	68.4	53.5	72.7	50.0
81.0	78.3	63.4	82.6	17.3
74.4	71.9	56.0	75.0	34.2
96.9	93.8	78.9	97.5	25.7
82.3	79.6	64.7	84.2	42.9
95.0	91.0	76.1	96.4	36.6
51.8	48.7	33.8	52.3	11.1
89.7	84.3	69.4	90.0	7.2
93.2	88.4	73.5	95.1	48.8
				DONE

Figure 8-5.   *A sample table produced by* Put_Data_Values

When the *Get—Data—Values* procedure is called, the user can use the arrow keys to move the highlight to the value that needs to be changed. Pressing RETURN then allows the user to change that data value. The applications program only needs to call the routine, and all changes that the user makes are accomplished inside of the *Get—Data—Values* procedures. When all required changes have been made, the user must use the arrow keys until the word **DONE** is the highlighted value.

```
procedure Put_Data_Values (ENTRY: DATA_ARRAY;
           NUM_ROWS, NUM_COLS,
           NUM_LENGTH, NUM_DEC,
           TOP_LINE, LEFT_COL: integer);
{
DESCRIPTION:
    This routine displays a group of data values that are used
    for data entry.  The numbers are in table form, and can be
    altered with the Get_Data_Values routine.

PARAMETERS:
    ENTRY (in) - table array containing data values
    NUM_ROWS (in) - total number of rows in the data array
    NUM_COLS (in) - total number of columns in the data array
    NUM_LENGTH (in) - total number of places for each real number
    NUM_DEC (in) - number of decimal places for each real number
    TOP_LINE (in) - topmost line to start data table
    LEFT_COL (in) - leftmost column to start data table

TYPES REQUIRED:
    DATA_ARRAY - for defining the table of values (must be real)

SAMPLE CALL:
    Put_Data_Values (TEST_SCORES, 18, 6, 7, 1, 4, 10);

NOTES:
    This routine automatically places the values in table form,
    using every line from the top line specified, and leaves
    two spaces between column entries.

-----------------------------------------------------------}


  var
    LINE, COL: integer;                     {counters for loops}

  begin

{display the entire table}
    for COL := 1 to NUM_COLS do
      for LINE := 1 to NUM_ROWS do
        begin

{leave two spaces between entries on each line}
          GotoXY (LEFT_COL + (COL-1) * (NUM_LENGTH+2), TOP_LINE + LINE - 1);
          write (ENTRY[LINE, COL]:NUM_LENGTH:NUM_DEC);
        end;
    end;
```

```
procedure Get_Data_Values (var ENTRY: DATA_ARRAY;
                NUM_ROWS, NUM_COLS,
                NUM_LENGTH, NUM_DEC,
                TOP_LINE, LEFT_COL: integer);
{
DESCRIPTION:
    This routine allows the user to alter entries in a table of real
    numbers.  Control is returned to the calling procedure only after
    all desired changes have been made.

PARAMETERS:
    ENTRY (in/out) - table array containing data values
    NUM_ROWS (in) - total number of rows in the data array
    NUM_COLS (in) - total number of columns in the data array
    NUM_LENGTH (in) - total number of places for each real number
    NUM_DEC (in) - number of decimal places for each real number
    TOP_LINE (in) - topmost line to start data table
    LEFT_COL (in) - leftmost column to start data table

TYPES REQUIRED:
    RESPONSE_TYPE - type of input (from Get_Response)
    MOVEMENT - direction of arrow key input (from Get_Response)
    STRING79 - used for all strings
    DATA_ARRAY - for defining the table of values (must be real)

LIBRARY ROUTINES USED:
    Get_Response - gets a response from the user
    Get_Real - gets a real number from the user
    Put_Real - outputs a real number to the screen
    Put_String - outputs a string at a given location on the screen

SAMPLE CALL:
    Get_Data_Values (TEST_SCORES, 18, 6, 7, 1, 4, 10);

NOTES:
    This routine assumes the data entries have already been
    displayed by Put_Data_Values.
    All arrow keys change the highlighted data entry.

-----------------------------------------------------------}

  const
    BELL      = 7;                   {ASCII character for bell}

  var
    RESPONSE : RESPONSE_TYPE;        {keyboard response - see Get_Response}
    DIR      : MOVEMENT;             {direction of arrow key hit}
    KEYCH    : char;                 {character entered by user}
    LINE, COL: integer;             {current cursor location in table}

  begin

{data entry continues until the user uses the arrow keys to get
to the DONE at the bottom right of the table}
    Put_String ('DONE', TOP_LINE + NUM_ROWS,
        LEFT_COL + (NUM_COLS-1)*(NUM_LENGTH+2), 2);
    LINE := 1;
    COL := 1;
```

```
{loop until the line pointer gets to the DONE}
    while LINE <= NUM_ROWS do
      begin

{highlight the current entry}
      Put_Real (ENTRY[LINE, COL], TOP_LINE + LINE-1,
          LEFT_COL + (COL-1)*(NUM_LENGTH+2), 1, NUM_LENGTH, NUM_DEC);
      Get_Response (RESPONSE, DIR, KEYCH);
      case RESPONSE of

{if an arrow key is hit, change the current entry accordingly}
        ARROW:
          begin
            Put_Real (ENTRY[LINE, COL], TOP_LINE + LINE-1,
                LEFT_COL + (COL-1)*(NUM_LENGTH+2), 0,
                NUM_LENGTH, NUM_DEC);
            case DIR of

{left arrow - move left with a wraparound}
              LEFT:  if COL = 1 then
                       COL := NUM_COLS
                     else
                       COL := COL - 1;

{right arrow - move right with a wraparound}
              RIGHT:  if COL = NUM_COLS then
                        COL := 1
                      else
                        COL := COL + 1;

{up arrow - move up with a wraparound}
              UP:  if LINE = 1 then
                     LINE := NUM_ROWS
                   else
                     LINE := LINE - 1;

{down arrow - move down with a wraparound}
              DOWN:  begin
                       if LINE = NUM_ROWS then
                         LINE := 1
                       else
                         LINE := LINE + 1;

{if user hits a down arrow from the bottom right of the table,
set the line pointer to get out of the loop}
                       if (LINE = 1) and (COL = NUM_COLS) then
                         LINE := NUM_ROWS + 1;
                     end;
            end; {case}
          end;  {ARROW}

{if user enters a carriage return, call routine to change the number}
        RETURN: Get_Real (ENTRY[LINE, COL], TOP_LINE + LINE,
                LEFT_COL + (COL-1)*(NUM_LENGTH+2), 1,
                NUM_LENGTH, NUM_DEC);

{otherwise, ring the bell}
        KEY: write (Chr(BELL));
      end;   {case}
    end;  {while}
  end;
```

Forms

The final set of routines in this chapter allows the programmer to display an entire screen without having to call *Put—String* for each string. Like the routines in the previous section, these routines will be complemented by the routines in Chapter 10.

The form for the routines is simply that of an array of strings, defined as

```
type
   FORM_TYPE = array[1..25] of STRING79;
```

After a form is read from a file into an array, the *Put—Form* will display all 25 strings on the screen. Separate prompted-input routines (from Chapter 7) can then be used to get the appropriate user inputs. The *Get—Form* routine "reads" the screen and places the characters into a form. It uses some of the routines found in Chapter 9.

```
procedure Put_Form (FORM: FORM_TYPE;
                ATTRIBUTE: integer);
{
DESCRIPTION:
    This routine places a form on the screen.  Anything that was
    previously on the screen is destroyed.

PARAMETERS:
    FORM (in) - the form to be displayed
    ATTRIBUTE (in) - video attribute of the form

TYPES REQUIRED:
    FORM_TYPE - string array that contains a form

LIBRARY ROUTINES USED:
    Put_String - outputs a string at a given location on the screen

SAMPLE CALL:
    Put_Form (JOB_APPLICATION, 0);

NOTES:
    See Set_Video for the key to the video attributes.

-----------------------------------------------------------}

   var
     I: integer;                    {counter for loops}

   begin

{print all 25 lines, one at a time}
     for I := 1 to 25 do
        Put_String (FORM[I], I, 1, ATTRIBUTE);

   end;
```

```
procedure Get_Form (var FORM: FORM_TYPE);
{
DESCRIPTION:
    This routine reads a form from the screen.  Attributes
    are ignored.

PARAMETERS:
    FORM (out) - the form to be displayed

TYPES REQUIRED:
    FORM_TYPE - string array that contains a form

LIBRARY ROUTINES USED:
    Get_Character_at_Cursor - reads the screen for a character
    at a given location on the screen
    Get_Active_Display_Page - returns the active video display
    page

SAMPLE CALL:
    Get_Form (JOB_APPLICATION);

--------------------------------------------------------}

  var
    DUMMY,
    DISPLAY_PAGE,                   {active display page}
    I, J: integer;                  {counters for loops}

  begin
    DISPLAY_PAGE := Get_Active_Display_Page;

{go to each location on the screen and read the character}
    for I := 1 to 25 do
      for J := 1 to 79 do
        begin
          GotoXY (J, I);
          Get_Character_at_Cursor (DISPLAY_PAGE, FORM[I][J], DUMMY);
        end;
      FORM[I][0] := Chr(J);
    end;
end;
```

C H A P T E R

9

ROM-BIOS and DOS Interface

A major goal in program development is to write as much of the program as possible in a high-level language. The advantages of using a high-level language over assembly language include

- Machine independence
- Ease of implementation and testing
- Ease of modification
- Increased readability.

Unfortunately, applications such as advanced file manipulation and interfacing to the operating system require developing low-level routines. The developers of Turbo Pascal recognized the need to simplify the interface to the operating system and to the underlying hardware. They have provided an access method that is consistent and easy to use. Even the novice Pascal programmer can quickly use these capabilities. If you take advantage of the ROM-BIOS and DOS services, your programs gain tremendous flexibility. This chapter will first review the structure of ROM-BIOS and DOS, before examining the routines that use them.

Interrupts

An *interrupt* is a signal to the processor from a program or a hardware device. Interrupts suspend the function of the processor temporarily so that the processor can perform a specific task. Each interrupt has a section of code, resident in memory, that the processor performs when the interrupt occurs. This code is called an *interrupt handler* or an *interrupt service routine*. When an interrupt occurs, the processor locates the associated interrupt handler and executes that segment of code. For example, when a user holds down the SHIFT and PRTSC keys, an interrupt handler prints the contents of the screen. When the processor completes the requested task, it continues the function it was performing prior to the interrupt.

The processor finds interrupt handlers by using *interrupt vectors.* You can visualize the vectors as a table with three columns and N rows, with N being the number of interrupts supported by the system. When an interrupt occurs, the processor uses the interrupt number as an index into the table to locate the interrupt handler's address. Before the system passes control to the interrupt handler, it stores information about the current program on the stack. This allows the system to regain control after it completes the interrupt handler.

This is a simplified view of interrupt handling. Nevertheless, using the ROM-BIOS and DOS services from Turbo Pascal requires only a general understanding of interrupt handling.

8088 Registers

Within the CPU, there is a set of memory locations called *registers*. Any values contained within these locations can be retrieved quickly, since the registers are part of the processor itself. The 8088 has 14 registers, each capable of storing 16 bits of data. The built-in procedures **Hi** and **Lo** of Turbo Pascal allow easy access to the high and low bytes of each register. The 8088 register utilization appears as follows:

General-Purpose Registers

	AH	AL			CH	CL
AX				CX		

	BH	BL			DH	DL
BX				DX		

Base and Index Registers

SP
Stack pointer

SI
Source index

BP
Base pointer

DI
Destination index

Special-Purpose Registers

Flags register

IP
Instruction pointer

Segment Registers

CS
Code segment

SS
Stack segment

DS
Data segment

ES
Extended segment

The ROM-BIOS and DOS services require the use of a record to simulate the registers that are accessible only in assembly language. The following shows the format that these subroutines will use.

```
type
  REGISTERS = record
    AX, BX, CX, DX, BP, SI, DI, DS, ES, FLAGS: integer;
  end;
```

Values are assigned to each field, and the record is passed to the routines **Intr** and **MSDos**. **Intr** and **MSDos** extract the values from the record and assign them to the correct registers before invoking the desired interrupt. When the interrupt is complete, **Intr** and **MSDos** place the values returned to the calling routine into the correct fields of the record.

Many of the following routines use the **FLAGS** register for error detection. Like the other 8088 registers, the **FLAGS** register is a 16-bit register. Each bit has a specific meaning that you can interrogate to determine the status of the previous operation. For example, many of the DOS services in this chapter set the carry flag when an error occurs. If you develop applications to interrogate the values of these flags, error detection becomes very simple. The meaning of each bit in the **FLAGS** register is as follows:

Bit	0	Carry flag
Bit	1	Not used
Bit	2	Parity flag
Bit	3	Not used
Bit	4	Auxiliary flag (used in binary-coded decimal arithmetic)
Bit	5	Not used
Bit	6	Zero flag
Bit	7	Sign flag (sign of the last arithmetic operation)
Bit	8	Trap flag (used in debugging)
Bit	9	Interrupt flag (enables and disables interrupts)
Bit	10	Direction flag (if set, string operations increment the index register; otherwise, the register is decremented)
Bit	11	Overflow flag
Bits	12-15	Not used

The following routines return a Boolean value of true if the previous operation set a specific flag; otherwise, they return false:

```
{ FLAG REGISTER INFORMATION FUNCTIONS

DESCRIPTION:
    The following routines return a boolean true if
    the specific flag within the FLAGS register has
    been set.

VALUES RETURNED:
    a boolean value.  Returns true if the flag is set,
    otherwise false.
```

```
TYPES REQUIRED:
    REGISTERS - used in all ROM-BIOS and DOS interrupts

NOTES:
    The current setting of the flags of interest is
    determined by ANDing the contents of the FLAGS register
    with specific powers of two.

------------------------------------------------------------}

function CARRY_FLAG_SET (FLAGS: integer): boolean;

  begin
    CARRY_FLAG_SET := (1 and FLAGS) = 1;
  end;

function PARITY_FLAG_SET (FLAGS: integer): boolean;

  begin
    PARITY_FLAG_SET := (4 and FLAGS) = 1;
  end;

function AUX_FLAG_SET (FLAGS: integer): boolean;

  begin
    AUX_FLAG_SET := (16 and FLAGS) = 1;
  end;

function ZERO_FLAG_SET (FLAGS: integer): boolean;

  begin
    ZERO_FLAG_SET := (64 and FLAGS) = 1;
  end;

function SIGN_FLAG_SET (FLAGS: integer): boolean;

  begin
    SIGN_FLAG_SET := (128 and FLAGS) = 1;
  end;

function TRAP_FLAG_SET (FLAGS: integer): boolean;

. begin
    TRAP_FLAG_SET := (256 and FLAGS) = 1;
  end;

function INTERRUPT_FLAG_SET (FLAGS: integer): boolean;

  begin
    INTERRUPT_FLAG_SET := (512 and FLAGS) = 1;
  end;

function DIRECTION_FLAG_SET (FLAGS: integer): boolean;

  begin
    DIRECTION_FLAG_SET := (1024 and FLAGS) = 1;
  end;

function OVERFLOW_FLAG_SET (FLAGS: integer): boolean;

  begin
    OVERFLOW_FLAG_SET := (2048 and FLAGS) = 1;
  end;

{------------------------------------------------------------}
```

ROM-BIOS

Every computer comes with built-in procedures that boot the operating system when you turn the computer on or reboot. The processor reads these procedures from *read-only memory* (ROM) each time the system boots. With the IBM-PC and PC compatibles, this collection of routines also contains services that support input and output. The *Basic Input/Output Services* (BIOS) are responsible for handling all I/O requests. When a character is read from the keyboard, a ROM-BIOS interrupt is responsible for controlling the actual input.

The processor accesses ROM-BIOS routines through interrupts. Many Turbo routines use the built-in procedure **Intr** to access the ROM services. The format of a calling sequence for **Intr** is

Intr (*interrupt number***, REGISTERS);**

For example, the statement

Intr (5, REGISTERS);

invokes the print-screen interrupt. The following program uses **Intr** to print the contents of the screen:

```
program Print_Screen;

type
  REGISTERS = record
    AX, BX, CX, DX, BP, SI, DI, DS, ES, FLAGS: integer;
  end;

var
  REGS : REGISTERS;

begin
  Intr (5, REGS);
end;
```

Several of the ROM interrupts return values in the registers passed to the routine **Intr**. In addition, some routines use the registers to request specific operations. You will use ROM interrupts in many of the routines throughout the remainder of this chapter.

DOS Services

The developers of DOS created routines that manipulate files, access system information, and control the execution of processes. All of these routines are available to applications programs in the form of interrupts. (Be careful not to confuse these routines with the ROM-BIOS interrupts that the processor uses when the system boots. Each set of services performs distinct tasks and is invoked differently from Turbo Pascal: the ROM services perform the system startup and control I/O, while the DOS services allow the manipulation of files and processes.)

To access DOS interrupts, you use the built-in Turbo procedure **MSDos**. This procedure uses the value contained in register **AH** to determine the operation desired. For example, the following program obtains the current disk drive (drive A is 0, drive B is 1, drive C is 2, and so on):

```
program Obtain_Disk_Drive;

type
  REGISTERS = record
    AX, BX, CX, DX, BP, SI, DI, DS, ES, FLAGS: integer;
  end;

var
  REGS: REGISTERS;

begin
  with REGS do
    begin
      AX := $1900; {interrupt $19 in AH}
      MSDos (REGS);
      Writeln ('The current drive is ', Lo(AX));
    end;
end.
```

Several DOS interrupts return information in the registers. One important and often-overlooked piece of information is the success status of the operation performed. For example, if a program sets the default directory to a nonexistent path, the DOS service will return an error status. The calling routine should always examine the return status before continuing. The following are several common status values that are returned by the DOS interface routines.

    2 File not found
    3 Path not found
    4 Too many open files
    5 Access denied
  16 Cannot remove current directory
  18 No more files

(Be sure to read the section on DOS function calls in the Turbo Pascal reference manual.)

The System Clock

DOS provides access to the system date and time, as shown in the following procedures. The DOS services perform date and time validation, and they do not modify the system clock if the calling routine passes an invalid date. Although there are ROM-BIOS services that access the system clock, you should use the DOS services whenever you set the system date and time, so that you can use the DOS services' error checking.

```
procedure Get_Date (var DAY, MONTH, YEAR: integer);
{
DESCRIPTION:
    This routine accesses the time of day clock to obtain
    the current date.

PARAMETERS:
    DAY (out) - day of the month [1-31]
    MONTH (out) - month of the year [1-12]
    YEAR (out) - [1980-2099]

TYPES REQUIRED:
    REGISTERS - used in all ROM-BIOS and DOS interrupts

SAMPLE CALL:
    Get_Date (DAY, MONTH, YEAR);

----------------------------------------------------------}

  var
    REGS: REGISTERS;  {AX, BX, CX, DX, BP, SI, DI, DS, ES, FLAGS}

  begin
    with REGS do
      begin

{set AH to set the current date contained in the time of day clock}
        AX := $2A00;           {DOS function code}

{invoke the DOS interrupt that returns the date}
        MSDos (REGS);
```

```
{return the current date as day, month, year}
        DAY   := Lo(DX);
        MONTH := Hi(DX);
        YEAR  := CX;
      end;
  end;
```

```
procedure Set_Date (DAY, MONTH, YEAR: integer;
                    var STATUS: byte);
{
DESCRIPTION:
    This routine sets the system clock to the date
    specified.

PARAMETERS:
    DAY (in) - day of the month [1-31]
    MONTH (in) - month of the year [1-12]
    YEAR (in) - [1980-2099]
    STATUS (out) - success status of the routine 0 = successful
                                                  1 = invalid date

TYPES REQUIRED:
    REGISTERS - used in all ROM-BIOS and DOS interrupts

SAMPLE CALL:
    Set_Date (25, 12, 1986, STATUS);


NOTES:
    Invalid dates have no effect on the system date.

----------------------------------------------------------}

    var
      REGS: REGISTERS;   {AX, BX, CX, DX, BP, SI, DI, DS, ES, FLAGS}

    begin
      with REGS do
        begin

{set the registers to set the date contained in the
 system clock}
        AX := $2B00;               {DOS function code}
        DX := (MONTH shl 8) + DAY; {DH contains month - DL day}
        CX := YEAR;

{invoke the DOS interrupt that sets the system clock}
        MSDos (REGS);

{return the success status based upon a valid date}
        if (LO(AX) = $FF) then
          STATUS := 1
        else
          STATUS := 0;
        end;
    end;
```

```
procedure Get_Time (var HOURS, MINUTES, SECONDS, HUNDREDTHS: integer);
{
DESCRIPTION:
    This routine accesses the time of day clock to obtain
    the current time of day.

PARAMETERS:
    HOURS (out) - hour of the day [0-23]
    MINUTES (out) - [0-59]
    SECONDS (out) - [0-59]
    HUNDREDTHS (out) - hundredths of seconds [0-99]

TYPES REQUIRED:
    REGISTERS - used in all ROM-BIOS and DOS interrupts

SAMPLE CALL:
    Get_Time (HOUR, MINUTE, SECOND, HUNDREDTH);

-------------------------------------------------------}

  var
    REGS: REGISTERS;   {AX, BX, CX, DX, BP, SI, DI, DS, ES, FLAGS}

  begin
    with REGS do
      begin

{set AH to request the current time contained in the
 time of day clock}
        AX := $2C00;                {DOS function code}

{invoke the DOS function that returns the current time}
        MSDos (REGS);

{return the current time as hours, minutes, seconds, and
 hundredths of seconds}
        HOURS := Hi(CX);
        MINUTES := Lo(CX);
        SECONDS := Hi(DX);
        HUNDREDTHS := Lo(DX);
      end;
  end;
```

```
procedure Set_Time (HOURS, MINUTES, SECONDS, HUNDREDTHS: integer;
                                          var STATUS: byte);
{
DESCRIPTION:
    This routine sets the system clock to the time
    specified.

PARAMETERS:
    HOURS (in) - hour of the day (0-23)
    MINUTES (in) - (0-59)
    SECONDS (in) - (0-59)
    HUNDREDTHS (in) - (0-99)
    STATUS (out) - success status of the routine 0 = successful
                                                  1 = invalid time
```

```
TYPES REQUIRED:
    REGISTERS - used in all ROM-BIOS and DOS interrupts

SAMPLE CALL:
    Set_Time (12, 30, 0, 0, STATUS);

NOTES:
    Invalid times have no effect on the system clock.

------------------------------------------------------------}

  var
    REGS: REGISTERS;   {AX, BX, CX, DX, BP, SI, DI, DS, ES, FLAGS}

  begin
    with REGS do
      begin

{set the registers to set the time in the system clock}
        AX := $2D00;
        CX := (HOURS shl 8) + MINUTES;
        DX := (SECONDS shl 8) + HUNDREDTHS;

{invoke the DOS interrupt that sets the current time}
        MSDos (REGS);

{return the success status based upon the current time}
        if (Lo(AX) = $FF) then
          STATUS := 1
        else
          STATUS := 0;
      end;
  end;
```

ASCIIZ

All routines that pass strings to the DOS interface must use *ASCIIZ strings*. An ASCIIZ string is a character string terminated by a byte of zeros, which is the NUL character. (This structure is different from the way Turbo Pascal normally stores its character strings.) To convert a string to an ASCIIZ string, concatenate a NUL character to the end of the string by using this format:

$$FILE\_NAME := FILE\_NAME + Chr(0);$$

Chr(0) creates a NUL character. The assembly language routines that return pointers to strings also reference ASCIIZ strings. The maximum size of an ASCIIZ string is 128 characters.

File Handles

Early versions of DOS performed all file access by using *file control blocks* (FCBs). Each time DOS opened a file, it created a file control block. Many programmers realized they could control file attributes by circumventing the DOS function calls. Unfortunately, many of these clever routines were much more difficult to modify and were less portable than routines that used the DOS services.

To increase file integrity, DOS versions 3.0 and greater have introduced the concept of a *file handle.* The file handle is an integer value that identifies the file or device to manipulate. Newer DOS services require file handles for all file accesses. These services expand previous capabilities by allowing the manipulation of files contained in directories other than the default directory. DOS interrupt **$3D00** returns a file handle.

The following routines use file handles to access files:

```
procedure Open_File (FILENAME: STRING79;
                            MODE: byte;
                 var FILE_HANDLE: integer;
                      var STATUS: byte);
{
DESCRIPTION:
    This routine opens the file specified and returns
    a file handle that is required by many of the
    newer DOS file manipulation routines.

PARAMETERS:
    FILENAME (in) - name of the desired file
    FILE_HANDLE (out) - the file handle
    STATUS (out) - success status of the procedure
                        (0 is a successful operation)
    MODE (in) - the mode to open the file in
                (0 read only, 1 write only, 2 read/write)

LIBRARY ROUTINES USED:
    Carry_Flag_Set - returns true if the carry flag in the FLAGS
                        register has been set; false if not

TYPES REQUIRED:
    REGISTERS - used in all ROM-BIOS and DOS interrupts
    STRING79 - used in all string operations

SAMPLE CALL:
    Open_File ('LIB.PAS', 0, FILE_HANDLE, STATUS);

NOTES:
    Common Return Status Values:
        2 - File not found     3 - Path not found
        4 - Too many files open  5 - Access denied

----------------------------------------------------------}
```

```
    var
      REGS: REGISTERS;   {AX, BX, CX, DX, BP, SI, DI, DS, ES, FLAGS}

    begin
      with REGS do
        begin

{convert the file name to open to ASCIIZ and set the registers
 to open the file specified}
          FILENAME := FILENAME + Chr(0);
          AX := $3D00 + MODE;                {mode is in AL}
          DS := Seg(FILENAME[1]);
          DX := Ofs(FILENAME[1]);

{invoke the DOS interrupt that opens a file and returns a file
 handle}
          MSDos (REGS);

{test the status of the operation and return the file handle
 if the operation was successful}
          if Carry_Flag_Set (FLAGS) then    {error in operation}
            STATUS := Lo(AX)
          else
            begin
              FILE_HANDLE := AX;             {successful operation}
              STATUS := 0;
            end;
        end;
    end;
```

```
      procedure Get_File_Date_Time (FILE_HANDLE: integer;
                var DAY, MONTH, HOURS, MINUTES,
                         SECONDS, YEAR: integer;
                             var STATUS: byte);
      {
      DESCRIPTION:
          This routine returns the date and time stamp
          of the file specified (creation/modificaton date).

      PARAMETERS:
          FILE_HANDLE (in) - file handle from the routine Open_File
          DAY (out) - day of the month [1-31]
          MONTH (out) - month of the year [1-12]
          HOURS (out) - hour of the day [0-23]
          MINUTES (out) - [0-59]
          SECONDS (out) - [0-59]
          YEAR (out) - [1980-2099]
          STATUS (out) - success status of the procedure
                         (0 is a successful operation)

      LIBRARY ROUTINES USED:
          Carry_Flag_Set - returns true if the carry flag in the FLAGS
                           register has been set; false if not

      TYPES REQUIRED:
          REGISTERS - used in all ROM-BIOS and DOS interrupts
```

```
SAMPLE CALL:
    Get_File_Date_Time (FILE_HANDLE, DAY, MONTH,
                        HOURS, MINUTES, SECONDS,
                        YEAR, STATUS);

NOTES:
    This routine requires a file handle.
    Common Return Status Values:
        2 - File not found      3 - Path not found
        5 - Access denied

----------------------------------------------------------}

  var
    REGS: REGISTERS;  {AX, BX, CX, DX, BP, SI, DI, DS, ES, FLAGS}

  begin
    with REGS do
      begin

{set the registers to request the date and time stamp for a file}
        AX := $5700;
        BX := FILE_HANDLE;

{invoke the DOS interrupt that returns the date and time stamp}
        MSDos (REGS);

{test the status of the operation and return the file's date and
 time stamp if the operation was successful}
        if Carry_Flag_Set (FLAGS) then      {error in operation}
          STATUS := Lo(AX)
        else
          begin
            STATUS := 0;                     {successful operation}
            YEAR  := (Hi(DX) shr 1) + 1980;
            MONTH := (DX and $1E0) shr 5;
            DAY   := DX and $1F;
            HOURS := Hi(CX) shr 3;
            MINUTES := (CX and $7E0) shr 5;
            SECONDS := (CX and $1F) * 2;
          end;
      end;
  end;
```

```
procedure Set_File_Date_Time (FILE_HANDLE, DAY, MONTH,
                              HOURS, MINUTES, SECONDS, YEAR: integer;
                                         var STATUS: byte);
{
DESCRIPTION:
    This routine modifies the time stamp of the
    file associated with the file handle provided.

PARAMETERS:
    FILE_HANDLE (in) - file handle from the routine Open_File
    DAY (in) - day of the month [1-31]
    MONTH (in) - month of the year [1-12]
    HOURS (in) - hour of the day [0-23]
```

```
        MINUTES (in) - [0-59]
        SECONDS (in) - [0-59]
        YEAR (in) - [1980-2099]
        STATUS (out) - success status of the procedure
                       (0 is a successful operation)

LIBRARY ROUTINES USED:
    Carry_Flag_Set - returns true if the carry flag in the FLAGS
                     has been set; false if not
TYPES REQUIRED:
    REGISTERS - used in all ROM-BIOS and DOS interrupts

SAMPLE CALL:
    Set_File_Date_Time (FILE_HANDLE, 25, 12, 12, 0, 0, 1986, STATUS);

NOTES:
    This routine requires a file handle.
    Common Return Status Values:
      2 - File not found                   3 - Path not found
      5 - Access denied

----------------------------------------------------------------}

   var
     REGS: REGISTERS;   {AX, BX, CX, DX, BP, SI, DI, DS, ES, FLAGS}

   begin
     with REGS do
       begin

{set the registers to set the date and time stamp of a file}
         AX := $5701;
         BX := FILE_HANDLE;
         DX := (YEAR - 1980) shl 9;
         DX := DX + (MONTH shl 5);
         DX := DX + DAY;
         CX := HOURS shl 11;
         CX := CX + (MINUTES shl 5);
         CX := CX + SECONDS div 2;

{invoke the DOS interrupt that sets a files date and time stamp}
         MSDos (REGS);

{return the status of the operation}
         if Carry_Flag_Set (FLAGS) then      {error in operation}
           STATUS := Lo(AX)
         else
           STATUS := 0;                       {successful operation}
       end;
   end;
```

```
procedure Close_File (FILE_HANDLE: integer;
                      var STATUS: byte);
{
DESCRIPTION:
    This routine closes the file associated with the
    file handle specified.
```

```
PARAMETERS:
    FILE_HANDLE (in) - file handle from the routine Open_File
    STATUS (out) - success status of the procedure
                  (0 is a successful operation)

LIBRARY ROUTINES USED:
    Carry_Flag_Set - returns True if the carry flag in the FLAGS
                     register has been set; false if not

TYPES REQUIRED:
    REGISTERS - used in all ROM-BIOS and DOS interrupts

SAMPLE CALL:
    Close_File (FILE_HANDLE, STATUS);

------------------------------------------------------------}

  var
    REGS: REGISTERS;   {AX, BX, CX, DX, BP, SI, DI, DS, ES, FLAGS}

  begin
    with REGS do
      begin

{set the registers to close a file via file handle}
        AX := $3E00;
        BX := FILE_HANDLE;

{invoke the DOS interrupt that closes the file}
        MSDos (REGS);

{return the status of the operation}
        if Carry_Flag_Set (FLAGS) then      {error in operation}
```

The DTA

The *disk transfer area* (DTA) is an area in memory that the operating system sets aside to buffer disk I/O. The routines *Find—First* and *Find—Next* use the DTA. When the routines find a file that matches the search specification passed from the calling routine, the following information is offset from the DTA:

DTA + 21 bytes   A 1-byte value containing the file's attributes
DTA + 22 bytes   A 2-byte value containing the file's time stamp
DTA + 24 bytes   A 2-byte value containing the file's date stamp
DTA + 26 bytes   A 2-byte value containing the low word of the file's size
DTA + 28 bytes   A 2-byte value containing the high word of the file's size.

You can use the following routine to find out what the current DTA is.

```
procedure Get_Disk_Transfer_Area (var SEGMENT, OFFSET: integer);
{
DESCRIPTION:
     This routine returns the current disk transfer
     area which is an area in memory set aside for
     all files transactions.  The disk transfer area
     (DTA) is used by the routines Find_First and
     Find_Next in support of wild card file
     specifications.

PARAMETERS:
     SEGMENT (out) - segment address of the current DTA
     OFFSET (out) - offset address of the current DTA

TYPES REQUIRED:
     REGISTERS - used in all ROM-BIOS and DOS interrupts

SAMPLE CALL:
     Get_Disk_Transfer_Area (SEGMENT, OFFSET);

--------------------------------------------------------}
   var
     REGS: REGISTERS;  {AX, BX, CX, DX, BP, SI, DI, DS, ES, FLAGS}

   begin
     with REGS do
       begin

{set AX to request the disk transfer area}
         AX := $2F00;

{invoke the DOS interrupt that returns the disk transfer area}
         MSDos (REGS);

{return the segment and offset addresses}
         SEGMENT := ES;
         OFFSET  := BX;
       end;
   end;
```

The routines *Find—First* and *Find—Next* use the values offset from the disk transfer area to obtain information about the files that match the search specification. These two routines are the two most powerful file manipulation services in this chapter. The routines return file specifications for files that match the search specification provided. The *file specification* is a record containing the following:

```
DTA_INFO = record
  ATTRIBUTES : byte;
  FILE_SIZE  : real;
  NAME       : STRING79;
end;
```

The search specification can use the DOS wild-card characters as follows:

```
Find_First ('*.*', ATTRIBUTES, FILESPEC, STATUS);
```

Here are the *Find—First* and *Find—Next* routines:

```
procedure Find_First (SEARCH_SPEC: STRING79;
                      ATTRIBUTES: byte;
                  var FILESPEC: DTA_INFO;
                  var STATUS: byte);
{
DESCRIPTION:
    This routine places the name and attributes
    of the first file meeting the search specification
    provided into the field DTA_INFO.NAME.  The routine
    allows us to search for a specific file or access a file
    via wild-card specifications.

PARAMETERS:
    SEARCH_SPEC (in) - specifies the name of the file to search
                       for (wild-cards are supported)
    FILESPEC (out) - the file name and attributes of the first
                     file found which matches the search specification
    ATTRIBUTES (in) - attributes desired for the file
                      (see Set_File_Attributes for a listing
                       of attributes)
    STATUS (out) - success status of the procedure
                   (0 is a successful operation)

TYPES REQUIRED:
    REGISTERS - used in all ROM-BIOS and DOS interrupts
    DTA_INFO
    STRING79 - used in all string operations

LIBRARY ROUTINES USED:
    Carry_Flag_Set - returns True if the carry flag in the FLAGS
                     register has been set; false if not
    Get_Disk_Transfer_Area - returns the current disk transfer
                             area (DTA)
    Power - returns the result of a value raised to a power

SAMPLE CALL:
    Find_First ('*.PAS', 0, FILESPEC, STATUS);


NOTES:
    Common Return Status Values:
       2 - File not found      3 - Path not found
      18 - No more files

------------------------------------------------------------}

   var
     REGS     : REGISTERS;  {AX, BX, CX, DX, BP, SI,
                             DI, DS, ES, FLAGS}
     DTA_SEG,
     DTA_OFS : integer;  {address of disk transfer area}
     I       : integer;  {counter for loops}
```

```
    begin
      with REGS do
        begin

{convert the search specification to ASCIIZ and set the registers
  to find the first occurrence of a file meeting the file specification}
          SEARCH_SPEC := SEARCH_SPEC + Chr(0);
          AX := $4E00;                        {DOS function code}
          DS := Seg(SEARCH_SPEC[1]);
          DX := Ofs(SEARCH_SPEC[1]);
          CX := ATTRIBUTES;

{invoke the DOS interrupt that finds the first matching file}
          MSDos (REGS);
          if Carry_Flag_Set (FLAGS) then      {error in operation}
            STATUS := Lo(AX)
          else
            begin
              STATUS := 0;                     {successful operation}

{all file information is offset from the DTA}
            Get_Disk_Transfer_Area (DTA_SEG, DTA_OFS);

            with FILESPEC do
              begin
                ATTRIBUTES :=  Mem [DTA_SEG:DTA_OFS+21];

                FILE_SIZE  := 1.0 * Mem [DTA_SEG:DTA_OFS+26] +
                              Mem [DTA_SEG:DTA_OFS+27] * 256.0 +
                              Mem [DTA_SEG:DTA_OFS+28] * Power (256.0, 2) +
                              Mem [DTA_SEG:DTA_OFS+29] * Power (256.0, 3);

{convert the file name from ASCIIZ}
                I := 0;
                while ((I < 13) and (Mem[DTA_SEG:DTA_OFS+30+I] <> 0)) do
                  begin
                    name[I + 1] := Chr(Mem[DTA_SEG:DTA_OFS+30+I]);
                    I := I + 1;
                  end;

                name[0] := Chr(I);
              end; {with FILESPEC}
          end;
      end;            {with REGS}
  end;
```

```
      procedure Find_Next (var FILESPEC: DTA_INFO;
                           var STATUS: byte);
      {
      DESCRIPTION:
          This routine returns the next file matching the
          search specification provided to the routine
          Find_First.  This routine provides the capability to
          retrieve files based upon the wild-card specifications.

      PARAMETERS:
          FILESPEC (out) - the name and attributes of the next file
                           that matches the search specification
          STATUS (out) - success status of the procedure
                         (0 is a successful operation)
```

```
TYPES REQUIRED:
    REGISTERS - used in all ROM-BIOS and DOS interrupts
    DTA_INFO

LIBRARY ROUTINES USED:
    Carry_Flag_Set - returns True if the carry flag in the FLAGS
                     register has been set; false if not
    Get_Disk_Transfer_Area - returns the current disk transfer
                             area (DTA)
    Power - returns the result of a value raised to a power

SAMPLE CALL:
    Find_Next (FILE_SPECIFICATION, STATUS);

NOTES:
    This routine is used extensively in the file manipulation
    routines to allow the routines to be applied to all of the
    files in a directory or disk (containing subdirectories).
    Common Return Status Values:
        5 - Access denied          18 - No more files

----------------------------------------------------------}

  var
    REGS     : REGISTERS;   {AX, BX, CX, DX, BP, SI,
                             DI, DS, ES, FLAGS}
    DTA_SEG,
    DTA_OFS : integer;      {address of disk transfer area}
    i       : integer;      {counter for loops}

  begin
    with REGS do
      begin

{set AX to request the next matching file specification}
        AX := $4F00;

{invoke the DOS interrupt that returns the next matching file}
        MSDos (REGS);

{test the status of the operation and return the information on
 the file found if the operation was successful}
        if Carry_Flag_Set (FLAGS) then    {error in operation}
          STATUS := Lo(AX)
        else
          begin
            STATUS := 0;                      {successful operation}

{all file information is offset from the DTA}
        Get_Disk_Transfer_Area (DTA_SEG, DTA_OFS);

          with FILESPEC do
            begin
              ATTRIB          Get_Disk_Transfer_Area (DTA_SEG, DTA_OFS);

          with FILESPEC do
            begin
              ATTRIBUTES :=  Mem [DTA_SEG:DTA_OFS+21];

              FILE_SIZE  := 1.0 * Mem [DTA_SEG:DTA_OFS+26] +
                            Mem [DTA_SEG:DTA_OFS+27] * 256.0 +
                            Mem [DTA_SEG:DTA_OFS+28] * Power (256.0, 2) +
                            Mem [DTA_SEG:DTA_OFS+29] * Power (256.0, 3);
```

```
{convert the file name from ASCIIZ}
            I := 0;
            while ((I < 13) and (Mem[DTA_SEG:DTA_OFS+30+I] <> 0)) do
              begin
                name[I + 1] := Chr(Mem[DTA_SEG:DTA_OFS+30+I]);
                I := I + 1;
              end;

            name[0] := Chr(I);
          end; {with FILESPEC}
        end;
      end;           {with REGS}
    end;
```

Video Display Control

One of the largest distinguishing factors between professional and hobbyist programs is video enhancement. Professionals write programs that control the monitor and capitalize on all available video capabilities. Hobbyists, however, often allow the screen to control their programs, instead of actively controlling its built-in capabilities themselves.

Chapter 7 focused on I/O and screen management. Several examples in that chapter illustrate programmer control of the screen. The following routines use ROM-BIOS interrupts to provide the basis of screen management:

```
procedure Get_Video_Mode (var MODE, SCREEN_WIDTH,
                                   PAGE: integer);
{
DESCRIPTION:
    This routine obtains the current video mode.

PARAMETERS:
    MODE (out) - video mode number as described below [0-15]
    SCREEN_WIDTH (out) - width of screen in characters
                         either 40 or 80 column
    PAGE (out) - active display page [0-3 in 80 column text mode]
                 [0-7 in 40 column text mode]

TYPES REQUIRED:
    REGISTERS - used in all ROM-BIOS and DOS interrupts

SAMPLE CALL:
    Get_Video_Mode (MODE, SCREEN_WIDTH, ACTIVE_PAGE);

NOTES:
    Video mode numbers
        0 - 40 column black and white text
        1 - 40 column 16 color text
        2 - 80 column black and white text
        3 - 80 column 16 color text
```

```
       4 - 4 color medium resolution graphics
       5 - 4 grey color medium resolution graphics
       6 - black and white high resolution graphics
       7 - 80 column monochrome
       8 - 15 graphics modes for the extended graphics adapter

---------------------------------------------------------}

   var
     REGS: REGISTERS;   {AX, BX, CX, DX, BP, SI, DI, DS, ES, FLAGS}

   begin
     with REGS do
       begin

{set AH to request the current video mode}
         AX := $0F00;

{invoke the ROM-BIOS interrupt that returns the current video mode}
         Intr ($10, REGS);

{return the current mode, screen width, and display page}
         MODE := Lo(AX);                {current video mode}
         SCREEN_WIDTH := Hi(AX);        {current screen width}
         PAGE := Hi(BX);                {active display page}
       end;
   end;
```

```
   procedure Set_Video_Mode (MODE: integer);
   {
   DESCRIPTION:
       This routine sets the current graphics mode.

   PARAMETERS:
       MODE (in) - video mode as described in
                   Get_Video_Mode [0-15]

   TYPES REQUIRED:
       REGISTERS - used in all ROM-BIOS and DOS interrupts

   SAMPLE CALL:
       Set_Video_Mode (3);   [80 column 16 color]

   NOTES:
       See video mode description in Get_Video_Mode.

   ---------------------------------------------------------}

   var
     REGS: REGISTERS;   {AX, BX, CX, DX, BP, SI, DI, DS, ES, FLAGS}

   begin
     with REGS do
       begin

{set AX to set the current video mode AH = 0, AL = MODE}
         AX := MODE;

{invoke the ROM-BIOS interrupt}
         Intr ($10, REGS);
       end;
   end;
```

The routines *Set_Active_Display_Page* and *Get_Active_Display_Page* cause screen output to appear instantaneously. For example, while an application displays page 0, it can use the routine *Write_Character* to write information to another page. When the user is finished with the current page, the application simply selects the page it has been writing to as active, and the data will appear instantaneously.

```
procedure Set_Active_Display_Page (PAGE: integer);
{
DESCRIPTION:
    This routine selects the active video display page.

PARAMETERS:
    PAGE (in) - video display page desired [0-7]

TYPES REQUIRED:
    REGISTERS - used in all ROM-BIOS and DOS interrupts

SAMPLE CALL:
    Set_Active_Display_Page (1);

NOTES:
    In 80 column mode pages 0 to 3 can be selected.
    In 40 column mode pages 0 to 7 are available.  If
    output is written to a specific page via the routine
    Write_Character and the page is selected as the
    active display, the output will appear to be
    instantaneous.

-----------------------------------------------------------}

   var
     REGS: REGISTERS;   {AX, BX, CX, DX, BP, SI, DI, DS, ES, FLAGS}

   begin
     with REGS do
       begin

{set the registers to change the active display page}
         AX := $0500 + PAGE;   {AL contains the display page desired}

{invoke the ROM-BIOS interrupt that changes the active display page}
         Intr ($10, REGS);
       end;
   end;
```

```
function Get_Active_Display_Page: integer;
{
DESCRIPTION:
    This routine obtains the active display page. [0-7]

VALUE RETURNED:
    Integer value containing the active display page.
```

```
TYPES REQUIRED:
    REGISTERS - used in all ROM-BIOS and DOS interrupts

SAMPLE CALL:
    ACTIVE_PAGE := Get_Active_Display_Page;

-----------------------------------------------------------}


  var
    REGS: REGISTERS;  {AX, BX, CX, DX, BP, SI, DI, DS, ES, FLAGS}

  begin
    with REGS do
      begin

{set AH to request the current video mode}
      AX := $0F00;

{invoke the ROM-BIOS interrupt that returns the current video mode}
      Intr ($10, REGS);

{return the active display page}
      Get_Active_Display_Page := Hi(BX);
    end;
  end;
```

```
procedure Write_Character (LETTER: char;
                  ATTRIBUTE, PAGE: integer;
                             COUNT: integer);
{
DESCRIPTION:
    This routine writes a character to the display
    page specified based upon the count (number of
    times to display) and attributes provided.

PARAMETERS:
    LETTER (in) - character to be displayed
    ATTRIBUTE (in) - attributes of the character [0-255]
    PAGE (in) - video display page number [0-7]
    COUNT (in) - number of times to display the character

TYPES REQUIRED:
    REGISTERS - used in all ROM-BIOS and DOS interrupts

SAMPLE CALL:
    Write_Character ('A', 128, 0, 1);
    (write 'A' (blinking) on page 0 one time)

NOTES:
    See the description of character attributes in the
    routine Get_Character_At_Cursor.

-----------------------------------------------------------}


  var
    REGS: REGISTERS;  {AX, BX, CX, DX, BP, SI, DI, DS, ES, FLAGS}

  begin
    with REGS do
      begin
```

```
{set the registers to write a character at given page, line,
 and column with the attributes given}
         AX := $0900 + Ord(LETTER);       {convert to a byte}
         BX := (PAGE shl 8) + ATTRIBUTE;  {page desired is in BH}
                                          {attributes are in BL}
         CX := COUNT;          {number of times to print character}

{invoke the ROM-BIOS interrupt to write the character}
         Intr ($10, REGS);
      end;
   end;
```

The ROM-BIOS services provide a great deal of information about the cursor and about video attributes at the current cursor osition. The routines *Set—Cursor—Position* and *Get—Cursor— Position* set and obtain the cursor position for any of the video display pages. The procedure *Get—Character—At—Cursor* returns the character (and its attributes) being displayed at the current cursor position. You can use this routine to read and save the current contents of the screen for later display.

```
procedure Set_Cursor_Position (LINE, COLUMN, PAGE: integer);
{
DESCRIPTION:
    This routine sets the cursor position to a
    given line, column position on the display page
    specified.

PARAMETERS:
    LINE (in) - line (vertical) position of the cursor [0-24]
    COLUMN (in) - column (horizontal) cursor position  [0-79]
    PAGE (in) - display page of the cursor             [0-7]

TYPES REQUIRED:
    REGISTERS - used in all ROM-BIOS and DOS interrupts

SAMPLE CALL:
    Set_Cursor_Position (12, 40, 0);

----------------------------------------------------------}

  var
    REGS: REGISTERS;   {AX, BX, CX, DX, BP, SI, DI, DS, ES, FLAGS}

  begin
    with REGS do
      begin

{set the registers to set the cursor position}
         AX := $0200;                  {function code}
         DX := (LINE shl 8) + COLUMN;  {DH contains the desired line}
                                       {DL contains the desired column}
         BX := PAGE shl 8;             {cursor page number}

{invoke the ROM-BIOS interrupt that sets the cursor position}
         Intr ($10, REGS);
      end;
   end;
```

```
procedure Get_Cursor_Position (PAGE: integer;
                  var LINE, COLUMN,
                      TOP, BOTTOM: integer);
{
DESCRIPTION:
    This routine returns the current cursor position
    (line, column) along with the top and bottom scan
    lines for the display page specified.

PARAMETERS:
    PAGE (in) - page the cursor position is desired for [0-7]
    LINE (out) - current line position of the cursor [0-24]
    COLUMN (out) - current column position of the cursor [0-79]
    TOP (out) - top scan line of the cursor [0-13]
    BOTTOM (out) - bottom scan line of the cursor [0-13]

TYPES REQUIRED:
    REGISTERS - used in all ROM-BIOS and DOS interrupts

SAMPLE CALL:
    Get_Cursor_Position (3, LINE, COLUMN, TOP, BOTTOM);

NOTES:
    See Set_Cursor_Size for an explanation of scan lines.

-----------------------------------------------------------}

  var
    REGS: REGISTERS;   {AX, BX, CX, DX, BP, SI, DI, DS, ES, FLAGS}

  begin
    with REGS do
      begin

{set the registers to read the current cursor position}
        AX := $0300;         {function code}
        BX := PAGE shl 8;    {page desired is in BH}

{invoke the ROM-BIOS interrupt that reads the current cursor position}
        Intr ($10, REGS);

{return information about the current cursor}
        LINE   := Hi(DX);
        COLUMN := Lo(DX);
        PAGE   := Hi(BX);
        TOP    := Hi(CX);        {upper scan line}
        BOTTOM := Lo(CX);        {bottom scan line}
      end;
  end;
```

```
procedure Get_Character_At_Cursor (PAGE: integer;
                       var LETTER: char;
                       var ATTR: integer);
{
DESCRIPTION:
    This routine returns the character being displayed
    at the current cursor position of the page specified.

PARAMETERS:
    PAGE (in) - display page of interest [0-7]
    LETTER (out) - character displayed at the current cursor position
    ATTR (out) - attributes of the character  [0-255]
```

```
TYPES REQUIRED:
    REGISTERS - used in all ROM-BIOS and DOS interrupts

SAMPLE CALL:
    Get_Character_At_Cursor (0, LETTER, ATTRIBUTES);

NOTES:
    Character attributes are
        1 - Blue foreground on      2 - Green foreground on
        4 - Red  foreground on      8 - Foreground intensity on
       16 - Blue background on     32 - Green background on
       64 - Red  background on    128 - Blinking

---------------------------------------------------------------}

  var
    REGS: REGISTERS;   {AX, BX, CX, DX, BP, SI, DI, DS, ES, FLAGS}

  begin
    with REGS do
      begin

{set the registers to read the character at the cursor}
        AX := $0800;          {function code}
        BX := PAGE shl 8;     {page desired}

{invoke the ROM-BIOS interrupt that reads the character}
        Intr ($10, REGS);

{return the character and attributes at the cursor position}
        LETTER := Chr(Lo(AX));
        ATTR   := Hi(AX);     {attributes of the character}
      end;
  end;
```

There are many applications in which it is convenient to remove the cursor from the screen. You can do this by modifying the cursor scan lines with the routine *Set — Cursor — Size*. The routine controls the cursor size by adjusting the number of scan lines used to represent the cursor. To remove the cursor from the screen, you change the top scan line so that it is greater than the bottom scan line. The cursor then becomes invisible. Cursor scan lines specify the cursor size as shown here:

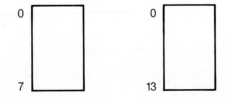

Color graphics monitor   Monochrome monitor

Here is the *Set_Cursor_Size* routine:

```
procedure Set_Cursor_Size (TOP, BOTTOM: integer);
{
DESCRIPTION:
    This routine sets the cursor size in the same
    fashion as the LOCATE function in BASIC.

PARAMETERS:
    TOP (in) - upper cursor scan line (default is 6) [0-13]
    BOTTOM (in) - lower cursor scan line (default is 7) [0-13]

TYPES REQUIRED:
    REGISTERS - used in all ROM-BIOS and DOS interrupts

SAMPLE CALL:
    Set_Cursor_Size (8, 7); [Make cursor invisible]

NOTES:
    If the top scan line is greater than the bottom scan
    line the cursor becomes invisible.

------------------------------------------------------------}

   var
     REGS: REGISTERS;   {AX, BX, CX, DX, BP, SI, DI, DS, ES, FLAGS}

   begin
     with REGS do
       begin

{set the registers to define the cursor size}
       AX := $0100;              {function code}
       CX := (TOP shl 8) + BOTTOM; {AH contains top scan line}
                                 {AL contains bottom scan line}
{invoke the ROM-BIOS interrupt that sets the cursor size}
       Intr ($10, REGS);
       end;
   end;
```

The routine *Scroll_Region* scrolls a region of the video display without affecting the remainder of the screen:

```
procedure Scroll_Region (ULINE, LLINE, LCOL, RCOL, NUMBER_OF_LINES,
                    FILL_ATTR, DIRECTION: integer);
{
DESCRIPTION:
    This routine allows you to scroll a specific region
    of the screen without affecting the remainder of the
    screen.

PARAMETERS:
    ULINE (in) - upper line of the scrolling region [0-24]
    LLINE (in) - lower line of the scrolling region [0-24]
    LCOL (in) - leftmost column of the scrolling region [0-79]
    RCOL (in) - rightmost column of the scrolling region [0-79]
    NUMBER_OF_LINES (in) - number of lines to scroll
    FILL_ATTR (in) - attribute of the fill character
    DIRECTION (in) - 1 is scroll up, 0 is scroll down
```

```
TYPES REQUIRED:
    REGISTERS - used in all ROM-BIOS and DOS interrupts

SAMPLE CALL:
    Scroll_Region (20, 24, 0, 79, 4, 0, 1);

NOTES:
    The empty lines as result of the scroll are filled
    with blanks.  See Get_Character_At_Cursor for the
    fill attributes.

-------------------------------------------------------------}
  const
    UP = 1;

  var
    REGS: REGISTERS;   {AX, BX, CX, DX, BP, SI, DI, DS, ES, FLAGS}

  begin
    with REGS do
      begin

{determine the direction to scroll}
        if DIRECTION = UP then
          AX := $0600                  {scroll up}
        else
          AX := $0700;                 {scroll down}

{specify the scrolling region and number lines to scroll}
        AX := AX + NUMBER_OF_LINES;  {number of lines to scroll}
        BX := FILL_ATTR shl 8;       {character to fill empty region with}
        CX := ULINE shl 8;           {upper line of scrolling region}
        CX := CX + LCOL;             {left hand column}
        DX := LLINE shl 8;           {lower line of scrolling region}
        DX := DX + RCOL;             {right hand column}

{invoke the ROM-BIOS interrupt to scroll the region as specified}
        Intr ($10, REGS);
      end;
  end;
```

Directory Manipulation

A convenient feature provided by Turbo Pascal is *directory manipulation*. Many applications require data contained in directories other than the current default directory. Although the Turbo Pascal routines **RmDir**, **MkDir**, **ChDir**, and **GetDir** make it possible to remove, make, change, and get the current directory, the following routines are provided for two reasons. First, while Turbo Pascal provides similar routines, these procedures simplify error checking. For example, if you call *Make—Directory* with a directory name that already exists, DOS returns an error status. The routine that called the function examines the status value and continues processing accordingly. Each of the following routines provides the error status as a parameter, which reinforces the desire to perform error testing. Turbo Pascal requires that the status be tested via the function **IOresult**. Second, these routines provide complete examples of DOS interfaces to the directory structure.

```
procedure Get_Current_Directory (var DIRECTORY: STRING79;
                                     DRIVE: byte;
                                 var STATUS: byte);
{
DESCRIPTION:
    This routine returns the name of the current directory.

PARAMETERS:
    DIRECTORY (out) - the current directory
    DRIVE (in) - drive containing the directory
    STATUS (out) - success status of the procedure
                  (0 is a successful operation)

LIBRARY ROUTINES USED:
    Carry_Flag_Set - returns true if the carry flag in the FLAGS
                     register has been set; false if not

TYPES REQUIRED:
    REGISTERS - used in all ROM-BIOS and DOS interrupts
    STRING79 - used in all string operations

SAMPLE CALL:
    Get_Current_Directory (DIRECTORY, 1, STATUS);

NOTES:
    The drive is specified as A = 0, B = 1, C = 2.

------------------------------------------------------------}

   var
     REGS: REGISTERS;   {AX, BX, CX, DX, BP, SI, DI, DS, ES, FLAGS}
     I   : integer;     {counter for loop}

   begin
     with REGS do
       begin

{set the registers to request the current directory}
          AX := $4700;                    {DOS function code}
          DS := Seg(DIRECTORY[1]);
          SI := Ofs(DIRECTORY[1]);
          DX := DRIVE;                     {drive desired}

{invoke the DOS interrupt that returns the current directory}
          MSDos (REGS);

{test the status of the DOS operation and return the current
  directory if the operation was successful}
          if Carry_Flag_Set (FLAGS) then    {error in operation}
             STATUS := Lo(AX)
          else
             STATUS := 0;
```

```
{successful operation so convert name from ASCIIZ to string}
        I := 1;
        while Ord(DIRECTORY[I]) <> 0 do
          I := I + 1;
        DIRECTORY[0] := Chr(I - 1);          {length of name}
      end;
  end;
```

```
procedure Change_Directory (DIRECTORY: STRING79;
                            var STATUS: byte);
{
DESCRIPTION:
    This routine changes the current default directory
    to the one specified.

PARAMETERS:
    DIRECTORY (in) - the desired directory path
    STATUS (out) - success status of the procedure
                   (0 is a successful operation)

LIBRARY ROUTINES USED:
    Carry_Flag_Set - returns true if the carry flag in the FLAGS
                     register has been set; false if not

TYPES REQUIRED:
    REGISTERS - used in all ROM-BIOS and DOS interrupts
    STRING79 - used in all string operations

SAMPLE CALL:
    Change_Directory ('\TURBO', STATUS);

NOTES:
    Common Return Status Values:
        3 - Path not found        5 - Access denied

---------------------------------------------------------}

  var
    REGS: REGISTERS;   {AX, BX, CX, DX, BP, SI, DI, DS, ES, FLAGS}

  begin
    with REGS do
      begin

{set the registers to change the current default directory to
 the directory provided}
        DIRECTORY := DIRECTORY + Chr(0);   {convert to ASCIIZ}
        AX := $3B00;                       {DOS function code}
        DS := Seg(DIRECTORY[1]);
        DX := Ofs(DIRECTORY[1]);

{invoke the DOS interrupt that changes the default directory}
        MSDos (REGS);

{return the status of the operation}
        if Carry_Flag_Set (FLAGS) then     {error in operation}
          STATUS := Lo(AX)
        else
          STATUS := 0;                     {successful operation}
      end;
  end;
```

```
procedure Make_Directory (DIRECTORY: STRING79;
                          var STATUS: byte);
{
DESCRIPTION:
    This routine creates a directory with the name
    specified.

PARAMETERS:
    DIRECTORY - name of the new directory
    STATUS - STATUS - success status of the procedure
             (0 is a successful operation)

LIBRARY ROUTINES USED:
    Carry_Flag_Set - returns true if the carry flag in the FLAGS
                     register has been set; false if not

TYPES REQUIRED:
    REGISTERS - used in all ROM-BIOS and DOS interrupts
    STRING79 - used in all string operations

SAMPLE CALL:
    Make_Directory ('\TOOLS', STATUS);

NOTES:
    Common Return Status Values:
       3 - Path not found        5 - Access denied

----------------------------------------------------------}

  var
    REGS: REGISTERS;  {AX, BX, CX, DX, BP, SI, DI, DS, ES, FLAGS}

  begin
    with REGS do
      begin

{convert the desired directory name to ASCIIZ and set the registers
 to make the new directory}
        DIRECTORY := DIRECTORY + Chr(0);      {convert to ASCIIZ}
        AX := $3900;                          {DOS function code}
        DS := Seg(DIRECTORY[1]);
        DX := Ofs(DIRECTORY[1]);

{invoke the DOS operation that makes a new directory}
        MSDos (REGS);

{return the status of the operation}
        if Carry_Flag_Set(FLAGS) then         {error in operation}
          STATUS := Lo(AX)
        else
          STATUS := 0;                         {successful operation}
      end;
  end;
```

```
procedure Remove_Directory (DIRECTORY: STRING79;
                            var STATUS: byte);
{
DESCRIPTION:
    This routine removes the directory specified.

PARAMETERS:
    DIRECTORY - the directory to remove.
    STATUS - STATUS - success status of the procedure
             (0 is a successful operation)

LIBRARY ROUTINES USED:
    Carry_Flag_Set - returns true if the carry flag in the FLAGS
                     register has been set; false if not

TYPES REQUIRED:
    REGISTERS - used in all ROM-BIOS and DOS interrupts
    STRING79 - used in all string operations

SAMPLE CALL:
    Remove_Directory ('\BASIC', STATUS);

NOTES:
    Common Return Status Values:
       2 - File not found   3 - Path not found
       5 - Access denied    16 - Cannot remove current directory

--------------------------------------------------------------}

   var
     REGS: REGISTERS;  {AX, BX, CX, DX, BP, SI, DI, DS, ES, FLAGS}

   begin
     with REGS do
       begin

{convert the name of the directory to delete to ASCIIZ and
 set the registers to delete the directory}
         DIRECTORY := DIRECTORY + Chr(0);      {convert to ASCIIZ}
         AX := $3A00;                          {DOS function code}
         DS := Seg(DIRECTORY[1]);
         DX := Ofs(DIRECTORY[1]);

{invoke the DOS interrupt that removes directories}
         MSDos (REGS);

{return the status of the operation}
         if Carry_Flag_Set (FLAGS) then        {error in operation}
           STATUS := Lo(AX)
         else
           STATUS := 0;                        {successful operation}
       end;
   end;
```

File Manipulation

Most programming applications require the creation and manipulation of data files. The following routines provide control over these files. For example, many applications use temporary files. The routines *Rename_File* and *Delete_File* rename and dispose of these files as you may desire.

In addition, there are routines that set and return file attributes. One of the best uses of these routines is for file protection. Most end-users are not "computer literate." If they are allowed to reach the DOS prompt, they can delete and rename files, which can leave applications inoperative. The routines *Set_File_Attributes* and *Get_File_Attributes* are therefore critical. These routines give you several alternatives for protecting files. The first is to make a file *read-only*. Read-only files can be accessed in any manner that does not affect their contents or characteristics. The second alternative is to make the files invisible to the DOS commands. This prevents DOS commands from affecting hidden files and does not allow the files to show up in directory listings.

```
procedure Set_File_Attributes (FILENAME: STRING79;
                               ATTRIBUTES: byte;
                               var STATUS: byte);
{
DESCRIPTION:
    This routine sets the attributes of the given file
    as specified.

PARAMETERS:
    FILENAME (in) - name of the file to set the attributes
    ATTRIBUTES (in) - file attributes desired [0-255]
    STATUS (out) - success status of the procedure
                   (0 is a successful operation)

LIBRARY ROUTINES USED:
    Carry_Flag_Set - returns True if the carry flag in the FLAGS
                     register has been set; false if not
TYPES REQUIRED:
    REGISTERS - used in all ROM-BIOS and DOS interrupts
    STRING79 - used in all string operations

SAMPLE CALL:
    Set_File_Attributes ('AAR.PAS', 2, STATUS); [make the file hidden]

NOTES:
    File attributes are as follows:
        1 - read only (cannot be deleted)
        2 - hidden file (hidden to DOS commands)
        4 - system attribute (not used by DOS)
        8 - volume label
       16 - subdirectory
```

```
        32 - archive
        64 and 128 are unused

     Common Return Status Values:
        2 - File not found              3 - Path not found
        5 - Access denied

--------------------------------------------------------------}

   var
      REGS: REGISTERS;   {AX, BX, CX, DX, BP, SI, DI, DS, ES, FLAGS}

   begin
     with REGS do
       begin

{convert the file name to ASCIIZ and set the registers to
 assign the file the attributes specified}
        FILENAME := FILENAME + Chr(0);      {convert to ASCIIZ}
        AX := $4301;                        {DOS function code}
        DS := Seg(FILENAME[1]);
        DX := Ofs(FILENAME[1]);
        CX := ATTRIBUTES;

{invoke the DOS interrupt that assigns the file attributes}
        MSDos (REGS);

{return the status of the DOS operation}
        if Carry_Flag_Set (FLAGS) then     {error in operation}
          STATUS := Lo(AX)
        else
          STATUS := 0;                      {successful operation}
      end;
   end;
```

```
procedure Get_File_Attributes (FILENAME: STRING79;
                  var ATTRIBUTES, STATUS: byte);
{
DESCRIPTION:
    This routine retrieves the attributes of the
    file specified.

PARAMETERS:
    FILENAME (in) - the file name desired
    ATTRIBUTES (out) - the attributes of the file [0-255]
    STATUS (out) - success status of the procedure
                   (0 is a successful operation)

LIBRARY ROUTINES USED:
    Carry_Flag_Set - returns true if the carry flag in the FLAGS
                     register has been set; false if not

TYPES REQUIRED:
    REGISTERS - used in all ROM-BIOS and DOS interrupts
    STRING79 - used in all string operations

SAMPLE CALL:
    Get_File_Attributes ('DOS.PAS', ATTRIBUTES, STATUS);
```

```
NOTES:
    See the file attributes listed in Set_File_Attributes.
    Common Return Status Values:
       2 - File not found        3 - Path not found
       5 - Access denied

-------------------------------------------------------------}

  var
    REGS: REGISTERS;  {AX, BX, CX, DX, BP, SI, DI, DS, ES, FLAGS}

  begin
    with REGS do
      begin

{convert the file name to ASCIIZ and set the registers to
 request the attributes of the file provided}
        FILENAME := FILENAME + Chr(0);     {convert to ASCIIZ}
        AX := $4300;                       {DOS function code}
        DS := Seg(FILENAME[1]);
        DX := Ofs(FILENAME[1]);

{invoke the DOS interrupt that returns the attributes of a file}
        MSDos (REGS);

{test the status of the DOS operation and return the attributes
 if it was successful}
        if Carry_Flag_Set (FLAGS) then    {error in operation}
          STATUS := Lo(AX)
        else
          begin
            STATUS := 0;                      {successful operation}
            ATTRIBUTES := Lo(CX);
          end;
      end;
  end;
```

```
procedure Delete_File (FILENAME: STRING79;
                       var STATUS: byte);
{
DESCRIPTION:
    This routine deletes the file specified.

PARAMETERS:
    FILENAME (in) - the file to delete
    STATUS (out) -  success status of the procedure
                    (0 is a successful operation)

LIBRARY ROUTINES USED:
    Carry_Flag_Set - returns true if the carry flag in the FLAGS
                     register has been set; false if not

TYPES REQUIRED:
    REGISTERS - used in all ROM-BIOS and DOS interrupts
    STRING79 - used in all string operations

SAMPLE CALL:
    Delete_File ('TEST.BAK');
```

```
NOTES:
    Common Return Status Values:
        2 - File not found                    3 - Path not found
        5 - Access denied

------------------------------------------------------------}

  var
    REGS: REGISTERS;   {AX, BX, CX, DX, BP, SI, DI, DS, ES, FLAGS}

  begin
    with REGS do
      begin

{convert the file name to delete to ASCIIZ and set the registers
 to delete the file}
        FILENAME := FILENAME + Chr(0);        {convert to ASCIIZ}
        AX := $4100;                          {DOS function code}
        DS := Seg(FILENAME[1]);
        DX := Ofs(FILENAME[1]);

{invoke the DOS interrupt that deletes files}
        MSDos (REGS);

{return the status of the operation}
        if Carry_Flag_Set (FLAGS) then        {error in operation}
          STATUS := Lo(AX)
        else
          STATUS := 0;                        {successful operation}
      end;
  end;
```

```
procedure Rename_File (OLD_NAME, NEW_NAME: STRING79;
                                var STATUS: byte);
{
DESCRIPTION:
    This routine renames the file specified by OLD_NAME
    to the name provided in NEW_NAME.

PARAMETERS:
    OLD_NAME (in) - current file name
    NEW_NAME (in) - desired file name
    STATUS (out) -  success status of the procedure
                    (0 is a successful operation)

LIBRARY ROUTINES USED:
    Carry_Flag_Set - returns true if the carry flag in the FLAGS
                     register has been set; false if not

TYPES REQUIRED:
    REGISTERS - used in all ROM-BIOS and DOS interrupts
    STRING79 - used in all string operations

SAMPLE CALL:
    Rename_File ('TURBO.DAT', '\ARCHIVE\TURBO.DAT');

NOTES:
    This routine can be used to rename files across
    subdirectories within a drive.
```

```
          Common Return Status Values:
             2 - File not found    3 - Path not found
             5 - Access denied

      ----------------------------------------------------------}

      var
         REGS: REGISTERS;   {AX, BX, CX, DX, BP, SI, DI, DS, ES, FLAGS}

      begin
        with REGS do
          begin
   {convert the old and new names to ASCIIZ and set the registers
    to rename the file}
            OLD_NAME := OLD_NAME + Chr(0);
            NEW_NAME := NEW_NAME + Chr(0);
            AX := $5600;                      {DOS function code}
            DS := Seg(OLD_NAME[1]);
            DX := Ofs(OLD_NAME[1]);
            ES := Seg(NEW_NAME[1]);
            DI := Ofs(NEW_NAME[1]);

   {invoke the DOS interrupt that renames a file}
            MSDos (REGS);
   {return the status of the operation}
            if Carry_Flag_Set (FLAGS) then    {error in operation}
               STATUS := STATUS
            else
               STATUS := 0;                    {successful operation}
        end;
      end;
```

Accessing the Hardware Configuration

Too often, because of assumptions made by the programmer about the hardware configuration of the target computer, programs fail when they are moved to a different system. The following routines provide access to the list of equipment contained in the system. In addition, there are two routines that return the machine type and ROM-BIOS date. You can use these two values to determine the functions supported by the computer. The following record contains the equipment list:

```
EQUIPMENT_LIST = record
   NUMBER_OF_PRINTERS,
   NUMBER_OF_RS232_PORTS,
   NUMBER_OF_FLOPPY_DRIVES,
   INITIAL_VIDEO_MODE,
   SYSTEM_BOARD_RAM: byte;
```

```
  DMA_CHIP_INSTALLED,
  SERIAL_PRINTER_INSTALLED,
  GAME_ADAPTER_INSTALLED,
  DISK_INSTALLED : boolean;
end;
```

In addition to the routines that return the current hardware configuration, routines are presented here to provide greater control over disk I/O operations. For example, the routines *Set__Current__ Drive* and *Get__Current__Drive* set and obtain the current default disk drive. The routine *Get__Free__Disk__Space* returns the amount of free disk space remaining on the selected drive. If your application writes many files to disk, it should invoke this routine to ensure that ample disk space exists.

```
procedure Get_Equipment_List (var LIST: EQUIPMENT_LIST);
{
DESCRIPTION:
    This routine invokes a ROM-BIOS interrupt that returns
    the current configuration of the system.

PARAMETERS:
    LIST (out) - the equipment configuration of the system

TYPES REQUIRED:
    REGISTERS - used in all ROM-BIOS and DOS interrupts
    EQUIPMENT_LIST - list containing the system configuration

SAMPLE CALL:
    Get_Equipment_List (LIST_OF_HARDWARE);

NOTES:
    It is possible to obtain this information by directly
    referencing the section of memory that contains the
    equipment list; however, there is no guarantee that future
    releases of the operating system will store the list in
    the same location.  Utilizing the interrupt service
    routine increases the probability that applications
    will run successfully in the future.


------------------------------------------------------------}

  var
    REGS: REGISTERS;   {AX, BX, CX, DX, BP, SI, DI, DS, ES, FLAGS}

  begin
    with REGS do
      with LIST do
        begin

{invoke the ROM-BIOS interrupt that returns the current
 system hardware configuration}
          Intr ($11, REGS);

{return the number of printers, RS232 ports, and floppy drives}
          NUMBER_OF_PRINTERS        := Hi(AX) shr 6;
          NUMBER_OF_RS232_PORTS     := (Hi(AX) and $E) shr 1;
          NUMBER_OF_FLOPPY_DRIVES   := ((AX and $C0) shr 6) + 1;
```

```
{return the initial video mode (at boot time)}
        INITIAL_VIDEO_MODE      := (AX and $30) shr 4;

{return the amount of memory contained on the system board}
        SYSTEM_BOARD_RAM        := ((AX and $C) shr 2);
        case SYSTEM_BOARD_RAM of
          0: SYSTEM_BOARD_RAM := 16; {16K}
          1: SYSTEM_BOARD_RAM := 32; {32K}
          2: SYSTEM_BOARD_RAM := 64; {64K}
        end;

{return that boards are installed}
        DMA_CHIP_INSTALLED      := (Hi(AX) and 1) = 1;
        SERIAL_PRINTER_INSTALLED := (AX and $2000) = 1;
        GAME_ADAPTER_INSTALLED  := (AX and $1000) = 1;
        DISK_INSTALLED          := (AX and 1) = 1;
      end;
  end;
```

```
procedure Get_ROM_Date (var DATE: STRING79);
{
DESCRIPTION:
    This routine returns the date associated with the ROM
    (Read Only Memory) chip contained in the PC.

PARAMETERS:
    DATE (out) - the date of the ROM chip

TYPES REQUIRED:
    STRING79 - used for all string operations

SAMPLE CALL:
    Get_ROM_Date (MACHINE_ROM_DATE);

NOTES:
    Some IBM compatibles do not provide the ROM date.
    From Peter Norton's Programmer's Guide to the IBM PC, the
    following dates apply:
        04/24/81 -- Original PC ROM
        10/19/81 -- Updated PC ROM
        08/16/82 -- Original IBM XT
        10/27/82 -- PC Upgrade to XT ROM
        11/08/82 -- PC Portable
        06/01/83 -- PC Jr
        01/10/84 -- PC AT

-----------------------------------------------------------}

  var
    I: integer;    {counter for loop}

  begin

{assign the 8 consecutive characters in memory that specify
 the date of the ROM chip to the string DATE}
    for I := 0 to 7 do
      DATE[I + 1] := Chr(Mem[$F000:$FFF5 + I]);
    DATE[0] := Chr(8);  {date is 8 characters}
  end;
```

```
function Get_Machine_Id: byte;
{
DESCRIPTION:
    This routine returns a byte that can be used to
    determine the machine's type.

SAMPLE CALL:
    MACHINE_TYPE := Get_Machine_Id;

NOTES:
    Some IBM compatibles do not provide a machine ID.
    From Peter Norton's Programmer's Guide to the IBM PC,
    the following types apply:
        255 -- Original PC
        254 -- XT and PC Portable
        253 -- PC Jr
        252 -- PC AT

------------------------------------------------------------}

  begin
    Get_Machine_Id := Mem[$F000:$FFFE];
  end;
```

```
function Get_Memory_Size: integer;
{
DESCRIPTION:
    This routine returns the amount of memory present in
    the system in K bytes.

VALUE RETURNED:
    integer value containing the amount of memory
    in K bytes

TYPES REQUIRED:
    REGISTERS - used in all ROM-BIOS and DOS interrupts

SAMPLE CALL:
    MEMORY_PRESENT := Get_Memory_Size;

NOTES:
    The value returned is in K bytes.  The value
    512 therefore means (512 * 1024) or 524,288 bytes.

------------------------------------------------------------}

  var
    REGS: REGISTERS;  {AX, BX, CX, DX, BP, SI, DI, DS, ES, FLAGS}

  begin
    with REGS do
      begin

{invoke the ROM-BIOS interrupt that returns the amount of
 memory present in the system}
        Intr ($12, REGS);

{return the amount of memory present in K bytes}
        Get_Memory_Size := AX;
      end;
  end;
```

```
function Get_Keyboard_Status: byte;
{
DESCRIPTION:
     This routine returns the current status of the
     keyboard (shift key, num-lock set etc.).

VALUE RETURNED:
     The byte returned specifies the current status
     of the keyboard.

TYPES REQUIRED:
     REGISTERS - used in all ROM-BIOS and DOS interrupts

SAMPLE CALL:
     KEYBOARD_STATUS := Get_Keyboard_Status;

NOTES:
     The status values returned are:
     1 - Right Hand Shift Key      2 - Left Hand Shift Key
     4 - Control Shift depressed   8 - Alt Shift depressed
     16 - Scroll Lock on          32 - Num-Lock on
     64 - Caps Lock on            128 - Insert Mode on

-----------------------------------------------------------}

   var
     REGS: REGISTERS;   {AX, BX, CX, DX, BP, SI, DI, DS, ES, FLAGS}

   begin
     with REGS do
       begin

{set AH to get the current keyboard status}
         AX := $0200;       {DOS function code}

{invoke the ROM-BIOS interrupt that returns the keyboard status}
         Intr ($16, REGS);

{return the current keyboard status}
         Get_Keyboard_Status := Lo(AX);
       end;
   end;
```

```
procedure Set_Current_Drive (DRIVE: byte);
{
DESCRIPTION:
     This routine selects the current default drive.

PARAMETERS:
     DRIVE (in) - the desired default drive

TYPES REQUIRED:
     REGISTERS - used in all ROM-BIOS and DOS interrupts

SAMPLE CALL:
     Set_Current_Drive (1);
```

```
NOTES:
    Drives are selected based on A = 0, B = 1, C = 2.
    Invalid drives have no effect on the current drive.

-----------------------------------------------------------}

  var
    REGS: REGISTERS;   {AX, BX, CX, DX, BP, SI, DI, DS, ES, FLAGS}

  begin
    with REGS do
      begin
{set the registers to select the current drive}
        AX := $E00;          {DOS function code}
        DX := DRIVE;

{invoke the DOS interrupt that selects the current drive}
        MSDos (REGS);
      end;
  end;
```

```
function Get_Current_Drive: byte;
{
DESCRIPTION:
    This routine returns the current drive.

VALUE RETURNED:
    A byte value that specifies the current drive.

TYPES REQUIRED:
    REGISTERS - used in all ROM-BIOS and DOS interrupts

SAMPLE CALL:
    if (Get_Current_Drive <> 1) then
      Set_Current_Drive (1);

NOTES:
    Drives are identified as A = 0, B = 1, C = 2.

-----------------------------------------------------------}

  var
    REGS: REGISTERS;   {AX, BX, CX, DX, BP, SI, DI, DS, ES, FLAGS}

  begin
    with REGS do
      begin

{set AX to request the current drive}
        AX := $1900;

{invoke the DOS interrupt that returns the current drive}
        MSDos (REGS);

{return the current drive}
        Get_Current_Drive := Lo(AX);
      end;
  end;
```

```
procedure Get_Free_Disk_Space (DRIVE: byte;
                               var SPACE: real;
                               var STATUS: byte);
{
DESCRIPTION:
    This routine returns the amount of free disk
    space on the drive specified.

PARAMETERS:
    SPACE (out) - amount of free disk space in bytes
    DRIVE (in) - drive the free space is desired for
    STATUS (out) - success status of the procedure
                   (0 is a successful operation)

TYPES REQUIRED:
    REGISTERS - used in all ROM-BIOS and DOS interrupts

SAMPLE CALL:
    Get_Free_Disk_Space (1, SPACE, STATUS);

NOTES:
    The value returned must be the type real because
    integer values cannot exceed the value 32,767.


----------------------------------------------------------}


   var
     REGS: REGISTERS;   {AX, BX, CX, DX, BP, SI, DI, DS, ES, FLAGS}

   begin
     with REGS do
       begin

{set AX to request the current free disk space for the drive
 specified in DX}
         AX := $3600;
         DX := DRIVE;

{invoke the DOS interrupt that returns the free disk space}
         MSDos (REGS);

{test the status of the operation and return the amount of
 free disk space if the operation was successful}
         if (AX = $FFFF) then    {error in operation}
           begin
             STATUS := 1;           {return error status code}
             SPACE := -1;
           end
         else
           begin                   {successful operation}
             STATUS := 0;
             SPACE := 1.0 * AX * BX * CX;   {free space}
           end;
       end;
   end;
```

Process Information and Control

The following routines allow Turbo programs to exit to DOS with a return status, reboot the system, and invoke ROM BASIC. In addition, the routine *Get__Program__Segment__Prefix* returns the address of the *program segment prefix* (PSP). Program information such as the disk transfer area and the control break vector are offsets of the PSP.

```
procedure Reboot_System ;
{
DESCRIPTION:
     This routine invokes the DOS system reboot procedures.

TYPES REQUIRED:
     REGISTERS - used in all ROM-BIOS and DOS interrupts

SAMPLE CALL:
     Reboot_System;

NOTES:
     Close all files before invoking this procedure or
     their contents may be destroyed.

--------------------------------------------------------}

  var
     REGS: REGISTERS;   {AX, BX, CX, DX, BP, SI, DI, DS, ES, FLAGS}

  begin

{reboot the operating system}
     Intr ($19, REGS);
     end;
```

The routine *Exit__To__DOS* terminates a program and returns a status value to DOS or to the particular routine invoking the process. This status can be accessed from DOS .BAT files via the **ERRORLEVEL** condition handler. For example, if a series of programs executes within a batch file, the status value can provide conditional execution as follows:

```
GetData
if ERRORLEVEL 3 Goto Done
SortData
Print Data.Dat
:Done
```

```
procedure Invoke_ROM_BASIC ;
{
DESCRIPTION:
    This routine invokes ROM BASIC.

TYPES REQUIRED:
    REGISTERS - used in all ROM-BIOS and DOS interrupts

SAMPLE CALL:
    Invoke_ROM_BASIC;

NOTES:
    Once control is passed to ROM BASIC the system must
    be rebooted to return to DOS.

---------------------------------------------------------}

  var
    REGS: REGISTERS;    {AX, BX, CX, DX, BP, SI, DI, DS, ES, FLAGS}

  begin

{invoke ROM BASIC}
    Intr ($18, REGS);
  end;
```

```
procedure Exit_To_DOS (LEVEL: integer);
{
DESCRIPTION:
    This routine terminates a program and returns control
    to DOS (or the invoking process) with a return status.
    The status value can be examined to determine the
    success of the terminated program.

PARAMETERS:
    LEVEL (in) - The status value to be returned to DOS

TYPES REQUIRED:
    REGISTERS - used in all ROM-BIOS and DOS interrupts

SAMPLE CALL:
    if (RESPONSE = 'QUIT') then
      Exit_To_DOS (1);            [1 is a successful termination]

---------------------------------------------------------}

  var
    REGS: REGISTERS;   {AX, BX, CX, DX, BP, SI, DI, DS, ES, FLAGS}

  begin
    with REGS do
      begin
```

```
{set AX to return control to DOS with the return status specified}
        AX := $4C00 + LEVEL;    {return status code is in AL}

{invoke the DOS interrupt with the exit status}
        MSDos (REGS);
      end;
   end;
```

```
function Get_Program_Segment_Prefix: integer;
{
DESCRIPTION:
    This routine returns the program segment prefix of the
    current program.  When a program is executed, DOS creates
    a control region at the beginning of the memory area
    referenced by the code segment register. This region of
    memory contains information about the program such as the
    control break vector, disk transfer area, and terminate
    vector.  Each field contained within the program segment
    prefix can be referenced as an offset of the segment
    address returned.

VALUE RETURNED:
    The address of the program segment prefix

TYPES REQUIRED:
    REGISTERS - used in all ROM-BIOS and DOS interrupts

SAMPLE CALL:
    SEGMENT_ADDRESS := Get_Program_Segment_Prefix;

NOTES:
    The actual fields of the program segment prefix (PSP) are
    well documented in the IBM Technical Reference Manual
    or Peter Norton's Programmer's Guide to the IBM PC.

    ---------------------------------------------------------}

  var
    REGS: REGISTERS;   {AX, BX, CX, DX, BP, SI, DI, DS, ES, FLAGS}

  begin
    with REGS do
      begin

{set the registers to get the program segment prefix}
        AX := $6200;                     {DOS function code}

{invoke the DOS interrupt that returns the PSP}
        MSDos (REGS);

{return the address of the program segment prefix}
        Get_Program_Segment_Prefix := BX;
      end;
   end;
```

Printer Control

The following routines test and reset the status of the printer. The routine *Initialize—Printer* resets the printer to its default values. Many programs open files and write directly to the printer. If the printer is offline or not present on the system, the DOS I/O error handler will gain control. The routine *Get—Printer—Status* examines the current printer status and continues processing accordingly.

```
function Initialize_Printer: byte;
{
DESCRIPTION:
    This routine resets the printer.

VALUE RETURNED:
    byte value containing the current printer status

TYPES REQUIRED:
    REGISTERS - used in all ROM-BIOS and DOS interrupts

SAMPLE CALL:
    STATUS := Initialize_Printer;

NOTES:
    This routine will reset all of the printer characteristics
    to their defaults such as width, formfeeds, etc. See the
    routine Get_Printer_Status for the possible return
    status values.  The printer number is placed in register
    DX.  If only one printer is present the DX is set to 0.
    If you have multiple printers you must modify this routine
    to accept the printer number as a parameter.  If the printer
    is turned off, or does not exist, these routines return a
    status value that can be tested.

    -------------------------------------------------------------}

  var
    REGS: REGISTERS;   {AX, BX, CX, DX, BP, SI, DI, DS, ES, FLAGS}

  begin
    with REGS do
      begin

{set the registers to initialize the printer}
        DX := 0;                          {printer number}
        AX := $0100;                      {function code}

{invoke the ROM-BIOS interrupt that initializes the printer}
        Intr ($17, REGS);

{return the current printer status}
        Initialize_Printer := Hi(AX);  {printer status}
      end;
  end;
```

```
function Get_Printer_Status:byte;
{
DESCRIPTION:
    This routine returns the current printer status.

TYPES REQUIRED:
    REGISTERS - used in all ROM-BIOS and DOS interrupts

SAMPLE CALL:
    Get_Printer_Status;

NOTES:
    From Peter Norton's Programmer's Guide to the IBM PC
    Printer status return codes:
        1  printer time-out           2  not used
        4  not used                    8  I/O error
        16 printer selected           32 out of paper
        64 acknowledge               128 not busy

    The printer number is placed in register DX.  If only one
    printer is present the DX is set to 0. If you have multiple
    printers this routine must be modified to accept the printer
    number as a parameter.  Unlike Initialize_Printer this
    routine does not reset the printer attributes.

----------------------------------------------------------}

    var
      REGS: REGISTERS;  {AX, BX, CX, DX, BP, SI, DI, DS, ES, FLAGS}

    begin
      with REGS do
        begin

{initialize the registers to return the current printer status}
        DX := 0;                      {printer number}
        AX := $0200;                  {function code}

{invoke the ROM-BIOS interrupt that returns the printer status}
        Intr ($17, REGS);

{return the printer status}
        Get_Printer_Status := Hi(AX);  {printer status}
        end;
      end;
```

```
procedure .Print_Screen ;
{
DESCRIPTION:
    This routine prints the contents of the screen in the
    same fashion as the shift-PrtSc function.

TYPES REQUIRED:
    REGISTERS - used in all ROM-BIOS and DOS interrupts

SAMPLE CALL:
    Print_Screen;

----------------------------------------------------------}
```

```
var
   REGS: REGISTERS;  {AX, BX, CX, DX, BP, SI, DI, DS, ES, FLAGS}

begin

{print the contents of the screen}
   Intr ($5, REGS);
end;
```

Miscellaneous DOS Services

The following routines perform miscellaneous DOS services: returning the major and minor DOS version numbers, setting interrupt vectors, and returning extended information on DOS errors.

Many of the previous routines set the carry flag and return a status value when an error occurs. The routine *Get__Extended__Error* provides additional information about the status value, as shown in this list of the more common errors returned by *Get__Extended__Error*:

1. Invalid function number

2. File not found

3. Path not found

4. No file handles available

5. Access denied

6. Insufficient memory.

DOS further categorizes each by class. The following classes are returned by *Get__Extended__Error*:

1. No resources available

2. Temporary error

3. Authorization error

4. Internal software error

5. Hardware error

6. System failure

7. Application software error

8. Item not found

9. Invalid format

10. Item locked

11. Media error

12. Item already exists

13. Unknown error.

DOS provides recommended actions for errors, as shown here:

1. Retry operation

2. Delay and retry operation

3. User retry

4. Abort processing with cleanup

5. Immediate exit no cleanup

6. Ignore error

7. Retry with user intervention.

Finally, to help locate the source of the error, DOS provides the following Locus information:

1. Unknown source

2. Block device error (disk)

3. Network error

4. Serial device error

5. Memory error.

Here are the routines that perform miscellaneous DOS services:

```
procedure Get_DOS_Version (var MAJOR, MINOR: integer);
{
DESCRIPTION:
    This routine returns the major and minor version of
    the current DOS.

PARAMETERS:
    MAJOR (out) - the major version of the operating system
    MINOR (out) - the minor version of the operating system

TYPES REQUIRED:
    REGISTERS - used in all ROM-BIOS and DOS interrupts
```

```
SAMPLE CALL:
    Get_DOS_Version (MAJOR_VERSION, MINOR_VERSION);

NOTES:
    Given DOS version 3.1, 3 is the major version and 1 is
    the minor version.

---------------------------------------------------------}

    var
       REGS: REGISTERS;  {AX, BX, CX, DX, BP, SI, DI, DS, ES, FLAGS}

    begin
      with REGS do
        begin

{set AX to request the DOS version number}
        AX := $3000;      {DOS function code}

{invoke the DOS interrupt that returns the current DOS version}
        MSDos (REGS);

{return the major and minor version numbers}
        MAJOR := Lo(AX);
        MINOR := Hi(AX);
      end;
    end;
```

```
procedure Set_Interrupt_Vector (INTERRUPT, SEGMENT, OFFSET: integer);
{
DESCRIPTION:
    This routine modifies ROM BIOS and DOS interrupts by
    reassigning the address of the routine that services
    the interrupt.

PARAMETERS:
    INTERRUPT (in) - interrupt service number to reassign
    SEGMENT (in) - segment address of the new routine
    OFFSET (in) - offset address of the service routine

TYPES REQUIRED:
    REGISTERS - used in all ROM-BIOS and DOS interrupts

SAMPLE CALL:
    Set_Interrupt_Vector ($24, $F000, $FF54);

NOTES:
    Thorough understanding of the DOS memory map and the
    interrupt structure and handling is required
    before attempting to modify interrupt vectors.

---------------------------------------------------------}

    var
       REGS: REGISTERS;  {AX, BX, CX, DX, BP, SI, DI, DS, ES, FLAGS}

    begin
      with REGS do
        begin
```

```
{set the registers to redefine an interrupt vector}
        AX := $2500 + interrupt;  {interrupt number is in AL}
        DS := SEGMENT;
        DX := OFFSET;

{invoke the DOS interrupt that redefines an interrupt vector}
        MSDos (REGS);
      end;
  end;
```

```
procedure Get_Extended_Error (ERROR: integer;
         var CLASS, ACTION, LOCUS: integer);
{
DESCRIPTION:
    This routine returns more information on DOS errors
    that can in turn be examined in the IBM technical
    reference manual or Peter Norton's Programmer's Guide for
    the IBM PC.

PARAMETERS:
    ERROR (in) - error value
    CLASS (out) - class of error (hardware, DOS, etc.)
    ACTION (out) - recommended action
    LOCUS (out) - error locus

TYPES REQUIRED:
    REGISTERS - used in all ROM-BIOS and DOS interrupts

SAMPLE CALL:
    Get_Extended_Error (5, CLASS, ACTION, LOCUS);

--------------------------------------------------------}

  var
    REGS: REGISTERS;  {AX, BX, CX, DX, BP, SI, DI, DS, ES, FLAGS}

  begin
    with REGS do
      begin

{set the registers to request information on a specific error}
        AX := $5900;        {DOS function code}
        BX := 0;            {0 for DOS 3.0 and 3.1}

{invoke the DOS interrupt that returns information on an error}
        MSDos (REGS);

{return the extended error information}
        CLASS  := Hi(BX);
        ACTION := Lo(BX);
        LOCUS  := Hi(CX);
      end;
  end;
```

10

File Manipulation Routines

In your work with a computer, files serve as the means of storing and retrieving information from one work session to another. Since data control is now considered to be the primary function of computers—even over the function of high-speed calculation—most computer applications require a set of file manipulation routines. This chapter provides a generic set of routines that complement the ones found in Turbo Pascal. These routines include an introduction to the use of wild-card file specifications and command-line processing.

Getting Text-File Information

The standard type **text** is defined as a file of characters. Turbo Pascal files can also be files of records, known as *random access files*. Turbo Toolbox provides a set of subroutines to insert, delete, and change records within random access files, as shown in Chapter 12. This chapter will therefore deal primarily with text files. Text files can store any type of information, whereas all random access files must have the same structure.

All of the routines in this section have a few common characteristics. First, the routines pass only the name of the file of interest as a parameter to the subroutines. Each subroutine assigns the name to a text-file variable, opens the file, manipulates it as required, and closes the file. To avoid problems with the file buffer, do *not* pass to these routines the name of a file that is already open.

Second, the routines in this section, like those in the rest of the chapter, are heavily *I/O bound*. Text files are defined as

```
ANY_FILE: text[$FFF];
```

The **$FFF** increases the size of the text-file buffer from 128 bytes to 4K bytes. The growth in buffer size increases the amount of the file in resident memory and decreases the number of times that the routine physically has to read from the disk.

Third, the routines in this section also allow the programmer to channel output to any destination file. Since standard devices like the terminal and the printer are treated as files, you can use this parameter to the subroutines in order to display the information that you need on the screen, print it on the printer, or save it in a text file. Thus, the routines increase flexibility and help you avoid the chore of writing multiple procedures to accomplish similar tasks.

The first routine in this section, *Text—FileSize*, returns the number of lines in a text file. Each line can contain a different number of bytes, so the only way to find out how many lines there are is to count them one at a time.

Extract—Lines reads through a file and extracts a given set of lines. You can use this routine to display the first few lines of a file to remind you of its contents, or to display the last few lines to show where you left off.

The *Browse—File* routine allows you to page interactively through a text file. This procedure is handy as a stand-alone program, since the DOS "type" command is so cumbersome. When first called, *Browse—File* displays the first page on the screen; you can press the PGUP and PGDN keys to move around within the file.

```
function Text_FileSize (TEXT_FILE: STRING79): integer;
{
DESCRIPTION:
      This procedure determines the number of lines in
        a text file.

PARAMETERS:
      TEXT_FILE (in) - the name of the file of interest

VALUE RETURNED:
      the size of the text file

TYPES REQUIRED:
      STRING79 - used for all strings

SAMPLE CALL:
      SIZE := Text_FileSize ('sample.txt');

NOTES:
      If the file does not exist, the size returned is -1.
      If the file is empty, the size is 0.

      ------------------------------------------------------}

   var
      IN_TEXT  : text[$FFF];       {the actual input file}
      TEMP_LINE: STRING79;         {the string on the current line}
      LINE_NUM : integer;          {the number of lines read so far}

   begin
      {$I-}

{attempt to open the file}
      assign (IN_TEXT, TEXT_FILE);
      reset (IN_TEXT);

{if the file could not be opened, return 0}
      if IOResult > 0 then
        Text_FileSize := 0
      else
        begin

{read through the input file, counting the lines}
           LINE_NUM := 0;
           while not eof (IN_TEXT) do

             begin
               readln (IN_TEXT, TEMP_LINE);
               LINE_NUM := LINE_NUM + 1;
             end;
           Text_FileSize := LINE_NUM;
        end;
```

```
{close the input file}
   close (IN_TEXT);
   {$I+}
 end;
```

```
procedure Extract_Lines (IN_FILE: STRING79;
            FIRST_LINE, LAST_LINE: integer;
                      OUT_FILE: STRING79;
                   var SUCCESS: byte);
{
DESCRIPTION:
    This procedure extracts a series of lines from one file to the
destination specified.  The destination can be 'prn' or 'trm:' to
print or display the lines, respectively.

PARAMETERS:
    IN_FILE (in) - the name of the file containing the lines
    FIRST_LINE (in) - the first line of interest
    LAST_LINE (in) - the last line of interest
    OUT_FILE (in) - the name of the output destination
    SUCCESS (out) - status byte (0 is successful)

TYPES REQUIRED:
    STRING79 - used for all strings

SAMPLE CALL:
    Extract_Lines ('sample.txt', 1, 24, 'trm:', SUCCESS);

------------------------------------------------------------}

  var
    IN_TEXT,                    {the actual input file}
    OUT_TEXT : text[$FFF];      {the actual output file}
    TEMP_LINE: STRING79;        {the string on the current line}
    LINE_NUM : integer;         {the number of lines read so far}

  begin
    {$I-}

{open the input file}
    Assign (IN_TEXT, IN_FILE);
    reset (IN_TEXT);
    SUCCESS := IOResult;

{open the output file by trying to first append an existing file}
    if (SUCCESS = 0) then
      begin
        Assign (OUT_TEXT, OUT_FILE);
        append (OUT_TEXT);
        SUCCESS := IOResult;
        if SUCCESS <> 0 then
          begin
            rewrite (OUT_TEXT);
            SUCCESS := IOResult;
          end;
      end;
```

```
{go through the file looking for the first line to extract}
    LINE_NUM := 1;
    while (LINE_NUM < FIRST_LINE) and (SUCCESS = 0) do
      begin
        readln (IN_TEXT, TEMP_LINE);
        SUCCESS := IOResult;
        LINE_NUM := LINE_NUM + 1;
      end;

{read and write the lines of interest}
    while (LINE_NUM <= LAST_LINE) and (SUCCESS = 0) and
          (not eof (IN_TEXT)) do
      begin
        readln (IN_TEXT, TEMP_LINE);
        SUCCESS := IOResult;
        if SUCCESS = 0 then
          begin
            writeln (OUT_TEXT, LINE_NUM:4, ' ', TEMP_LINE);
            SUCCESS := IOResult;
          end;
        LINE_NUM    := LINE_NUM + 1;
      end;

{warn if end of file reached}
    if eof (IN_TEXT) then
      writeln (OUT_TEXT, '***** end of file detected.');

{close both files}
    close (IN_TEXT);
    close (OUT_TEXT);
    {$I+}
  end;
```

```
procedure Browse_File (IN_FILE: STRING79);
{
DESCRIPTION:
    This procedure allows a user to browse through a text file
    by displaying the file a screen at a time.

PARAMETERS:
    IN_FILE (in) - the name of the file to browse

TYPES REQUIRED:
    STRING79 - used for all strings

LIBRARY ROUTINES USED:
    Put_String - writes a string at a given location on the screen

SAMPLE CALL:
    Browse_File ('sample1.pas');

NOTES:
    The "PgUp" and "PgDn" keys are used to move through
    the file.  The "Q" key terminates the routine.

-------------------------------------------------------------}
```

```
const
  MAX_PAGES = 20;

type
  BUFFER_TYPE = array [1..MAX_PAGES, 1..24] of STRING79;

var
  IN_TEXT      : text[$FFF];       {the actual input file}
  TEMP_STR,                        {temporary string}
  TOP_LINE     : STRING79;         {the string on the current line}
  BUFFER       : BUFFER_TYPE;      {buffer holding part of the file}
  CURRENT_PAGE,                    {the page being looked at}
  TEMP_PAGE,                       {temporary page}
  FIRST_PAGE,                      {the first page in the buffer}
  LAST_PAGE_IN_BUFFER,             {the last page in the buffer}
  LAST_PAGE_IN_FILE,               {the last page in the file}
  LINE         : integer;          {temporary line indicator}
  IN_CHAR      : char;             {the keyboard character input}
  BUFFER_EMPTY: boolean;           {do we need to reload the buffer?}

begin
  {$I-}

{open the input file}
  Assign (IN_TEXT, IN_FILE);
  reset (IN_TEXT);

  if IOResult <> 0 then
    writeln ('File not found.')

{initialize to the first page of the file}
  else
    begin
      Put_String ('Checking file size...', 25, 1, 3);
      LAST_PAGE_IN_FILE := Text_Filesize(IN_FILE) div 24 + 1;
      CURRENT_PAGE := 1;
      BUFFER_EMPTY := true;
      IN_CHAR := 'j';

{loop until user wants to quit}
      while IN_CHAR <> 'Q' do
        begin

{fill the buffer with the required part of the input file}
          if BUFFER_EMPTY then
            begin
              BUFFER_EMPTY := false;
              Put_String ('Filling buffer...', 25, 1, 3);
              ClrEol;

{place the current page in the center of the buffer}
              FIRST_PAGE := CURRENT_PAGE - MAX_PAGES div 2;
              if FIRST_PAGE < 1 then
                FIRST_PAGE := 1;

{skip first pages that won't fit}
              TEMP_PAGE := 1;
```

```
                    reset (IN_TEXT);
                    while (TEMP_PAGE < FIRST_PAGE) do
                      begin
                        for LINE := 1 to 24 do
                          readln (IN_TEXT, TEMP_STR);
                        TEMP_PAGE := TEMP_PAGE + 1;
                      end;

{read the next pages into the buffer}
                    LINE := 1;
                    TEMP_PAGE := 1;
                    while (FIRST_PAGE + TEMP_PAGE - 1 <= LAST_PAGE_IN_FILE)
                          and (TEMP_PAGE <= MAX_PAGES) do
                      begin
                        readln (IN_TEXT, BUFFER[TEMP_PAGE, LINE]);
                        LINE := LINE + 1;
                        if LINE > 24 then
                          begin
                            TEMP_PAGE := TEMP_PAGE + 1;
                            LINE := 1;
                          end;
                      end;
                    LAST_PAGE_IN_BUFFER := FIRST_PAGE + TEMP_PAGE - 2;
                  end;

{display the header line}
                  ClrScr;
                  Str (CURRENT_PAGE, TOP_LINE);
                  Str (LAST_PAGE_IN_FILE, TEMP_STR);
                  TOP_LINE := 'File: ' + IN_FILE +
                    '                              Page: ' + TOP_LINE +
                    ' of ' + TEMP_STR;
                  Put_String (TOP_LINE, 1, 1, 2);
{display the current page}
                  LINE := 1;
                  while (LINE <= 24) and (not KeyPressed) do
                    begin
                      Put_String (BUFFER[CURRENT_PAGE-FIRST_PAGE+1, LINE],
                                  LINE+1, 1, 0);
                      LINE := LINE + 1;
                    end;

{get a character from the keyboard}
                  read (kbd, IN_CHAR);

{check for escape sequences}
                  if (IN_CHAR = Chr(27)) then      {escape character}
                    begin
                      read (kbd, IN_CHAR);

{check for page down; refill buffer if backed up too far}
                      if (IN_CHAR = Chr(81)) and
                            (CURRENT_PAGE < LAST_PAGE_IN_FILE) then
                        begin
                          CURRENT_PAGE := CURRENT_PAGE + 1;
                          if CURRENT_PAGE > LAST_PAGE_IN_BUFFER then
                            BUFFER_EMPTY := true;
                        end
```

```
{check for page up; refill buffer if gone too far}
            else if (IN_CHAR = Chr(73)) and
                    (CURRENT_PAGE > 1) then
                begin
                  CURRENT_PAGE := CURRENT_PAGE - 1;
                  if CURRENT_PAGE < FIRST_PAGE then
                      BUFFER_EMPTY := true;
                end;

              IN_CHAR := 'j';
          end
{not an escape sequence -- check for quitting}
          else
              IN_CHAR := UpCase (IN_CHAR);
        end;
    end;
  close (IN_TEXT);

  {$I+}
 end;
```

The next three procedures are used to find occurrences of a string within a file. The first one, *Search—for—String*, is the basic routine that goes through an entire file and extracts the lines that contain the string from the file. As with the other routines in the chapter, you can use the routine to display the lines on the screen, print them, or save them to a file.

The second procedure, *Wild—Search—for—String*, demonstrates the use of the wild-card character in a file specification. The procedure uses the routines *Find—First* and *Find—Next*, introduced in the previous chapter, to search the current directory for files that meet the given specification. For example, suppose a directory contains the following six files:

TEST1.PAS	TEST2.PAS	TEST1.TST
SAMPLE1.TXT	SAMPLE.PAS	SAMPLE1.PAS

The subroutine call

```
Wild_Search_for_String ('*.pas', 'function', true, 'trm:');
```

would display on the screen all lines in all four .PAS files that contain the word "function," regardless of case. You may wish to make modifications to the rest of the file manipulation routines to support wild-card file specifications.

The third routine, *Command—Search—for—String*, is a stand-alone program that analyzes the parameters passed to it from DOS.

The first parameter must be the file specification, and the second must be the string to search for. These parameters are retrieved through the standard Turbo functions **ParamCount** and **ParamStr**. Even if you are a novice programmer, you should be able to take the shell of this program and modify it to call other subroutines in a similar fashion.

```
procedure Search_for_String (IN_FILE, FIND_STRING: STRING79;
                                        IGNORE_CASE: boolean;
                                        OUT_FILE: STRING79);
{
DESCRIPTION:
    This procedure outputs the lines of a file where a
given string has been found.

PARAMETERS:
    IN_FILE (in) - the name of the file of interest
    FIND_STRING (in) - the string being searched for
    IGNORE_CASE (in) - boolean to ignore the case of the string
    OUT_FILE (in) - the name of the output destination

TYPES REQUIRED:
    STRING79 - used for all strings

LIBRARY ROUTINES USED:
    Str_Count - returns the number of occurrences of a target
    string within an object string

SAMPLE CALL:
    Search_for_String ('sample.txt', 'HI', false, 'prn');

NOTES:

-------------------------------------------------------------}


    var
       IN_TEXT,                     {the actual input file}
       OUT_TEXT : text[$FFF];       {the actual output file}
       TEMP_LINE: STRING79;         {the string on the current line}
       LINE_NUM : integer;          {the number of lines read so far}

    begin
    {$I-}

{open the output file}
       Assign (OUT_TEXT, OUT_FILE);
       append (OUT_TEXT);
       if IOResult <> 0 then
         rewrite (OUT_TEXT);

{open the input file}
       if IOResult = 0 then
         begin
           Assign (IN_TEXT, IN_FILE);
           reset (IN_TEXT);
         end;
```

```
       if IOResult > 0 then
         writeln (OUT_TEXT, 'File not found')
       else

         begin

{loop through the input file}
         LINE_NUM := 0;
         while not eof (IN_TEXT) do
           begin
             readln (IN_TEXT, TEMP_LINE);
             LINE_NUM := LINE_NUM + 1;

{if the string is found on the line, output the line}
             if Str_Count (FIND_STRING, TEMP_LINE, IGNORE_CASE) > 0 then
               writeln (OUT_TEXT, LINE_NUM:4, '  ', TEMP_LINE);
           end;
       end;
     close (OUT_TEXT);
     close (IN_TEXT);
     {$I+}
   end;
```

```
   procedure Wild_Search_for_String (IN_FILE_SPEC,
                              FIND_STRING: STRING79;
                              IGNORE_CASE: boolean;
                                 OUT_FILE: STRING79);
   {
   DESCRIPTION:
       This procedure outputs the lines of all files where a
   given string has been found.  Wildcards are supported in
   the file specification.

   PARAMETERS:
       IN_FILE_SPEC (in) - the name of the files of interest
       FIND_STRING (in) - the string being searched for
       IGNORE_CASE (in) - boolean to ignore the case of the string
       OUT_FILE (in) - the name of the file to contain the lines

   TYPES REQUIRED:
       DTA_INFO - information on a file

   LIBRARY ROUTINES USED:
       Search_for_String - searches for all occurrences of a
           string in a file
       Find_First - finds the first file that meets the required
           specifications
       Find_Next - finds the next file that meets the required
           specifications

   SAMPLE CALL:
       Wild_Search_for_String ('*.txt', 'HI', false, 'prn');

   ----------------------------------------------------------}
```

```
  var
    FILE_FOUND: DTA_INFO;        {the file meeting specifications}
    SUCCESS   : byte;            {return status}
    OUT_TEXT  : text;            {actual output file}

  begin
    {$I-}

{open the output file}
    Assign (OUT_TEXT, OUT_FILE);
    append (OUT_TEXT);
    if IOResult <> 0 then
      rewrite (OUT_TEXT);

{if unsuccessful, use the terminal screen}
    if IOResult <> 0 then
      begin
        Assign (OUT_TEXT, 'trm:');
        rewrite (OUT_TEXT);
        writeln (OUT_TEXT, 'Unable to open output file.');
      end;

{find the first input file}
    Find_First (IN_FILE_SPEC, 0, FILE_FOUND, SUCCESS);
    if SUCCESS <> 0 then
      writeln (OUT_TEXT, 'No files found.');

{search for the string with every file found}
    while SUCCESS = 0 do
      begin
        writeln (OUT_TEXT, '    File: ', FILE_FOUND.NAME);
        Search_for_String (FILE_FOUND.NAME, FIND_STRING, IGNORE_CASE,
            OUT_FILE);
        Find_Next (FILE_FOUND, SUCCESS);
      end;
    {$I+}
  end;
```

```
  procedure Command_Search_for_String;
  {
  DESCRIPTION:
      This procedure outputs the lines of all files where a
  given string has been found.  Wildcards are supported in
  the file specification.  All parameters come from the
  command line.

  PARAMETERS (from DOS):
      1 - the name of the input file spec
      2 - the string to search for
      3 - the name of the output file

  TYPES REQUIRED:
      STRING79 - used for all strings
```

```
LIBRARY ROUTINES USED:
    Wild_Search_for_String - searches for all occurrences of a
        string in a set of files

SAMPLE CALL FROM DOS (assuming SEARCH.COM was created):
    Search  *.txt 'hi' trm:

NOTES:
    If the final parameter is not included, "trm:" is
    assumed.

------------------------------------------------------------}

   var
      SUCCESS    : byte;                {return status}
      IN_FILE_SPEC,                     {input file specifications}
      FIND_STRING,                      {the string to search for}
      OUT_FILE  : STRING79;             {the name of the output file}
      NUM_PARAMS: integer;              {number of command parameters}

   begin

{check for minimum parameters}
    NUM_PARAMS := ParamCount;
    if NUM_PARAMS < 2 then
       writeln ('Not enough parameters')

       else
          begin

{assign each parameter to the proper variable}
          IN_FILE_SPEC := ParamStr(1);
          FIND_STRING := ParamStr(2);

{default output to the terminal screen}
          if NUM_PARAMS = 2 then
             OUT_FILE := 'trm:'
          else
             OUT_FILE := ParamStr(3);

{call the proper subroutine}
          Wild_Search_for_String (IN_FILE_SPEC, FIND_STRING, true,
             OUT_FILE);
       end;
   end;
```

Changing Text Files

Unfortunately, Pascal does not support the ability to make small changes in a text file. You can open text files for reading or clear them for writing, but you cannot combine the two. Consequently, procedures that change text files must create a temporary file where the new file contents can be stored. To avoid writing over a file that already exists in the process, the procedure *Create_ Unique_File* calls a DOS function that creates a new file.

Create—Unique—File is used by the other routines in this chapter. One of these routines is *Replace—String*. The complement of *Search—for—String*, this procedure finds all occurrences of a string in a file and replaces them with a different string. This subroutine is handy for changing a variable or similar name that is used in more than one file in a directory. As the lines are read from the file, they are changed as required and stored in the temporary file. When the file has been read completely, it is deleted, and the temporary file is renamed to the original file's name. Used by *Replace—String*, the procedures *Delete—File* and *Rename—File* are given in Chapter 9.

The other file-changing routine, *Remove—Lines*, takes a given set of lines completely out of a file. This procedure uses the temporary file scheme in the same way that *Replace—String* did.

```
procedure Create_Unique_File (PATH: STRING79;
                    ATTRIBUTES: integer;
                var FILE_NAME: STRING79;
                var FILE_HANDLE: integer;
                var STATUS: byte);
{
DESCRIPTION:
    This routine creates a file with a unique name
    in the path specified.  The new file name is
    appended to the path.

PARAMETERS:
    PATH (in) - contains the name of the path
                to create the file in.
    ATTRIBUTES (in) - the attributes to assign to the new file
    FILE_NAME (out) - the unique file name created
    FILE_HANDLE (out) - the file handle used to access the file
    STATUS (out) - success status of the procedure
                (0 is a successful operation)

TYPES REQUIRED:
    STRING79 - used in all string operations

LIBRARY ROUTINES USED:
    Carry_Flag_Set - returns True if the carry flag in the FLAGS
                register has been set, otherwise False

SAMPLE CALL:
    Create_Unique_File ('\TURBO', 2, FILE_NAME, FILE_HANDLE, STATUS);

NOTES:
    If the carry flag is set the register AX contains the error
    status code, otherwise AX contains the file handle of the
    unique file.

-------------------------------------------------------------}
```

```
var
  REGS: REGISTERS;       {AX, BX, CX, DX, BP, SI, DI, DS, ES, FLAGS}
  I   : integer;         {counter for loops}

begin
  with REGS do
    begin

{set the registers to request a unique file name}
      AX := $5A00;
      PATH := PATH + Chr(0);      {asciiz}
      DS := Seg (PATH[1]);
      DX := Ofs (PATH[1]);
      CX := ATTRIBUTES;

{invoke the DOS interrupt which returns a unique file name}
      MSDos (REGS);

{if no error occurred return the file name and handle}
      if Carry_Flag_Set (FLAGS) then
        STATUS := AX
      else
        begin
          STATUS := 0;            {successful operation}
          FILE_HANDLE := AX;

{get the file name}
          i := 1;
          while Ord (PATH[I]) <> 0 do
            begin
              FILE_NAME[I] := PATH[I];
              I := I + 1;
            end;
          FILE_NAME[0] := Chr (I-1);    {length of new file name}
        end;
    end; {with REGS}
end;
```

```
procedure Replace_String (IN_FILE,
          FIND_STRING, NEW_STRING: STRING79;
                    IGNORE_CASE: boolean;
                        OUT_FILE: STRING79);
{
DESCRIPTION:
    This procedure replaces all occurrences of a string with
    another string in a given file, and outputs the changed
    lines.

PARAMETERS:
    IN_FILE (in) - the name of the file of interest
    FIND_STRING (in) - the string being searched for
    NEW_STRING (in) - the string that will replace the old string
    IGNORE_CASE (in) - boolean to ignore the case of the string
    OUT_FILE (in) - the name of the output destination

TYPES REQUIRED:
    STRING79 - used for all strings
```

```
    LIBRARY ROUTINES USED:
        Str_Replace_All - replaces all occurrences of one string with
          another
        Create_Unique_File - creates a temporary file
        Delete_File - deletes a specified file
        Rename_File - renames a file from one name to another

    SAMPLE CALL:
        Replace_String ('sample.txt', 'HI', 'HOWDY', false, 'prn');

    NOTES:

    -----------------------------------------------------------}


      var
        IN_TEXT,                        {the actual input file}
        TEMP_TEXT,                      {a temporary file}
        OUT_TEXT : text[$FFF];          {the actual output file}
        TEMP_FILE,                      {temporary file name}
        TEMP_LINE: STRING79;            {the string on the current line}
        NUM_REPLACEMENTS,               {the number of replacements of a string}
        FILE_HANDLE,                    {handle of the temporary file}
        LINE_NUM : integer;             {the number of lines read so far}
        SUCCESS  : byte;                {return status}

      begin
        {$I-}
    {open the output file}
        Assign (OUT_TEXT, OUT_FILE);
        Append (OUT_TEXT);
        if IOResult <> 0 then
          Rewrite (OUT_TEXT);

    {open the temporary file}
        if IOResult = 0 then
          begin
            Create_Unique_File ('\', 0, TEMP_FILE, FILE_HANDLE, SUCCESS);
            Assign (TEMP_TEXT, TEMP_FILE);
            rewrite (TEMP_TEXT);
          end;

    {open the input file}
        if IOResult = 0 then
          begin
            Assign (IN_TEXT, IN_FILE);
            reset (IN_TEXT);
          end;

        if IOResult > 0 then
          writeln (OUT_TEXT, 'File not found')
        else
          begin

    {loop through the input file}
            LINE_NUM := 0;
            while not eof (IN_TEXT) do
              begin
                readln (IN_TEXT, TEMP_LINE);
                LINE_NUM := LINE_NUM + 1;
                Str_Replace_All (TEMP_LINE, FIND_STRING, NEW_STRING,
                    IGNORE_CASE, NUM_REPLACEMENTS);
```

```
{if the string was replaced, output the line}
            if NUM_REPLACEMENTS > 0 then
                writeln (OUT_TEXT, LINE_NUM:4, ' ', TEMP_LINE);
            writeln (TEMP_TEXT, TEMP_LINE);
        end;
    end;
  Close (OUT_TEXT);
  Close (TEMP_TEXT);
  Close (IN_TEXT);

{delete the input file and rename the temporary file as the
input file}
    Delete_File (IN_FILE, SUCCESS);
    Rename_File (TEMP_FILE, IN_FILE, SUCCESS);

    {$I+}
  end;
```

```
procedure Remove_Lines (TEXT_FILE: STRING79;
            FIRST_LINE, LAST_LINE: integer;
                var SUCCESS: byte);
{
DESCRIPTION:
    This procedure removes a series of lines from a file.

PARAMETERS:
    TEXT_FILE (in) - the name of the file containing the lines
    FIRST_LINE (in) - the first line of interest
    LAST_LINE (in) - the last line of interest
    SUCCESS (out) - status byte (0 is successful)

TYPES REQUIRED:
    STRING79 - used for all strings

LIBRARY ROUTINES USED:
    Create_Unique_File - creates a temporary file
    Delete_File - deletes a specified file
    Rename_File - renames a file from one name to another

SAMPLE CALL:
    Remove_Lines ('sample.txt', 1, 24, SUCCESS);

NOTES:

------------------------------------------------------------}

  var
    IN_TEXT,                        {the actual input file}
    TEMP_TEXT: text[$FFF];          {a temporary file}
    TEMP_FILE,                      {the name of the temporary file}
    TEMP_LINE: STRING79;            {the string on the current line}
    FILE_HANDLE,                    {the handle of the temporary file}
    LINE_NUM : integer;             {the number of lines read so far}
```

```
    begin
      {$I-}

{create a temporary file}
    Create_Unique_File ('\', 0, TEMP_FILE, FILE_HANDLE, SUCCESS);
    if SUCCESS = 0 then
      begin
        assign (TEMP_TEXT, TEMP_FILE);
        rewrite (TEMP_TEXT);
        SUCCESS := IOResult;
      end;

{open the input file}
    if SUCCESS = 0 then
      begin
        assign (IN_TEXT, TEXT_FILE);
        reset (IN_TEXT);
        SUCCESS := IOResult;
      end;

{read through the input file until the first line of interest is
found; echo these lines to the temporary file}
    LINE_NUM := 1;
    while (LINE_NUM < FIRST_LINE) and (SUCCESS = 0) do
      begin
        readln (IN_TEXT, TEMP_LINE);
        SUCCESS := IOResult;
        if SUCCESS = 0 then
          begin
            writeln (TEMP_TEXT, TEMP_LINE);
            SUCCESS := IOResult;
          end;
        LINE_NUM := LINE_NUM + 1;
      end;

{read through the lines to be removed}
    while (LINE_NUM <= LAST_LINE) and (SUCCESS = 0) do
      begin
        readln (IN_TEXT, TEMP_LINE);
        SUCCESS := IOResult;
        LINE_NUM    := LINE_NUM + 1;
      end;

{read the remaining lines of the file, echoing to the
temporary file}
    while (not eof(IN_TEXT)) and (SUCCESS = 0) do
      begin
        readln (IN_TEXT, TEMP_LINE);
        SUCCESS := IOResult;
        if SUCCESS = 0 then
          begin
            writeln (TEMP_TEXT, TEMP_LINE);
            SUCCESS := IOResult;
          end;
      end;

{close both files}
    close (IN_TEXT);
    close (TEMP_TEXT);
```

```
{delete the input file and rename the temporary file as the
input file}
    if SUCCESS = 0 then
      Delete_File (TEXT_FILE, SUCCESS);
    if SUCCESS = 0 then
      Rename_File (TEMP_FILE, TEXT_FILE, SUCCESS);

    {$I+}
  end;
```

Appending Files

Applications often arise that require the appending of several files into one file. Turbo Pascal does not provide this capability directly, but it does provide the standard procedure **Append**. This procedure opens a file and places the file pointer at the end of the file so that you can add new text. The file-searching routines presented earlier used **Append** so that *Search—for—String* could be called in a loop and the results from multiple searches could be stored in the same file.

The *Append—Files* procedure given in this section appends one file to another. The loop

```
for COUNT := 1 to ParamCount-1 do
  Append_Files (ParamStr[I+1], ParamStr[I], SUCCESS);
```

could be used by a program that reads the command-line parameters and appends a group of files together in the order specified.

Append—Includes, which is a slightly more complicated procedure, is useful only for Turbo Pascal programs because it searches the file for the include compiler directive {**$I**}. After the directive is found, the procedure searches for the file and copies the entire include module into the destination file. *Append—Includes* is handy for printing an entire program with its include modules in proper order.

```
procedure Append_Files (IN_FILE, DEST_FILE: STRING79;
                                    var SUCCESS: byte);
{
DESCRIPTION:
    This procedure appends one text file onto another.
```

```
PARAMETERS:
    IN_FILE (in) - the name of the file that will go at the
    end of the destination file
    DEST_FILE (in) - the name of the file that will be appended
    SUCCESS (out) - return status (0 is successful)

TYPES REQUIRED:
    STRING79 - used for all strings

SAMPLE CALL:
    Append_Files ('sample1.txt', 'sample2.txt', ERROR);

NOTES:

-----------------------------------------------------------}

  var
    IN_TEXT,                      {the actual input file}
    DEST_TEXT: text[$FFF];        {the actual destination file}
    TEMP_LINE: STRING79;          {the string on the current line}

    begin
      {$I-}

  {open the output file and go the beginning of a new line}
      Assign (DEST_TEXT, DEST_FILE);
      Append (DEST_TEXT);
      writeln (DEST_TEXT);
      SUCCESS := IOResult;

  {open the input file}
      if SUCCESS = 0 then
        begin
          Assign (IN_TEXT, IN_FILE);
          reset (IN_TEXT);
          SUCCESS := IOResult;
        end;

      if SUCCESS = 0 then
        begin

  {loop through the input file, appending the output file}
          while (not eof (IN_TEXT)) and (SUCCESS = 0) do
            begin
              readln (IN_TEXT, TEMP_LINE);
              SUCCESS := IOResult;
              if SUCCESS = 0 then
                begin
                  writeln (DEST_TEXT, TEMP_LINE);
                  SUCCESS := IOResult;
                end;
            end;
        end;
      close (DEST_TEXT);
      close (IN_TEXT);

      {$I+}
    end;
```

```
procedure Append_Includes (IN_FILE, OUT_FILE: STRING79;
                               var SUCCESS: byte);
{
DESCRIPTION:
    This procedure appends one text file onto another.

PARAMETERS:
    IN_FILE (in) - the name of the main program
    OUT_FILE (in) - the name of the file to contain the complete
      program
    SUCCESS (out) - return status (0 is successful)
TYPES REQUIRED:
    STRING79 - used for all strings

LIBRARY ROUTINES USED:
    Next_Pos - locates the next occurrence of one string within
      another

SAMPLE CALL:
    Append_Includes ('sample1.pas', 'prn', ERROR);

NOTES:

-----------------------------------------------------------}

  var
    IN_TEXT,                      {the actual input file}
    INCLUDE_TEXT,                 {the include file}
    OUT_TEXT : text[$FFF];        {the actual output file}
    INCLUDE_NAME,                 {the name of the include file}
    TEMP_LINE: STRING79;          {the string on the current line}
    LOC     : integer;            {location of $I in string}

  begin
    {$I-}
{open the output file}
    Assign (OUT_TEXT, OUT_FILE);
    rewrite (OUT_TEXT);
    SUCCESS := IOResult;

{open the input file}
    if SUCCESS = 0 then
      begin
        Assign (IN_TEXT, IN_FILE);
        reset (IN_TEXT);
        SUCCESS := IOResult;
      end;

    if SUCCESS = 0 then
      begin

{loop through the input file, appending the output file}
        while (not eof (IN_TEXT)) and (SUCCESS = 0) do
          begin
            readln (IN_TEXT, TEMP_LINE);
            SUCCESS := IOResult;
            if SUCCESS = 0 then
              begin
                writeln (OUT_TEXT, TEMP_LINE);
                SUCCESS := IOResult;
              end;
```

```
{search for the include compiler directive}
        LOC := Next_Pos ('{$I', TEMP_LINE, 0, true);
        if (LOC > 0) and ((TEMP_LINE[LOC+3] >= 'A')
            or (TEMP_LINE[LOC+3] = ' ')) then
          begin

{determine the name of the include file, eliminating spaces}
            LOC := LOC + 3;
            while TEMP_LINE[LOC] = ' ' do
              LOC := LOC + 1;
            INCLUDE_NAME := Copy (TEMP_LINE, LOC,
                Pos ('}', TEMP_LINE) - LOC);

{set the default extension to .pas}
            if Pos ('.', INCLUDE_NAME) = 0 then
              INCLUDE_NAME := INCLUDE_NAME + '.pas';
            Assign (INCLUDE_TEXT, INCLUDE_NAME);

{open include file}
            reset (INCLUDE_TEXT);
            SUCCESS := IOResult;
            if SUCCESS = 0 then

{echo include file}
              while not eof (INCLUDE_TEXT) do
                begin
                  readln (INCLUDE_TEXT, TEMP_LINE);
                  writeln (OUT_TEXT, TEMP_LINE);
                end
              else
                writeln (OUT_TEXT, '{***** Include not found.}');
          end;
        end;
      end;
    close (OUT_TEXT);
    close (IN_TEXT);

    {$I+}
  end;
```

Support for Special I/O

Chapter 8 presented several routines that display and manipulate entire screens of information. Here is a set of procedures that support those routines by loading and saving the associated data structures to files.

The routines *Load__Data__Values* and *Save__Data__Values*, as given here, retrieve and store the data-entry tables that are displayed and changed by the routines *Put__Data__Values* and *Get__Data__Values*, given in Chapter 8. Since the real-number table is stored in the file as one large record, it can be loaded and saved quickly.

The procedures *Load—Form* and *Save—Form* support the *Put—Form* and *Get—Form* routines from Chapter 8. These four routines work together to allow you to design, display, save, and recall a complete form.

```
procedure Load_Data_Values (var ENTRY: DATA_ARRAY;
                                FILE_NAME: STRING79;
                                var SUCCESS: byte);
{
DESCRIPTION:
    This procedure loads a group of data values that are
    used for data entry.  The numbers are in table form,
    and must have been saved with Save_Data_Values.

PARAMETERS:
    ENTRY (out) - the table array to contain the data values
    FILE_NAME (in) - the name of the file containing the
      values
    SUCCESS (out) - return status (0 is successful)

TYPES REQUIRED:
    STRING79 - used for all strings
    DATA_ARRAY - used for defining the table of real values

SAMPLE CALL:
    Load_Data_Values (SCORES, 'scores.dat', ERROR);

NOTES:
    See Get_Data_Values and Put_Data_Values for more information.

------------------------------------------------------------}


  var
    ENTRY_FILE: file of DATA_ARRAY;        {actual data file}

  begin
    {$I-}

{open the data file}
    Assign (ENTRY_FILE, FILE_NAME);
    reset (ENTRY_FILE);
    SUCCESS := IOResult;

    if SUCCESS = 0 then
      begin

{read in the entire array}
        read (ENTRY_FILE, ENTRY);
        SUCCESS := IOResult;
      end;

    close (ENTRY_FILE);
    {$I+}
  end;
```

```
procedure Save_Data_Values (ENTRY: DATA_ARRAY;
                            FILE_NAME: STRING79;
                            var SUCCESS: byte);
{
DESCRIPTION:
    This procedure saves a group of data values that are
    used for data entry.  The numbers are in table form.

PARAMETERS:
    ENTRY (in) - the table array containing the data values
    FILE_NAME (in) - the name of the file to contain the
      values
    SUCCESS (out) - return status (0 is successful)

TYPES REQUIRED:
    STRING79 - used for all strings
    DATA_ARRAY - used for defining the table of real values

SAMPLE CALL:
    Save_Data_Values (SCORES, 'scores.dat', ERROR);

NOTES:
    See Get_Data_Values and Put_Data_Values for more information.

------------------------------------------------------------}

  var
    ENTRY_FILE: file of DATA_ARRAY;        {actual data file}

  begin
    {$I-}

{open an empty file}
    Assign (ENTRY_FILE, FILE_NAME);
    rewrite (ENTRY_FILE);
    SUCCESS := IOResult;

    if SUCCESS = 0 then
      begin

{write out the entire array}
        write (ENTRY_FILE, ENTRY);
        SUCCESS := IOResult;
      end;

    close (ENTRY_FILE);
    {$I+}
  end;
```

```
procedure Load_Form (var FORM: FORM_TYPE;
                     FILE_NAME: STRING79;
                     var SUCCESS: byte);
{
DESCRIPTION:
    This procedure loads a screen of information into an
    array for later display.  The form must have been
    previously saved with Save_Form.
```

```
PARAMETERS:
    FORM (out) - the array to contain the form
    FILE_NAME (in) - the name of the file containing the form
    SUCCESS (out) - return status (0 is successful)
TYPES REQUIRED:
    STRING79 - used for all strings
    FORM_TYPE - used for defining the form

SAMPLE CALL:
    Load_Form (FORM_LETTER, 'letter.dat', ERROR);

NOTES:
    See Get_Form and Put_Form for more information.

    ------------------------------------------------------------}


  var
    FORM_FILE: file of FORM_TYPE;      {actual form file}

  begin
    {$I-}

{open the existing file}
    Assign (FORM_FILE, FILE_NAME);
    reset (FORM_FILE);
    SUCCESS := IOResult;

    if SUCCESS = 0 then
      begin

{read in the entire form}
        read (FORM_FILE, FORM);
        SUCCESS := IOResult;
      end;

    close (FORM_FILE);
    {$I+}
  end;
```

```
procedure Save_Form (FORM: FORM_TYPE;
              FILE_NAME: STRING79;
              var SUCCESS: byte);
{
DESCRIPTION:
    This procedure saves an array of screen information
    for later retrieval.

PARAMETERS:
    FORM (in) - the array containing the form
    FILE_NAME (in) - the name of the file to contain the form
    SUCCESS (out) - return status (0 is successful)

TYPES REQUIRED:
    STRING79 - used for all strings
    FORM_TYPE - used for defining the form
```

```
SAMPLE CALL:
    Save_Form (FORM_LETTER, 'letter.dat', ERROR);

NOTES:
    See Get_Form and Put_Form for more information.

-----------------------------------------------------------}

  var
    FORM_FILE: file of FORM_TYPE;     {the actual file}

  begin
    {$I-}

{open and clear a file}
    Assign (FORM_FILE, FILE_NAME);
    rewrite (FORM_FILE);
    SUCCESS := IOResult;

    if SUCCESS = 0 then
      begin

{write out the entire form}
        write (FORM_FILE, FORM);
        SUCCESS := IOResult;
      end;

    close (FORM_FILE);
    {$I+}
  end;
```

11

Programming The Pipe

The pipe is a tool, supported by UNIX and DOS, that allows a user to make the output of one program become the input of a second program. For example, the command

```
DIR | SORT
```

causes the output of the directory command to become the input of the sort command. Since the origin of the pipe lies in UNIX, most programmers associate the pipe with C programs. However, Turbo Pascal makes this useful tool readily available to programs with a few simple compiler directives.

When you run a program, the operating system defines several default sources of input and output. Normally, the default input points to the keyboard and the default output to the screen. UNIX and DOS define these sources as **stdin** (standard input) and **stdout** (standard output). When you use the pipe, the operating system directs the input source of the second program to point to the output of the first program. For example, with the command

```
DIR | SORT
```

the operating system directs **stdout** of the directory command to **stdin** of the sort command, as shown here:

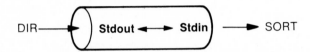

In addition to the pipe, UNIX and DOS support another form of I/O redirection that allows **stdin** and **stdout** to be modified so that they access data from or write data to a file. The command

```
DIR > X.DAT
```

writes the output of the directory command to the file X.DAT, instead of to the screen. Similarly, the command

```
SORT < X.DAT
```

allows the sort routine to obtain its input from the file X.DAT. You can include several pipes and redirections in the same command line, as shown here:

```
TAB < X.DAT | SORT > SRTTAB.DAT
```

This command line is equivalent to

```
TYPE X.DAT | TAB | SORT > SRTTAB.DAT
```

The >> operator allows users to append the output of a program to a file:

```
DIR *.PAS >> PASFILES.DAT
```

As you can see, the pipe and I/O redirection allow almost endless combinations.

Using the Pipe With Turbo Pascal

Two compiler directives enable the I/O redirection required to implement the pipe with Turbo Pascal. Input redirection is enabled through the **G** compiler directive (GET), and output redirection is enabled through the **P** (PUT).

To support redirection, the program must specify the buffer sizes used for I/O. By default, the buffer sizes are 0. The following compiler directive creates buffer sizes of 256 bytes. It should be placed at the beginning of programs that support I/O redirection.

```
{$G256, I256}
```

Consider the following program, which prints each line input from **stdin** preceded by line numbers. The program is invoked by using the pipe as follows:

```
DIR *.TOL | LINENUM
```

If the directory contains

```
 Volume in drive C has no label
 Directory of  C:\TURBO

COMMLINE TOL      1179    1-03-80    7:42p
STRINGS  TOL     13907    1-03-80    8:35a
MENUS    TOL     33844    1-03-80    8:42a
INOUT    TOL     25608    1-03-80    8:39a
         4 File(s)     739328 bytes free
```

then the output of the program is

```
1:
2:   Volume in drive C has no label
3:   Directory of  C:\TURBO
4:
5: COMMLINE TOL      1179    1-03-80    7:42p
6: STRINGS  TOL     13907    1-03-80    8:35a
7: MENUS    TOL     33844    1-03-80    8:42a
8: INOUT    TOL     25608    1-03-80    8:39a
9:          4 File(s)     737280 bytes free
```

Note the difference in the number of free bytes remaining in the two directory listings. When the pipe is used, the operating system creates temporary files. In this case, the size of the files was 2048 total bytes.

The program *LINENUM* is implemented in Turbo Pascal as follows:

```
{$G256,P256}

program Line_Number (input, output);

type
  STRING79 = string[79];

var
  LINE : STRING79;          {line read from stdin}
  COUNT: integer;           {current line number}

begin
  COUNT := 0;

{read each line from stdin and display it preceded by its line number}
  while (not EOF) do
    begin
      COUNT := COUNT + 1;
      Readln (LINE);
      Writeln (COUNT, ': ', LINE);
    end;
end.
```

The program *LINECNT* displays the total number of lines input from **stdin**. If the user issues the command

```
DIR *.TOL | LINECNT
```

the output is

```
linecnt: the number of lines is 9
```

Try invoking the routine without the pipe by typing **LINECNT** and pressing the ENTER key. The program will continue to read the data you input until you enter an end of file by pressing CTRL-Z. Since the pipe is not used, the operating system does not redirect **stdin** from the keyboard.

Here is the program *LINECNT*.

```
{$G256,P256}

program Line_Count (input, output);

type
   STRING79 = string[79];

var
   LINE : STRING79;          {line read from stdin}
   COUNT: integer;           {count of number of lines read}

begin

   COUNT := 0;

{read each record from stdin incrementing the count of the
 number of lines until end of file occurs}
   while (not EOF) do
     begin
       COUNT := COUNT + 1;
       Readln (LINE);
     end;
   writeln ('linecnt: the number of lines is ', COUNT);
end.
```

The redirection operators can be used with all of the remaining routines.

```
MORE < LINENUM.PAS
```

The routine *MORE*, similar to the **more** provided by UNIX and DOS, can be used like this: It will read and display text from **stdin** until a screen of information has been displayed. The program will then pause and prompt the user to press RETURN to continue. *MORE* must read the carriage return from **kbd**, instead of **stdin**. Since the operating system has redirected **stdin** away from the keyboard, the **read** statement must explicitly request user input from the keyboard. Here is the *MORE* routine:

```
{$G256,P256}

program More (input, output);

const
   SCREEN_SIZE = 24;          {number of lines to display on a screen}

type
   STRING79 = string[79];
```

```
var
  LINE : STRING79;            {line read from stdin}
  COUNT: integer;             {count of lines displayed}
begin
  COUNT := 0;

{read lines from stdin displaying them a page at a time.  Prompt the
user to press return with each screen of data}
  while (not EOF) do
    begin
      COUNT := COUNT + 1;
      Readln (LINE);
      Writeln (LINE);

{if a screen of information has been displayed, prompt the user
to press return}
      if (COUNT mod SCREEN_SIZE = 0) then
        begin
          Write ('more: <enter> to continue ');

{read the carriage return from the keyboard as opposed to stdin,
which has been redirected by the operating system}
          Readln (KBD);
          Writeln;
        end;

    end;
end.
```

The routine *TAB* allows the user to place tabs at the beginning of each line of text. The program is invoked as follows:

```
SOMEPROG | TAB [SPACES]
```

The **[SPACES]** is an optional command-line argument that specifies the number of spaces to place at the beginning of each line. The value must be in the range 0 to 31. If the user does not specify a value, the default value is 7. Here is the *TAB* routine:

```
{$G256,P256}

program Tab (input, output);

const
  DEFAULT_SPACES = 7;         {default number of spaces to tab}

type
  STRING79 = string[79];
  STRING131 = string[131];

{************************************************************}
function Add_Tabs (LINE: STRING131;
                   NUM_SPACES: integer): STRING131;
{
```

```
DESCRIPTION:
    This function pads the string contained in LINE with
    the number of spaces specifed.

VALUE RETURNED:
    The padded string

PARAMETERS:
    LINE: the string to pad with blanks
    NUM_SPACES: the number of blanks to pad the string with

TYPES REQUIRED:
    STRING132: string[131]

SAMPLE CALL:
    NEW_LINE := Add_Tabs ("UNTABBED LINE", 10);

-------------------------------------------------------------}

var
  TEMP: STRING131;       {the string returned to the calling routine}

begin
  FillChar (TEMP, NUM_SPACES, ' ');    {pad the string with the
                                        number of blanks specified}
  TEMP[0] := Chr(NUM_SPACES);          {new string length}
  Add_Tabs := TEMP + LINE;
end;


var
  LINE : STRING79;        {line read from stdin}
  NEW_LINE: STRING131;    {line padded with blanks}

  NUM_SPACES,             {number of spaces to pad}
  STATUS: integer;        {status of ASCII to integer conversion}

begin

{see if the user specified the number of spaces to tab}
  if (ParamCount = 0) then
    begin
      NUM_SPACES := DEFAULT_SPACES;
      STATUS := 0;
    end
  else
{user specified the number of spaces so convert it from ASCII}
    Val (ParamStr(1), NUM_SPACES, STATUS);

{make sure the number of spaces is valid}
  if ((STATUS <> 0) or (NUM_SPACES > 32)) then
    Writeln ('tab: invalid spacing ', ParamStr(1))
  else

{read each record from stdin and pad it with blanks}
    while (not EOF) do
      begin
        Readln (LINE);
        NEW_LINE := Add_Tabs (LINE, NUM_SPACES);
        Writeln (NEW_LINE);
      end;
end.
```

The program *COMP* compares the data input from **stdin** to a file. The program is invoked as follows:

```
SOMEPROG | COMP DATAFILE
```

The program compares the lines read from **stdin** to the contents of the file specified, and it displays either the line number and character location of the first difference, or the following message:

```
comp: program output is identical to file
```

Here is the program *COMP*:

```
{$G256,P256}

program Comp (input, output);

type
  STRING79 = string[79];

{$I STRINGS.TOL}

var
  FILE_LINE,              {line read from the file}
  PIPE_LINE: STRING79;    {line read from stdin}
  COMP_FILE: text;        {file to compare stdin to}

  DIFFERENT: boolean;     {true when a difference occurs}
  DIFF,                   {character location of the difference}
  LINE: integer;          {line location of the difference}

begin

{make sure the user has provided a file to compare stdin to}
  if (ParamCount = 0) then
    Writeln ('comp: invalid usage: comp filename')

{a file has been provided so compare each line from stdin to the
  contents of the file specified}
  else
    begin
      LINE := 1;
      DIFFERENT := false;

      Assign (COMP_FILE, ParamStr(1));
      {$I-} Reset (COMP_FILE) {$I+};
      if (IOresult <> 0) then
        Writeln ('comp: error opening the file ', ParamStr(1))
      else
        begin
          while (not DIFFERENT and (not Eof) and (not Eof(COMP_FILE))) do
            begin
              Readln (PIPE_LINE);
              Readln (COMP_FILE, FILE_LINE);
              DIFF := First_Difference (PIPE_LINE, FILE_LINE, false);
```

```
       if (DIFF <> 0) then
           DIFFERENT := true
       else if (Eof and (not Eof(COMP_FILE))) then
          begin
             DIFF := 0;
             DIFFERENT := true;
             LINE := LINE + 1;
          end
       else if (Eof(COMP_FILE) and (not Eof)) then
          begin
             DIFF := 0;
             DIFFERENT := true;
             LINE := LINE + 1;
          end
       else
          LINE := LINE + 1;
     end;

   if DIFFERENT then
     begin
        Writeln ('comp: first difference is line ', LINE,

                 ' character ', DIFF);

     if (not Eof) then
        begin
           if (Eof(COMP_FILE)) then
              Readln (PIPE_LINE);
           Writeln ('pipe input: ', PIPE_LINE);
        end;

     if (not Eof(COMP_FILE)) then
        begin
           if (Eof) then
              Readln (COMP_FILE, FILE_LINE);
           Writeln ('file input: ', FILE_LINE);
        end;
   end
 else
     Writeln ('comp: program output is identical to file');
 end;

  Close (COMP_FILE);
 end;
end.
```

The program *FINDWORD* examines each line input from **stdin** for a specific character string. The program is invoked in this manner:

```
SOMEPROG | FINDWORD WORD
```

However, the program can also be invoked by using

```
FINDWORD WORD < SOMEFILE
```

Here is the program *FINDWORD*:

```
{$G256,P256}

program Find_Word (input, output);

type
  STRING79 = string[79];

{$I STRINGS.TOL}

var
  LINE,                        {line read from stdin}
  SEARCH_STRING : STRING79;    {string to search for}

begin

{make sure the user provided a string to search for}
  if (ParamCount = 0) then
    Writeln ('findword: invalid useage: findword word')

{a string was provided so examine each record input from stdin
and print the records containing the word desired}
  else
    begin
      SEARCH_STRING := ParamStr(1);
      while (not EOF) do
        begin
          Readln (LINE);
          if (Str_Count (SEARCH_STRING, LINE, 0, true) <> 0) then
            Writeln (LINE);
        end;
    end;
end.
```

The *Str—Count* routine is defined in the chapter on strings.

PCRYPT allows the user to encrypt the output of a program as follows:

```
SOMEPROG | PCRYPT KEY
```

The program uses a key specified by the user to encrypt or decrypt data. The encryption is performed by exclusive ORing a letter from **stdin** with a letter from the key. To decrypt the data, the same key is used, and the exclusive OR reverses the processes. Following the exclusive OR of the characters, the only check performed by the program is a test for control characters. If the exclusive OR creates a control character, the output character is converted back to the original value. This prevents two characters from combining to form a CTRL-Z (end of file), which causes the program to terminate prematurely during decryption. Since the encryption algorithm is quite simplistic, you should use a complex key, such as ,./;'[]\.

Here is the *PCRYPT* routine:

```
{$G256,P256}

program Pcrypt (input, output);

type
  STRING79 = string [79];

var
  LINE,                        {line read from standard input}
  KEY : STRING79;              {the encryption/decryption key}
  I,                           {index into the line read}
  KEY_INDEX,                   {index into the encryption key}
  KEY_LENGTH: integer;         {length of the encryption key}

begin

{make sure the user provided an encryption/decryption key}
  if (ParamCount = 0) then
    Writeln ('pcrypt: no key specified')

{key provided so encrypt/decrypt the file}
  else
    begin
      KEY_INDEX := 1;
      KEY := ParamStr(1);
      KEY_LENGTH := Length(KEY);

{encrypt/decrypt each record read from stdin}
      while (not EOF) do
        begin
          Readln (LINE);
          for I := 1 to Length (LINE) do
            begin
              LINE[I] := Chr (Ord (LINE[I]) xor  Ord(KEY[KEY_INDEX]));

{if the new character is a control character, convert it back to the
 original character.  This prevents a CTRL-Z from indicating a
premature end of file.}
              if (Ord(LINE[I]) in [0..31]) then
                LINE[I] := Chr (Ord(LINE[I]) xor Ord(KEY[KEY_INDEX]));

{increment the key index to point to the next letter in the key}
              KEY_INDEX := (KEY_INDEX + 1) mod KEY_LENGTH;
            end;
          Writeln (LINE);
        end;
    end;
end.
```

The program *TEE* completes the piping concept by allowing output to proceed through the pipe to an output file. The command

```
DIR | TEE DIR.DAT | MORE
```

displays the directory one screen at a time. In addition, the directory contents are written to the file DIR.DAT. You can imagine the "tee" as follows:

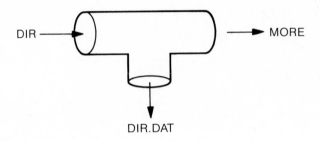

Here is the *TEE* program:

```
{$G256,P256}

program Tee (input, output);

type
  STRING79 = string[79];

var
  LINE    : STRING79;          {line read from stdin}
  TEE_FILE: text;              {the tee output file}

begin

{make sure the user provided an output file for the tee}
  if (ParamCount = 0) then
    Writeln ('tee: invalid useage: tee filename')

{an output file was provided so read each record from stdin and
 write it stdout and the output file}
    else
    begin
      Assign (TEE_FILE, ParamStr(1));
      {$I-} Rewrite (TEE_FILE) {$I+};
      if (IOresult <> 0) then
        Writeln ('tee: error opening the file ', ParamStr(1))
      else
        while (not EOF) do
          begin
            Readln (LINE);                {read from stdin}
            Writeln (TEE_FILE, LINE);     {write to tee output file}
            Writeln (LINE);               {write to stdout}
          end;
        Close (TEE_FILE);
    end;
end.
```

12

Turbo Toolbox

Any book on Turbo Pascal tools would be incomplete if it failed to mention Borland International's *Turbo Toolbox*. The Toolbox is a three-module package that allows even a novice Pascal programmer to develop programs of professional quality quickly. The package provides access to indexed files through the use of B-trees, a quick sort for files of records, and a terminal installation package that is generic.

Turbo ISAM

Most database packages require a great deal of disk access. Therefore, the retrieval speed of a program depends heavily on the time it takes the disk access routine to retrieve the desired record. For example, consider a database program that allows a telephone operator in a small town to look up phone numbers contained in a file like this one:

Adams, Alan K.	989-3331
Anderson, John A.	933-3443
Barnes, Terrie A.	443-3432
Byrd, James	453-1233
⋮	
Zane, Charles C.	542-3221

Imagine that the program reads each record in the file sequentially to search for the desired record. This method is called *sequential file access*. In this case, the program can quickly retrieve the number for Adams. However, if the operator must find Charles Zane's number, the retrieval time will be very long, because the program must read all of the preceding records. If the program were used in a large city like New York instead of in a small city, sequential access would be inappropriate.

In addition to sequential file access, most Pascal compilers support *random file access*, which retrieves records based upon record number. For example, each record in this random access file has a unique number that indicates its position in the file:

Record Number	Data	
0	Adams, Alan K.	989-3331
1	Anderson, John A.	933-3443
2	Barnes, Terrie A.	443-3432
3	Byrd, James	453-1233
⋮	⋮	
10003	Zane, Charles C.	542-3221

The routine **Seek** retrieves records based on the record number:

```
Seek (FILE_POINTER, RECORD_NUMBER);
```

To retrieve the phone number for Terrie Barnes in this example, a database program would perform the following statements.

```
Seek (FILE_POINTER, 2);
Get (PHONE_RECORD);
```

The disk access routine does not have to read each record preceding Barnes, so the retrieval time is much faster.

Although random access has decreased the retrieval time for a given record, it introduces a new problem: how is a particular name associated with a record number? Turbo's *ISAM* (Indexed Sequential Access Method) files solve this problem.

ISAM files use *keys* to retrieve specific records. For example, if you use the small-town phone book example, the key could be the name:

Key Field	*Other Data Fields*
Adams, Alan K.	989-3331
Anderson, John A.	933-3443
Barnes, Terrie A.	443-3432
Byrd, James	453-1233
:	
:	
Zane, Charles C.	542-3221

As shown in the following illustration, to retrieve a phone number, the operator simply specifies the name desired, which then becomes the key. Next, the ISAM disk access routines map the key to a record number and then retrieve the record by using random access.

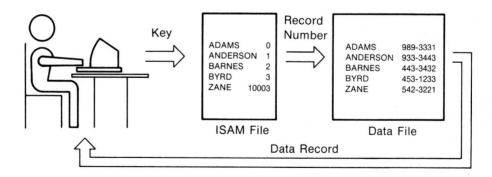

ISAM file applications often use two files. The first contains the actual data, as shown here:

Record Number	Data	
0	Adams, Alan K.	989-3331
1	Anderson, John A.	933-3443
2	Barnes, Terrie A.	443-3432
3	Byrd, James	453-1233
.	.	
.	.	
.	.	
10003	Zane, Charles C.	542-3221

The second contains indexes into the file, based upon keys:

Key Field	Record Number
Adams, Alan K.	0
Anderson, John A.	1
Barnes, Terrie A.	2
Byrd, James	3
.	.
.	.
.	.
Zane, Charles C.	10003

The format of the ISAM file is crucial to the speed of record retrieval. Each key and record-number combination is stored in a tree structure, as shown here:

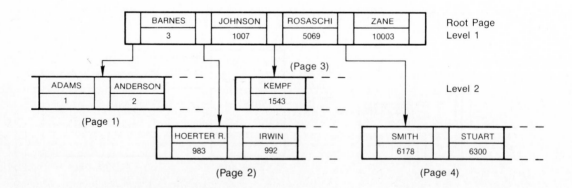

The tree is composed of several levels. The first level (level 1) is called the *root*. Each level contains items grouped into *pages*. Each entry in the page can point to additional levels; this creates paths that the routines use to locate key values. Pages with no references to lower levels are called *terminal pages*.

To locate a key, the retrieval algorithm starts at level 1 of the tree and sequentially examines each entry in the page for that particular key or another key that is larger than the key desired. If a larger key is found, the routine follows the pointer to the next level and continues the same process. The search for the key ends if the desired key is found or if the page does not contain pointers to other levels.

In the example just given, if the operator needs the phone number for R. Hoerter, the access routines can retrieve the record number by first reading Johnson and then reading Hoerter.

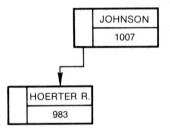

Before examining the Turbo Tools implementation of ISAM files, you should examine several concepts that are critical to the tree structure. As previously stated, each key and record-number combination is an entry in the tree, with the key and the record number forming separate fields. Turbo ISAM defines this entry as an item and adds to it a third field, which acts as an index to help manipulate the tree structure, as shown here:

	Key	
Internal Reference	Data File Record Number	

While it is apparent that storing the indexes to records in this manner speeds up file access, there are several factors that can adversely affect retrieval speed. If the page size is too large, time will be wasted while the routine sequentially searches for items in the page for a matching key. If the page size is too small, the increased number of traversals required to access a key will slow retrieval time.

The *B-tree* (not to be confused with the binary tree) is a multidirectional tree that minimizes retrieval time by restricting the number of nodes in any page to a value between n and $2n$. The value of n equals the order of the tree. B-trees of order n have these four characteristics:

1. Each page contains a maximum of $2n$ keys.

2. Each page, except the root page, contains at least n keys.

3. Each page either is a terminal page (one with no descendents) or has $k+1$ descendents, where k is the number of keys in the page.

4. All terminal pages occur at the same level.

Turbo ISAM requires that you define the following constants with each application:

- **MaxDataRecSize**, the maximum size (in bytes) of the largest record that the program will access. If the routine uses multiple data files, set **MaxDataRecSize** to the largest record to be used.

- **MaxKeyLen**, the maximum size (in bytes) of the largest key that the program will use. If the program uses multiple files, set **MaxKeyLen** to the largest key to be used.

- **PageSize**, the maximum number of items allowed in each page. **PageSize** must be the same for all of the files accessed by a program, and it should be set to an integer value between 4 and 254. A value of 16 or 32 will usually be sufficient; a smaller value will require more disk accesses, which slows the process.

- **Order**, the minimum number of items allowed in a page. **Order** should be defined as half of **PageSize**.

- **PageStackSize**, the number of pages kept in memory at one time. Increasing **PageStackSize** usually decreases the access time. Increasing this value consumes the memory available to a program. The minimum **PageStackSize** is 3; for best performance make **PageStackSize** as large as you can.

- **MaxHeight**, the maximum number of levels in the B-tree.

Establishing the correct values for many of these parameters is not an easy task. Larger databases may require some trial and error before the file parameters are efficient.

The skeleton program of the phone book example is as follows:

```
program Phone_Company ;

 const
{ required TURBO ISAM constants }
    MaxDataRecSize = 240;   { 3 fields of 80 characters }
    MaxKeyLen = 30;         { maximum length of key }
    PageSize = 16;          { number of entries in a page }
    Order = 8;              { half of PageSize - mimimum number of }
                            { entries in a page }
    PageStackSize = 5;      { number of pages in memory }
    MaxHeight = 5;          { maximum number of levels in the tree }

{ user-defined constants }
    NO_DUPLICATES = 0;      { no duplicate records allowed }
    DUPLICATES = 1;         { duplicate records allowed }
type
    STRING79 = string[79];

    LISTING = record
      NAME,
      ADDRESS,
      PHONE   : STRING79;
    end;


{$I ACCESS3.BOX}
{$I GETKEY.BOX}
{$I ADDKEY.BOX}
{$I DELKEY.BOX}

{ user-defined routines }

var
   PHONE_BOOK : DataFile;
   PHONE_INDEX: IndexFile;

begin

{ main program here }

end.
```

Most database applications require the following capabilities:

- Adding records to the database
- Deleting records from the database
- Retrieving records from the database
- Updating records in the database.

Turbo Toolbox provides functions to support each of these requirements. However, before examining these routines, this chapter will outline the routines that create, open, and initialize both indexed and data files.

Data File Routines

The following routines support database management of data files for Turbo ISAM:

```
procedure Make (FILE_POINTER, FILE_NAME, RECORD_LENGTH);
{
DESCRIPTION:
    This routine creates a new data file for processing
    by TURBO ISAM.

PARAMETERS:
    FILE_POINTER (out) - pointer to the data file
    FILE_NAME (in) - the name of the data file
    RECORD_LENGTH (in) - the number of bytes in each record

TYPES REQUIRED:
    DataFile - FILE_POINTER must be the type DataFile.

SAMPLE CALL:
    MakeFile (FILE_POINTER, 'DATA.DAT', Sizeof (RECORD_USED));

NOTES:
    FILE_NAME is string[14].
    RECORD_LENGTH is type integer.

---------------------------------------------------------}
```

```
OpenFile (FILE_POINTER, FILE_NAME, RECORD_LENGTH);
{
DESCRIPTION:
    This routine opens an existing file and prepares it for
    processing by TURBO ISAM.

PARAMETERS:
    FILE_POINTER (out) - pointer to the data file
    FILE_NAME (in) - the name of the data file
    RECORD_LENGTH (in) - the number of bytes in each record

TYPES REQUIRED:
    DataFile - FILE_POINTER must be the type DataFile.

SAMPLE CALL:
    OpenFile (FILE_POINTER, 'DATA.DAT', Sizeof (RECORD_USED));

NOTES:
    FILE_NAME is string[14].
    RECORD_LENGTH is type integer.

---------------------------------------------------------}
```

```
CloseFile (FILE_POINTER);
{
DESCRIPTION:
    This routine closes a data file.

PARAMETERS:
    FILE_POINTER (in) - pointer to the data file

TYPES REQUIRED:
    DataFile - FILE_POINTER must be the type DataFile.

SAMPLE CALL:
    CloseFile (FILE_POINTER);

------------------------------------------------------------}
```

Indexed File Routines
For Turbo ISAM

The following routines support database maintenance of indexed files for Turbo ISAM:

```
InitIndex ;
{
DESCRIPTION:
    This routine initializes the tables used by the indexed
    files.

PARAMETERS:
    NONE

TYPES REQUIRED:
    NONE

SAMPLE CALL:
    InitIndex;

NOTES:
    This routine must be called prior to all of the TURBO
    ISAM indexed file routines.  The routine is invoked
    once, normally as the first statement of a program.

------------------------------------------------------------}
```

```
procedure MakeIndex (FILE_INDEX, FILE_NAME, KEY_LENGTH, STATUS);
{
DESCRIPTION:
    This routine creates a new indexed file for processing
    by TURBO ISAM.

PARAMETERS:
    FILE_INDEX (out) - pointer to the indexed file
```

```
        FILE_NAME (in) - the name of the indexed file
        RECORD_LENGTH (in) - the number of bytes in the key
        STATUS (in) - 1 if duplicate keys are allowed
                      0 if no duplicate keys are allowed

TYPES REQUIRED:
    IndexFile - FILE_INDEX must be the type IndexFile.

SAMPLE CALL:
    MakeIndex (FILE_INDEX, 'DATA.IDX', MaxKeyLen, 1);

NOTES:
    FILE_NAME is string[14].
    KEY_LENGTH and STATUS are type integer.

------------------------------------------------------------}
```

```
OpenIndex (FILE_INDEX, FILE_NAME, KEY_LENGTH, STATUS);
{
DESCRIPTION:
    This routine opens an existing indexed file and prepares
    it for processing by TURBO ISAM.

PARAMETERS:
    FILE_INDEX (out) - pointer to the indexed file
    FILE_NAME (in) - the name of the indexed file
    RECORD_LENGTH (in) - the number of bytes in the key
    STATUS (in) - 1 if duplicate keys are allowed
                  0 if no duplicate keys are allowed

TYPES REQUIRED:
    IndexFile - FILE_INDEX must be the type IndexFile.

SAMPLE CALL:
    MakeIndex (FILE_INDEX, 'DATA.IDX', MaxKeyLen, 1);

NOTES:
    FILE_NAME is string[14].
    KEY_LENGTH and STATUS are type integer.

------------------------------------------------------------}
```

```
CloseIndex (FILE_INDEX);
{
DESCRIPTION:
    This routine closes an indexed file.

PARAMETERS:
    FILE_INDEX (in) - pointer to the indexed file.

TYPES REQUIRED:
    IndexFile - FILE_INDEX must be the type IndexFile.

SAMPLE CALL:
    CloseIndex (FILE_INDEX);

------------------------------------------------------------}
```

Data File Routines of Turbo Toolbox

The following Turbo Toolbox routines support database maintenance of data files:

```
AddRec (FILE_POINTER, RECORD_NUMBER, DATA_RECORD);
{
DESCRIPTION:
    This routine adds a record to a data file.

PARAMETERS:
    FILE_POINTER (in) - pointer to the data file
    RECORD_NUMBER (in) - record number of the new entry
    DATA_RECORD (in) - data record to be added to the file

TYPES REQUIRED:
    DataFile - FILE_POINTER must be the type DataFile.

SAMPLE CALL:
    AddRec (FILE_POINTER, RECORD_NUMBER, DATA_RECORD);

NOTES:
    DATA_RECORD is passed to AddRec as an untyped variable.

-----------------------------------------------------------}
```

```
DelRec (FILE_POINTER, RECORD_NUMBER)
{
DESCRIPTION:
    This routine deletes a record from a data file.

PARAMETERS:
    FILE_POINTER (in) - pointer to the data file
    RECORD_NUMBER (in) - record number to delete

TYPES REQUIRED:
    DataFile - FILE_POINTER must be the type DataFile.

SAMPLE CALL:
    DelRec (FILE_POINTER, RECORD_NUMBER);

NOTES:
    The record is added to the deleted record list so the file
    space can be reused before the file is expanded for future
    records.

-----------------------------------------------------------}
```

```
GetRec (FILE_POINTER, RECORD_NUMBER, DATA_RECORD);
{
DESCRIPTION:
    This routine returns a record contained in a data file.

PARAMETERS:
    FILE_POINTER (in) - pointer to the data file
    RECORD_NUMBER (in) - record number to retrieve
    DATA_RECORD (in) - data record retrieved from the file

TYPES REQUIRED:
    DataFile - FILE_POINTER must be the type DataFile.

SAMPLE CALL:
    GetRec (FILE_POINTER, RECORD_NUMBER, DATA_RECORD);

NOTES:
    DATA_RECORD is passed to GetRec as an untyped variable.

-----------------------------------------------------------}
```

```
PutRec (FILE_POINTER, RECORD_NUMBER, DATA_RECORD)
{
DESCRIPTION:
    This routine replaces a record in a data file.

PARAMETERS:
    FILE_POINTER (in) - pointer to the data file
    RECORD_NUMBER (in) - record number to delete
    DATA_RECORD (in) - data record retrieved from the file

TYPES REQUIRED:
    DataFile - FILE_POINTER must be the type DataFile.

SAMPLE CALL:
    PutRec (FILE_POINTER, RECORD_NUMBER, DATA_RECORD);

NOTES:
    DATA_RECORD is passed to GetRec as an untyped variable.

-----------------------------------------------------------}
```

```
function FileLen (FILE_POINTER): integer;
{
DESCRIPTION:
    This routine returns the number of records in a data
    file.

PARAMETERS:
    FILE_POINTER (in) - pointer to the data file

TYPES REQUIRED:
    DataFile - FILE_POINTER must be the type DataFile.
```

```
SAMPLE CALL:
    writeln ('Number of records ', FileLen (FILE_POINTER));

NOTES:
    The length returned includes records contained in the
    deleted record list.

    ----------------------------------------------------------}
```

```
function UsedRecs (FILE_POINTER): integer;
{
DESCRIPTION:
    This routine returns the number of records in a data
    file that are being used.

PARAMETERS:
    FILE_POINTER (in) - pointer to the data file

TYPES REQUIRED:
    DataFile - FILE_POINTER must be the type DataFile.

SAMPLE CALL:
    writeln ('Number of records used ', UsedRecs (FILE_POINTER));

    ----------------------------------------------------------}
```

Indexed File Routines
Of Turbo Toolbox

The following Turbo Toolbox routines support database maintenance
for indexed files:

```
AddKey (FILE_INDEX, RECORD_NUMBER, KEY);
{
DESCRIPTION:
    This routine adds a key string to an indexed file.

PARAMETERS:
    FILE_INDEX (in) - pointer to the indexed file.
    RECORD_NUMBER (in) - record number of the data record
                         associated with the key.
    KEY (in) - key associated with the data record.

TYPES REQUIRED:
    IndexFile - FILE_INDEX must be the type IndexFile.

SAMPLE CALL:
    AddKey (FILE_INDEX, RECORD_NUMBER, KEY);
```

```
NOTES:
     RECORD_NUMBER is type integer.
     KEY is passed to AddKey as an untyped variable.
     The global variable OK is set to true if the
     key is successfully added; otherwise it is false.

----------------------------------------------------------}
```

```
DelKey (FILE_INDEX, RECORD_NUMBER, KEY);
{
DESCRIPTION:
     This routine deletes a key string from an indexed file.

PARAMETERS:
     FILE_INDEX (in) - pointer to the indexed file
     RECORD_NUMBER (in) - record number of the data record
                          associated with the key
     KEY (in) - key associated with the data record

TYPES REQUIRED:
     IndexFile - FILE_INDEX must be the type IndexFile.

SAMPLE CALL:
     DelKey (FILE_INDEX, RECORD_NUMBER, KEY);

NOTES:
     RECORD_NUMBER is type integer.
     KEY is passed to AddKey as an untyped variable.
     The global variable OK is set to true if the
     key is successfully deleted; false if not.

----------------------------------------------------------}
```

```
FindKey (FILE_INDEX, RECORD_NUMBER, KEY);
{
DESCRIPTION:
     This routine returns the record number associated with
     a key string to an indexed file.

PARAMETERS:
     FILE_INDEX (in) - pointer to the indexed file
     RECORD_NUMBER (out) - record number of the data record
                           associated with the key
     KEY (in) - key associated with the data record

TYPES REQUIRED:
     IndexFile - FILE_INDEX must be the type IndexFile.

SAMPLE CALL:
     FindKey (FILE_INDEX, RECORD_NUMBER, KEY);

NOTES:
     RECORD_NUMBER is type integer.
```

```
    KEY is passed to AddKey as an untyped variable.
    The global variable OK is set to true if the
    key is found; false if not.
    If duplicate records are allowed, FindKey will
    return the record number of the first match.

------------------------------------------------------------}
```

```
    SearchKey (FILE_INDEX, RECORD_NUMBER, KEY);
    {
    DESCRIPTION:
        This routine returns the record number associated with
        the first key string that is greater to or equal to
        the key specified.

    PARAMETERS:
        FILE_INDEX (in) - pointer to the indexed file
        RECORD_NUMBER (out) - record number of the data record
                              associated with the key
        KEY (in) - key associated with the data record

    TYPES REQUIRED:
        IndexFile - FILE_INDEX must be the type IndexFile.

    SAMPLE CALL:
        SearchKey (FILE_INDEX, RECORD_NUMBER, KEY);

    NOTES:
        RECORD_NUMBER is type integer.
        KEY is passed to AddKey as an untyped variable.
        The global variable OK is set to true if the
        key is found; false if not.

------------------------------------------------------------}
```

```
    NextKey (FILE_INDEX, RECORD_NUMBER, KEY);
    {                                          `
    DESCRIPTION:
        This routine returns the record number associated with
        the next key in the indexed file.

    PARAMETERS:
        FILE_INDEX (in) - pointer to the indexed file
        RECORD_NUMBER (in/out) - record number of the data record
                                 associated with the key
        KEY (in) - key associated with the data record

    TYPES REQUIRED:
        IndexFile - FILE_INDEX must be the type IndexFile.

    SAMPLE CALL:
        NextKey (FILE_INDEX, RECORD_NUMBER, KEY);
```

```
NOTES:
    RECORD_NUMBER is type integer.
    KEY is passed to AddKey as an untyped variable.
    The global variable OK is set to true if the
    key is found; false if not.

    ------------------------------------------------------------}
```

```
PrevKey (FILE_INDEX, RECORD_NUMBER, KEY);
{
DESCRIPTION:
    This routine returns the record number associated with
    the preceding key in the indexed file.

PARAMETERS:
    FILE_INDEX (in) - pointer to the indexed file
    RECORD_NUMBER (in/out) - record number of the data record
                             associated with the key
    KEY (in) - key associated with the data record

TYPES REQUIRED:
    IndexFile - FILE_INDEX must be the type IndexFile.

SAMPLE CALL:
    PrevKey (FILE_INDEX, RECORD_NUMBER, KEY);

NOTES:
    RECORD_NUMBER is type integer.
    KEY is passed to AddKey as an untyped variable.
    The global variable OK is set to true if the
    key is found; false if not.

    ------------------------------------------------------------}
```

```
ClearKey (FILE_INDEX);
{
DESCRIPTION:
    This routine resets the pointer to the beginning of an
    indexed file for sequential processing.

PARAMETERS:
    FILE_INDEX (out) - pointer to the indexed file

TYPES REQUIRED:
    IndexFile - FILE_INDEX must be the type IndexFile.

SAMPLE CALL:
    ClearKey (FILE_INDEX);

    ------------------------------------------------------------}
```

A Complete Phone Book Program

The complete phone book program allows the operator to add, delete, list, and update entries in the phone book. In addition, the procedure *Display—Database—Statistics* displays the number of records contained and being used in the database. The program uses several of the programming tools introduced in previous chapters.

```
program Phone_Company ;

label END_PROGRAM;

const
  MaxDataRecSize = 240;   { 3 fields of 80 characters }
  MaxKeyLen = 30;         { maximum length of key }
  PageSize = 16;          { number of entries in a page }
  Order = 8;              { half of PageSize }
  PageStackSize = 5;      { number of pages in memory }
  MaxHeight = 5;          { maximum number of levels in the tree }
  NO_DUPLICATES = 0;      { no duplicate records allowed }

{ define video attributes }
  BOLD = 1;

type
  STRING79 = string[79];

type

  LISTING = record
    NAME,
    ADDRESS,
    PHONE  : STRING79;
  end;


{$I ACCESS3.BOX}    {TURBO TOOLBOX DECLARATIONS}
{$I GETKEY.BOX}
{$I ADDKEY.BOX}
{$I DELKEY.BOX}


{$I STRINGS.TOL}    {DECLARATIONS FROM CHAPTER 5}
{$I INOUT.TOL}      {DECLARATIONS FROM CHAPTER 7}
{$I MENUS.TOL}      {DECLARATIONS FROM CHAPTER 8}

const

  MAIN_MENU : MENU_REC = (
    NUM_CHOICES : 6;           { number of menu choices }
    MENU_WIDTH : 45;
    CHOICES    : '12345E      ';
```

```
            DESCRIPTIONS: ('Display A Phone Listing',
                           'Add A New Listing',
                           'Delete A Current Listing',
                           'Update A Current Listing',
                           'View Database Statistics',
                           'Exit Phone Company Program',
                           '','', '','','','','','');
            TITLE        : 'PHONE COMPANY MAIN MENU';
            PROMPT       : 'Type in choice: or use arrows and press <ENTER>');


procedure Display_Phone_Listing (var PHONE_BOOK : DataFile;
                                 var PHONE_INDEX: IndexFile);
var
   PHONE_LISTING : LISTING;
   RESPONSE      : STRING79;   { user response to prompt }
   ENTRY_NUMBER,              { record number }
   I             : integer;

begin
   with PHONE_LISTING do
     begin
        ClrScr;
        Display_Frame (7, 70);
        Put_Centered_String ('Display Phone Listing', 9, 2);

{ get the name to display }
        NAME := '';
        Put_String ('Name:    ' + NAME, 11, 10, 0);
        Get_Prompted_String (NAME, BOLD, 30, 'NAME:     ', 11, 10,
          'Type in the name to display', 23, 2);

{ pad the name with blanks }
        for I := Length (NAME) to MaxKeyLen do
          NAME := NAME + ' ';

{ convert the name to UPPERCASE }
        Str_To_Uppercase (NAME);

{ find the entry in the file }
        FindKey (PHONE_INDEX, ENTRY_NUMBER, NAME);

        if OK then   { entry exists }
          begin
            GetRec (PHONE_BOOK, ENTRY_NUMBER, PHONE_LISTING);
            Put_String ('Name:    ' + NAME, 11, 10, 0);
            Put_String ('Phone:   ' + PHONE, 12, 10, 0);
            Put_String ('Address: ' + ADDRESS, 13, 10, 0);
          end
        else
          Put_String ('Entry not found in phone book', 13, 10, 0);

        RESPONSE := '';
        Get_Prompted_String (RESPONSE, BOLD, 1, '', 23, 30,
          'Press <enter> to continue', 23, 2);

     end;  { with }
   end;


procedure Duplicate_Record (NAME: STRING79);
var
   RESPONSE: STRING79;   { user response }
```

```
   begin
     ClrScr;
     Display_Frame (8, 70);
     Put_Centered_String ('Duplicate Listing', 9, 2);

     Put_String ('Duplicate Name ' + NAME, 11, 10, 0);
     Put_String ('Record will not be added', 13, 10, 0);

     RESPONSE := '';
     Get_Prompted_String (RESPONSE, BOLD, 1, '', 23, 30,
       'Press <enter> to continue', 23, 2);
   end;


procedure Add_Phone_Listing (var PHONE_BOOK : DataFile;
                             var PHONE_INDEX: IndexFile);
var
  DONE, NAME_OK, PHONE_OK, ADDRESS_OK: boolean;
  NEW_LISTING : LISTING;
  RESPONSE    : STRING79;   { user response to prompt }
  ENTRY_NUMBER,            { record number }
  I           : integer;

begin
  with NEW_LISTING do
    begin
      ClrScr;
      Display_Frame (7, 70);
      Put_Centered_String ('Add Phone Listing', 9, 2);

      NAME := ''; PHONE := ''; ADDRESS := '';
      NAME_OK := false; PHONE_OK := false; ADDRESS_OK := false;
      DONE := false;  { true when all entries are valid }
{ get the name, phone number, and address of the new entry }
      repeat
        Put_String ('Name:    ' + NAME, 11, 10, 0);
        Put_String ('Phone:   ' + PHONE, 12, 10, 0);
        Put_String ('Address: ' + ADDRESS, 13, 10, 0);

        if (not NAME_OK) then
          begin
            Get_Prompted_String (NAME, BOLD, 30, 'NAME:    ', 11, 10,
              'Type in the name of the new listing', 23, 2);
            NAME_OK := true;
            for I := Length (NAME) to MaxKeyLen do
              NAME := NAME + ' ';
            Str_To_Uppercase (NAME);  { convert the name to UPPERCASE }
          end;

        if (not PHONE_OK) then
          begin
            Get_Prompted_String (PHONE, BOLD, 8, 'PHONE:   ', 12, 10,
              'Type in the phone number of the new listing', 23, 2);
            PHONE_OK := true;
          end;

        if (not ADDRESS_OK) then
          begin
            Get_Prompted_String (ADDRESS, BOLD, 50, 'ADDRESS: ', 13, 10,
              'Type in the address of the new listing', 23, 2);
            ADDRESS_OK := true;
          end;
```

```
                    Put_String ('Press <Enter>; or type N, P, A to modify an entry',
                      23, 2, 0);

        { highlight the options N P A in bold }
                    Put_String ('N', 11, 10, 2);
                    Put_String ('P', 12, 10, 2);
                    Put_String ('A', 13, 10, 2);
                    Put_String ('N', 23, 25, 2);
                    Put_String ('P', 23, 28, 2);
                    Put_String ('A', 23, 31, 2);

                    RESPONSE := '';
                    Get_Prompted_String (RESPONSE, BOLD, 1, '', 23, 55, '', 23, 55);

                    if (Length(RESPONSE) = 0) then
                      DONE := true
                    else
                      case (Upcase(RESPONSE[1])) of
                        'N' : NAME_OK    := false;
                        'P' : PHONE_OK   := false;
                        'A' : ADDRESS_OK := false;
                        else writeln (Chr(7)); { bell }
                      end;

              until DONE;

        { find out if the user wants to store the record }
              repeat
                    Put_String ('Type Y to add entry; Q to quit', 23, 2, 0);
                    Put_String ('Y', 23, 7, 2);
                    Put_String ('Q', 23, 23, 2);
                    Get_Prompted_String (RESPONSE, BOLD, 1,
                      'Store New Listing (Y/Q)? ', 15, 10, '', 23, 35);

                    if (Length (RESPONSE) = 0) then
                      write(Chr(7))
                    else if (not (RESPONSE[1] in ['Y','Q','y', 'q'])) then
                      write(Chr(7));
                    until (RESPONSE[1] in ['Y', 'Q', 'y', 'q']);

                if (RESPONSE[1] in ['Y', 'y']) then
                  begin

        { check for a duplicate record }

                        FindKey (PHONE_INDEX, ENTRY_NUMBER, NAME);
                        if OK then
                          Duplicate_Record (NAME)
                        else
                          begin

        { add the record and index }
                            AddRec (PHONE_BOOK, ENTRY_NUMBER, NEW_LISTING);
                            AddKey (PHONE_INDEX, ENTRY_NUMBER, NAME);
                          end;
                  end;

              end; { with }
            end;
```

```
procedure Delete_Phone_Listing  (var PHONE_BOOK : DataFile;
                                 var PHONE_INDEX: IndexFile);
var
  DONE, NAME_OK, PHONE_OK, ADDRESS_OK: boolean;
  PHONE_LISTING: LISTING;
  RESPONSE     : STRING79;  { user response to prompt }
  ENTRY_NUMBER,            { record number }
  I            : integer;

begin
  with PHONE_LISTING do
    begin
      ClrScr;
      Display_Frame (7, 70);
      Put_Centered_String ('Delete Phone Listing', 9, 2);

{ get the name to delete }
      NAME := '';
      Put_String ('Name:    ' + NAME, 11, 10, 0);
      Get_Prompted_String (NAME, BOLD, 30, 'NAME:     ', 11, 10,
        'Type in the name to display', 23, 2);

{ pad the name with blanks }
      for I := Length (NAME) to MaxKeyLen do
        NAME := NAME + ' ';

{ convert the name to UPPERCASE }
      Str_To_Uppercase (NAME);

{ see if the entry exists }
      FindKey (PHONE_INDEX, ENTRY_NUMBER, NAME);

      if OK then   { entry exists }
        begin
          GetRec (PHONE_BOOK, ENTRY_NUMBER, PHONE_LISTING);
          Put_String ('Name:    ' + NAME, 11, 10, 0);
          Put_String ('Phone:   ' + PHONE, 12, 10, 0);
          Put_String ('Address: ' + ADDRESS, 13, 10, 0);

{ make sure the user wants to delete the entry }
          Put_String ('Type <enter> to continue; D to delete record',
            23, 2, 0);
          Put_String ('D', 23, 28, 2);

          RESPONSE := '';
          Get_Prompted_String (RESPONSE, BOLD, 1, '', 23, 50,
            '', 23, 50);

          if (Length(RESPONSE) > 0) then
            if (RESPONSE[1] in ['D', 'd']) then
              begin
                DeleteKey (PHONE_INDEX, ENTRY_NUMBER, NAME);
                DeleteRec (PHONE_BOOK, ENTRY_NUMBER);
              end;

        end
      else
        Put_String (NAME + ' not found in phone book', 13, 10, 0);

    end; { with }
end;
```

```
procedure Update_Phone_Listing (var PHONE_BOOK : DataFile;
                                var PHONE_INDEX: IndexFile);
var
  DONE, NAME_OK, PHONE_OK, ADDRESS_OK: boolean;
  PHONE_LISTING        : LISTING;
  RESPONSE             : STRING79;   { user response to prompt }
  ORIGINAL_ENTRY_NUMBER,             { record number of record to update }
  ENTRY_NUMBER,                      { used to check for duplicate record }
  I                    : integer;

begin
  with PHONE_LISTING do
    begin
      ClrScr;
      Display_Frame (7, 70);
      Put_Centered_String ('Update Phone Listing', 9, 2);

      NAME := '';
      NAME_OK := false; PHONE_OK := false; ADDRESS_OK := false;
      DONE := false;  { true when all entries are valid }

{ get the name to update }
      Put_String ('Name:    ' + NAME, 11, 10, 0);
      Get_Prompted_String (NAME, BOLD, 30, 'NAME:    ', 11, 10,
        'Type in the name to update', 23, 2);

{ pad the name with blanks }
      for I := Length (NAME) to MaxKeyLen do
        NAME := NAME + ' ';

{ convert the name to UPPERCASE }
      Str_To_Uppercase (NAME);

{ see if the record exists }
      FindKey (PHONE_INDEX, ORIGINAL_ENTRY_NUMBER, NAME);

      if OK then    { record exists }
        begin
          GetRec (PHONE_BOOK, ORIGINAL_ENTRY_NUMBER, PHONE_LISTING);
          Put_String ('Name:    ' + NAME, 11, 10, 0);
          Put_String ('Phone:   ' + PHONE, 12, 10, 0);
          Put_String ('Address: ' + ADDRESS, 13, 10, 0);

{ update the name, phone number, and address of the entry }
          repeat
            Put_String ('Name:    ' + NAME, 11, 10, 0);
            Put_String ('Phone:   ' + PHONE, 12, 10, 0);
            Put_String ('Address: ' + ADDRESS, 13, 10, 0);

            if (not NAME_OK) then
              begin
                Get_Prompted_String (NAME, BOLD, 30, 'NAME:    ', 11, 10,
                  'Type in the name of the updated listing', 23, 2);
                for I := Length (NAME) to MaxKeyLen do
                  NAME := NAME + ' ';
                NAME_OK := true;
              end;

            if (not PHONE_OK) then
              begin
                Get_Prompted_String (PHONE, BOLD, 8, 'PHONE:   ', 12, 10,
                  'Type in the phone number of the updated listing', 23, 2);
                PHONE_OK := true;
              end;
```

```
                  if (not ADDRESS_OK) then
                    begin
                      Get_Prompted_String (ADDRESS, BOLD, 50, 'ADDRESS: ', 13, 10,
                        'Type in the address of the updated listing', 23, 2);
                      ADDRESS_OK := true;
                    end;

                  Put_String ('Press <Enter>; or type N, P, A to modify an entry',
                    23, 2, 0);

{ highlight the options N P A in bold }
                  Put_String ('N', 11, 10, 2);
                  Put_String ('P', 12, 10, 2);
                  Put_String ('A', 13, 10, 2);
                  Put_String ('N', 23, 25, 2);
                  Put_String ('P', 23, 28, 2);
                  Put_String ('A', 23, 31, 2);

{ does the user want to modify fields? }
                  RESPONSE := '';
                  Get_Prompted_String (RESPONSE, BOLD, 1, '', 23, 55, '', 23, 55);

                  if (Length(RESPONSE) = 0) then
                    DONE := true
                  else
                    case (Upcase(RESPONSE[1])) of
                      'N' : NAME_OK    := false;
                      'P' : PHONE_OK   := false;
                      'A' : ADDRESS_OK := false;
                      else writeln (Chr(7)); { bell }
                    end;

              until DONE;

{ make sure the user wants to store the entry }
              repeat
                Put_String ('Type Y to add entry; Q to quit', 23, 2, 0);
                Put_String ('Y', 23, 7, 2);
                Put_String ('Q', 23, 23, 2);
                Get_Prompted_String (RESPONSE, BOLD, 1,
                  'Store New Listing (Y/Q)? ', 15, 10, '', 23, 35);

                if (Length (RESPONSE) = 0) then
                  write(Chr(7))
                else if (not (RESPONSE[1] in ['Y','Q','y', 'q'])) then
                  write(Chr(7));
              until (RESPONSE[1] in ['Y', 'Q', 'y', 'q']);

              if (RESPONSE[1] in ['Y', 'y']) then
                begin
{ check for duplicate records }
                  FindKey (PHONE_INDEX, ENTRY_NUMBER, NAME);
                  if (OK and (ORIGINAL_ENTRY_NUMBER <> ENTRY_NUMBER))  then
                    Duplicate_Record (NAME)
                  else
                    PutRec (PHONE_BOOK, ENTRY_NUMBER, PHONE_LISTING);
                end;

            end
          else
            begin
              Put_String ('Entry not found in phone book', 13, 10, 0);
```

```
                    RESPONSE := '';
                    Get_Prompted_String (RESPONSE, BOLD, 1, '', 23, 30,
                      'Press <enter> to continue', 23, 2);
                 end;

        end;  { with }
    end;

procedure Display_Database_Statistics (var PHONE_BOOK : DataFile);
var
   RESPONSE: STRING79;

begin
   ClrScr;
   Display_Frame (8, 70);
   Put_Centered_String ('Database Statistics', 9, 2);

   gotoxy (10, 11);
   writeln ('The database contains ', FileLen (PHONE_BOOK), ' records');
   gotoxy (10, 13);
   writeln ('The number of records used is ', UsedRecs (PHONE_BOOK));
   RESPONSE := '';
   Get_Prompted_String (RESPONSE, BOLD, 1, '', 23, 30,
      'Press <enter> to continue', 23, 2);
end;


{------------------------------------------------------------------------}
{                        M A I N    P R O G R A M                        }
{------------------------------------------------------------------------}

var
   MAIN_CHOICE: char;      { user choice from menu }
   RESPONSE   : STRING79;

   PHONE_BOOK : DataFile;
   PHONE_INDEX: IndexFile;

begin
        RESPONSE := '';
        InitIndex ;

{ open the data and indexed file }
        OpenFile (PHONE_BOOK, 'PHONE.DAT', Sizeof (LISTING));
        if OK then
           OpenIndex (PHONE_INDEX, 'PHONE.IDX', MaxKeyLen, NO_DUPLICATES);

{ files do not exist.  does user want to create them? }
        if not OK then
           begin
             ClrScr;
             Display_Frame (5, 60);

             repeat
                Put_String ('Type Y to create files N to exit', 23, 2, 0);
                Put_String ('Y', 23, 7, 2);
                Put_String ('N', 23, 25, 2);
                Get_Prompted_String (RESPONSE, BOLD, 1,
                   'Data Files do not exist. Create them (Y/N)? ', 11, 15,
                   '', 23, 35);
```

```
         if (Length (RESPONSE) = 0) then
             write(Chr(7))
         else if (not (RESPONSE[1] in ['Y','N','y', 'n'])) then
             write(Chr(7));
     until (RESPONSE[1] in ['Y', 'N', 'y', 'n']);

     if (RESPONSE[1] in ['Y', 'y']) then
       begin
         Put_String ('Creating Data and Index Files', 13, 15, 2);

         MakeFile (PHONE_BOOK, 'PHONE.DAT', Sizeof (LISTING));
         MakeIndex (PHONE_INDEX, 'PHONE.IDX', MaxKeyLen, NO_DUPLICATES);
       end
     else
       goto END_PROGRAM;  { user wants to quit }
   end;


 repeat
   Display_Menu (MAIN_MENU);
   Get_Menu_Response (MAIN_MENU, MAIN_CHOICE);

   case MAIN_CHOICE of
     '1': Display_Phone_Listing (PHONE_BOOK, PHONE_INDEX);
     '2': Add_Phone_Listing (PHONE_BOOK, PHONE_INDEX);
     '3': Delete_Phone_Listing (PHONE_BOOK, PHONE_INDEX);
     '4': Update_Phone_Listing (PHONE_BOOK, PHONE_INDEX);
     '5': Display_Database_Statistics (PHONE_BOOK);
   end;
 until (MAIN_CHOICE = 'E');

 CloseFile (PHONE_BOOK);
 CloseIndex (PHONE_INDEX);


END_PROGRAM:
end.
```

TurboSort

Although Chapter 4 provides several array-sorting routines, many applications require the sorting of multiple keys or of files of records. The Turbo Toolbox provides a quick sort called **TurboSort** that you can easily modify for specific applications. **TurboSort** works in three phases:

- Input phase
- Sorting phase
- Output phase.

Since the sort routines work with any type of data, you must write the input (**Inp**) and output (**OutP**) procedures, as well as the function **Less**, which actually compares the records being sorted. These procedures use **forward** declarations and are called by the Toolbox routine **TurboSort**; therefore, the names of the procedures are unchangeable.

Here is a program that uses the Toolbox **TurboSort** to read a file of employee records, sort them, and display the sorted information on the screen. The employee records will have the following structure:

```
EMPLOYEE_INFO = record
  NAME  : STRING79;
  AGE   : integer;
  SALARY: real;
end;
```

Here is the skeleton program:

```
program SortDemo ;

type
  STRING79 = string[79];

  EMPLOYEE_INFO = record
    NAME  : STRING79;
    AGE   : integer;
    SALARY: real;
  end;
{ define the type SORTRECORDS }
  SORTRECORDS = EMPLOYEE_INFO;

var
  SORT_FILE: file of SORTRECORDS;  { must be global }

{$I SORT.BOX}

{ procedure Inp here }
{ function Less here }
{ procedure OutP here }

var
  RESULT: integer; { result of the sort }

begin
  Assign (SORT_FILE, 'SORTDEMO.DAT');
  Reset (SORT_FILE);

  RESULT := TurboSort(Sizeof(SORTRECORDS));
  Close (SORT_FILE);
end.
```

The input procedure (**Inp**) simply reads each record in the data file and passes it to the routine **SortRelease**. The routine is based on the record type **SORTRECORDS**, which increases the routine's generic nature. Modifying the file type should not require a modification to the procedure **Inp**.

```
procedure Inp;
var
   SORT_RECORD: SORTRECORDS;

begin
  repeat
    Read (SORT_FILE, SORT_RECORD);
    SortRelease (SORT_RECORD);
  until EOF (SORT_FILE);
end;
```

The output procedure (**OutP**) obtains records from the procedure **SortRelease** until the routine sets the variable **SortEOS** to true. Like **Inp**, **OutP** is based on the record type **SORTRECORDS**, which minimizes the amount of code that needs to be modified with new applications:

```
procedure OutP;
var
   SORT_RECORD: SORTRECORDS;

begin
  with SORT_RECORD do
    repeat
      SortReturn (SORT_RECORD);

{ this portion is application-dependent }
      writeln (NAME, ' ', AGE, ' ', SALARY);

    until SortEOS;
end;
```

The function **Less** compares the records to be sorted:

```
function Less ;
var
  FIRST_RECORD : SORTRECORDS absolute X;
  SECOND_RECORD: SORTRECORDS absolute Y;

begin

{ this portion is application-dependent }
  Less := FIRST_RECORD.NAME <SECOND_RECORD.NAME;

end;
```

Less uses the variables **X** and **Y** (defined in **SORT.BOX**) during the comparison. Since the routine is based on the record type **SORT-RECORDS**, the statement

```
Less := FIRST_RECORD.NAME < SECOND_RECORD.NAME;
```

is the only statement that you must modify for your applications. For example, if employees are to be sorted first by age and then by name, the test becomes

```
Less := (FIRST_RECORD.AGE < SECOND_RECORD.AGE) or
        ((FIRST_RECORD.AGE = SECOND_RECORD.AGE) and
         (FIRST_RECORD.NAME < SECOND_RECORD.NAME));
```

Here is the complete application:

```
program SortDemo ;

type
  STRING79 = string[79];

  EMPLOYEE_INFO = record
    NAME  : STRING79;
    AGE   : integer;
    SALARY: real;
  end;

{ define the type SORTRECORDS }
  SORTRECORDS = EMPLOYEE_INFO;

var
  SORT_FILE: file of SORTRECORDS;  { must be global }

{$I SORT.BOX}

procedure Inp;
var
  SORT_RECORD: SORTRECORDS;

begin
  repeat
    Read (SORT_FILE, SORT_RECORD);
    SortRelease (SORT_RECORD);
  until EOF (SORT_FILE);
end;

function Less ;
var
  FIRST_RECORD : SORTRECORDS absolute X;
  SECOND_RECORD: SORTRECORDS absolute Y;

begin

{ this portion is application-dependent }
  Less := FIRST_RECORD.NAME <SECOND_RECORD.NAME;

end;
```

```
procedure OutP;
var
  SORT_RECORD: SORTRECORDS;

begin
  with SORT_RECORD do
    repeat
      SortReturn (SORT_RECORD);

{ this portion is application-dependent }
      writeln (NAME, ' ', AGE, ' ', SALARY);

    until SortEOS;
end;

var
  RESULT: integer; { result of the sort }

begin
  Assign (SORT_FILE, 'SORTDEMO.DAT');
  Reset (SORT_FILE);

  RESULT := TurboSort(Sizeof(SORTRECORDS));
  Close (SORT_FILE);
end.
```

TurboSort is invoked as a function and returns these status values to report on the success of the sort:

Value	Meaning
0	Successful sort
3	Insufficient memory for sort
8	Invalid item length (must be at least 2 bytes)
9	Too many input records (must be $<=$ **MaxInt**)
10	Unexpected error during sort (check disk space)
11	Read error during sort (check disk)
12	File creation error (check directory)

GINST

Many routines presented in this book illustrate the advantages of generic routines. Therefore, when you develop a routine, you try to maximize the number of applications it can be used in without modification. Similarly, when developing a program, you should maximize the number of computers on which the program can run successfully. One of the biggest factors influencing whether or not a program runs on a different computer is *video control*. The Turbo Tools *GINST* (General Installation) program is an excellent tool for moving programs from one computer to another.

GINST allows a program user to specify the type of terminal on which the program will be run. Each time an application runs, it will use the terminal setup commands specified by installation procedures. The setup commands include

- Display modes
- Cursor positioning commands
- Clear screen/line commands
- Video intensity commands.

The example given in this section will create a terminal installation for **DEMO.COM**. The names of the installation files will be **DEMOINST.COM**, **DEMOINST.DTA**, and **DEMOINST.MSG**.

To develop a terminal installation routine for a specific application, type **GINST** at the DOS prompt. The following will appear on the screen:

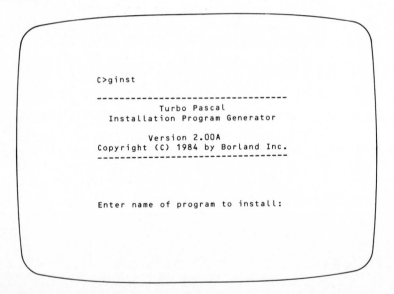

```
C>ginst

-----------------------------------
             Turbo Pascal
    Installation Program Generator

           Version 2.00A
   Copyright (C) 1984 by Borland Inc.
-----------------------------------



    Enter name of program to install:
```

For the example presented here, type the name **demo**. GINST then prompts you for the name of the installation files. In this case, type **demoinst**, and GINST displays the following:

```
Creating DEMOINST.COM
Creating DEMOINST.DTA
Creating DEMOINST.MSG

Installation program for DEMO.COM created
```

The screen should now contain this:

```
--------------------------------------
              Turbo Pascal
       Installation Program Generator

            Version 2.00A
   Copyright (C) 1984 by Borland Inc.
--------------------------------------

   Enter name of program to install: demo

   Enter first name for installation files: demoinst

   Creating DEMOINST.COM
   Creating DEMOINST.DTA
   Creating DEMOINST.MSG

   Installation program for DEMO.COM created

   C>
```

To define the terminal for the application, a user simply types **demoinst** at the DOS prompt. The terminal installation package **DEMOINST.COM** then displays the following:

```
Choose one of the following terminals:

    1) ADDS 20/25/30          15) RC-855 (ITT)
    2) ADDS 40/60             16) Soroc IQ-120
    3) ADDS Viewpoint-1A      17) Soroc new models
    4) Ampex D80              18) SSM-UB3
    5) ANSI                   19) Tandberg TDV 2215
    6) Hazeltine 1500         20) Teletex 3000
    7) Kaypro 10              21) Televideo 912/920/92
    8) Kaypro II and 4        22) Texas Instrument Pro
    9) Lear-Siegler ADM-20    23) Visual 200
   10) Lear-Siegler ADM-31    24) Wyse WY-100/200/300
   11) Liberty                25) Zenith, Victor 9000
   12) Morrow MDT-20          26) None of the above
   13) Otrona Attache         27) Delete a definition
   14) Qume

Which terminal? (Enter no. or ^Q to exit):
```

If the user's terminal is listed, the user simply enters the number associated with the terminal. Otherwise, the user must select option 26, **None of the above**.

The terminal installation program requires several terminal-specific escape sequences, which should be defined in the manual that accompanies the particular terminal. To enter an escape sequence, simply press the ESC key on the keyboard or type **27**. **<ESC>** should now be displayed on the screen. The following shows what the terminal installation program will prompt you for:

Typical Prompt	*Response*
Terminal Type	Enter the name of the terminal you are installing. This name will later appear on the list of terminals supported.
Send an initialization string to the terminal?	If you type **Y**, you can enter up to 13 characters to download commands to the programmable function keys.
Send a reset string to the terminal?	If you type **Y**, you can define the string of characters sent to the terminal each time the application terminates.
Cursor Lead-In Command	This is a special sequence of characters that tells the terminal that the following string is the address of the location on the screen at which the cursor should be placed.

The following are related to the cursor lead-in command:

Typical Prompt	*Response*
Cursor Positioning Command to send between line and column	Some terminals require a command between the numbers that define the cursor position by row and column.
Cursor Positioning Command to send after line and column	Some terminals require a command after the numbers that define the cursor position by row and column.

Typical Prompt	*Response*
Column First	If you type **Y**, the first number specified is the column position; if you type **N**, it is the row position.
Offset to add to line	Enter the offset to be added to the row address.
Offset to add to column	Enter the offset to be added to the column address.
Binary Address	If you type **Y**, the address must be specified in binary form.

The following are associated with the binary address:

Typical Prompt	*Response*
2 or 3 ASCII digits	Enter the number of digits in the cursor address.

Here are some other installation questions:

Typical Prompt	*Response*
Clear Screen	Enter the sequence that clears your screen.
Does Clear Screen also Home Cursor?	If you type **N**, the installation program will prompt you for the sequence that sets the cursor to the home position.
Delete Line Command	Enter the command that deletes the line at the cursor position.
Insert Line	Enter the sequence that inserts a line at the current cursor position.
Erase to End of Line	Enter the sequence that deletes the contents of the line from the current cursor position.
Start of Low Video Command	Enter the sequence that specifies low-density video. You will then have to enter the sequence that specifies normal video.
Number of lines on your screen	Enter the number of rows on the terminal (normally 25).

Typical Prompt	*Response*
Number of columns on your screen	Enter the number of columns on the terminal (normally 80).
Delay after Cursor Address	Enter 0-255ms. 0 says no delay.
Delay after Clear, Delete, or Insert	Enter 0-255ms. 0 says no delay.
Delay after erase to end of line or Highlight on/off	Enter 0-255ms. 0 says no delay.
Is this definition correct?	If you type **N**, you will start the installation specification again with the values just entered as defaults. If you type **Y**, the program will prompt for the processor speed in MHz.

The installation is now complete.

13

Using Turbo Graphix

Turbo Pascal's extended graphics package, called GRAPH.P, includes several basic graphics routines that you can combine to do more complex graphics. However, adding the Turbo Graphix Toolbox gives you most of the higher-level routines. This package provides a tremendous set of routines for manipulating graphics images, windows, screens, and complex curves.

This chapter provides a brief review of graphics coordinate systems, a set of routines (including a complete application) designed to complement Turbo Graphix, and a brief description of each Turbo

Graphix routine and how to use it. If you are unfamiliar with the Turbo Graphix Toolbox, you probably should read the first section and then skip ahead to the Turbo Graphix routines before studying the supplemental procedures provided.

Graphics Review

The Turbo Graphix Toolbox contains almost a hundred subroutines. Some are for internal use only, but if you understand the way that these work, you will be able to use the high-level routines more effectively.

Turbo Graphix uses four different coordinate systems, each with its own unique purpose. The simplest of these is the *screen-coordinate system*. This system allows you to address individual pixels on the screen. The IBM graphics screen is 640 pixels wide and 200 pixels high. Horizontal screen coordinates on the X-axis go from 0 on the far left to 639 on the far right. However, the vertical coordinates on the Y-axis go from 0 on the top of the screen to 199 on the bottom. The vertical coordinates in the screen-coordinate system are reversed from those on the traditional Euclidean coordinate system. The lowest-level Turbo Graphix routines use the screen-coordinate system so that they can manipulate the graphics quickly and accurately. Here is the screen-coordinate system:

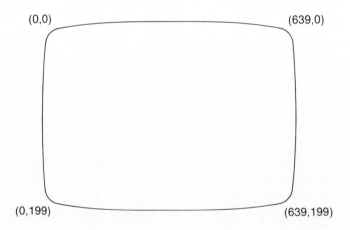

Turbo Pascal's *window-coordinate system* is based on the internal representation of screen memory. Each byte in the graphics memory stores 8 pixels from one line. Therefore, the window-coordinate system becomes 80 pixels wide and 200 pixels high. Used in Turbo Graphix routines that define and manipulate windows, this window-coordinate system speeds up window manipulation: if bit masking and bit shifting are not required, windows can be moved and stored much more quickly and easily.

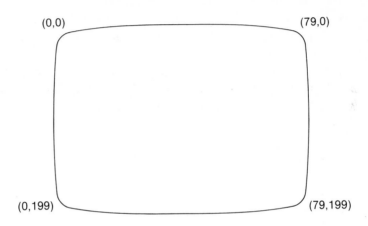

Of the four coordinate systems, the most important is the *world-coordinate system* because it offers almost complete control to the programmer. The *world-coordinate system* defines the boundary coordinates within the active window that fit the application. For example, suppose that you want to plot on the screen a set of data points, with the X-coordinates ranging from 50 to 100 and the Y-coordinates ranging from 0 to 3. If you plotted these points with screen coordinates, all points would appear in the upper-left corner of the screen. However, the call

```
DefineWorld (1, 40.0, 4.0, 120.0, -1.0);
```

defines a world or screen in which the data points will be spread out throughout most of the screen. Also, if the first Y-coordinate of the definition happens to be larger than the second, the entire system is flipped over, allowing you to model the traditional coordinate axes. The world-coordinate system defined by the call given earlier would cause the screen to be defined like this:

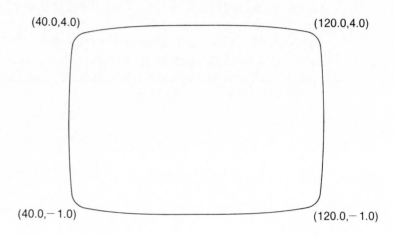

(40.0,4.0)   (120.0,4.0)

(40.0,− 1.0)   (120.0,− 1.0)

The final coordinate system found in the Turbo Graphix package is the 80-column by 25-row screen that is used to draw internal text characters. The **GotoXY** procedure is used to move the text cursor to the proper screen location.

Supplemental Routines

Unfortunately, with Turbo Pascal 3.0 and Turbo Graphix 1.03, most of Turbo Pascal's "IBM-PC Goodies" graphics routines cannot be used with the Turbo Graphix routines. However, the following routines, written by using the Turbo Graphix routines, have the same functions as the extended graphics in Turbo Pascal.

Probably the most useful routine omitted by Turbo Graphix is an arc-drawing routine. The routine **DrawCircleSegment** that is provided does draw an arc, but it also draws lines from the beginning and end of the arc to the center, forming a pie-shaped piece. The routine *Draw_Arc* given in this section draws an arc of a circle, the line of which follows the 8-bit line pattern set by **SetLineStyle**.

Another routine left out of Turbo Graphix is a routine that fills a random shape. The **SetBackground** procedure that Turbo Graphix has can only fill in squares (defined as windows). The procedure *Fill_Shape* given later starts at a center point and fills a closed shape with a given background pattern. For example, for the W shape given here,

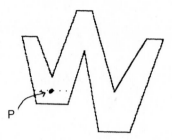

when you select an inside point, P, the routine fills the line that the point is on and moves up. If you use a diagonal-line pattern, the diagonal lines move up until they reach a "fork" in the letter:

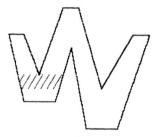

At this point, the routine saves its position by recursively calling the *Fill—Up* procedure to continue to fill only the right fork:

When the lines that fill the right side are finished, the routine then must call the *Fill—Down* procedure, which eventually calls the *Fill—Up* procedure. Calling *Fill—Up* in this way is called *indirect recursion*. After the third call to the *Fill—Up* procedure reaches a

dead end, as shown here,

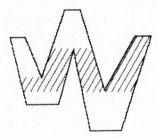

the procedure returns, and the *Fill—Down* procedure fills the bottom of the right side of the W:

Fill—Down soon completes its task and returns to the *Fill—Up* section, and eventually the entire W is filled.

Problems arise when you use fill patterns that have no lines that go straight across. For example, in the O shape shown here,

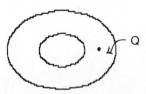

if the *Fill—Up* procedure starts at point Q, it will have to call the *Fill—Down* procedure to fill the left side of the O. A sparse pattern would yield this:

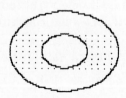

Since no straight lines have been drawn, the *Fill—Down* procedure would attempt to refill the right side of the O, and an infinite loop would result. Thus, the *Fill—Shape* procedure given later uses more complicated logic: because *Fill—Shape* searches for smaller spaces, it can fill the O completely, although it will take slightly longer.

```
procedure Draw_Arc (XCENTER, YCENTER, RADIUS: real;
                    START_ANGLE, STOP_ANGLE: integer);
{
DESCRIPTION:
    This routine draws an arc of a circle.  The arc can be
made elliptical by using the SetAspect procedure.

PARAMETERS:
    XCENTER (in) - the x-coordinate (world) of the center point
    YCENTER (in) - the y-coordinate (world) of the center point
    RADIUS (in) - the radius (world scale) of the arc
    START_ANGLE (in) - the start angle in degrees
    STOP_ANGLE (in) - the final angle in degrees

SAMPLE CALL:
    Draw_Arc (0.0, 0.0, 5, 90, 180);

NOTES:
    The circle used follows the mathematical standard of
        0 degrees - three o'clock
       90 degrees - twelve o'clock
      180 degrees - nine o'clock
      270 degrees - six o'clock

------------------------------------------------------------}

  const
    PI = 3.1416;

  var
    ANGLE,                      {the current angle}
    X1, Y1,                     {the start point of the current line}
    X2, Y2: real;               {the end point of the current line}

  begin

{calculate the first point on the arc}
    X1 := XCENTER + RADIUS * COS(START_ANGLE * PI/180);
    Y1 := YCENTER + RADIUS * SIN(START_ANGLE * PI/180) * AspectGlb;

{loop through each angle}
    ANGLE := START_ANGLE;
    while ANGLE < STOP_ANGLE do
      begin

{draw more lines on larger circles, fewer lines for small circles}

        ANGLE := ANGLE + 360/RADIUS;

{do not go past the end of the arc}
        if ANGLE > STOP_ANGLE then
          ANGLE := STOP_ANGLE;
        X2 := XCENTER + RADIUS * COS(ANGLE * PI/180);
        Y2 := YCENTER + RADIUS * SIN(ANGLE * PI/180) * AspectGlb;
```

```
{draw a line that simulates the arc}
        DrawLine (X1, Y1, X2, Y2);
        X1 := X2;
        Y1 := Y2;
      end;
  end;
```

```
procedure Fill_Shape (XINSIDE, YINSIDE: real;
                                 BACK: BackgroundArray);
{
DESCRIPTION:
    This routine fills any closed shape with a given
background pattern.  If the shape is not closed, the filling
will "spill" into the rest of the screen.

PARAMETERS:
    XINSIDE (in) - the x-coordinate (world) of an inside point
    YINSIDE (in) - the y-coordinate (world) of an inside point
    BACK (in) - the background pattern (see SetBackground8)

SAMPLE CALL:
    Fill_Shape (10.0, 5.0, DIAGONAL);

NOTES:
    Background patterns that contain zeros (blank lines) will
take slightly longer to fill due to the search constraints.
    This routine uses indirect recursion to handle all possible
shapes.

-----------------------------------------------------------}


  var
    FIRSTLEFT, FIRSTRIGHT: integer;    {x-coordinates of first line}
```

```
procedure Fill_Line (X, Y: integer;
        var XLEFT, XRIGHT: integer);
{
DESCRIPTION:
    This routine fills a line a with a given background pattern.
It returns the coordinates of the endpoints that it found.

PARAMETERS:
    X (in) - the x-coordinate (screen) of an inside point
    Y (in) - the y-coordinate (screen) of an inside point
    XLEFT (out) - the x-coordinate (screen) of the leftmost point
        on the line
    XRIGHT (out) - the x-coordinate (screen) of the rightmost
        point on the line
```

```
    SAMPLE CALL:
        Fill_Line (34, 45, LEFT, RIGHT);

    NOTES:
        This routine is for internal use by Fill_Shape.

--------------------------------------------------------------}

    var
      I: integer;                        {counter for loops}

    begin
      XLEFT := X;
      XRIGHT := X;

{if the inside point is already filled, do not fill anything}
        if not PD (X, Y) then
          begin

{find the left-most point to fill on the line}
            while (not PD (XLEFT-1, Y)) and (XLEFT > 0) do
                XLEFT := XLEFT - 1;

{find the right-most point to fill on the line}
            while (not PD (XRIGHT, Y)) and (XRIGHT < 639) do
                XRIGHT := XRIGHT + 1;

{draw the line}
            if BACK[Y and 7] = $FF then
                DrawStraight (XLEFT, XRIGHT, Y)
            else if BACK[Y and 7] <> 0 then
                for I := XLEFT to XRIGHT do

{use the pattern specified by the background array}
                if (128 shr (I and 7)) and (BACK[Y and 7]) <> 0 ther
                  DP (I, Y);

          end;
      end;

    procedure Fill_Down (XINSIDE, YINSIDE,
                           XLEFT, XRIGHT: integer); forward;
```

```
procedure Fill_Up (XINSIDE, YINSIDE,
                     XLEFT, XRIGHT: integer);
{
DESCRIPTION:
    This routine checks to see if a shape can be filled
above the current line.

PARAMETERS:
    XINSIDE (in) - the x-coordinate (screen) of an inside point
    YINSIDE (in) - the y-coordinate (screen) of an inside point
    XLEFT (out) - the x-coordinate (screen) of the leftmost point
        on the current line
    XRIGHT (out) - the x-coordinate (screen) of the rightmost
        point on the current line
```

```
    SAMPLE CALL:
        Fill_Up (34, 45, 30, 38);

    NOTES:
        This routine is for internal use by Fill_Shape.

    -----------------------------------------------------------}


    var
      I,                                {counter for loops}
      TLEFT, TRIGHT,                    {temporary left and right}
      NEWLEFT, NEWRIGHT: integer;       {left and right of the next line}

    begin
{fill the section going up}
    while (XLEFT < XRIGHT) and (YINSIDE > 0) do
        begin
          if PD (XLEFT, YINSIDE-1) then
            while (PD (XLEFT, YINSIDE-1)) and (XLEFT < XRIGHT) do
              XLEFT := XLEFT + 1;
          Fill_Line (XLEFT, YINSIDE-1, NEWLEFT, NEWRIGHT);

{if the new line went further left, check below}
          if NEWLEFT < XLEFT - 1 then
            begin
              I := NEWLEFT;
              while I < XLEFT do
                begin
                  Fill_Line (I, YINSIDE, TLEFT, TRIGHT);
                  if TLEFT+7 < TRIGHT then
                    Fill_Down (I, YINSIDE, TLEFT, TRIGHT);
                  I := TRIGHT + 2;
                end;
            end;

{if the new line did not go far enough right, check above}
          if NEWRIGHT + 1 < XRIGHT then
            begin
              I := NEWRIGHT + 2;
              while I <= XRIGHT do
                begin
                  Fill_Line (I, YINSIDE-1, TLEFT, TRIGHT);
                  if TLEFT+7 < TRIGHT then
                    Fill_Up (I, YINSIDE-1, TLEFT, TRIGHT);
                  I := TRIGHT + 2;
                end;
            end;

{if the new line went further right, check below}
          if NEWRIGHT > XRIGHT + 1 then
            begin
              I := XRIGHT + 2;
```

```
            while I <= NEWRIGHT do
               begin
                  Fill_Line (I, YINSIDE, TLEFT, TRIGHT);
                  if TLEFT+7 < TRIGHT then
                    Fill_Down (I, YINSIDE, TLEFT, TRIGHT);
                  I := TRIGHT + 2;
               end;
           end;

{go up one line}
         XLEFT := NEWLEFT;
         XRIGHT := NEWRIGHT;
         YINSIDE := YINSIDE - 1;
       end;
   end;
```

```
procedure Fill_Down;
{
DESCRIPTION:
    This routine checks to see if a shape can be filled
above the current line.

PARAMETERS:
    XINSIDE (in) - the x-coordinate (screen) of an inside point
    YINSIDE (in) - the y-coordinate (screen) of an inside point
    XLEFT (out) - the x-coordinate (screen) of the leftmost point
       on the current line
    XRIGHT (out) - the x-coordinate (screen) of the rightmost
       point on the current line

SAMPLE CALL:
    Fill_Down (34, 45, 30, 38);

  NOTES:
      This routine is for internal use by Fill_Shape.

---------------------------------------------------------}


  var
    I,                             {counter for loops}
    TLEFT, TRIGHT,                 {temporary left and right}
    NEWLEFT, NEWRIGHT: integer;    {left and right of the next line}


    begin
```

```
    {fill the section going down}
        while (XLEFT < XRIGHT) and (YINSIDE < 200) do
          begin
            if PD (XLEFT, YINSIDE+1) then
              while (PD (XLEFT, YINSIDE+1)) and (XLEFT < XRIGHT) do
                XLEFT := XLEFT + 1;
            Fill_Line (XLEFT, YINSIDE+1, NEWLEFT, NEWRIGHT);

    {if the new line went further left, check above}
            if NEWLEFT < XLEFT - 1 then
              begin
                I := NEWLEFT;
                while I < XLEFT - 1 do
                  begin
                    Fill_Line (I, YINSIDE, TLEFT, TRIGHT);
                    if TLEFT+7 < TRIGHT then
                      Fill_Up (I, YINSIDE, TLEFT, TRIGHT);
                    I := TRIGHT + 2;
                  end;
              end;

    {if the new line did not go far enough right, check below}
            if NEWRIGHT + 1 < XRIGHT then
              begin
                I := NEWRIGHT + 2;
                while I <= XRIGHT do
                  begin
                    Fill_Line (I, YINSIDE+1, TLEFT, TRIGHT);
                    if TLEFT+7 < TRIGHT then
                      Fill_Down (I, YINSIDE+1, TLEFT, TRIGHT);
                    I := TRIGHT + 2;
                  end;
              end;

    {if the new line went further right, check above}
            if NEWRIGHT > XRIGHT + 1 then
              begin
                I := XRIGHT + 2;
                while I <= NEWRIGHT do
                  begin
                    Fill_Line (I, YINSIDE, TLEFT, TRIGHT);
                    if TLEFT+7 < TRIGHT then
                    Fill_Up (I, YINSIDE, TLEFT, TRIGHT);
                    I := TRIGHT + 2;
                  end;
              end;

{go up one line}
        XLEFT := NEWLEFT;
        XRIGHT := NEWRIGHT;
        YINSIDE := YINSIDE + 1;
      end;
  end;


  begin                    {Fill_Shape}
    SetWindowModeOff;
```

```
{fill the first line}
    Fill_Line (WindowX (XINSIDE), WindowY (YINSIDE), FIRSTLEFT, FIRSTRIGHT);

{fill above the first line}
    Fill_Up (WindowX (XINSIDE), WindowY (YINSIDE), FIRSTLEFT, FIRSTRIGHT);

{fill below the first line}
    Fill_Down (WindowX (XINSIDE), WindowY (YINSIDE), FIRSTLEFT, FIRSTRIGHT);
    SetWindowModeOn;
  end;
```

The next set of routines further supplements the Turbo Graphix Toolbox. The procedures *Draw_Ascii_Down* and *Draw_Ascii_Up* are used internally by *Draw_TextW_Vertical* to draw the Turbo Graphix 4×6 font either up or down. As with the **Draw-TextW** procedure, which Turbo Graphix provides, this routine allows you to specify a scale to produce large characters.

The *Invert_Square* routine converts every pixel to reverse video in a square that is defined by world coordinates. Turbo Graphix provides **InvertWindow**, but the procedure restricts you to 8-pixel byte boundaries in the horizontal direction. By using world coordinates, *Invert_Square* sacrifices some speed because it must address each individual pixel. Thus, large squares may take several seconds to change.

```
procedure Draw_Ascii_Down (var XLOC, YLOC: integer;
                               CHAR_SIZE, ASCII: byte);
{
DESCRIPTION:
    This routine draws a character downward using the 4x6
font.  It can be scaled to draw large characters.  A
simulated graphics cursor (the character location) gets
updated automatically.

PARAMETERS:
    XLOC (in/out) - the x-coordinate (screen) of the character
    YLOC (in/out) - the y-coordinate (screen) of the character
    CHAR_SIZE (in) - the size of the character
    ASCII (in) - the ascii value of the character

SAMPLE CALL:
    Draw_Ascii_Down (100, 50, 2, 65);      (draws an 'A')

NOTES:
    This routine is primarily for internal use by
Draw_TextW_Vertical.

-------------------------------------------------------------}
```

```pascal
var
  I,                             {counter for loops}
  XLINE, YBIT,                   {the isolated bit of the character}
  XLEFT, XRIGHT,                 {the x-coordinates of the bit square}
  YTOP, YBOTTOM: integer;        {the y-coordinates of the bit square}
  NIBBLE      : byte;            {the nibble read from the font}

begin

{go through each line of the character}
  for XLINE := 0 to 5 do
    begin

{isolate the nibble from the font array}
      if Odd (XLINE) then
        NIBBLE := CharSet[ASCII, XLINE div 2 + 1] and 15
      else
        NIBBLE := CharSet[ASCII, XLINE div 2 + 1] shr 4;

{go through each bit on each line}
      for YBIT := 0 to 3 do
        if NIBBLE and (8 shr YBIT) <> 0 then
          begin

{draw a square (based on scale) for each bit}
            XLEFT := XLOC + 1 + (XLINE-3)*CHAR_SIZE*2;
            XRIGHT := XLEFT + CHAR_SIZE*2 - 1;
            YTOP := YLOC + YBIT*CHAR_SIZE;
            YBOTTOM := YTOP + CHAR_SIZE - 1;

{draw in a filled square in screen coordinates}
            for I := YTOP to YBOTTOM do
              DrawStraight (XLEFT, XRIGHT, I);
          end;
    end;

{advance the graphic cursor}
  YLOC := YLOC + CHAR_SIZE*6;
  end;
```

```pascal
procedure Draw_Ascii_Up (var XLOC, YLOC: integer;
                CHAR_SIZE, ASCII: byte);
{
DESCRIPTION:
    This routine draws a character upward using the 4x6
font.  It can be scaled to draw large characters.  A
simulated graphics cursor (the character location) gets
updated automatically.

PARAMETERS:
    XLOC (in/out) - the x-coordinate (screen) of the character
    YLOC (in/out) - the y-coordinate (screen) of the character
    CHAR_SIZE (in) - the size of the character
    ASCII (in) - the ascii value of the character
```

```
SAMPLE CALL:
    Draw_Ascii_Up (100, 50, 2, 65);       (draws an 'A')

NOTES:
    This routine is primarily for internal use by
Draw_TextW_Vertical.

---------------------------------------------------------}


   var
     I,                        {counter for loops}
     XLINE, YBIT,              {the isolated bit of the character}
     XLEFT, XRIGHT,            {the x-coordinates of the bit square}
     YTOP, YBOTTOM: integer;   {the y-coordinates of the bit square}
     NIBBLE        : byte;     {the nibble read from the font}

   begin

{go through each line of the character}
    for XLINE := 0 to 5 do   {right to left}
     begin

{isolate the nibble from the font array}
       if Odd (XLINE) then
          NIBBLE := CharSet[ASCII, XLINE div 2 + 1] and 15
       else
          NIBBLE := CharSet[ASCII, XLINE div 2 + 1] shr 4;

{go through each bit on each line}
       for YBIT := 0 to 3 do
         if NIBBLE and (8 shr YBIT) <> 0 then
         begin

{draw a square (based on scale) for each bit}
          XRIGHT := XLOC - 1 - (XLINE-3)*CHAR_SIZE*2;
          XLEFT := XRIGHT - CHAR_SIZE*2 + 1;
          YTOP := YLOC - YBIT*CHAR_SIZE;
          YBOTTOM := YTOP - CHAR_SIZE + 1;

{draw in a filled square in screen coordinates}
          for I := YBOTTOM to YTOP do
             DrawStraight (XLEFT,XRIGHT,I);
          end;
       end;

{advance the graphic cursor}
    YLOC := YLOC - CHAR_SIZE*6;
   end;


procedure Draw_TextW_Vertical (X_START, Y_START: real;
                               SCALE, DIRECTION: integer;
                               TEXT_STR: WrkString);
   {
```

```
DESCRIPTION:
     This routine draws a text string upward or downward
using the 4x6 font.  It can be scaled to draw large
characters.

PARAMETERS:
     X_START (in) - the x-coordinate (world) of the start of text
     Y_START (in) - the y-coordinate (world) of the start of text
     SCALE (in) - the size of the text string [1-16]
     DIRECTION (in) - the direction to draw [0-1]
     TEXT_STR (in) - the text string to draw

LIBRARY ROUTINES USED:
     Draw_Ascii_Up - draws one character upward
     Draw_Ascii_Down - draws one character downward

SAMPLE CALL:
     Draw_TextW_Vertical (100, 50, 2, 1, 'hi');       (draws hi up)

NOTES:
     If DIRECTION is 1, the text will be drawn upward.
Otherwise it will drawn downward.

----------------------------------------------------------}


  var
    X_SCREEN, Y_SCREEN,            {the screen coordinates of the text}
    I: integer;                    {counter for loops}

  begin

{determine the screen coordinates of the starting point}
    X_SCREEN := WindowX (X_START);
    Y_SCREEN := WindowY (Y_START);

{loop through each character of the text}
    for I := 1 to Length (TEXT_STR) do
      if DIRECTION = 1 then
        Draw_Ascii_Up (X_SCREEN, Y_SCREEN, SCALE, Ord(TEXT_STR[I]))
      else
        Draw_Ascii_Down (X_SCREEN, Y_SCREEN, SCALE, Ord(TEXT_STR[I]));

    end;
```

```
procedure Invert_Square (X1, Y1, X2, Y2: real);
{
DESCRIPTION:
     This routine inverts all of the pixels within a rectangular
area.

PARAMETERS:
     X1 (in) - the leftmost column of the box (world coordinates)
     Y1 (in) - the top row of the box (world coordinates)
     X2 (in) - the rightmost column of the box (world coordinates)
     Y2 (in) - the bottom row of the box (world coordinates)
```

```
SAMPLE CALL:
    Invert_Square (2.0, 3.0, 5.0, 5.0);

NOTES:
    As with many special graphics routines, this routine takes
much longer to invert large squares.

------------------------------------------------------------}

  var
    X, Y: integer;                              {counters for loops}

  begin

{loop through every pixel of the entire box}
    for X := WindowX (X1) to WindowX (X2) do
      for Y := WindowY (Y1) to WindowY (Y2) do

{if the point is not drawn, draw it}
        if not PD(X,Y) then
          DP(X,Y)

{if the point is drawn, erase it}
        else
          begin
            SetColorBlack;
            DP(X,Y);
            SetColorWhite;
          end;
  end;
```

Cursor Routines

Often, you will encounter an application that requires the user to specify a location on the screen. A *graphics cursor* would enable users to see exactly where they are pointing to. Following the standard set by Turbo Graphix, these routines require two global variables:

```
var
  X_CURSOR, Y_CURSOR: integer;
```

These variables represent the screen location of the graphics cursor. The *Draw—Cursor* routine given later is primarily for internal use by the other procedures. *Init—Cursor* is called with world coordinates to place the cursor in a desired position. *Blink—Cursor* will cause the cursor to blink slowly until the user presses a key.

Moving the graphics cursor all over the screen could easily erase the screen contents. To avoid this problem, you must save a window that includes the screen before drawing the cursor. Every time that the cursor is moved, the window is replaced with its former contents. The procedure *Move —Cursor* takes care of this step when it moves the cursor.

One of the biggest drawbacks of the graphics modes in Turbo Pascal is that they do not provide a cursor for text positions. If a menu is displayed in high-resolution graphics mode, nothing on the screen indicates to the user where input will occur. The routine *Blink —Text —Cursor* simulates the cursor shown in normal text mode. The two-line cursor blinks rapidly at the desired screen position (defined by text coordinates) until the user presses a key.

The routine *Get —String —With —Cursor* goes one step further. When a program needs to get a string from the user and the screen is in high-resolution graphics mode, *Get —String —With —Cursor* reads in characters one at a time. Each time a valid character is entered, it is echoed to the screen and the text cursor is moved right one column. The user probably will not realize that the entire process is simulated.

```
procedure Draw_Cursor;
{
DESCRIPTION:
    This routine draws a large graphic cursor on the screen
at the current cursor position.

SAMPLE CALL:
    Draw_Cursor;

NOTES:
    This routine uses the global variables X_CURSOR and
Y_CURSOR that contain the screen coordinates of the current
cursor location.

------------------------------------------------------------}

   begin

{draw the actual cursor point}
    DP (X_CURSOR, Y_CURSOR);

{draw four lines out from the cursor point}
    DrawLineClipped (X_CURSOR+4, Y_CURSOR, X_CURSOR+14, Y_CURSOR);
    DrawLineClipped (X_CURSOR-4, Y_CURSOR, X_CURSOR-14, Y_CURSOR);
    DrawLineClipped (X_CURSOR, Y_CURSOR+3, X_CURSOR, Y_CURSOR+7);
    DrawLineClipped (X_CURSOR, Y_CURSOR-3, X_CURSOR, Y_CURSOR-7);
   end;
```

```
procedure Init_Cursor (XCURS, YCURS: real);
{
DESCRIPTION:
    This routine initializes a large graphics cursor and draws
```

it, clipping as necessary. Before drawing, the contents of the
area where the cursor is located are saved.

```
PARAMETERS:
    XCURS (in) - x-coordinate (world) of the new cursor position
    YCURS (in) - y-coordinate (world) of the new cursor position

LIBRARY ROUTINES USED:
   Draw_Cursor - displays the graphic cursor

SAMPLE CALL:
    Init_Cursor (1.2, 3.4);

NOTES:
    This routine sets the global variables X_CURSOR and
Y_CURSOR that contain the screen coordinates of the current
cursor location.

-----------------------------------------------------------}


   var
      XSCREEN, YSCREEN,                   {the screen coordinates of the point}
      X1_WINDOW, Y1_WINDOW,               {coordinates of the cursor window}
      X2_WINDOW, Y2_WINDOW: integer;

   begin

{determine the screen coordinates of the cursor location}
      XSCREEN := WindowX (XCURS);
      YSCREEN := WindowY (YCURS);

{clip the x-coordinate of the cursor within the active window}
      if XSCREEN <= X1RefGlb shl 3 then          {too far left}
         X_CURSOR := X1RefGlb shl 3
      else if XSCREEN >= X2RefGlb shl 3 + 7 then     {too far right}
         X_CURSOR := X2RefGlb shl 3 + 7
      else
         X_CURSOR := XSCREEN;

{clip the y-coordinate of the cursor within the active window}
      if YSCREEN <= Y1RefGlb then                {too far up}
         Y_CURSOR := Y1RefGlb
      else if YSCREEN >= Y2RefGlb then              {too far down}
         Y_CURSOR := Y2RefGlb
      else
         Y_CURSOR := YSCREEN;

{determine the x-coordinates of a window that includes the entire
graphic cursor, clipping within the screen}
      X1_WINDOW := X_CURSOR div 8 - 2;
      if X1_WINDOW < 0 then                      {too far left}
         X1_WINDOW := 0;
      X2_WINDOW := X_CURSOR div 8 + 3;
      if X2_WINDOW > XMaxGlb then                {too far right}
         X2_WINDOW := XMaxGlb;

{determine the x-coordinates of a window that includes the entire
graphic cursor, clipping within the screen}
      Y1_WINDOW := Y_CURSOR - 8;
      if Y1_WINDOW < 0 then                      {too far up}
         Y1_WINDOW := 0;
      Y2_WINDOW := Y_CURSOR + 8;
      if Y2_WINDOW > YMaxGlb then                {too far down}
         Y2_WINDOW := YMaxGlb;
```

```
{define and save the window that includes the cursor so that the
window can be redrawn when the cursor moves}
    DefineWindow (2, X1_WINDOW, Y1_WINDOW, X2_WINDOW, Y2_WINDOW);
    StoreWindow (2);

{draw the cursor}

    Draw_Cursor;
  end;
```

```
procedure Blink_Cursor;
{
DESCRIPTION:
    This routine blinks a large graphics cursor on the screen
until the user presses any key.

LIBRARY ROUTINES USED:
    Draw_Cursor - displays the graphic cursor

SAMPLE CALL:
    Blink_Cursor;

NOTES:
    This routine should only be used after the cursor is
initialized with Init_Cursor.

----------------------------------------------------------}

  begin

{repeat the blinking until a key is pressed}
    while not KeyPressed do
      begin
        Delay (500);
        if not KeyPressed then
          begin

{turn the cursor off, wait, and turn it back on}
            SetColorBlack;
            Draw_Cursor;
            Delay (300);
            SetColorWhite;
            Draw_Cursor;
          end;
      end;
  end;
```

```
procedure Move_Cursor (DELTA_X, DELTA_Y: real);
{
DESCRIPTION:
    This routine moves a large graphics cursor and redraws
it, clipping as necessary.  The area where the cursor was
is replaced with its original contents.
```

```
PARAMETERS:
    DELTA_X (in) - the change in x (world scale) of the cursor
    DELTA_Y (in) - the change in y (world scale) of the cursor

LIBRARY ROUTINES USED:
    Draw_Cursor - displays the graphic cursor
    Init_Cursor - reinitializes the graphic cursor

SAMPLE CALL:
    Move_Cursor (1.5, 0);

NOTES:
    This routine uses the global variables X_CURSOR and
Y_CURSOR that contain the screen coordinates of the current
cursor location.

-----------------------------------------------------------}


   begin

{erase the current cursor}
    SetColorBlack;
    Draw_Cursor;

{redraw the window of where the cursor was}
    SetColorWhite;
    RestoreWindow (2, 0, 0);

{move the cursor, converting the deltas to screen coordinates}
    Init_Cursor (X_CURSOR + BxGlb*DELTA_X, Y_CURSOR - ByGlb*DELTA_Y);
    end;
```

```
procedure Blink_Text_Cursor (LINE, COL: integer);
{
DESCRIPTION:
    This routine simulates the text cursor in high resolution
graphics mode.  The cursor blinks rapidly until a key is
pressed by the user.

PARAMETERS:
    LINE (in) - the text line of the cursor [1-25]
    COL (in) - the text column of the cursor [1-80]

SAMPLE CALL:
    Blink_Text_Cursor (23, 1);

-----------------------------------------------------------}
   begin

{move to the correct cursor location}
    GotoXY (COL, LINE);

{blink until a key is pressed}
    while not KeyPressed do
      begin
```

```
{draw the pair of lines below the position}
        SetColorWhite;
        DrawStraight (COL*8 - 8, COL*8 - 1, LINE*8);
        DrawStraight (COL*8 - 8, COL*8 - 1, LINE*8 - 1);
        Delay (150);

{erase the cursor; it should be gone when a key is pressed}
        SetColorBlack;
        DrawStraight (COL*8 - 8, COL*8 - 1, LINE*8);
        DrawStraight (COL*8 - 8, COL*8 - 1, LINE*8 - 1);
        Delay (100);
        SetColorWhite;
      end;
  end;
```

```
procedure Get_String_With_Cursor (var TEXT_STR: WrkString;
                                      LINE, COL: integer);
{
DESCRIPTION:
    This routine gets a string from the user in high
resolution graphics mode.  A simulated cursor blinks rapidly
in the current cursor location.

PARAMETERS:
    TEXT_STR (in) - the string input by the user
    LINE (in) - the text line of the start of input [1-25]
    COL (in) - the text column of the start of input [1-80]

SAMPLE CALL:
    Get_String_With_Cursor (NAME_STRING, 23, 1);

NOTES:
    Tabs and other special characters are ignored.

---------------------------------------------------------}


  var
    COUNT: integer;                {the number of characters input}
    IN_CHAR: char;                 {the current character input}

  begin

{initialize the character and the input string}
    IN_CHAR := ' ';
    COUNT := 0;
    TEXT_STR := '';

{loop until the user presses the carriage return}
    while IN_CHAR <> Chr(13) do
      begin

{display the cursor at the current position}
        Blink_Text_Cursor (LINE, COL);
        read (kbd, IN_CHAR);
```

```
{if a legitimate character is input, add it to the input string}
      if Ord(IN_CHAR) >= 32 then
         begin
           write (IN_CHAR);
           COUNT := COUNT + 1;
           TEXT_STR[COUNT] := IN_CHAR;
           TEXT_STR[0] := Chr(COUNT);

{move the cursor one space to the right}
           COL := COL + 1;
         end;
      end;
   end;
```

The Turbo Key Program

This chapter includes one complete application. The Turbo Key program displays the keyboard on the screen and enables the user to redefine the function keys visually.

Each of the 83 IBM-PC keyboard keys is listed in the file shown here. Each line contains in the first two columns on the left the keyboard scan codes for a particular key when it is pressed alone and when it is pressed with the ALT key. If 0 is displayed in either of the columns, that particular key cannot be redefined in that mode. A set of world coordinates forms the square that is the key's location on the keyboard. These coordinates are given in columns 3 through 6. The next two columns give the coordinates of the text that will be displayed inside the square. Finally, the key's text is given in the column on the far right.

59	104	0.1	0.1	1.0	0.9	0.2	0.4	F1
61	106	0.1	1.1	1.0	1.9	0.2	1.4	F3
63	108	0.1	2.1	1.0	2.9	0.2	2.4	F5
65	110	0.1	3.1	1.0	3.9	0.2	3.4	F7
67	112	0.1	4.1	1.0	4.9	0.2	4.4	F9
60	105	1.2	0.1	2.1	0.9	1.3	0.4	F2
62	107	1.2	1.1	2.1	1.9	1.3	1.4	F4
64	109	1.2	2.1	2.1	2.9	1.3	2.4	F6
66	111	1.2	3.1	2.1	3.9	1.3	3.4	F8
68	113	1.2	4.1	2.1	4.9	1.2	4.4	F10
71	174	17.7	1.1	18.6	1.9	17.7	1.4	HME
79	182	17.7	3.1	18.6	3.9	17.7	3.4	END
82	185	16.6	4.1	18.6	4.9	17.0	4.4	INS
73	176	19.9	1.1	20.9	1.9	19.85	1.4	PGUP
81	184	19.9	3.1	20.9	3.9	19.85	3.4	PGDN
83	186	18.8	4.1	20.9	4.9	19.4	4.4	DEL
0	120	3.6	0.1	4.4	0.9	3.7	0.4	1

0	16	4.1	1.1	4.9	1.9	4.2	1.4	Q
0	30	4.3	2.1	5.1	2.9	4.4	2.4	A
0	44	4.8	3.1	5.6	3.9	4.9	3.4	Z
0	121	4.6	0.1	5.4	0.9	4.7	0.4	2
0	17	5.1	1.1	5.9	1.9	5.2	1.4	W
0	31	5.3	2.1	6.1	2.9	5.4	2.4	S
0	45	5.8	3.1	6.6	3.9	5.9	3.4	X
0	122	5.6	0.1	6.4	0.9	5.7	0.4	3
0	18	6.1	1.1	6.9	1.9	6.2	1.4	E
0	32	6.3	2.1	7.1	2.9	6.4	2.4	D
0	46	6.8	3.1	7.6	3.9	6.9	3.4	C
0	123	6.6	0.1	7.4	0.9	6.7	0.4	4
0	19	7.1	1.1	7.9	1.9	7.2	1.4	R
0	33	7.3	2.1	8.1	2.9	7.4	2.4	F
0	47	7.8	3.1	8.6	3.9	7.9	3.4	V
0	124	7.6	0.1	8.4	0.9	7.7	0.4	5
0	20	8.1	1.1	8.9	1.9	8.2	1.4	T
0	34	8.3	2.1	9.1	2.9	8.4	2.4	G
0	48	8.8	3.1	9.6	3.9	8.9	3.4	B
0	125	8.6	0.1	9.4	0.9	8.7	0.4	6
0	21	9.1	1.1	9.9	1.9	9.2	1.4	Y
0	35	9.3	2.1	10.1	2.9	9.4	2.4	H
0	49	9.8	3.1	10.6	3.9	9.9	3.4	N
0	126	9.6	0.1	10.4	0.9	9.7	0.4	7
0	22	10.1	1.1	10.9	1.9	10.2	1.4	U
0	36	10.3	2.1	11.1	2.9	10.4	2.4	J
0	50	10.8	3.1	11.6	3.9	10.9	3.4	M
0	127	10.6	0.1	11.4	0.9	10.7	0.4	8
0	23	11.1	1.1	11.9	1.9	11.2	1.4	I
0	37	11.3	2.1	12.1	2.9	11.4	2.4	K
0	128	11.6	0.1	12.4	0.9	11.7	0.4	9
0	24	12.1	1.1	12.9	1.9	12.2	1.4	O
0	38	12.3	2.1	13.1	2.9	12.4	2.4	L
0	129	12.6	0.1	13.4	0.9	12.7	0.4	0
0	25	13.1	1.1	13.9	1.9	13.2	1.4	P
0	130	13.6	0.1	14.4	0.9	13.7	0.4	—
0	131	14.6	0.1	15.4	0.9	14.7	0.4	=
0	0	2.5	0.1	3.4	0.9	2.5	0.4	ESC
0	0	2.5	1.1	3.9	1.9	2.8	1.4	TAB
0	0	2.5	2.1	4.1	2.9	2.7	2.4	CTRL
0	0	2.5	3.1	3.6	3.9	2.5	3.4	SHFT
0	0	3.8	3.1	4.6	3.9	3.9	3.4	\
0	0	2.5	4.1	4.3	4.9	2.9	4.4	ALT
0	0	4.5	4.1	14.4	4.9	8.1	4.4	SPACE BAR
0	0	11.8	3.1	12.6	3.9	11.9	3.4	,
0	0	13.3	2.1	14.1	2.9	13.4	2.4	;
0	0	12.8	3.1	13.6	3.9	12.9	3.4	.
0	0	14.1	1.1	14.9	1.9	14.2	1.4	[
0	0	14.3	2.1	15.1	2.9	14.4	2.4	'
0	0	13.8	3.1	14.6	3.9	13.9	3.4	/

0	0	15.1	1.1	16.3	1.9	15.2	1.4	]
0	0	15.3	2.1	16.3	2.9	15.5	2.4	'
0	0	14.6	4.1	16.3	4.9	14.6	4.4	CAPLOCK
0	0	14.8	3.1	16.3	3.9	14.9	3.4	SHFT
0	0	16.5	3.1	17.4	3.9	16.7	3.4	*
0	0	16.5	1.1	17.4	2.9	16.5	1.9	RET
0	0	15.6	0.1	17.4	0.9	15.6	0.4	BKSPACE
0	0	17.7	0.1	19.7	0.9	17.9	0.4	NUMLOCK
0	0	19.9	0.1	21.9	0.9	20.1	0.4	SCROLL
0	0	17.7	2.1	18.6	2.9	17.7	2.4	LFT
0	0	18.8	1.1	19.7	1.9	18.9	1.4	PG UP
0	0	19.9	2.1	20.9	2.9	20.0	2.4	RIT
0	0	18.8	3.1	19.7	3.9	18.9	3.4	PG DN
0	0	18.8	2.1	19.7	2.9	18.9	2.4	
0	0	21.1	1.1	21.9	1.9	21.2	1.4	—
0	0	21.1	2.1	21.9	4.9	21.2	3.4	+

If the entire keyboard is read in and displayed, the screen appears like this:

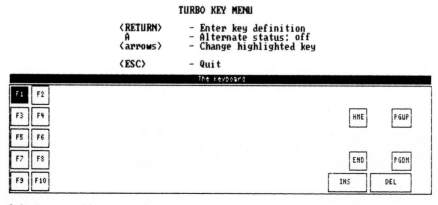

When Turbo Key first comes up, only the 16 keys that can be redefined without the ALT key appear:

The first one, F1, is displayed in reverse video. A menu appears at
the top of the screen, and the user can either redefine the current
key, set the ALT mode on, change the highlighted key, or quit the
program. When ALT mode is turned on, the additional 38 keys that
can be redefined with the ALT key depressed appear on the keyboard. Thus, the user can make a total of 70 redefinitions.

The Turbo Key application requires you to use the ANSI driver,
and a few routines that are provided in the next chapter.

```
{$P256}
program Turbo_Key;
{
DESCRIPTION:
     This program draws certain keys of the keyboard on the
screen and enables the user to redefine those keys using
the ANSI driver.

LIBRARY ROUTINES USED:
     Set_Cursor - sets the ANSI driver cursor position
     Invert_Square - inverts all pixels within a box
     Blink_Text_Cursor - simulates the text cursor
     Get_String_With_Cursor - gets a string using the
               simulated cursor
     Redefine_Function_Key - redefines any key that returns
          an escape sequence (see Chapter 14)

NOTES:
     This routine requires a file, KEYS.DAT, that contains
the information on each key for both displaying it and
redefining it.
     The compiler directive ($P256) must be used to
redirect the output through the ANSI driver.

----------------------------------------------------------}

const
   CARRIAGE_RETURN = 13;          {ascii code of a carriage return}

type
   ANY_KEY = record
      KEY_CODE,                   {escape sequence returned by the key}
      ALT_KEY_CODE: integer;      {sequence returne by ALT and the key}
      X1, Y1,                     {world coordinates of the box}
      X2, Y2,                         {formed by the key}
      XTEXT, YTEXT: real;         {the location of the key text}
      KEY_LABEL   : string[10];   {the text written on the key}
   end;
   ALL_KEYS = array [1..83] of ANY_KEY;

var
   CURRENT_KEY    : integer;      {the current key to redefine}
   KEYS           : ALL_KEYS;     {the entire keyboard}
   IN_CHAR        : char;         {the character input from the user}
   ALTERNATE_MODE : boolean;      {is the alternate key depressed?}
   READ_STRING    : WrkString;    {the string input from the user}
   DEFINITION     : STRING79;     {the string to redefine}
```

```
procedure Setup_Keyboard;
{
DESCRIPTION:
     This routine sets up a display menu and does the required
initializations for the high resolution graphics screen.

SAMPLE CALL:
     Setup_Keyboard;

NOTES:
     This routine is for internal use by the Turbo_Key
program.

-----------------------------------------------------------}


begin
   InitGraphic;                               {initialize the graphics system}
{setup the keyboard world and window}
   SetHeaderOn;
   DefineWindow (1, 0, 60, 79, 150);
   DefineWindow (2, 10, 71, 58, 140);
   DefineHeader(1,'The Keyboard'); {give it a header}
   DefineWorld(1, 0, 5, 22, 0);
   SelectWorld(1);
   SelectWindow(1);
   DrawBorder;

{display the Turbo Key menu}
   Set_Cursor (1, 33);
   writeln ('TURBO KEY MENU');
   Set_Cursor (3, 22);
   Writeln ('<RETURN>      - Enter key definition');
   Set_Cursor (4, 22);
   Writeln (' A           - Alternate status: OFF');
   Set_Cursor (5, 22);
   Writeln ('<arrows>     - Change highlighted key');
   Set_Cursor (7, 22);
   Writeln ('<ESC>        - Quit');

{display the menu prompt}
   Set_Cursor (21, 1);
   Writeln ('Select menu option: ');
 end;
```

```
procedure Load_Keyboard (var KEYBOARD: ALL_KEYS);
{
DESCRIPTION:
     This routine reads in the keyboard file and loads an
array with information for each key.

PARAMETERS:
     KEYBOARD (out) - the array of records containing the
        information about each key
```

```
SAMPLE CALL:
    Setup_Keyboard;

NOTES:
    This routine is for internal use by the Turbo_Key
program.

------------------------------------------------------------}



    var
      KEY_TEXT: text;                    {the file with keyboard specs}
      I       : integer;                 {counter for loops}

    begin

{open the keyboard file}

    Assign (KEY_TEXT, 'keys.dat');
    Reset (KEY_TEXT);

{read in the specifications for all 83 keys}
    for I := 1 TO 83 do
      with KEYBOARD[I] do
        Readln (KEY_TEXT, KEY_CODE, ALT_KEY_CODE, X1, Y1, X2, Y2,
                XTEXT, YTEXT, KEY_LABEL);
    Close (KEY_TEXT);
    end;
```

```
    procedure Display_Keyboard (KEYBOARD: ALL_KEYS;
                  FIRST_KEY, LAST_KEY: integer);
    {
    DESCRIPTION:
        This routine displays a series of keys on the graphics
    screen.

    PARAMETERS:
        KEYBOARD (in) - the array of records containing the
            information about each key
        FIRST_KEY (in) - the index of the first key to display
        LAST_KEY (in) - the index of the last key to display

    SAMPLE CALL:
        Setup_Keyboard;

    NOTES:
        This routine is for internal use by the Turbo_Key
    program.

    ------------------------------------------------------------}



    var
      I: integer;                    {counter for loops}

    begin
```

```
{display only the keys desired}
    for I := FIRST_KEY to LAST_KEY do
       with KEYBOARD[I] do
          begin

{draw a box around the key and display the text}
          DrawSquare (X1, Y1, X2, Y2, false);
          DrawTextW (XTEXT, YTEXT, 1, KEY_LABEL);
          end;
    end;


begin

{load the keyboard specifications from the keyboard file}
  Load_Keyboard (KEYS);

{setup the screen to draw the keyboard keys}
  Setup_Keyboard;

{display the keyboard keys that can be redefined directly}
  Display_Keyboard (KEYS, 1, 16);

{highlight the first key}
  CURRENT_KEY := 1;
  with KEYS[CURRENT_KEY] do
    Invert_Square (X1, Y1, X2, Y2);
  ALTERNATE_MODE := false;
  READ_STRING := '';

{loop until the proper exit -- the escape key}
  repeat

{get an input from the user}
    Blink_Text_Cursor (21, 21);
    read (kbd, IN_CHAR);

{if a carriage return was pressed, get the new definition string}
    if IN_CHAR = Chr(CARRIAGE_RETURN) then
      begin
        Set_Cursor (23, 3);
        Write ('Enter string: ');
        Get_String_With_Cursor (READ_STRING, 23, 17);
        DEFINITION := READ_STRING;

{redefine the key, depending on whether the alternate key will
be pressed}
        if ALTERNATE_MODE then
          Redefine_Function_Key (KEYS[CURRENT_KEY].ALT_KEY_CODE,
                    DEFINITION)
        else
          Redefine_Function_Key (KEYS[CURRENT_KEY].KEY_CODE,
                    DEFINITION);
        GotoXY (1,23);
        ClrEol;
      end

{if the A was pressed, turn on or off ALTernate mode}
    else if (IN_CHAR = 'a') or (IN_CHAR = 'A') then
      begin
        Set_Cursor (4, 55);
```

```
        ALTERNATE_MODE := not ALTERNATE_MODE;
        if ALTERNATE_MODE then
          begin
            writeln ('ON ');

{display the keyboard keys that can be redefined with ALTernate}
                Display_Keyboard (KEYS, 17, 54);
                end

          else
            begin
              writeln ('OFF');

{clear the ALTernate only keys off the screen}
                SelectWindow (2);
                SetBackground (0);
                SelectWindow (1);
              end
          end

{if an escape sequence was entered, see if only the escape key
was pressed}
        else if (IN_CHAR = Chr(ESC)) then
          begin
            Delay (100);
            if KeyPressed then
              begin

{if not, check for up or down arrows}
                read (kbd, IN_CHAR);
                case ord(IN_CHAR) of
                  80: begin   {down arrow}

{de-highlight the current key}
                    with KEYS[CURRENT_KEY] do
                      Invert_Square (X1, Y1, X2, Y2);
                    CURRENT_KEY := CURRENT_KEY + 1;

{if key is F10 and alternate is enabled, make next key the 1}
                    if ALTERNATE_MODE and (CURRENT_KEY = 11) then
                      CURRENT_KEY := 17

{if key is DEL, wrap around to F1}
                    else if CURRENT_KEY = 17 then
                      CURRENT_KEY := 1

{if key is =, set to HOME}
                    else if CURRENT_KEY = 55 then
                      CURRENT_KEY := 11;

{highlight the new current key}
                    with KEYS[CURRENT_KEY] do
                      Invert_Square (X1, Y1, X2, Y2);
                  end;
                  72: begin   {up arrow}

{de-highlight the current key}
                    with KEYS[CURRENT_KEY] do
                      Invert_Square (X1, Y1, X2, Y2);
                    CURRENT_KEY := CURRENT_KEY - 1;
```

```
{if key is HOME and alternate is enabled, set key to =}
            if ALTERNATE_MODE and (CURRENT_KEY = 10) then
                CURRENT_KEY := 54

{if key is 1, set to F10}
            else if CURRENT_KEY = 16 then
                CURRENT_KEY := 10

{if key is F1, wrap back to DEL}
            else if CURRENT_KEY = 0 then
                CURRENT_KEY := 16;

{highlight the new current key}
            with KEYS[CURRENT_KEY] do
                Invert_Square (X1, Y1, X2, Y2);
         end;
         else;

        end;  {case}
      end;
   end;


  until IN_CHAR = Chr(ESC);

  LeaveGraphic;                           {leave the graphics system}

end.
```

The Turbo Graphix Routines

Here is a summary of each of the Turbo Graphix routines.

Preparatory Routines

To compile a Turbo Graphix routine successfully, you must include the following files in this order:

```
{$I TYPEDEF.SYS}
{$I GRAPHIX.SYS}
{$I KERNEL.SYS}
```

You must also include a fourth file when manipulating windows:

```
{$I WINDOWS.SYS}
```

To use the Turbo Graphix Toolbox, you must use a few procedure calls for required initializations. The primary initialization routine is **InitGraphic**. This routine sets up all variables, initializes the windows to be full-screen, and initializes the world coordinates to match the screen coordinates.

After the screen is initialized and cleared, you must select the portion of the screen in which the graphics images will be displayed. You can make your selection with **DefineWindow**. This window can have a header line, which can be set by **DefineHeader**.

After the window is defined, you should select the world-coordinate system. Although defined by **DefineWorld**, the actual system is not set until a call to **SelectWorld** is made. This call should be followed by a call to **SelectWindow**, which associates the world system and activates the window.

You can draw a border (along with the header) by a call to **DrawBorder**. After using these calls in the order discussed, you are ready to draw graphics images.

```
procedure InitGraphic;
{
DESCRIPTION:
    This routine initializes all of the Turbo Graphix variables
and prepares the terminal for graphic commands.

SAMPLE CALL:
    InitGraphic;

NOTES:
    This routine must be the first Turbo Graphix routine
called.  It should be called only once per application
program.

-----------------------------------------------------------}
```

```
procedure DefineWorld (WORLD_INDEX: integer;
    XLEFT, YTOP, XRIGHT, YBOTTOM: real);
{
DESCRIPTION:
    The routine defines a world coordinate system that is used
when drawing and plotting.  The default world system is the
same as the screen coordinates.

PARAMETERS:
    XLEFT (in) - world coordinate of the leftmost column
    YTOP (in) - world coordinate of the top line
    XRIGHT (in) - world coordinate of the rightmost column
    YBOTTOM (in) - world coordinate of the bottom line
```

```
SAMPLE CALL:
    DefineWorld (1, -1.6, 1, 1.6, -1);          (defines world 1 so
                           that a circle of radius 1 will take as much
                           of the screen as possible)

NOTES:
    If YBOTTOM is less than YTOP, the coordinate system will be
inverted (bottom to top).
    A ratio between the Y-span and the X-span of 1.6 will guarantee
that perfect circles will come out right.
    This routine does not enable the world coordinate system -- this
is done by SelectWorld.

---------------------------------------------------------}
```

```
procedure SelectWorld (WORLD_INDEX: integer);
{
DESCRIPTION:
    This routine enables a world coordinate system defined
by DefineWorld.  All future graphic commands will be associated
with that coordinate system.

PARAMETERS:
    WORLD_INDEX (in) - the index of the world to enable [1-4]

SAMPLE CALL:
    SelectWorld (1);

NOTES:
    This routine must be called BEFORE SelectWindow to
associate the world coordinate system with a particular
window.

---------------------------------------------------------}
```

```
procedure DefineWindow (INDEX, XLEFT, YTOP,
                          XRIGHT, YBOTTOM: integer);
{
DESCRIPTION:
    This routine defines the limits of a window.  All
subsequent graphics calls will be confined to that portion
of the screen.

PARAMETERS:
    INDEX (in) - the index of the window to create [1-16]
    XLEFT (in) - the leftmost window column [0-79]
    YTOP (in) - the top window line [0-199]
    XRIGHT (in) - the rightmost window column [0-79]
    YBOTTOM (in) - the bottom window line [0-199]

SAMPLE CALL:
    DefineWindow (2, 40, 100, 79, 199);     (Defines window 2 as
                           the lower right quarter of the screen)
```

```
NOTES:
     XRIGHT cannot be less than XLEFT.
     YBOTTOM cannot be less than YTOP.
     The actual window selection is accomplished by
SelectWindow.

-------- ---------------------------------------------------}
```

```
procedure DefineTextWindow (INDEX, LEFT_COL, TOP_LINE,
                RIGHT_COL, BOTTOM_LINE, TEXT_BORDER: integer);
{
DESCRIPTION:
     This routine creates a window based on text coordinates.  It
also enables you to fit machine-dependent text inside a given
window.

PARAMETERS:
     LEFT_COL (in) - the leftmost text column [1-80]
     TOP_LINE (in) - the top text line [1-25]
     RIGHT_COL (in) - the rightmost text column [1-80]
     BOTTOM_LINE (in) - the bottom text line [1-25]
     TEXT_BORDER (in) - the number of pixels that the actual
        graphics window will exceed the desired text window
        on all sides

SAMPLE CALL:
     DefineTextWindow (1, 1, 40, 12, 1);   (defines window 1 as
                                top left quarter of the screen)

NOTES:
     This routine is especially useful for the Hercules version
of Turbo Graphix, where the relationship between window
coordinates and screen coordinates is not as obvious.
     This routine does not enable the window -- that is done
by SelectWindow.

     ---------------------------------------------------------}
```

```
procedure SelectWindow (INDEX: integer);
{
DESCRIPTION:
     This routine enables a window, or portion of the screen,
defined by DefineWindow or DefineTextWindow.  All future
graphic commands will be confined to that window.

PARAMETERS:
     INDEX (in) - the index of the window to enable [1-16]
```

```
SAMPLE CALL:
    SelectWindow (1);
```

NOTES:
    This routine must be called AFTER SelectWorld to
associate a world coordinate system with a window.

--}

```
procedure DefineHeader (INDEX: integer;
                        HEADER: WrkString);
{
```
DESCRIPTION:
    This routine associates a string with a given window. This
header is centered on either the top or bottom of the window.

PARAMETERS:
    INDEX (in) - the number of the window [1-16]
    HEADER (in) - the header text

```
SAMPLE CALL:
    DefineHeader (1, 'THIS IS A WINDOW');
```

NOTES:
    This routine does NOT display the header -- that is done
by DrawBorder.

--}

```
procedure DrawBorder;
{
```
DESCRIPTION:
    This routine draws a box and an optional header
around the active window.

```
SAMPLE CALL:
    DrawBorder;
```

NOTES:
    The header must have be previously defined by
DefineHeader.
    The box is drawn with the line style set by
SetLineStyle.

--}

```
procedure LeaveGraphic;
{
DESCRIPTION:
    This routine clears the screen and returns to the
text mode enabled before the call to InitGraphic.

SAMPLE CALL:
    LeaveGraphic;

NOTES:
    This routine should be called before leaving any
applications program.

--------------------------------------------------------------}
```

```
procedure EnterGraphic;

{
DESCRIPTION:
    This routine clears the screen and sets the terminal
screen in high resolution graphics mode.  In addition, the
screen colors are changed to white and black.

SAMPLE CALL:
    EnterGraphic;

NOTES:
    This routine will not initialize all required parameters
to successfully use other Turbo Graphix routines -- InitGraphic
must be used for this purpose.

--------------------------------------------------------------}
```

Basic Graphics Routines

Turbo Graphix includes high-level routines to draw points, lines, squares, circles, and text. Each set of these routines includes lower-level routines that draw the shapes by using screen coordinates. You should only use these routines when speed and accuracy down to the pixel are critical. *Never* mix the routines and attempt to juggle the two coordinate systems.

You can draw lines by using any 8-bit pattern set by **SetLineStyle** and fill squares automatically. A call to **SetAspect** can make circles into ellipses. All of these extras make the Turbo Graphix Toolbox a must for programmers who realize the importance of high-quality graphics.

```
procedure ClearScreen;
{
DESCRIPTION:
     This routine clears the current screen, either the
terminal screen or the RAM screen.

SAMPLE CALL:
     ClearScreen;

-----------------------------------------------------------}
```

```
procedure SetForegroundColor (COLOR_INDEX: integer);
{
DESCRIPTION:
     This routine changes the foreground, or "white" color.  All
objects on the screen get changed to the new color, and all future
graphics calls will be done in that color.

PARAMETERS:
     COLOR_INDEX (in) - the index of the new foreground color [1-15]

SAMPLE CALL:
     SetForegroundColor (4);     (sets "white" to red)

NOTES:
     See the Turbo Graphix Toolbox manual p. 238ff for colors
for the various graphics adapters.

-----------------------------------------------------------}
```

```
procedure SetColorWhite;
{
DESCRIPTION:
     This routine sets the drawing color to "white".  All
further graphics call will be done in "white" until a call
to SetColorBlack.

SAMPLE CALL:
     SetColorWhite;

NOTES:
     "White" may be any non-black color.  It is changed by
SetForegroundColor.

-----------------------------------------------------------}
```

```
procedure SetColorBlack;
{
DESCRIPTION:
    This routine sets the drawing color to black.  All
further graphics call will be done in black until a call
to SetColorWhite.

SAMPLE CALL:
    SetColorBlack;

NOTES:
    This routine is most useful for drawing in an inverted
screen or window.

------------------------------------------------------------}
```

```
procedure DrawPoint (XPT, YPT: real);
{
DESCRIPTION:
    This routine draws a point at a given location in world
coordinates.  If the point lies outside of the active
window, no point is drawn.

PARAMETERS:
    XPT (in) - the x-coordinate (world) of the point
    YPT (in) - the y-coordinate (world) of the point

SAMPLE CALL:
    DrawPoint (3.5, 6.0);

------------------------------------------------------------}
```

```
function PointDrawn (XPT, YPT: real):boolean;
{
DESCRIPTION:
    This routine determines if a point at a given location
in world coordinates has been drawn.

VALUE RETURNED:
    true if the pixel is set to the current drawing color,
otherwise false.

PARAMETERS:
    XPT (in) - the x-coordinate (world) of the point
    YPT (in) - the y-coordinate (world) of the point

SAMPLE CALL:
    if not PointDrawn (XLOC, YLOC) then
        DrawPoint (XLOC, YLOC);

------------------------------------------------------------}
```

```
procedure DrawLine (XSTART, YSTART, XEND, YEND: real);
{
DESCRIPTION:
    This routine draws a line in world coordinates.  The
line can drawn as a pattern set by SetLineStyle and is
clipped in the active window.

PARAMETERS:
    XSTART (in) - the x-coordinate (world) of the start point
    YSTART (in) - the y-coordinate (world) of the start point
    XEND (in) - the x-coordinate (world) of the end point
    YEND (in) - the y-coordinate (world) of the end point

SAMPLE CALL:
    DrawLine (0, 0, 1.2, 1.8);

------------------------------------------------------------}
```

```
procedure SetLineStyle (STYLE: integer);
{
DESCRIPTION:
    This routine sets a pattern that future calls to DrawLine
and DrawSquare will follow when drawing lines.

PARAMETERS:
    STYLE (in) - the line style or byte pattern to follow

SAMPLE CALL:
    SetLineStyle (2);       (set pattern to dashed line)

NOTES:
    If STYLE is between 0 and 4, a preset pattern is followed:
        0 - full line
        1 - dotted line
        2 - dashed line
        3 - dash-dotted line
        4 - short dashed line
When STYLE is 5 or greater, the number represents the actual
byte pattern to follow.

------------------------------------------------------------}
```

```
procedure DrawSquare (XLEFT, YTOP, XRIGHT, YBOTTOM: real;
                                        FILL: boolean);
{
DESCRIPTION:
    This routine draws a box in world coordinates.  The box
may be filled completely if desired.  The lines of the box
are drawn according to the line style set by SetLineStyle.

PARAMETERS:
    XLEFT (in) - world coordinate of the leftmost column of the box
    YTOP (in) - world coordinate of the top line of the box
    XRIGHT (in) - world coordinate of the rightmost column of the box
    YBOTTOM (in) - world coordinate of the bottom line of the box
    FILL (in) - flag to determine if the box should be filled
```

```
SAMPLE CALL:
    DrawSquare (1.0, 1.0, 10.0, 10.0, true);

----------------------------------------------------------}
```

```
procedure DrawCircle (XCENTER, YCENTER, RADIUS: real);

{
DESCRIPTION:
    This routine draws a circle in the current drawing color.
An ellipse may be drawn by setting the aspect factor with
SetAspect.

PARAMETERS:
    XCENTER (in) - the x-coordinate (world) of the center point
    YCENTER (in) - the y-coordinate (world) of the center point
    RADIUS (in) - radius of the circle in world coordinates

SAMPLE CALL:
    DrawCircle (0.0, 0.0, 5.0);

NOTES:
    SetAspect should be called before drawing the first
circle.

----------------------------------------------------------}
```

```
procedure SetAspect (ASPECT_RATIO: real);
{
DESCRIPTION:
    This routine sets the aspect ratio, the ratio of the
heighth of an ellipse to its width, of all future circles
and arcs.

PARAMETERS:
    ASPECT_RATIO (in) - the desired aspect ratio

SAMPLE CALL:
    SetAspect (1);    (sets the aspect ratio for perfect circles)

----------------------------------------------------------}
```

```
procedure DrawTextW (XLOC, YLOC: real;
               SCALING_FACTOR: integer;
                  TEXT_STR: WrkString;
{
```

```
DESCRIPTION:
    This routine displays a text string at a given location
in world coordinates.  The text is written in the Turbo
Graphix 4x6 font, and can be scaled to make it larger.

PARAMETERS:
    XLOC (in) - the x-coordinate (world) of the start of text
    YLOC (in) - the y-coordinate (world) of the start of text
    RADIUS (in) - muliplying factor for text [1-33]
    TEXT_STR (in) - the string to be displayed

SAMPLE CALL:
    DrawTextW (3.4, 5.0, 2, 'Hi There');          (draws text in
                                                  8x12 characters)

NOTES:
    The first character of the text string is located just to
the right of the point, and is centered on the y-coordinate.
    To display the normal 8x8 text characters, use the standard
Turbo procedures GotoXY and Write.

-----------------------------------------------------------}
```

Window Manipulation Routines

Window management is one of the most useful tools in creating a visually appealing program. The Turbo Graphix Toolbox makes manipulating windows easy. The routines **MoveHor** and **MoveVer** allow the user to see a window move across the screen. The contents of a window can be copied, saved to a file, stored in memory, and restored—each process accomplished by one simple procedure call.

```
procedure SetHeaderToBottom;
{
DESCRIPTION:
    This routine sets an internal flag so that all future
window borders have their header drawn at the bottom of
the window.

SAMPLE CALL:
    SetHeaderToBottom;

NOTES:
    This routine does not draw any headers -- this is
done by DrawBorder.

-----------------------------------------------------------}
```

```
procedure SetHeaderToTop;
{
DESCRIPTION:
    This routine sets an internal flag so that all future
window borders have their header drawn at the top of
the window.

SAMPLE CALL:
    SetHeaderToTop;

NOTES:
    This routine does not draw any headers -- this is
done by DrawBorder.

-------------------------------------------------------------}
```

```
procedure RemoveHeader (INDEX: integer);
{
DESCRIPTION:
    This routine sets an internal flag so that the header
of a given window is no longer drawn.

PARAMETERS:
    INDEX (in) - the index of the window of interest [1-16]

SAMPLE CALL:
    RemoveHeader (2);

NOTES:
    This routine does not actually remove the header on
the screen -- a call to DrawBorder will do that.

-------------------------------------------------------------}
```

```
procedure RedefineWindow (INDEX, XLEFT, YTOP,
                          XRIGHT, YBOTTOM: integer);
{
DESCRIPTION:
    This routine redefines the location of a particular
window without affecting the header information.

PARAMETERS:
    INDEX (in) - the index of the window to redefine [1-16]
    XLEFT (in) - the leftmost window column [0-79]
    YTOP (in) - the top window line [0-199]
    XRIGHT (in) - the rightmost window column [0-79]
    YBOTTOM (in) - the bottom window line [0-199]
```

```
SAMPLE CALL:
    RedefineWindow (2, 40, 100, 79, 199);    (Redefines window 2
                           as the lower right quarter of the screen)

NOTES:
    XRIGHT cannot be less than XLEFT.
    YBOTTOM cannot be less than YTOP.
    The actual window selection is accomplished by
SelectWindow.

    -----------------------------------------------------------}
```

```
procedure SetBackground (PATTERN: byte);
{
DESCRIPTION:
    This routine fills the active window with a specified
pattern.  It can be used to clear a window or completely
fill a window.

PARAMETERS:
    PATTERN (in) - the 8-bit pattern to fill the window with

SAMPLE CALL:
    SetBackground ($55);    (fills in every other pixel)

NOTES:
    The same 8-bit pattern is repeated throughout the
window.  For a more versatile background, use SetBackground8.

    -----------------------------------------------------------}
```

```
procedure SetBackground8 (PATTERN: BackgroundArray);
{
DESCRIPTION:
    This routine fills the active window with a specified
pattern.  The pattern is an 8x8 square that is repeated
throughout the window.

PARAMETERS:
    PATTERN (in) - an array of bytes to specify the pattern

SAMPLE CALL:
    for I := 0 to 7 do
      DIAGONAL[I] := 1 shl I;
    SetBackground8 (DIAGONAL);

    -----------------------------------------------------------}
```

```
procedure MoveHor (DELTAX: integer;
            SCREEN_COPY: boolean);
{
DESCRIPTION:
     This routine moves the active window a given number of
bytes horizontally.  The area behind the window can be
either cleared or filled with the contents of the RAM
screen.

PARAMETERS:
     DELTAX (in) - number of bytes (8 pixels) to move window
     SCREEN_COPY (in) - flag indicating whether the uncovered
        area is to be filled with the corresponding area of
        the RAM screen.

SAMPLE CALL:
     MoveHor (10, true);

NOTES:
     The RAM screen must be allocated for successful
copying of the background.

     ------------------------------------------------------------}
```

```
procedure MoveVer (DELTAY: integer;
            SCREEN_COPY: boolean);
{
DESCRIPTION:
     This routine moves the active window a given number of
pixels vertically.  The area behind the window can be
either cleared or filled with the contents of the RAM
screen.  The speed and smoothness is set by SetVStep.

PARAMETERS:
     DELTAY (in) - number of pixels to move window
     SCREEN_COPY (in) - flag indicating whether the uncovered
        area is to be filled with the corresponding area of
        the RAM screen.

SAMPLE CALL:
     MoveVer (40, true);

NOTES:
     The RAM screen must be allocated for successful
copying of the background.

     ------------------------------------------------------------}
```

```
procedure SetVStep (NUM_PIXELS: integer);
{
DESCRIPTION:
     This routine determines the speed of vertical moves
```

(with MoveVer) by setting the number a pixels to move
each time.

PARAMETERS:
    NUM_PIXELS (in) - the number of pixels per step

SAMPLE CALL:
    SetVStep (8);

--}

procedure CopyWindow (FROM_SCREEN, TO_SCREEN: byte;
                                    XLEFT, YTOP: integer);
{
DESCRIPTION:
    This routine copies the current window from its screen
to a specified location on either the terminal screen or the
RAM screen.

PARAMETERS:
    FROM_SCREEN (in) - the screen the current window is on [1-2]
    TO_SCREEN (in) - the screen where the new window will be [1-2]
    XLEFT (in) - the left column of the new window [0-79]
    YTOP (in) - the top screen row of the new window [0-199]

SAMPLE CALL:
    CopyWindow (1, 1, 0, 0); (copies the current window to
                        the upper left corner of the screen)

NOTES:
    The RAM screen must be allocated for successful
copies to or from screen 2.

--}

procedure InvertWindow;
{
DESCRIPTION:
    This routine inverts each pixel in the active window --
pixels that were "white" become "black" and vice versa.

SAMPLE CALL:
    InvertWindow;

--}

```
function WindowSize (INDEX: integer): integer;
{
DESCRIPTION:
    This routine determines the size of a given window.
The size is rounded up to the nearest 1024 so that the
programmer can determine if the window can be saved on
the stack.

VALUE RETURNED:
    the size of the desired window

PARAMETERS:
    INDEX (in) - the index of the window to check [1-16]

SAMPLE CALL:
  if WindowSize (2) < Maxavail*16 then
    StoreWindow (2);

---------------------------------------------------------}
```

```
procedure StoreWindow (INDEX: integer);
{
DESCRIPTION:
    This routine stores a given window on the stack for
later retrieval.

PARAMETERS:
    INDEX (in) - the index of the window to store [1-16]

SAMPLE CALL:
    StoreWindow (2);

NOTES:
    If a window with the same index is already on the
stack, the new window replaces it.
    This routine does not affect the display.

--------------------------------------------------------}
```

```
procedure RestoreWindow (INDEX,
            DELTAX, DELTAY: integer);
{
```

```
DESCRIPTION:
    This routine takes a window that was stored on the stack
and displays it on the active screen.  The window position
may be offset by a set of deltas.

PARAMETERS:
    INDEX (in) - the index of the window to restore [1-16]
    DELTAX (in) - the number of bytes (8 pixels) to move
      horizontally
    DELTAY (in) - the number of pixels to move vertically

SAMPLE CALL:
    RestoreWindow (1, 4, -30);        (restores window 1 and
                                       moves it right and up)

NOTES:
    If INDEX is negative, the restored window is removed
from the stack.

-----------------------------------------------------------}
```

```
procedure SaveWindow (INDEX: integer;
            SAVE_FILE_NAME: WrkString);
{
DESCRIPTION:
    This routine saves the contents of a window to a
file.  The size and location of the window are included
in the file.

PARAMETERS:
    INDEX (in) - the index of the window to save [1-16]
    SAVE_FILE_NAME (in) - the name of the file to create

SAMPLE CALL:
    SaveWindow (4, 'FRANK.WDW');

NOTES:
    As always, if the file name given already exists, it
will be written over.

----------------------------------------------------------}
```

```
procedure LoadWindow (INDEX, XLEFT, YTOP: integer;
                LOAD_FILE_NAME: WrkString);
{
```

DESCRIPTION:
     This routine loads and displays a window saved by the
SaveWindow procedure. The window can be loaded back to its
original position or set in a new location.

PARAMETERS:
     INDEX (in) - the index of the window to save [1-16]
     XLEFT (in) - the left column of the new window [0-79]
     YTOP (in) - the top screen row of the new window [0-199]
     LOAD_FILE_NAME (in) - the name of the file to load

SAMPLE CALL:
     LoadWindow (3, -1, -1, 'FRANK.WDW');   (loads window 3
                                                into former position)

NOTES:
     If either coordinate is negative, the routine will
place the window in its original coordinate position.

     --}


```
procedure SaveWindowStack (STACK_FILE: WrkString);
{
```
DESCRIPTION:
     This routine writes the entire window stack to
disk.

PARAMETERS:
     STACK_FILE (in) - the name of the files to create

SAMPLE CALL:
     SaveWindowStack ('TABLES');

NOTES:
     This routine creates two files with different
extensions, and therefore STACK_FILE should not
include an extension.
     As always, if the file name given already exists, it
will be written over.

     --}


```
procedure LoadWindowStack (STACK_FILE: WrkString);
{
```
DESCRIPTION:
     This routine loads the entire window stack from
disk.

PARAMETERS:
     STACK_FILE (in) - the name of the files to load

```
SAMPLE CALL:
    LoadWindowStack ('TABLES');

NOTES:
    This routine searches for two files with different
extensions, and therefore STACK_FILE should not
include an extension.
    The new window stack replaces the current one.

----------------------------------------------------------}
```

```
procedure ClearWindowStack (INDEX: integer);
{
DESCRIPTION:
    This routine erases a window from the stack.

PARAMETERS:
    INDEX (in) - the index of the window to erase [1-16]

SAMPLE CALL:
    ClearWindowStack (2);

NOTES:
    If the window is not on the stack, no operation will
take place.

----------------------------------------------------------}
```

```
procedure ResetWindowStack;
{
DESCRIPTION:
    This routine clears the entire window stack.

SAMPLE CALL:
    ResetWindowStack;

----------------------------------------------------------}
```

Screen Manipulation Routines

As speed becomes increasingly important in applications today, screen manipulation is used more and more. Turbo Graphix automatically defines a RAM screen, which exactly duplicates the memory used to control the terminal screen. You can make changes to the RAM screen without any changes to the display. If you later copy or swap the RAM screen, large graphics changes will appear almost instantaneously.

Also included in the Turbo Graphix Toolbox are routines that save and load an entire screenful of information. Although the files created are large, you can use them to bring up complex graphics images (such as company logos) quickly and easily.

```
procedure InvertScreen;

{
DESCRIPTION:
    This routine inverts each pixel in the active screen --
pixels that were "white" become "black" and vice versa.

SAMPLE CALL:
    InvertScreen;

------------------------------------------------------------}
```

```
procedure SelectScreen (SCREEN_NUMBER: integer);
{
DESCRIPTION:
    This routine selects either the terminal screen or the
RAM screen as the active screen.  All future graphic commands
will be accomplished on the active screen.

PARAMETERS:
    SCREEN_NUMBER (in) - 1 for terminal, 2 for RAM screen

SAMPLE CALL:
    SelectScreen (2);

NOTES:
    Graphic calls when the RAM screen is active have no
affect on the terminal display.

------------------------------------------------------------}
```

```
procedure CopyScreen;
{
DESCRIPTION:
    This routine copies the active screen onto the inactive
screen.  In other words, it can be used to save the terminal
screen for later retrieval, or to retrieve the RAM screen.
```

```
SAMPLE CALL:
    CopyScreen;

NOTES:
    The RAM screen must be allocated for successful
completion.

----------------------------------------------------------}
```

```
procedure SwapScreen;
{
DESCRIPTION:
    This routine exchanges the terminal screen and the
RAM screen.

SAMPLE CALL:
    SwapScreen;

NOTES:
    The RAM screen must be allocated for successful
completion.
    The pointer to the active window is unaffected by
this call.

----------------------------------------------------------}
```

```
procedure SaveScreen (SCREEN_FILE: WrkString);
{
DESCRIPTION:
    This routine saves the entire contents of the active
screen to disk.

PARAMETERS:
    SCREEN_FILE (in) - the name of the file to create

SAMPLE CALL:
    SaveScreen ('MENU.PIC');

NOTES:
    As always, if the file name given already exists, it
will be written over.

----------------------------------------------------------}
```

```
procedure LoadScreen (SCREEN_FILE: WrkString);
{
DESCRIPTION:
    This routine loads in a file and replaces the active
```

```
screen with the contents of the file.

PARAMETERS:

    SCREEN_FILE (in) - the name of the file to load

SAMPLE CALL:
    LoadScreen ('MENU.PIC');

-------------------------------------------------------------}
```

```
procedure HardCopy (BLACK_WHITE_REVERSE: boolean;
                    PRINT_MODE: byte);
{
DESCRIPTION:
    This routine copies the terminal screen to a local
printer.  The densities can vary, if the printer supports
them.

PARAMETERS:
    BLACK_WHITE_REVERSE: flag to indicate whether the screen
        colors should be reversed when printed
    PRINT_MODE (in) - special print mode (see below)

SAMPLE CALL:
    HardCopy (true, 1);

NOTES:
    This routine only supports EPSON-compatible printers.
    Print modes are as follows:
       1 - 960 points/line   (for IBM-ready printers)
       3 - 1920 points/line
       5 - 640 points/line
       6 - 720 points/line

-------------------------------------------------------------}
```

Specialized Graphics Routines

In Turbo Graphix, the high-level graphics procedures are primarily used for the manipulation and display of two-dimensional data sets. The data sets can be plotted with coordinate axes either as a continuous line, in a bar graph, or as a smooth curve.

The following routines are in separate files on disk and must be included individually for successful compilation.

```
procedure DrawPolygon (POINTS: PlotArray;
     FIRST_POINT, LAST_POINT,
     SYMBOL, SCALE, BAR_CODE: integer);
{
DESCRIPTION:
     This routine draws a set of points on the active screen.
The points can be connected with lines defined by SetLineStyle.
The points themselves can be special symbols defined below.
In addition, vertical lines can be drawn from the axis to
the vertices.

PARAMETERS:
     POINTS (in) - the array of points to plot (two-dimensional)
     FIRST_POINT (in) - the index of the first point to plot [1-100]
     LAST_POINT (in) - the index of the last point to plot [1-100]
     SYMBOL (in) - the code for the symbol for each point [0-9]
     SCALE (in) - the size of the symbols [1-10]
     BAR_CODE (in) - the code for vertical bars [(-1)- 1]

SAMPLE CALL:
     DrawPolygon (GRADES, 1, NUM_GRADES, 3, 2, 0);

NOTES:
     The symbols are defined as follows:
          0 - line          5 - diamond
          1 - +             6 - Y
          2 - X             7 - *
          3 - square        8 - O
          4 - filled square 9 - .
     If BAR_CODE is less than 0, lines are drawn from the X axis to
each vertex.  If BAR_CODE is greater than 0, the lines are drawn
from the bottom of the window.
     If LAST_POINT is less than 0, full clipping is done on all lines.
Otherwise, only the vertices are clipped.

--------------------------------------------------------}
```

```
procedure ScalePolygon (var POINTS: PlotArray;
                    NUM_POINTS: integer;
                    XSCALE, YSCALE: real);
{
DESCRIPTION:
     This routine scales a set of points by multiplying a
constant by each of the coordinates.

PARAMETERS:
     POINTS (in/out) - the array of points to scale (two-dimensional)
     NUM_POINTS (in) - the number of points to scale [1-100]
     XSCALE (in) - the number to multiply each x-coordinate by
     YSCALE (in) - the number to multiply each y-coordinate by

SAMPLE CALL:
     ScalePolygon (CURVE, 50, 1, 1.1);          (makes CURVE
                                               slightly taller)

--------------------------------------------------------}
```

```
procedure RotatePolygon (var POINTS: PlotArray;
                             NUM_POINTS: integer;
                         ROTATION_ANGLE: real);
{
DESCRIPTION:
    This routine rotates a set of points around its geometric
center of gravity.


PARAMETERS:
    POINTS (in/out) - the array of points to rotate (two-dimensional)
    NUM_POINTS (in) - the number of points to rotate [1-100]
    ROTATION_ANGLE (in) - angle in degrees to rotate clockwise

SAMPLE CALL:
    RotatePolygon (CURVE, 75, 90);

----------------------------------------------------------}
```

```
procedure RotatePolygonAbout (var POINTS: PlotArray;
                                  NUM_POINTS: integer;
                         ROTATION_ANGLE, XLOC, YLOC: real);
{
DESCRIPTION:
    This routine rotates a set of points around a given
point.

PARAMETERS:
    POINTS (in/out) - the array of points to rotate (two-dimensional)
    NUM_POINTS (in) - the number of points to rotate [1-100]
    ROTATION_ANGLE (in) - angle in degrees to rotate clockwise
    XLOC (in) - the x-coordinate (world) of the rotation point
    YLOC (in) - the y-coordinate (world) of the rotation point

SAMPLE CALL:
    RotatePolygon (CURVE, 75, 90, 5.0, 5.0);

----------------------------------------------------------}
```

```
procedure TranslatePolygon (var POINTS: PlotArray;
                                NUM_POINTS: integer;
                            DELTAX, DELTAY: real);
{
DESCRIPTION:
    This routine moves a set of points a given distance in
both the x and y directions.
```

```
PARAMETERS:
    POINTS (in/out) - the array of points to translate (two-dimensional)
    NUM_POINTS (in) - the number of points to translate [1-100]
    DELTAX (in) - the change in X in world coordinates
    DELTAY (in) - the change in Y in world coordinates

SAMPLE CALL:
    TranslatePolygon (CURVE, 50, 2.0, 0.0);

    --------------------------------------------------------}
```

```
procedure FindWorld (WORLD_INDEX: integer;
                            POINTS: PlotArray;
                        NUM_POINTS: integer;
                    SCALEX, SCALEY: real;
{
DESCRIPTION:
    This routine finds a world coordinate system to fit a
set of points.  The system can be expanded by given scale
factors.

PARAMETERS:
    WORLD_INDEX (in) - the index of the world to create
    POINTS (in) - the array of points to use (two-dimensional)
    NUM_POINTS (in) - the number of points to rotate [1-100]
    SCALEX (in) - the scaling in the X direction
    SCALEY (in) - the scaling in the Y direction

SAMPLE CALL:
    FindWorld (2, CURVE, 80, 1.1, 1.1);        (finds world with
                                                10% extra space)

NOTES:
    This routine automatically calls DefineWorld and
SelectWorld.
```

```
procedure DrawAxis (XNUM_TICS, YNUM_TICS,
                    LEFT_SPACE, TOP_SPACE,
                  RIGHT_SPACE, BOTTOM_SPACE,
                   XLINE_STYLE, YLINE_STYLE: integer;
                             DRAW_ARROWS: boolean);
{
DESCRIPTION:
    This routine draws a set of coordinate axes in the
active window using the current world coordinates.  The
drawing area can be set away from the edges of the window.
```

PARAMETERS:

        XNUM_TICS (in) - relative number of tics on the x-axis [0-9]
        YNUM_TICS (in) - relative number of tics on the y-axis [0-9]
        LEFT_SPACE (in) - number of bytes (8 pixels) to leave on the left
        TOP_SPACE (in) - number of pixels to leave on the top
        RIGHT_SPACE (in) - number of bytes (8 pixels) to leave on the right
        BOTTOM_SPACE (in) - number of pixels to leave on the bottom
        XLINE_STYLE (in) - line style of the x-axis [0-256]
        YLINE_STYLE (in) - line style of the y-axis [0-256]
        DRAW_ARROWS (in) - flag to note placing arrows at the ends of
           the axes

SAMPLE CALL:
    DrawAxis (8, 8, 0, 0, 2, 2, 0, 0, false);

NOTES:
    If either XNUM_TICS or YNUM_TICS is negative, a border is drawn
around the newly-defined active area.
    The newly-defined active area is valid for one call to
DrawPolygon or DrawHistogram.

    ---}

```
procedure DrawHistogram (POINTS: PlotArray;
                    NUM_POINTS: integer;
                         HATCH: boolean;
                  HATCH_DENSITY: integer);
{
```
DESCRIPTION:
    This routine draws a histogram or bar chart, based on
a set of points. The bars can be hatched with various
densities.

PARAMETERS:
    POINTS (in) - the array of points to use (two-dimensional,
                although only the y-coordinates are used)
    NUM_POINTS (in) - the number of points to rotate [1-100]
    HATCH (in) - flag to enable hatching
    HATCH_DENSITY (in) - density of the hatching (see Hatch below)

SAMPLE CALL:

NOTES:
    If NUM_POINTS is negative, the bars are drawn from the
x-axis. If positive, they are drawn from the bottom of the
display area (and use absolute value so that values are
always positive).

    ---}

```
procedure Hatch (XLEFT, YTOP, XRIGHT, YBOTTOM: real;
                            HATCH_DENSITY: integer);
{
DESCRIPTION:
    This routine draws hatch marks in a rectangular area.
The density and direction can be varied.

PARAMETERS:
    XLEFT (in) - world coordinate of the leftmost column of the box
    YTOP (in) - world coordinate of the top line of the box
    XRIGHT (in) - world coordinate of the rightmost column of the box
    YBOTTOM (in) - world coordinate of the bottom line of the box
    HATCH_DENSITY (in) - distance between hatch lines

SAMPLE CALL:
    Hatch (1.1, 4.3, 6.8, 9.9, 3);        (hatches by drawing
                                           every third line)


NOTES:
    If HATCH_DENSITY is positive, lines will go up and to the right.
When negative, lines will go down and to the right.  The number
determines the number of dark lines -- 1 draws every line, 2 draws
every other line, 3 draws every third line, etc.


    -------------------------------------------------------}
```

```
procedure DrawCircleSegment (XCENTER, YCENTER: real;
                  var XSTART_END, YSTART_END: real;
          LABEL_INNER_RADIUS, LABEL_OUTER_RADIUS,
                       ANGLE, LABEL_VALUE: real;
                             LABEL_TEXT: WrkString;
                LABEL_OPTION, LABEL_SIZE: byte);
{
DESCRIPTION:

PARAMETERS:
    XCENTER (in) - the x-coordinate (world) of the center point
    YCENTER (in) - the y-coordinate (world) of the center point
    XSTART_END (in/out) - the x-coordinate (world) of the start
        point, the end point is returned in the same variable
    YSTART_END (in/out) - the y-coordinate (world) of the start
        point, the end point is returned in the same variable
    LABEL_INNER_RADIUS (in) - radius (world scale) of the start
        of the label line
    LABEL_OUTER_RADIUS (in) - radius (world scale) of the end
        of the label line
    ANGLE (in) - angle of segment in degrees counterclockwise
    LABEL_VALUE (in) - numeric value to use for label
    LABEL_TEXT (in) - text associated with numeric value
    LABEL_OPTION (in) - labelling option (see below) [0-3]
    LABEL_SIZE (in) - size of entire label [1-10]
```

```
SAMPLE CALL:
    DrawCircleSegment (0, 0, XLOC, YLOC, 0.8, 1.2, 90,
                        25, 'Percent of A''s: ', 2, 1);


NOTES:
    The aspect ratio, set by SetAspect is used so that
elliptical segments can be drawn.
    The label options are as follows:
        0 - no label
        1 - text label only
        2 - entire label (text and numeric)
        3 - numeric label only


-----------------------------------------------------------}
```

```
procedure DrawCartPie (XCENTER, YCENTER,
                       XSTART, YSTART,
        LABEL_INNER_RADIUS, LABEL_OUTER_RADIUS: real;
                       VALUES_AND_TEXT: PieArray;
              NUM_SEGMENTS, LABEL_OPTION,
                       LABEL_SIZE: integer);
{
DESCRIPTION:
    This routine draws a pie chart, given a center point and
a start point.  The size of the pie pieces are determined by
the sum of the given values forming 100% of the pie.  Each
segment can have an optional numeric or text label, with
a line in the center of the segment pointing to the label.

PARAMETERS:
    XCENTER (in) - the x-coordinate (world) of the center point
    YCENTER (in) - the y-coordinate (world) of the center point
    XSTART (in) - the x-coordinate (world) of the start point
    YSTART (in) - the y-coordinate (world) of the start point
    LABEL_INNER_RADIUS (in) - radius (world scale) of the start
        of the label line
    LABEL_OUTER_RADIUS (in) - radius (world scale) of the end
        of the label line
    VALUES_AND_TEXT (in) - array of text and numeric values to use
    NUM_SEGMENTS (in) - number of pie segments [1-10]
    LABEL_OPTION (in) - labelling option (see DrawCircleSegment)
    LABEL_SIZE (in) - size of entire label [1-10]

SAMPLE CALL:
    DrawCartPie (0.0, 0.0, 1.0, 0.0, 0.8, 1.2, GRADES, 5, 2, 1);


NOTES:

    This routine uses DrawCircleSegment, which must be
included for successful compilation.


-----------------------------------------------------------}
```

```
procedure DrawPolarPie (XCENTER, YCENTER,
                        RADIUS, START_ANGLE,
    LABEL_INNER_RADIUS, LABEL_OUTER_RADIUS: real;
                        VALUES_AND_TEXT: PieArray;
              NUM_SEGMENTS, LABEL_OPTION,
                        LABEL_SIZE: integer);
{
DESCRIPTION:
    This routine draws a pie chart, given a radius and an
initial angle.  The size of the pie pieces are determined by
the sum of the given values forming 100% of the pie.  Each
segment can have an optional numeric or text label, with
a line in the center of the segment pointing to the label.

PARAMETERS:
    XCENTER (in) - the x-coordinate (world) of the center point
    YCENTER (in) - the y-coordinate (world) of the center point
    RADIUS (in) - the radius (world scale) of the pie
    START_ANGLE (in) - the  start angle in degrees clockwise
    LABEL_INNER_RADIUS (in) - radius (world scale) of the start
        of the label line
    LABEL_OUTER_RADIUS (in) - radius (world scale) of the end
        of the label line
    VALUES_AND_TEXT (in) - array of text and numeric values to use
    NUM_SEGMENTS (in) - number of pie segments [1-10]
    LABEL_OPTION (in) - labelling option (see DrawCircleSegment)
    LABEL_SIZE (in) - size of entire label [1-10]

SAMPLE CALL:
    DrawPolarPie (0.0, 0.0, 1.0, 90.0, 0.8, 1.2, GRADES, 5, 2, 1);

NOTES:
    This routine uses DrawCircleSegment, which must be
included for successful compilation.

----------------------------------------------------------}
```

```
procedure Spline       (POINTS: PlotArray;
                        NUM_PTS: integer;
    FIRST_XVALUE, LAST_XVALUE: real;
                    var RESULT: PlotArray;
                   DESIRED_PTS: integer);
{
DESCRIPTION:
    This routine takes an array of points and computes a
spline function to fit those points.  The curve starts and
ends at points given.  Spline fits are often considered to
be the most accurate curve-fitting procedures.

PARAMETERS:
    POINTS (in) - the array of interest
    NUM_PTS (in) - the number of points in the array of interest [2-100]
```

```
     FIRST_XVALUE (in) - x-coordinate of first point for interpolation
     LAST_XVALUE (in) - x-coordinate of last point for interpolation
     RESULT (out) - the computed array
     DESIRED_PTS (in) - the number of points in the computed array [2-100]

SAMPLE CALL:
     Spline (MY_POINTS, 10, -10.0, 10.0, SPLINE_FIT, 50);

---------------------------------------------------------}
```

```
     procedure Bezier (POINTS: PlotArray;
                    NUM_PTS: integer;
                 var RESULT: PlotArray;
                 DESIRED_PTS: integer);
     {
DESCRIPTION:
     This routine takes an array of points and computes a
Bezier polynomial curve to fit those points.  The curve
passes as close to the original points as it can.

PARAMETERS:
     POINTS (in) - the array of interest
     NUM_PTS (in) - the number of points in the array of interest [2-100]
     RESULT (out) - the computed array
     DESIRED_PTS (in) - the number of points in the computed array [2-100]

SAMPLE CALL:
     Bezier (MY_ARRAY, 10, BEZIER_ARRAY, 50);

NOTES:
     This routine is only needed for applications requiring advanced
mathematical techniques.

---------------------------------------------------------}
```

14

Miscellaneous Routines

All of the routines presented in the previous chapters have fit into distinct categories. However, since the functions provided in this chapter are harder to classify, they are grouped under the category "miscellaneous routines," which completes this book's presentation of Turbo Pascal. The chapter examines several powerful programs that utilize the ANSI driver for video control, manipulate the keyboard buffer, trap interrupts, integrate assembly language routines into Turbo programs, and provide directory-wide manipulation of file attributes.

The ANSI Driver

The ANSI driver is a device driver that you must install into memory through the operating system when the system boots. (You will learn how to install it later in this section.) The driver is a collection of software routines that monitor input and output both from the keyboard and to the display monitor. The driver intercepts characters and examines them to see if they are ANSI driver commands. An ANSI driver command is distinguished by the following characters:

```
ESC, '['
```

The ESC character is the ASCII 27. After the driver finds these two characters, it continues to extract command parameters until the end-of-line character is found. For example, the command

```
ESC, '[H'
```

places the cursor at the home position.

To direct the operating system to install the ANSI driver at startup, you must modify the file CONFIG.SYS to include the following command:

```
DEVICE=ANSI.SYS
```

ANSI.SYS is the ANSI driver.

The following program uses the ANSI driver to place the cursor at the home position:

```
{$P256}

program Cursor_Home;

const
  ESC = 27;

begin
  writeln (Chr(ESC), '[H');
end.
```

To prevent output from bypassing the ANSI driver, you must place the compiler directive **{$P256}** at the beginning of your program.

As you will see, the ANSI driver provides tremendous capabilities. Several functions, such as redefining keys on the keyboard, can be performed *only* by the ANSI driver.

```
procedure Clear_Screen;
{
DESCRIPTION:
    This procedure uses the ANSI driver to clear the screen.

SAMPLE CALL:
    Clear_Screen;

NOTES:
    The cursor is placed in the home the position following
    the procedure call.

-------------------------------------------------------------}

begin
  writeln (Chr(ESC), '[H', Chr(ESC), '[J');
end;
```

```
procedure Save_Cursor;
{
DESCRIPTION:
    This procedure uses the ANSI driver to save the cursor
    position.  The cursor is placed at the location saved
    via the procedure Restore_Cursor.

SAMPLE CALL:
    Save_Cursor ;

-------------------------------------------------------------}

begin
  write (Chr(ESC), '[s');
end;
```

```
procedure Restore_Cursor;
{
DESCRIPTION:
    This procedure uses the ANSI driver to place the cursor
    at the location stored by the procedure Save_Cursor.

SAMPLE CALL:
    Restore_Cursor ;

-------------------------------------------------------------}

begin
  write (Chr(ESC), '[u');
end;
```

```
procedure Cursor_Up (ROWS: integer);
{
DESCRIPTION:
    This procedure uses the ANSI driver to move the cursor
    up the number of lines specified in ROWS.

PARAMETERS:
    ROWS (in): the number of rows to move the cursor up

SAMPLE CALL:
    Cursor_Up (5);

------------------------------------------------------------}

begin
  write (Chr(ESC), '[', ROWS, 'A');
end;
```

```
procedure Cursor_Down (ROWS: integer);
{
DESCRIPTION:
    This procedure uses the ANSI driver to move the cursor
    down the number of lines specified in ROWS.

PARAMETERS:
    ROWS (in): the number of rows to move the cursor down

SAMPLE CALL:
    Cursor_Down (5);

------------------------------------------------------------}

begin
  writeln (Chr(ESC), '[', ROWS, 'B');
end;
```

```
procedure Cursor_Right (COLUMNS: integer);
{
DESCRIPTION:
    This procedure uses the ANSI driver to move the cursor
    right the number of columns specified in COLUMNS.

PARAMETERS:
    COLUMNS (in): the number of columns to move the cursor right

SAMPLE CALL:
    Cursor_Right (5);

------------------------------------------------------------}

begin
  write (Chr(ESC), '[', COLUMNS, 'C');
end;
```

```
procedure Cursor_Left (COLUMNS: integer);
{
DESCRIPTION:
    This procedure uses the ANSI driver to move the cursor
    left the number of columns specified in COLUMNS.

PARAMETERS:
    COLUMNS (in): the number of columns to move the cursor left

SAMPLE CALL:
    Cursor_Left (5);

-----------------------------------------------------------}

begin
  write (Chr(ESC), '[', COLUMNS, 'D');
end;
```

```
procedure Cursor_Home ;
{
DESCRIPTION:
    This procedure uses the ANSI driver to move the cursor
    to the home position.

SAMPLE CALL:
    Cursor_Home;

-----------------------------------------------------------}

begin
  write (Chr(ESC), '[H');
end;
```

```
procedure Print_Blinking (STR: STRING79);
{
DESCRIPTION:
    This procedure uses the ANSI driver to print the
    string provided the calling routine blinking.

PARAMETERS:
    STR (in): the string to print blinking

SAMPLE CALL:
    Print_Blinking ('This line is blinking');

-----------------------------------------------------------}

begin
  write (Chr(ESC), '[5m', STR, Chr(ESC), '[m');
end;
```

```
procedure Print_Reverse_Video (STR: STRING79);
{
DESCRIPTION:
     This procedure uses the ANSI driver to print the
     string provided the calling routine in reverse video.

PARAMETERS:
     STR (in): the string to print in reverse video

SAMPLE CALL:
     Print_Reverse_Video ('This line is reverse video');

------------------------------------------------------------}

begin
  write (Chr(ESC), '[7m', STR, Chr(ESC), '[m');
end;
```

```
procedure Reverse_Video ;
{
DESCRIPTION:
     This procedure uses the ANSI driver to print
     subsequent characters in reverse video.

SAMPLE CALL:
     Reverse_Video ;

------------------------------------------------------------}

begin
  write (Chr(ESC), '[7m');
end;
```

```
procedure Reset_Character_Attributes;
{
DESCRIPTION:
     This procedure uses the ANSI driver to print
     subsequent characters in normal video.

SAMPLE CALL:
     Reset_Character_Attributes;

------------------------------------------------------------}

begin
  write (Chr(ESC), '[m');
end;
```

```
procedure Set_Cursor (ROW, COLUMN: integer);
{
DESCRIPTION:
    This procedure uses the ANSI driver to place the cursor
    in the row and column position specified.

PARAMETERS:
    ROW (in): the desired line for the cursor
    COLUMN (in): the desired column for the cursor

SAMPLE CALL:
    Set_Cursor (10, 10);

--------------------------------------------------------}

begin
  write (Chr(ESC), '[', ROW, ';', COLUMN, 'H');
end;
```

```
procedure Set_Color (FOREGROUND, BACKGROUND: integer);
{
DESCRIPTION:
    This procedure uses the ANSI driver to specify the
    foreground and blackground colors for subsequent characters.

PARAMETERS:
    FOREGROUND (in): the desired foreground color
    BACKGROUND (in): the desired background color

SAMPLE CALL:
    Set_Color (31, 44);   (red foreground, blue background)

NOTES:
    Use the following constants for colors:

    BLINK = 5                     REVERSE = 7
    INVISIBLE = 8                 BLACK_FOREGROUND = 30
    RED_FOREGROUND = 31           GREEN_FOREGROUND = 32
    YELLOW_FOREGROUND = 33        BLUE_FOREGROUND = 34
    MAGENTA_FOREGROUND = 35       CYAN_FOREGROUND = 36
    WHITE_FOREGROUND = 37         BLACK_BACKGROUND = 38
    RED_BACKGROUND = 41           GREEN_BACKGROUND = 42
    YELLOW_BACKGROUND = 43        BLUE_BACKGROUND = 44
    MAGENTA_BACKGROUND = 45       CYAN_BACKGROUND = 46
    WHITE_BACKGROUND = 47

--------------------------------------------------------}

begin
  write (Chr(ESC), '[', FOREGROUND, ';', BACKGROUND, 'm');
end;
```

```
procedure Redefine_Function_Key (KEY: integer;
                                 VALUE: STRING79);
{
DESCRIPTION:
    This procedure redefines the function key specified with
    the string contained in VALUE.  It is often referred to as
    the "Poor man's ProKey."

PARAMETERS:
    KEY: the function key to redefine
    VALUE: the new value of the key

TYPES REQUIRED:
    STRING79: the string type used in all string operations

SAMPLE CALL:
    Redefine_Function_Key (68, 'DIR *.PAS'); (redefine F10)

NOTES:
    See Appendix K of the Turbo Pascal Reference Guide
    for keyboard assignments.

-----------------------------------------------------------}

var
  ASCII: STRING79;    {ASCII representation of the key to redefine}

begin
  Str (KEY, ASCII);   {convert the key to ASCII}

  writeln (Chr(ESC), '[O;', ASCII, ';'''', VALUE, ''';13p');
end;
```

Keyboard Buffer

On the IBM PC and the PC compatibles, DOS places each keystroke that you make into a circular buffer. By default, the buffer size is large enough to contain 16 characters. As you type, each keystroke causes an interrupt that places both the character entered and its scan code into the buffer, as shown in the following diagram.

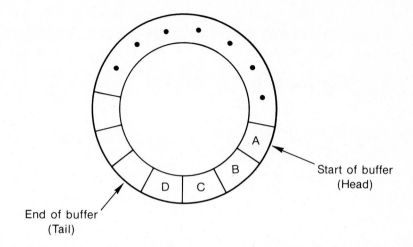

As the operating system processes the keystrokes, it removes them from the beginning of the buffer:

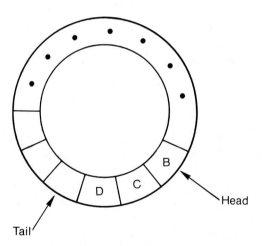

If you enter 16 characters before the operating system can process them, the buffer becomes full. When you try to enter another character, the operating system will notify you of the full buffer by sounding a bell, and it will ignore the additional character.

To support each of the keyboard operations, the operating system must know where the buffer is stored in memory, as well as the locations of the current head and tail of the buffer. DOS stores all of these values in locations that are easily accessible to Turbo Pascal programs, as shown here:

Memory Location	Memory
$480	Start of type-ahead buffer storage
$482	End of type-ahead buffer storage
. . .	• • •
$41A	Current head of buffer
$41C	Current tail of buffer

The following procedure allows a program to *flush*, or ignore, the characters in the type-ahead buffer. The procedure simply moves the tail of the type-ahead buffer so that it points to the head of the buffer, as shown here:

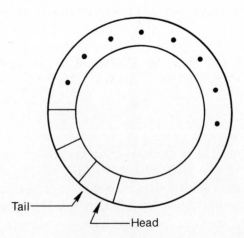

This tells the operating system that the buffer is empty.

```
procedure Flush_Type_Ahead_Buffer;
{
DESCRIPTION:
    This procedure flushes the type ahead buffer.
SAMPLE CALL:
    Flush_Type_Ahead_Buffer;

------------------------------------------------------------}

var
  BUFFER_HEAD : integer absolute $0000:$041A; {current head}
  BUFFER_TAIL : integer absolute $0000:$041C; {current tail}
begin

{flush the type ahead buffer by setting the tail of the
 circular queue to the head of the queue}
  BUFFER_TAIL := BUFFER_HEAD;

end;
```

The next program is more complex: it allows you to increase the size of the type-ahead buffer by changing the values that point to the head and tail of the buffer. Since the program changes the location of the buffer, you must be careful not to overwrite any information contained in memory. The program defines an array of 512 bytes, providing space for 256 characters and scan codes. It also modifies the keyboard buffers so that they point to the beginning and end of the array.

Next the program invokes DOS function **$3100**, which allows the program to terminate and remain resident in memory. This ensures that the type-ahead buffer will always reference the array created by the program, and it prevents any other memory locations from being overwritten. Note that several of the more popular editors and word processors scan the memory locations of the default keyboard buffer. These programs will hang after 15 characters have been entered (the default buffer size is 16).

```
program KeyBoard_Buffer;

const
  BUFFERSIZE = 512;        {new type ahead buffer size}
  PSP_SIZE = 256;          {program segment prefix in bytes}
  CODE_ESTIMATE = 16,024;  {estimated size of resident program}

{record structure to simulate 8088 registers}
type
  REGISTERS = record
    AX, BX, CX, DX, BP, SI, DI, DS, ES, FLAGS: integer;
  end;
```

```
var
  BUFFER        : array[1..BUFFERSIZE] of byte; {new buffer}

  BUFFER_BEGIN: integer absolute $0000:$0480; {starting location}
  BUFFER_END  : integer absolute $0000:$0482; {ending location}
  BUFFER_HEAD : integer absolute $0000:$041A; {current head}
  BUFFER_TAIL : integer absolute $0000:$041C; {current tail}

  REGS          : REGISTERS;

begin
{set the offsets of the buffer relative to segment 40}
  BUFFER_BEGIN := (Seg(BUFFER[1]) - $40) * 16 + Ofs(BUFFER[1]);
  BUFFER_END   := BUFFER_BEGIN + BUFFERSIZE;
  BUFFER_HEAD  := BUFFER_BEGIN;
  BUFFER_TAIL  := BUFFER_BEGIN;

{specify the amount of memory required for resident program}
  REGS.DX := (PSP_SIZE + BUFFERSIZE + CODE_ESTIMATE) div 16 + 1;

{terminate and remain resident}
  REGS.AX := $3100;
  MsDos (REGS);
end.
```

Ports

Much of the communication between the CPU and devices occurs through *ports*. In the 8088, each port is identified by a unique 16-bit address. You may notice that many ports reside at addresses normally reserved for ROM-BIOS. Do not confuse port addresses with memory addresses. The CPU distinguishes port addresses from memory addresses by placing a signal on the control lines when it addresses ports.

The ability to access ports directly provides programmers with several powerful tools. Turbo Pascal provides two predefined arrays, **Port** and **PortW**. Each element of the arrays corresponds to a port. Thus ports can be manipulated easily, as shown here:

CURRENT_VALUE := Port[DESIRED_PORT];
Port[DESIRED_PORT] := NEW_VALUE;

The next program displays and clears the following series of boxes until a keystroke is entered by the user:

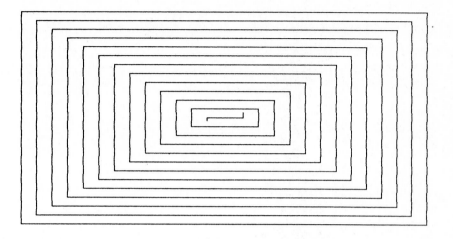

The program maps extended ASCII characters directly into the video display memory. If you run this program, you will notice a great deal of "flicker" appearing on the screen. This occurs because the video display memory is being updated while the CRT controller is performing video retrace. To remove the flicker, the screen update must be synchronized with the retrace. Although this may appear to be a difficult programming task at first, the ability to access ports directly will greatly simplify the programming required.

```
program Video_Synch;

const
  HORIZONTAL = 205;                    {extended ASCII horizontal bar}
  VERTICAL = 186;                      {extended ASCII vertical bar}
  LOWERLEFT_CORNER = 200;              {extended ASCII corner characters}
  UPPERLEFT_CORNER = 201;
  LOWERRIGHT_CORNER = 188;
  UPPERRIGHT_CORNER = 187;
  SPACE = 32;                          {ASCII blank character}

{define VIDEO segment addresses}
  MONOCHROM_SEG = $B000;
  COLOR_SEG = $B800;
  VIDEO_SEG = COLOR_SEG;         {demo the color graphics monitior}

Type

{define a record to simulate the 8088 registers}
  REGISTERS = record
    AX, BX, CX, DX, BP, SI, DI, DS, ES, FLAGS: integer;
  end;


{$I VIDEO.TOL}
```

```
{*************************************************************}
procedure Make_Move (ROW, COLUMN, SYMBOL: integer);
{
DESCRIPTION:
    This routine maps a screen row and column position to
    the correct location in the video display memory and
    places the character contained in symbol into that
    location.  The procedure waits for the vertical retrace
    to complete before moving the symbol into memory to
    prevent snow from appearing on the screen.

PARAMETERS:
    ROW (in): the screen line to display the character at
    COLUMN (in): the screen column to display the character at
    SYMBOL (in): the ASCII symbol to display

SAMPLE CALL:
    Make_Move (10, 15, 65); (displays A at row 10 column 15)

NOTES:
    Vertical retrace is found by examining bit 4 of port
    $3DA.  If the bit is 1, the retrace is in progress;
    otherwise the bit is 0.

--------------------------------------------------------}

var

   OFFSET: integer;    {the offset into display memory}

begin

{map the row and column to the correct display memory location}
   OFFSET := (ROW * 160) + (COLUMN * 2);

{wait for vertical retrace to complete}
   while ((Port[$3DA] and 8) <> 8);

{move the character to the display memory}
   Mem[VIDEO_SEG: OFFSET] := SYMBOL;
end;




{*************************************************************}
procedure Box (UROW, LROW, LCOL, RCOL: integer);
{
DESCRIPTION:
    This procedure draws a rectangle with sides specified by
    UROW (upper row), LROW (lower row), LCOL (leftmost column),
    RCOL (rightmost column).  The procedure will invoke itself
    recursively until the screen is filled with boxes.

PARAMETERS:
    UROW (in): the upper line of the rectangle
    LROW (in): the lower line of the rectangle
    LCOL (in): the leftmost column of the rectangle
    RCOL (in): the rightmost column of the rectangle

LIBRARY ROUTINES CALLED:
    Make_Move - moves a character into the display memory
                location associated with a row and column
```

```
SAMPLE CALL:
    Box (0, 24, 0, 79);

-------------------------------------------------------}

var
  ROW, COLUMN: integer;  {used in loops to create boxes}

begin

{draw upper row}
   for COLUMN := LCOL+1 to RCOL-1 do
     Make_Move (UROW, COLUMN, HORIZONTAL);

{draw upper right corner of the box}
   Make_Move (UROW, RCOL, UPPERRIGHT_CORNER);

{draw the right hand side of the box}
   for ROW := UROW+1 to LROW-1 do
     Make_Move (ROW, RCOL, VERTICAL);

{draw the lower right corner of the box}
   Make_Move (LROW, RCOL, LOWERRIGHT_CORNER);

{draw the bottom line of the box}
   for COLUMN := RCOL-1 downto LCOL+1 do
     Make_Move (LROW, COLUMN, HORIZONTAL);

{draw the lower left hand corner}
   Make_Move (LROW, LCOL, LOWERLEFT_CORNER);

{draw the left hand side of the box}
   for ROW := LROW-1 downto UROW+1 do
     Make_Move (ROW, LCOL, VERTICAL);

{draw the upper left corner of the box}
   Make_Move (UROW, LCOL, UPPERLEFT_CORNER);

{if the screen is not filled with boxes, invoke box recursivly}
   if (UROW < LROW) then
     Box (UROW + 1, LROW - 1, LCOL + 3, RCOL - 3);

{erase upper line of the box}
   for COLUMN := LCOL+1 to RCOL-1 do
     Make_Move (UROW, COLUMN, SPACE);

{erase the right hand side of the box}
   for ROW := UROW+1 to LROW-1 do
     Make_Move (ROW, RCOL, SPACE);

{erase the lower line of the box}
   for COLUMN := RCOL-1 downto LCOL+1 do
     Make_Move (LROW, COLUMN, SPACE);

{erase the left hand side of the box}
   for ROW := LROW-1 downto UROW+1 do
     Make_Move (ROW, LCOL, SPACE);

end;

begin
  ClrScr;
{make the cursor invisible}
  Set_Cursor_Size (8,7);
```

```
{fill the screen with boxes until a key is pressed}
  repeat
    box (0, 24, 0, 79);
  until keypressed;

{make the cursor visible again}
  Set_Cursor_Size (6, 7);
end.
```

Two bits in **Port[$3DA]** provide information on vertical and horizontal retrace for the color graphics adapter. When bit 0 is on, that is, **((Port[$3DA] and 1) = 1),** the CRT controller is performing horizontal retrace. When bit 3 is on, that is, **((Port[$3DA] and 8) = 8),** vertical retrace is being performed. Ideally you should synchronize your applications to the horizontal retrace, which occurs 12,000 times a second. To do so, wait for a retrace cycle to begin and complete as follows:

```
while ((Port[$3DA] and 1) <> 1) do ;   {wait for retrace to begin}
while ((Port[$3DA] and 1)  = 1) do ;   {wait for it to end}
```

Unfortunately, the small amount of time between updates does not allow much processing to occur. Therefore, to synchronize the box application, use the vertical retrace, which occurs 60 times a second. In this case, you simply wait for the retrace cycle to complete before performing the update of the display memory:

```
while ((Port[$3DA] and 8) = 8);
```

By synchronizing the move to the display memory in this fashion, you remove the flicker from the screen.

Interrupt Handling

A useful programming capability is the ability to trap and handle interrupts. To trap interrupts, you will use the routine *Set_ Interrupt_Vector,* which was introduced in Chapter 9. You will also use the **inline** compiler directive, which allows machine code to be embedded within Pascal source code.

Each interrupt handler must perform several startup steps when it is invoked. Therefore, the first line of the interrupt handler *must* be the following:

```
inline ($50/$53/$51/$52/$53/$56/$57/$1E/$06/$FB);
```

If you are familiar with 8088 assembly language, the equivalent code for the hex values in the **inline** statement are as follows:

```
$50   PUSH AX
$53   PUSH BX
$51   PUSH CX
$52   PUSH DX
$56   PUSH SI
$57   PUSH DI
$1E   PUSH DS
$06   PUSH ES
$FB   STI       ; enable interrupts
```

An interrupt must save the current state of the machine before it can perform its processing. The inline code stores the registers that were being used by the interrupted process; this step ensures that, upon completion of the interrupt, the previous process can resume its processing unaffected. The final line of code in the interrupt handler must restore the machine to the state it was in prior to the interrupt:

```
inline ($07/$1F/$5F/$5E/$5A/$59/$5B/$58/$8B/$E5/$5D/$CF);
```

The equivalent code for the hex values in the **inline** statement are as follows:

```
$07   POP ES
$1F   POP DS
$5F   POP DI
$5E   POP SI
$5A   POP DX
$59   POP CX
$5B   POP BX
$58   POP AX

$8B$E5   MOV BP, SP

$5D   POP BP
$CF   IRET
```

Here is a generic interrupt handler:

```
procedure Interrupt_Handler;
begin
  inline ($50/$53/$51/$52/$53/$56/$57/$1E/$06/$FB);

  {code to handle the interrupt here}

  inline ($07/$1F/$5F/$5E/$5A/$59/$5B/$58/$8B/$E5/$5D/$CF);
end;
```

The following routine returns the *interrupt vector* (segment and offset address) of a given interrupt:

```
procedure Get_Interrupt_Vector (INTERRUPT: integer;
                                var SEGMENT, OFFSET: integer);
{
DESCRIPTION:
    This routine returns the interrupt vector for the
    interrupt contained in INTERRUPT.

PARAMETERS:
    INTERRUPT (in) - interrupt service number to return
                     the vector for
    SEGMENT (in) - segment address of the interrupt handler
    OFFSET (in) - offset address of the interrupt handler

TYPES REQUIRED:
    REGISTERS - used in all ROM-BIOS and DOS interrupts

SAMPLE CALL:
    Get_Interrupt_Vector ($24, SEGMENT, OFFSET);

----------------------------------------------------------}

  var
    REGS: REGISTERS;  {AX, BX, CX, DX, BP, SI, DI, DS, ES, FLAGS}

  begin
    with REGS do
      begin

{set the registers to redefine an interrupt vector}
        AX := $3500 + interrupt;  {interrupt number is in AL}

{invoke the DOS interrupt which redefines an interrupt vector}
        MSDos (REGS);

        SEGMENT := ES;
        OFFSET := BX;
      end;
  end;
```

The following program traps and ignores the print-screen interrupt. Each time the interrupt occurs, the procedure *Ignore_ Interrupt* is invoked.

```
program Capture_Interrupt;

type
  REGISTERS = record
    AX, BX, CX, DX, BP, SI, DI, DS, ES, FLAGS: integer;
  end;

  STRING79 = string[79];

{$I SYSTEM.TOL}  {contains get and set interrupt vector}

procedure Ignore_Interrupt;
begin
  inline ($50/$53/$51/$52/$56/$57/$1E/$06/$FB);

  inline ($07/$1F/$5F/$5E/$5A/$59/$5B/$58/$8B/$E5/$5D/$CF);
end;


var
  SEGMENT,              {segment address of interrupt vector}
  OFFSET : integer;   {offset address of interrupt vector}

begin

{save the initial vector}
  Get_Interrupt_Vector ($05, SEGMENT, OFFSET);

{ignore the print screen interrupt}
  Set_Interrupt_Vector ($05, CSeg, Ofs(Ignore_Interrupt));

  Writeln ('Try print screen');
  Delay (5000);

{reset vector to its original value}
  Set_Interrupt_Vector ($05, SEGMENT, OFFSET);
end.
```

Unless your goal s to modify an interrupt vector for the entire user session and not just for a specific application, always restore the interrupt vectors to their original values before you terminate your applications. If you do not, you may have several unexpected results when DOS invokes interrupts handled by nonexistent interrupt handlers.

Integrating Assembly Language Routines With Turbo Pascal

In addition to the **inline** compiler directive, Turbo Pascal allows you to include assembly language routines in Turbo Pascal programs. So that Turbo Pascal can resolve the external references, your assembly language routines should take the following format:

```
code        segment
            assume    cs: code

; name is your routine name
name        proc      near

; save the environment
            PUSH  BP
            MOV   BP, SP

; your assembly languge code here

; restore the environment
            MOV   SP, BP
            POP   BP
            RET

name        endp
code        ends
            end
```

Assemble your procedure and link it. Ignore NO STACK SEG-
MENT warnings. Next, convert the .EXE file to a .COM file by
using **EXE2BIN**. If the assembly language procedure just given is
in a file called EXAMPLE.ASM, here is the entire process you
should follow:

```
ASM EXAMPLE
LINK EXAMPLE
EXE2BIN EXAMPLE EXAMPLE.COM
```

Within the Turbo Pascal program, the assembly language routine
must be declared as **external**:

```
procedure name [(optional parameters)]; external 'EXAMPLE.COM';
```

Turbo Pascal will open the file EXAMPLE.COM and include the
assembly language routine.

The following assembly language routine places the cursor at the
page, row, and column specified by the calling routine. It also displays the message it receives, pausing for the user to press any key.
The file containing the routine is assumed to be PAUSE.ASM.

```
; Pause prompting the user to hit return
;
code      segment
          assume  cs:code

pause     proc    near

; Save the environment
          PUSH    BP
          MOV     BP, SP

; Save the registers used
          PUSH    AX
          PUSH    BX
          PUSH    DX

; Place the cursor at page, row, column desired
          MOV     BH, [BP+8]       ; page
          MOV     DH, [BP+6]       ; row
          MOV     DL, [BP+4]       ; column
          MOV     AH, 2            ; service routine
          INT     10H

; Display the message
          MOV     DX, [BP+10]
          MOV     AH, 9            ; service routine
          INT     21H              ; display message

; Wait for keystroke
          MOV     AH, 8            ; service routine
          INT     21H              ; wait for input

; Restore the registers used
          POP     DX
          POP     BX
          POP     AX

; Restore the environment and return to calling routine
          MOV     SP, BP
          POP     BP
          RET     8

pause     ENDP
code      ENDS
          END
```

At the DOS prompt, perform the following:

```
ASM PAUSE
LINK PAUSE
EXE2BIN PAUSE PAUSE.COM
```

This program invokes a pause to display the message

```
Press any key to continue
```

Here is the program:

```
program Pause_Driver;
procedure Pause (PTR, page, row, column: integer); external
    'PAUSE.COM';
var
  MSG : string[79];

begin
 MSG := 'Press any key to continue $';

 Pause (Ofs(MSG[1]), 0, 10, 5);
end.
```

It is important to understand how Pascal passes parameters to the assembly language routine. Each time the routine is invoked, Pascal pushes the arguments that are passed to the routine onto the stack in the order in which they appear. Next Pascal places the contents of the instruction pointer (the return address) onto the stack. When control is passed to the assembly language routine, the stack will contain the following:

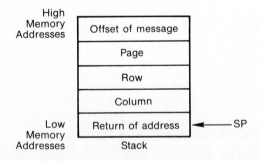

The **Pause** procedure pushes the contents of the base pointer (**BP**), which contains the starting address of the arguments passed from the calling routine on the stack. This simplifies the process of clearing the stackbefore returning to the calling routine.

At this point the stack contains the following:

```
BP+10   |  Offset of message  |

BP+8    |       Page          |

BP+6    |       Row           |

BP+4    |      Column         |

BP+2    |   Return address    |

BP      |   Base pointer      |  <------------ SP
        |    contents         |
```

You can offset from the contents of the base pointer (**BP**) to access any of the parameters passed to the routine:

[BP+4]   contains the column
[BP+6]   contains the row
[BP+8]   contains the page
[BP+10]   contains the offset of the first character
             of the message

After execution, the routine restores the stack to its original contents:

```
MOV   SP, BP
POP   BP
```

Although Turbo Pascal makes it easy to include assembly language routines within your programs, most applications can be performed from Pascal through the routines **Intr** and **MsDos** without any user-written assembly language routines. Using the Turbo Pascal interface routines will simplify development, testing, and debugging. Whenever possible, use a high-level language.

File Protection

The following routine allows you to protect files by setting their attribute byte. The routine is invoked as

PROTECT [FILESPEC] −h or −r or −n

The optional FILESPEC is the search specification used to identify the file to protect. It can be a specific name or wild-card combination. If omitted, the default is ∗.∗. The qualifiers −h, −r, and −n specify the desired attributes:

−h	hidden file
−r	read-only file
−n	no attributes

If you make a file hidden, it will not appear in directory listings and the delete command cannot find it. A read-only file cannot be modified or deleted without first changing its attributes. Here is the routine:

```
program Protect;

type
  REGISTERS = record
                AX, BX, CX, DX, BP, SI, DI, DS, ES, FLAGS: INTEGER;
              end;

  STRING79 = string[79];

  DTA_INFO = record
    ATTRIBUTES   : byte;        {file attributes}
    FILE_SIZE    : real;        {in bytes}
    NAME         : STRING79;
  end;

{$I FLAGS.TOL}
{$I MATH.TOL}
{$I FILES.TOL}
{$I STRINGS.TOL}
```

```
procedure Extract_Qualifiers (var SEARCH_SPEC: STRING79;
                              var CONTINUE: boolean;
                              var ATTRIBUTE: integer);
{
DESCRIPTION:
    This procedure extracts the parameters from the
    command line for the program Protect.
```

```
PARAMETERS:
    SEARCH_SPEC (out): the search specification for the
                       files to protect
    CONTINUE (out): a boolean flag used by the calling
                    routine that states whether or not the
                    command line parameters were valid
    ATTRIBUTE (out): the desired attributes of the files

TYPES REQUIRED:
    STRING79: used in all string routines

LIBRARY ROUTINES USED:
    Str_Count: returns the number of occurrences of a substring
               within a string

SAMPLE CALL:
    Extract_Qualifiers (SEARCH_SPEC, CONTINUE, ATTRIBUTE);

---------------------------------------------------------}

var
  QUALIFIER: STRING79;   {qualifier -n, -h, or -r}

begin
  CONTINUE := false;                   {assume the worst}
  QUALIFIER := ParamStr(ParamCount);   {get the qualifier}

{test for invalid command line}
  if (ParamCount < 1) then
    Writeln ('protect: invalid usage: protect [filespec] value')

{test for the command line protect attribute}
  else if (ParamCount = 1) then
      SEARCH_SPEC := '*.*'

  else
    SEARCH_SPEC := ParamStr(1);

{test for -n (no attribute) qualifier}
  if (Str_Count (QUALIFIER, '-n', true) <> 0) then
    begin
      ATTRIBUTE := 0;
      CONTINUE := true;
    end

{test for -r (read-only attribute) qualifier}
  else if (Str_Count (QUALIFIER, '-r', true) <> 0) then
    begin
      ATTRIBUTE := 1;
      CONTINUE := true;
    end

{test for -h (hidden attribute) qualifier}
  else if (Str_Count (QUALIFIER, '-h', true) <> 0) then
    begin
      ATTRIBUTE := 2;
      CONTINUE := true;
    end

{attribute is invalid}
  else if ParamCount > 0 then
    Writeln ('protect: invalid attribute ', ParamStr(ParamCount))
end;
```

```
Var
   SEARCH_SPEC: STRING79;   {search specification of files to protect}
   FILESPEC   : DTA_INFO;   {file name, size, attributes}
   ATTRIBUTE  : integer;    {new attribute of file}
   STATUS     : byte;       {status of file operations}
   CONTINUE   : boolean;    {continue processing}

begin

{ensure that the command line was valid}
   Extract_Qualifiers (SEARCH_SPEC, CONTINUE, ATTRIBUTE);

   if (CONTINUE) then
      begin

{find the first matching file}
      Find_First (SEARCH_SPEC, 0, FILESPEC, STATUS);

{as long as matching files exist, set their protection}
      while ((STATUS <> 18) and (STATUS <> 2) and (STATUS <> 3)) do
         begin
            Write (FILESPEC.NAME, '':(15-Length(FILESPEC.NAME)));
            Set_File_Attributes (FILESPEC.NAME, ATTRIBUTE, STATUS);
            if (STATUS = 0) then
               Writeln (' attributes modified')
            else
               Writeln (' *** attributes NOT modified ***');
{get the next matching file}
            FIND_NEXT (FILESPEC, STATUS);
         end;
      end;
end.
```

In the procedure *Extract—Qualifiers*, note the use of the variable
QUALIFIER. Turbo Pascal provides access to the command-line
parameters through the function **ParamStr**. If an application references a specific command-line parameter more than once, you
should place the value of the parameter into a variable. This
decreases the number of additional function calls required by the
program, which in turn increases the execution speed.

Directory Listing

The following program provides a complete directory listing of the
files specified in the command line. It is similar to the directory
listing provided by DOS; however, it also includes the file attributes.
In addition, the −t qualifier causes the program to display only files
created today. The complete command line for the program becomes

```
LS [FILESPEC] [-t]
```

Here is the program:

```
program Ls;

type
  REGISTERS = record
                AX, BX, CX, DX, BP, SI, DI, DS, ES, FLAGS: INTEGER;
              end;

  STRING79 = string[79];

  DTA_INFO = record
    ATTRIBUTES  : byte;        {attributes of the file}
    FILE_SIZE   : real;        {file size in bytes}
    NAME        : STRING79;    {file name}
  end;
{$I FLAGS.TOL}
{$I MATH.TOL}
{$I FILES.TOL}
{$I STRINGS.TOL}
{$I SYSTEM.TOL}

Var
  FILE_DAY, FILE_MONTH, FILE_YEAR,        {file date stamp}
  TODAYS_DAY, TODAYS_MONTH, TODAYS_YEAR,  {today's date}
  HOUR, MINUTES, SECONDS,                 {file time stamp}
  NUM_PARAMS,                             {# of command line params}
  FILE_HANDLE: integer;

  STATUS    : byte;                       {status of file operations}
  FILESPEC  : DTA_INFO;                   {name, size, attributes}

  DATE_QUALIFIER,                         {true if date qualifier.is present}
  DISPLAY_FILE: boolean;                  {true if this file should be displayed}

begin
  NUM_PARAMS := ParamCount;   {get the number of command line arguments}

{see if the date qualifier is present}
  if (NUM_PARAMS > 0) then
    DATE_QUALIFIER := Str_Count (ParamStr(NUM_PARAMS), '-t', true) <> 0
  else
    DATE_QUALIFIER := false;

{if so, get today's date}
  if (DATE_QUALIFIER) then
    Get_Date (TODAYS_DAY, TODAYS_MONTH, TODAYS_YEAR);

{test for the command line  LS or LS -t}
  if (NUM_PARAMS = 0) or ((NUM_PARAMS = 1) and DATE_QUALIFIER) then
    Find_First ('*.*', 0, FILESPEC, STATUS)

{the user specified a search specification  LS SPEC or LS spec -t}
  else
    Find_First (ParamStr(1), 0, FILESPEC, STATUS);

{list all of the matching files}
  while ((STATUS <> 18) and (STATUS <> 2) and (STATUS <> 3)) do
    begin
      DISPLAY_FILE := false;
```

```
            Open_File (FILESPEC.NAME, 0, FILE_HANDLE, STATUS);
            if (STATUS <> 0) then
              Writeln ('Error accessing date & time stamp')
            else
              begin
                Get_File_Date_Time (FILE_HANDLE, FILE_DAY,FILE_MONTH, HOUR,
                                    MINUTES, SECONDS, FILE_YEAR, STATUS);

                if (STATUS <> 0) then
                  Writeln ('Error accessing date & time stamp ', FILESPEC.NAME);

                Close_File (FILE_HANDLE, STATUS);
              end;

          if (not DATE_QUALIFIER) then
            DISPLAY_FILE := true

          else if (DATE_QUALIFIER) then
            if (TODAYS_DAY = FILE_DAY) and (TODAYS_MONTH = FILE_MONTH) and
               (TODAYS_YEAR = FILE_YEAR) then
              DISPLAY_FILE := true;

          if (DISPLAY_FILE) then
            begin
              Write (FILESPEC.NAME, '':(15-Length(FILESPEC.NAME)));

              case FILESPEC.ATTRIBUTES of
                0: Write ('NO ATTRIBUTES':15);
                1: Write ('READONLY':15);
                2: Write ('HIDDON':15);
                4: Write ('SYSTEM':15);
                16: Write ('SUBDIRECTORY':15);
                32: Write ('ARCHIVE':15);
              end;

              Write (FILESPEC.FILE_SIZE:10:0);

              if FILE_MONTH < 10 then
                Write (0:3, FILE_MONTH, '/')
              else
                Write (FILE_MONTH:4, '/');

              if FILE_DAY < 10 then
                Write (0, FILE_DAY:1, '/')
              else
                Write (FILE_DAY:2, '/');

              Write (FILE_YEAR:4);
              Write ((HOUR mod 12):4, ':');
              if (MINUTES < 10) then
                Write (0, MINUTES:1)
              else
                Write (MINUTES:2);

              if (HOUR div 12 = 1) then
                Writeln (' PM')
              else
                Writeln (' AM');
            end;

{get the next matching file}
      FIND_NEXT (FILESPEC, STATUS);
    end;
end.
```

A P P E N D I X

A

Built-In Turbo Pascal Procedures

This appendix provides the calling sequence and function of each built-in procedure of Turbo Pascal. Note that the parameter types are only meant to be informational and are not meant to be valid syntax. Therefore, interpret the type

string [1..255]

to mean a string from 1 to 255 characters in length. Also, the type

integer or real

means that the variable can be either of type **integer** or of type **real**.

Machine-Independent Procedures

The following procedures are machine-independent.

String Procedures

```
procedure Delete (var TARGET_STR: string[1..255];
                      POSITION,
                      NUM_CHARACTERS: integer);
{
DESCRIPTION:
    This procedure removes characters from TARGET_STR.  The
    characters start at POSITION.  The minimum of NUM_CHARACTERS
    and the number of characters remaining in TARGET_STR
    are removed.

PARAMETERS:
    TARGET_STR (in/out): the string to extract the characters from
    POSITION (in): the first character in TARGET_STR to delete
    NUM_CHARACTERS (in): the number of characters to delete

SAMPLE CALL:
    TARGET_STR := '123456789';
    Delete (TARGET_STR, 5, 1);   (assigns TARGET_STR '12346789')
    Delete (TARGET_STR, 5, 10);  (assigns TARGET_STR '1234')

-----------------------------------------------------------}
```

```
procedure Insert (STR_TO_INSERT: string [1..255];
                  var TARGET_STR: string [1..255];
                      POSITION: integer);
{
DESCRIPTION:
    This procedure inserts the substring STR_TO_INSERT into
    TARGET_STR at the character location contained in POSITION.

PARAMETERS:
    STR_TO_INSERT (in): the substring to insert
    TARGET_STR (in/out): the string STR_TO_INSERT is inserted into
    POSITION (in): the starting location for the substring within
              TARGET_STR

SAMPLE CALL:
    STR := '123456789';
    TGT := 'ABCDEFGHI';
    Insert (STR, TGT, 3);  (assigns TGT 'AB123456789CDEFGHI')
```

NOTES:
    If the insertion causes TARGET_STR to exceed its maximum
    length, the characters are truncated. If POSITION is
    greater than the length of TARGET_STR, STR_TO_INSERT is
    appended to TARGET_STR.

    --}

```
procedure Str (VALUE: integer or real;
      var ASCII_STR: string [1..255]);
{
DESCRIPTION:
    This procedure converts the numeric value contained in
    VALUE to its ASCII representation and stores the result
    in ASCII_STR.  The I/O formatting commands can be used
    in this procedure.

PARAMETERS:
    VALUE (in): the numeric value to be converted to ASCII
    ASCII_STR (out): the ASCII representation of VALUE

SAMPLE CALL:
    VALUE := 55;
    Str (VALUE:4, ASCII_STR);  (assigns ASCII_STR '  55')

    ------------------------------------------------------------}
```

```
procedure Val (ASCII_STR: string [1..255];
            var VALUE: integer or real;
            var STATUS: integer);
{
DESCRIPTION:
    This procedure converts the ASCII representation of a
    number to its actual value and stores the result
    in VALUE.  If no errors occur in the conversion, STATUS
    is set to 0; otherwise, status will contain the character
    location within ASCII_STR of the illegal character.

PARAMETERS:
    ASCII_STR (in): the ASCII representation of VALUE
    VALUE (out): the numeric equivalent
    STATUS (out): the error status code

SAMPLE CALL:
    ASCII_STR := '55';
    Val (ASCII_STR, VALUE, STATUS);  (assigns VALUE 55)

NOTES:
    You must remove leading and trailing blanks from ASCII_STR
    before invoking Val.

    ------------------------------------------------------------}
```

```
function Copy (ORIG_STR: string [1..255];
               POSITION,
          NUM_CHARACTERS: integer): string[1..255];
{
DESCRIPTION:
    This function returns a substring of ORIG_STR starting
    at POSITION.  The substring contains the minimum of
    NUM_CHARACTERS and the number of characters remaining
    in ORIG_STR.

VALUE RETURNED:
    The substring extracted from ORIG_STR

PARAMETERS:
    ORIG_STR (in/out): the string to remove the substring from
    POSITION (in): the starting position of the substring
                   within ORIG_STR
    NUM_CHARACTERS (in): the number of characters to place into the
                         substring

SAMPLE CALL:
    writeln ('The zip code is ', Copy ('LV, NV 89126', 8, 5));

NOTES:
    If POSITION exceeds the length of ORIG_STR, the empty
    string is returned.  If POSITION + NUM_CHARACTERS exceeds
    the length of ORIG_STR, only characters up to the end of
    the string are returned.  If POSITION is greater than
    255, a run-time error will occur.

    ------------------------------------------------------------}
```

```
function Concat (STR1, STR2..STRN: string [1..255]): string[1..255];
{
DESCRIPTION:
    This function concatenates 2 or more strings.

VALUE RETURNED:
    The string that is the concatenation of the arguments
    passed to Concat

PARAMETERS:
    STR1..STRN (in): the character strings to concatenate

SAMPLE CALL:
    writeln (Concat ('ABCDEF', 'GH'));
    writeln (Concat ('AB', 'CD', 'EF', 'GH'))

NOTES:
    The function will concatenate any number of string
    expressions that areseparated by commas and that are a
    maximum of 255 characters in total length.

    ------------------------------------------------------------}
```

```
function Length (OBJECT_STR: string[1..255]): integer;
{
DESCRIPTION:
    This function returns the number of characters in a
    string.

VALUE RETURNED:
    The number of characters in the string expression

PARAMETERS:
    OBJECT_STR (in): the string expression to be examined

SAMPLE CALL:
    writeln ('The length is ', Length ('TURBO'));
    (will display The length is 5)

-----------------------------------------------------------}
```

```
function Pos (OBJECT_STR, TARGET_STR: string[1..255]): integer;
{
DESCRIPTION:
    This function returns the first occurrence of OBJECT_STR
    within TARGET_STR.  If no match is found, 0 is returned.

VALUE RETURNED:
    The character location of the first occurrence of OBJECT_STR
    within TARGET_STR

PARAMETERS:
    OBJECT_STR (in): the string expression to search for
    TARGET_STR (in): the string to be examined

SAMPLE CALL:
    TARGET_STR := 'abcdeabcde';
    OBJECT_STR := 'de';
    writeln ('The first location is at ', Pos (OBJECT_STR, TARGET_STR));
    (will display The first location is at 4)

---------------------------------------------------------}
```

File Procedures

```
procedure Assign

 (var FILE_VAR: file of record;
                FILE_NAME: string [1..255]);
{
```

```
DESCRIPTION:
    This procedure assigns the file name contained in
    FILE_NAME to the file variable FILE_VAR.

PARAMETERS:
    FILE_VAR (out): a file variable to be used by the other file
                    manipulation routines
    FILE_NAME (in): a string expression containing the name of the
                    file to be manipulated

SAMPLE CALL:
    Assign (FP, 'TURBO.DAT');

NOTES:
    Do not use Assign with a file name that is already
    being used.

---------------------------------------------------------}
```

```
procedure Rewrite (FILE_VAR: file of record);
{
DESCRIPTION:
    This procedure creates a new disk file with the name
    assigned to the file variable FILE_VAR.  Existing files
    with the same name are erased.

PARAMETERS:
    FILE_VAR (in): the file variable returned by Assign, which
                   references the file to manipulate

SAMPLE CALL:
    Rewrite (FP);

--------------------------------------------------------}
```

```
procedure Reset (FILE_VAR: file of record);
{
DESCRIPTION:
    This procedure resets an existing disk file with the name
    assigned to the file variable FILE_VAR for input.  If the
    file does not exist, an I/O error occurs; if the file exists,
    the file pointer is placed at the beginning of the file.

PARAMETERS:
    FILE_VAR (in): the file variable returned by Assign, which
                   references the file to manipulate

SAMPLE CALL:
    Reset (FP);

---------------------------------------------------------}
```

```
procedure Read (FILE_VAR: file of record;
                VAR1..VARN);
{
DESCRIPTION:
    This procedure reads the file referenced by FILE_VAR.
    VAR1 through VARN are one or more variables of the
    component type FILE_VAR.  The procedure advances the
    file pointer to the next record upon completion.

PARAMETERS:
    FILE_VAR (in): the file variable returned by Assign, which
                   references the file to manipulate
    VAR1..VARN (out): component variables of the type FILE_VAR

SAMPLE CALL:
    Read (FP, CUSTOMER_RECORD);

------------------------------------------------------------}
```

```
procedure Write (FILE_VAR: file of record;
                 VAR1..VARN);
{
DESCRIPTION:
    This procedure writes the variables VAR1 through VARN
    to the file referenced by FILE_VAR. The procedure advances
    the file pointer to the next record upon completion.

PARAMETERS:
    FILE_VAR (in): the file variable returned by Assign, which
                   references the file to manipulate
    VAR1..VARN (in): component variables of the type FILE_VAR

SAMPLE CALL:
    Write (FP, CUSTOMER_RECORD);

------------------------------------------------------------}
```

```
procedure Seek (FILE_VAR: file of record;
                RECORD_NUMBER: integer);
{
DESCRIPTION:
    This procedure is used with random access files to move
    the file pointer to the desired record.  If the record
    number exceeds the number of records in the file, an I/O
    error occurs.

PARAMETERS:
    FILE_VAR (in): the file variable returned by Assign, which
                   references the file to manipulate
    RECORD_NUMBER (in): the desired record number
```

```
SAMPLE CALL:
    Seek (FP, 5);                    (moves the file pointer to record 5)
    Seek (FP, Sizeof(FIL_VAR)); (moves the file pointer to the end
                                      of the file)

------------------------------------------------------------}
```

```
procedure Flush (FILE_VAR: file of record);
{
DESCRIPTION:
    This procedure ensures that the internal buffer is
    written to disk.

PARAMETERS:
    FILE_VAR (in): the file variable returned by Assign, which
                   references the file to manipulate

SAMPLE CALL:
    Flush (FILE_VAR);

NOTES:
    Do not Flush a closed file.

------------------------------------------------------------}
```

```
procedure Close (FILE_VAR: file of record);
{
DESCRIPTION:
    This procedure closes the file referenced by FILE_VAR
    and updates the diskette directory.

PARAMETERS:
    FILE_VAR (in): the file variable returned by Assign, which
                   references the file to manipulate

TYPES REQUIRED:
    FILE_VAR - must be a file type

SAMPLE CALL:
    Close (FILE_VAR);

NOTES:
    Always close files opened for input or output.  Closing
    a file for output ensures the internal buffer is flushed
    and ensures adequate file handles are available.

------------------------------------------------------------}
```

```
procedure Erase (FILE_VAR: file of record);
{
DESCRIPTION:
    This procedure erases the contents of the file referenced
    by FILE_VAR.

PARAMETERS:
    FILE_VAR (in): the file variable returned by Assign,  which
                   references the file to manipulate

SAMPLE CALL:
    Erase (FILE_VAR);

------------------------------------------------------------}
```

```
procedure Rename (FILE_VAR: file of record;
                  NEW_NAME: string [1..255]);
{
DESCRIPTION:
    This procedure renames the file referenced by FILE_VAR
    to the name contained in NEW_NAME.

PARAMETERS:
    FILE_VAR (in): the file variable returned by Assign, which
                   references the file to manipulate
    NEW_NAME (in): a string expression containing the desired
                   file name

SAMPLE CALL:
    Rename (FILE_VAR, 'NEWNAME.DAT');

NOTES:
    Close the file referenced by FILE_VAR before invoking
    Rename.

----------------------------------------------------------}
```

```
function FilePos (FILE_VAR: file of record): integer;
{
DESCRIPTION:
    This function returns a integer value that specifies
    the record number the file pointer is currently referencing.

VALUE RETURNED:
    The current record number
```

```
PARAMETERS:
    FILE_VAR (in): the file variable returned by Assign, which
                   references the file to manipulate

SAMPLE CALL:
    CURRENT_RECORD := FilePos (FILE_VAR);

------------------------------------------------------------}
```

```
function Eof (FILE_VAR: file of record): boolean;
{
DESCRIPTION:
    This routine returns true if the end of the file referenced
    by FILE_VAR has been reached.

VALUE RETURNED:
    Boolean value that specifies whether or not end of file
    has occurred

PARAMETERS:
    FILE_VAR (in): the file variable returned by Assign, which
                   references the file to manipulate

SAMPLE CALL:
    while (not Eof (FILE_VAR))

------------------------------------------------------------}
```

```
function FileSize (FILE_VAR: file of record): integer;
{
DESCRIPTION:
    This function returns the number of records in a file.

VALUE RETURNED:
    The number of records in the file referenced by FILE_VAR

PARAMETERS:
    FILE_VAR (in): the file variable returned by Assign, which
                   references the file to manipulate

SAMPLE CALL:
    NUM_RECORDS := FileSize (FP);

NOTES:
    If the file is empty, the value 0 is returned.

------------------------------------------------------------}
```

Text File Routines

```
procedure Readln (FILE_VAR: text);
{
DESCRIPTION:
    This procedure skips to the beginning of the next line
    of a text file.

PARAMETERS:
    FILE_VAR (in): the file variable returned by Assign, which
                   references the file to manipulate

SAMPLE CALL:
    Readln (FP);

------------------------------------------------------------}
```

```
procedure Writeln (FILE_VAR: text);
{
DESCRIPTION:
    This procedure writes the end of line sequence (carriage
    return/line feed) to a text file.

PARAMETERS:
    FILE_VAR (in): the file variable returned by Assign, which
                   references the file to manipulate

SAMPLE CALL:
    Writeln (FP);

------------------------------------------------------------}
```

```
function Eoln (FILE_VAR: text): integer;
{
DESCRIPTION:
    This function returns true if the file pointer of a text
    file is currently pointing to the end of the current
    line; it returns false if not.

VALUE RETURNED:
    A boolean value that specifies whether or not the
    file pointer is pointing to the end of the current
    line.
```

```
PARAMETERS:
    FILE_VAR (in): the file variable returned by Assign, which
                   references the file to manipulate

SAMPLE CALL:
    if (not Eoln(FP)) then

----------------------------------------------------------}
```

```
function SeekEoln (FILE_VAR: text): integer;
{
DESCRIPTION:
    This function returns true if the file pointer of a text
    file is currently pointing to the end of the current
    line; it returns false if not.  SeekEoln skips leading
    blanks and tabs before testing .for end of line.

VALUE RETURNED:
    A boolean value that specifies whether or not the
    file pointer is pointing to the end of the current
    line

PARAMETERS:
    FILE_VAR (in): the file variable returned by Assign, which
                   references the file to manipulate

SAMPLE CALL:
    if (not SeekEoln(FP)) then

----------------------------------------------------------}
```

```
function SeekEof (FILE_VAR: text): integer;
{
DESCRIPTION:
    This function returns true if the file pointer of a text
    file is currently pointing to the end of the file;it returns
    false if not.  SeekEof skips leading blanks and tabs before
    testing for end of line.

VALUE RETURNED:
    A boolean value that specifies whether or not the
    file pointer is pointing to the end of the file

PARAMETERS:
    FILE_VAR (in): the file variable returned by Assign, which
                   references the file to manipulate

SAMPLE CALL:
    while (not SeekEof(FP)) then

----------------------------------------------------------}
```

Text Input/Output Procedures

```
procedure Read (VAR1..VARN);
{
DESCRIPTION:
    This procedure reads one or more variables of type
    integer, char, real, or string from the standard
    input.

PARAMETERS:
    VAR1..VARN (out): the variables to be input

SAMPLE CALL:
    Read (NUM_SCORES);
    Read (DATE, NAME, SCORE);

NOTES:
    Eoln is true if the next character is a carriage return
    or CTRL-Z.
    Eof is true if the next character is a CTRL-Z.

------------------------------------------------------------}
```

```
procedure Readln (VAR1..VARN);
{
DESCRIPTION:
    This procedure reads zero or more variables of type
    integer, char, real, or string to the standard
    input.  The routine is similar to the procedure Read
    except that after the last variable is read, Readln skips
    all of characters remaining on the line.

PARAMETERS:
    VAR1..VARN (out): the variables to be input

SAMPLE CALL:
    Readln (NUM_SCORES);
    Readln;

------------------------------------------------------------}
```

```
procedure Write (VAR1..VARN);
{
DESCRIPTION:
    This procedure writes one or more variables of type
    integer, char, real, or string to the standard
    output.

PARAMETERS:
    VAR1..VARN (out): the variables to be output
```

```
SAMPLE CALL:
    Write (NUM_SCORES);
    Write (DATE, NAME, SCORE);

------------------------------------------------------------}
```

```
procedure Writeln (VAR1..VARN);
{
DESCRIPTION:
    This procedure writes zero or more variables of type
    integer, char, real, or string to the standard output.
    This procedure is similar to the routine Write, except
    that the newline sequence (carriage return/linefeed) is
    written after the last variable.

PARAMETERS:
    VAR1..VARN (out): the variables to be output

SAMPLE CALL:
    Writeln ;
    Writeln (DATE, NAME, SCORE);

------------------------------------------------------------}
```

Untyped File Routines

```
procedure BlockRead (FILE_VAR: file;
                     var BUFFER: array [1..128] of byte;
                     NUM_RECORDS: integer;
                     [,var RESULT: integer]);
{
DESCRIPTION:
    This procedure performs a low-level read on the file
    referenced by FILE_VAR.  The routine will read the number
    of 128-byte records specified by NUM_RECORDS into the
    variable BUFFER.  The optional variable RESULT contains
    the actual number of records read.

PARAMETERS:
    FILE_VAR (in): the file variable returned by Assign, which
                   references the file to manipulate
    BUFFER (out): the variable to read the 128-byte records into
    NUM_RECORDS (in): the number of 128-byte records to retrieve
    RESULT (out): the actual number of records read

SAMPLE CALL:
    BlockRead (FP, BUFFER, N, RESULT);

------------------------------------------------------------}
```

```
procedure BlockWrite (FILE_VAR: file;
                        BUFFER: array [1..128] of byte;
                   NUM_RECORDS: integer;
                   [,var RESULT: integer]);
{
DESCRIPTION:
    This procedure performs a low-level write to the file
    referenced by FILE_VAR.  The routine will write the number
    of 128-byte records specified by NUM_RECORDS from the
    variable BUFFER.  The optional variable RESULT contains
    the actual number of records written.

PARAMETERS:
    FILE_VAR (in): the file variable returned by Assign, which
                    references the file to manipulate
    BUFFER (in): the variable containing the 128-byte records
    NUM_RECORDS (in): the number of 128-byte records to write
    RESULT (out): the actual number of records written

SAMPLE CALL:
    BlockWrite (FP, BUFFER, N, RESULT);

-----------------------------------------------------------}
```

Pointer Type Procedures

```
procedure New (RECORD_PTR: pointer variable);
{
DESCRIPTION:
    This procedure allocates memory dynamically and returns
    a pointer to the variable type it receives.

PARAMETERS:
    RECORD_PTR (out): a pointer to the variable type New is
                        creating the pointer to

SAMPLE CALL:
    New (STUDENT_PTR);

-----------------------------------------------------------}
```

```
procedure Mark (var HEAP_PTR: ^integer);
{
DESCRIPTION:
    This procedure aids in replacing allocated memory to the
    heap by assigning a heap pointer to the first free location
```

in the heap. Any dynamic variables created after Mark has
been invoked can be easily discarded by freeing all
of the memory locations above the address in HEAP_PTR.

PARAMETERS:
    HEAP_PTR (out): the location of the first free location in
                    the heap

SAMPLE CALL:
    Mark (HEAP_PTR);

---}

```
procedure Release (HEAP_PTR: ^integer);
{
DESCRIPTION:
    This procedure completes the replacement of allocated memory
    to the heap by returning all of the dynamic variables whose
    address is above HEAP_PTR in memory.

PARAMETERS:
    HEAP_PTR (in): a pointer to the heap, which is returned by
                   the routine Mark

SAMPLE CALL:
    Release (HEAP_PTR);
```

---}

```
procedure Dispose (RECORD_PTR: ^RECORD_TYPE);
{
DESCRIPTION:
    This routine returns allocated memory to the heap on
    a variable-by-variable basis as opposed to Mark/Release,
    which can manipulate large sections of the heap.

PARAMETERS:
    RECORD_PTR (in): a pointer to the variable type, which is
                     to be returned to the heap

SAMPLE CALL:
    Dispose (RECORD_PTR);
```

---}

```
procedure GetMem (BUFFER_PTR: pointer variable;
                  NUM_BYTES: integer);
```

```
{
DESCRIPTION:
    This routine allocates the number of bytes specified in
    the variable NUM_BYTES and assigns them to the memory
    location specified by BUFFER_PTR.

PARAMETERS:
    BUFFER_PTR (in): a pointer to the allocated memory
    NUM_BYTES (in): the number of bytes to allocate

SAMPLE CALL:
    GetMem (BUFFER_PTR, 256);

------------------------------------------------------------}
```

```
procedure FreeMem (BUFFER_PTR: pointer variable;
                   NUM_BYTES: integer);
{
DESCRIPTION:
    This routine returns the number of bytes specified in
    the variable NUM_BYTES to the heap.  FreeMem performs
    the opposite function of GetMem.  The memory locations
    pointed to by BUFFER_PTR are returned to the heap.

PARAMETERS:
    BUFFER_PTR (in): a pointer to the allocated memory
    NUM_BYTES (in): the number of bytes to release

SAMPLE CALL:
    FreeMem (BUFFER_PTR, 256);

------------------------------------------------------------}
```

```
function MaxAvail: integer;
{
DESCRIPTION:
    This function returns the size of the largest contiguous
    section of heap space.  For the IBM PC, and the PC
    compatibles, this value is in 16-byte paragraphs.

SAMPLE CALL:
    MaxAvail;

NOTES:
    If the value returned is negative, compute the correct
    number of paragraphs by 65536.0 - MaxAvail.

------------------------------------------------------------}
```

Standard Turbo Procedures

```
procedure ClrEol;
{
DESCRIPTION:
    This procedure clears all of the characters from the
    current cursor location to the end of the line.

SAMPLE CALL:
    ClrEol;

---------------------------------------------------------}
```

```
procedure ClrScr;
{
DESCRIPTION:
    This procedure clears the screen and places the cursor
    in the home position.

SAMPLE CALL:
    ClrScr;

---------------------------------------------------------}
```

```
procedure ClrInit;
{
DESCRIPTION:
    This procedure clears the screen and sends the initialization
    string defined in the terminal installation procedure
    to the screen.

SAMPLE CALL:
    ClrInit;

---------------------------------------------------------}
```

```
procedure ClrExit;
{
DESCRIPTION:
    This procedure clears the screen and sends the termination
    string defined in the terminal installation procedure
    to the screen.

SAMPLE CALL:
    ClrExit;

---------------------------------------------------------}
```

```
procedure Delay (TIME: integer);
{
DESCRIPTION:
    This routine delays for the number of milliseconds
    contained in the variable TIME.

PARAMETERS:
    TIME (in): the number of milliseconds to delay

SAMPLE CALL:
    Delay (2000);    (2-second delay)

----------------------------------------------------------}
```

```
procedure DelLine;
{
DESCRIPTION:
    This routine deletes the line containing the cursor
    and scrolls each line below that line up one.

SAMPLE CALL:
    DelLine;

----------------------------------------------------------}
```

```
procedure InsLine;
{
DESCRIPTION:
    This routine inserts a blank line at the current cursor
    position and scrolls each line below that line down one.

SAMPLE CALL:
    InsLine;

----------------------------------------------------------}
```

```
procedure GotoXY (COLUMN, LINE: integer);
{
DESCRIPTION:
    This routine places the cursor at the line and column
    specified.

PARAMETERS:
    COLUMN (in): the desired column location
    LINE (in): the desired line location

SAMPLE CALL:
    GotoXY (1, 25);    (bottom left corner)

----------------------------------------------------------}
```

```
procedure Exit;
{
DESCRIPTION:
    This routine exits the current block.  Within a program,
    the Exit routine terminates the program.  From a subroutine,
    the Exit routine returns control to the calling procedure.

SAMPLE CALL:
    if (CRITICAL_ERROR) then
        Exit;

-----------------------------------------------------------}
```

```
procedure Halt [(STATUS: integer)]
{
DESCRIPTION:
    This routine terminates a program and optionally returns
    a status value that can be tested by DOS or the calling
    process.

PARAMETERS:
    STATUS (out): the optional return status

SAMPLE CALL:
    if (CRITICAL_ERROR) then
        Halt(1);

NOTES:
    The status value can be examined in .BAT files with
    the ERRORLEVEL status.

-----------------------------------------------------------}
```

```
function KeyPressed: boolean;
{
DESCRIPTION:
    This function returns a boolean true if a key has been
    pressed, it returns false if not.

SAMPLE CALL:
    while (not KeyPressed) do ;

-----------------------------------------------------------}
```

```
procedure LowVideo;
{
DESCRIPTION:
    This procedure dims the video display.

SAMPLE CALL:
    LowVideo;

-----------------------------------------------------------}
```

```
procedure NormVideo;
{
DESCRIPTION:
    This procedure sets the video display to normal intensity.

SAMPLE CALL:
    NormVideo;

-----------------------------------------------------------}
```

```
procedure Randomize;
{
DESCRIPTION:
    This procedure initializes the random number generator
    for future calls to Random.

SAMPLE CALL:
    Randomize;

-----------------------------------------------------------}
```

```
procedure Move (VAR1, VAR2: any type;
                NUM_BYTES: integer)
{
DESCRIPTION:
    This procedure moves the number of bytes specified by
    NUM_BYTES starting with the first byte in VAR1 to VAR2.

PARAMETERS:
    VAR1 (in): contains the bytes to move
```

```
        VAR2 (out): destination of the move
        NUM_BYTES (in): the number of bytes to move

    SAMPLE CALL:
        Move (DATE, SAVE_DATE, Sizeof(DATE));

    ------------------------------------------------------------}
```

```
    procedure FillChar (TARGET_VAR: any type;
                        NUM_BYTES: integer;
                        FILL_VALUE: byte or char);
    {
    DESCRIPTION:
        This procedure fills the variable TARTGET_VAR with the
        FILL_VALUE based upon NUM_BYTES.

    PARAMETERS:
        TARGET_VAR (out): variable to be filled
        NUM_BYTES (in): the number of bytes to move
        FILL_VAR (in): value to be placed into TARGET_VAR

    SAMPLE CALL:
        FillChar (TAB_STRING, 10, ' ');

    ------------------------------------------------------------}
```

Mathematical Routines

```
    function Abs (EXPRESSION: integer or real): integer or real;
    {
    DESCRIPTION:
        This routine returns the absolute value of the value
        contained in EXPRESSION.

    PARAMETERS:
        EXPRESSION (in): the value to return the absolute value of

    SAMPLE CALL:
        X := Abs(X-Y);

    ------------------------------------------------------------}
```

```
function ArcTan (RADIANS: integer or real): real;
{
DESCRIPTION:
    This function returns the arctangent of the angle contained
    in RADIANS.

PARAMETERS:
    RADIANS (in): the angle to return the arctangent of

SAMPLE CALL:
    ARC := ArcTan (3.1415);

----------------------------------------------------------}
```

```
function Cos (RADIANS: integer or real): real;
{
DESCRIPTION:
    This function returns the cosine of the angle contained
    in RADIANS.

PARAMETERS:
    RADIANS (in): the angle to return the cosine of

SAMPLE CALL:
    Cosine := Cos (3.1415);

----------------------------------------------------------}
```

```
function Exp (VALUE: integer or real): real;
{
DESCRIPTION:
    This function returns the exponential of VALUE.

PARAMETERS:
    VALUE (in): the value to return the exponential of

SAMPLE CALL:
    RESULT := Exp (5.0);

----------------------------------------------------------}
```

```
function Frac (VALUE: integer or real): real;
{
DESCRIPTION:
    This function returns the fractional portion of a value (the
    values to the right of the decimal point).

PARAMETERS:
    VALUE (in): the value to return the fractional portion of

SAMPLE CALL:
    FRACTION := Frac (43.55);   (assigns FRACTION .55)

------------------------------------------------------------}
```

```
function Int (VALUE: integer or real): real;
{
DESCRIPTION:
    This function returns the integer portion of a value (the
    values to the left of the decimal point).

PARAMETERS:
    VALUE (in): the value to return the integer portion of

SAMPLE CALL:
    INT_PART := Int (43.55);   (assigns INT_PART 43)
```

```
function Ln (VALUE: integer or real): real;
{
DESCRIPTION:
    This function returns the natural logarithm of VALUE.

PARAMETERS:
    VALUE (in): the value to return the natural log of

SAMPLE CALL:
    LOG := Ln (5.6);

NOTES:
    If VALUE is less than 0, a run-time error occurs.

------------------------------------------------------------}
```

```
function Sin (RADIANS: integer or real): real;
{
DESCRIPTION:
    This function returns the sine of the angle contained
    in RADIANS.
```

```
PARAMETERS:
    RADIANS (in): the angle to return the sine of

SAMPLE CALL:
    SINE := Sin (3.1415);

---------------------------------------------------------}
```

```
function Sqr (VALUE: integer or real): real;
{
DESCRIPTION:
    This function returns the square of VALUE.

PARAMETERS:
    VALUE (in): the value to return the square of

SAMPLE CALL:
    RESULT := Sqr (5);   (assigns RESULT 25)

--------------------------------------------------------}
```

```
function Sqrt (VALUE: integer or real): real;
{
DESCRIPTION:
    This function returns the square root of VALUE.

PARAMETERS:
    VALUE (in): the value to return the square root of

SAMPLE CALL:
    ROOT := Sqrt (25);   (assigns ROOT 5)

--------------------------------------------------------}
```

```
function Pred (VALUE: scalar type): scalar type ;
{
DESCRIPTION:
    This function returns the predecessor of a scalar
    type.

PARAMETERS:
    VALUE (in): the value to return the predecessor of

SAMPLE CALL:
    PREV := Pred (25);      (assigns PREV 24)

-------------------------------------------------------}
```

```
function Succ (VALUE: scalar type): scalar type ;
{
DESCRIPTION:
    This function returns the successor of scalar type.

PARAMETERS:
    VALUE (in): the value to return the successor of

SAMPLE CALL:
    NEXT := Succ (25);      (assigns NEXT 26)

-----------------------------------------------------------}
```

```
function Odd (VALUE: integer): boolean;
{
DESCRIPTION:
    This function returns true if VALUE is odd; otherwise
    false if not.

PARAMETERS:
    VALUE (in): the value to examine for odd or even

SAMPLE CALL:
    if (Odd(VALUE)) then

----------------------------------------------------------}
```

Turbo Type-Conversion Functions

```
function Chr (VALUE: integer): char;
{
DESCRIPTION:
    This function returns the character with the ordinal
    value contained in VALUE.

PARAMETERS:
    VALUE (in): the value to convert to the type char

SAMPLE CALL:
    LTR := Chr (66);  (assigns LTR B)

----------------------------------------------------------}
```

```
function Ord (LETTER: char): integer;
{
DESCRIPTION:
    This function returns the ordinal value of LETTER.
```

```
PARAMETERS:
    LETTER (in): the character to return the ordinal value of

SAMPLE CALL:
    If (Ord(LETTER) = 13) then  (carriage return)

------------------------------------------------------------}
```

```
function Round (VALUE: real): integer;
{
DESCRIPTION:
    This function rounds the value contained in VALUE.

PARAMETERS:
    VALUE (in): the value to round

SAMPLE CALL:
    NEAREST_DOLLAR := Round (TAXES);

NOTES:
    0.5 or greater rounds up.

------------------------------------------------------------}
```

```
function Trunc (VALUE: integer): integer;
{
DESCRIPTION:
    This function truncates the value contained in VALUE.

PARAMETERS:
    VALUE (in): the value to truncate

SAMPLE CALL:
    LOWEST_DOLLAR := Trunc (TAXES);

------------------------------------------------------------}
```

Turbo Miscellaneous Functions

```
function Hi (VALUE: integer): integer;
{
DESCRIPTION:
    This function returns the high-order byte of VALUE.
```

```
PARAMETERS:
    VALUE (in): the value to return the high-order byte of

SAMPLE CALL:
    AH := Hi (regs.AX);

--------------------------------------------------------------}
```

```
function Lo (VALUE: integer): integer;
{
DESCRIPTION:
    This function returns the low-order byte of VALUE.

PARAMETERS:
    VALUE (in): the value to return the low-order byte of

SAMPLE CALL:
    AL := Lo (regs.AX);

--------------------------------------------------------------}
```

```
function Random: real;
{
DESCRIPTION:
    This function returns a random number that is greater
    than or equal to 0, and less than 1.

SAMPLE CALL:
    DATA := Random;

--------------------------------------------------------------}
```

```
function Random(LIMIT: integer): real;
{
DESCRIPTION:
    This function returns a random number that is greater
    than or equal to 0, and less than LIMIT.

PARAMETERS:
    LIMIT (in): upper limit of random number

SAMPLE CALL:
    DATA := Random(5);

--------------------------------------------------------------}
```

```
function ParamCount: integer;
{
DESCRIPTION:
    This function returns the number of parameters passed
    to the program in the command line.

SAMPLE CALL:
    for I := 1 to ParamCount do

-----------------------------------------------------------}
```

```
function ParamStr(INDEX: integer): string[1..255];
{
DESCRIPTION:
    This function returns the command-line argument indexed
    by INDEX.

PARAMETERS:
    INDEX (in): the index of the desired command-line buffer

SAMPLE CALL:
    for I := 1 to ParamCount do
      writeln (ParamStr(I));

-----------------------------------------------------------}
```

```
function Sizeof (OBJECT: any type): integer;
{
DESCRIPTION:
    This routine returns the number of bytes in the object
    provided.

PARAMETERS:
    OBJECT (in): the object to return the size (in bytes) of

SAMPLE CALL:
    NUM_BYTES := Sizeof (DATA_RECORD);

-----------------------------------------------------------}
```

```
function Swap (VALUE: integer): integer;
{
DESCRIPTION:
    This routine returns the result of VALUE after the high-order
    and low-order bytes are swapped.
```

```
PARAMETERS:
    VALUE (in): the value to swap the high-order and low-order
    bytes of

SAMPLE CALL:
    SWAPPED := Swap (regs.AX);

------------------------------------------------------------}
```

```
function Upcase (LETTER: char): char;
{
DESCRIPTION:
    This function returns the uppercase equivalent of LETTER
    if LETTER is a lowercase letter; otherwise, LETTER is
    unchanged if not.

PARAMETERS:
    LETTER (in): the letter to convert to uppercase

SAMPLE CALL:
    If (Upcase(LETTER) = 'Q') then

-----------------------------------------------------------}
```

IBM PC and PC Compatible Procedures

The following procedures are machine-dependent, and work only on the IBM PC and the PC compatibles.

Screen Mode Procedures

```
procedure  TextMode [(MODE: integer)];
{
DESCRIPTION:
    This procedure sets the screen to the mode specified.

PARAMETERS:
    MODE (in): the text mode desired

SAMPLE CALL:
    TextMode (C80);
    TextMode;
```

NOTES:
    The procedure uses 4 constants to determine the mode:
        BW40 - Black and white 40 column
        C40 - Color 40 column
        BW80 - Black and white 80 column
        C80 - Color 80 column

    If the optional mode is not specified, TextMode will
    clear the screen and resume the last active text mode.

    ---}

```
procedure  TextColor (COLOR: integer);
{
DESCRIPTION:
    This procedure sets the color of each character displayed
    in text mode.  The color is an integer value from 0 to 15.
    See the constants listed here.

PARAMETERS:
    COLOR (in): the desired text color

SAMPLE CALL:
    TextColor (Yellow);
    TextColor (Red);

NOTES:
    Turbo defines the following constants
    0 - Black        1 - Blue
    2 - Green        3 - Cyan
    4 - Red          5 - Magenta
    6 - Brown        7 - LightGray
    8 - DarkGray     9 - LightBlue
    10 - LightGreen  11 - LightCyan
    12 - LightRed    13 - LightMagenta
    14 - Yellow      15 - White

    In addition, Turbo defines an attribute called Blink.
    Here is the call for blinking red text:  TextColor (Red+Blink);

    -----------------------------------------------------------}
```

```
procedure  TextBackground (COLOR: integer);
{
DESCRIPTION:
    This procedure sets the background color of each character
    displayed in text mode.  The color is an integer value from
    0 to 8. See the constants listed below.

PARAMETERS:
    COLOR (in): the desired text background color
```

```
SAMPLE CALL:
    TextBackground (Blue);
    TextBackground (Red);

NOTES:
    Turbo defines the following constants
    0 - Black        1 - Blue
    2 - Green        3 - Cyan
    4 - Red          5 - Magenta
    6 - Brown        7 - LightGray

-----------------------------------------------------------}
```

Cursor Position Functions

```
function WhereX  ;
{
DESCRIPTION:
    This function returns the X-coordinate of the cursor.

SAMPLE CALL:
    XPOS := WhereX;

-----------------------------------------------------------}
```

```
function WhereY  ;
{
DESCRIPTION:
    This function returns the Y-coordinate of the cursor.

SAMPLE CALL:
    YPOS := WhereY;

-----------------------------------------------------------}
```

Graphics Mode Procedures

```
procedure GraphColorMode;
{
DESCRIPTION:
    This procedure places the screen into 320x200 pixel
    color graphics mode.

SAMPLE CALL:
    GraphColorMode;

-----------------------------------------------------------}
```

```
procedure GraphMode;
{
DESCRIPTION:
    This procedure places the screen into 320x200 pixel
    black-and-white graphics mode.

SAMPLE CALL:
    GraphMode;

------------------------------------------------------------}
```

```
procedure HiRes;
{
DESCRIPTION:
    This procedure places the screen into 640x200 pixel
    one-color high-resolution graphics mode.

SAMPLE CALL:
    HiRes;

-----------------------------------------------------------}
```

```
procedure HiResColor (COLOR: integer);
{
DESCRIPTION:
    This procedure sets the one available color in high
    resolution 640x200 pixel mode graphics.  See the
    constants below.

PARAMETERS:
    COLOR (in): the desired foreground color

SAMPLE CALL:
    HiResColor (BLUE);

NOTES:
    Turbo defines the following constants
     0 - Black         1 - Blue
     2 - Green         3 - Cyan
     4 - Red           5 - Magenta
     6 - Brown         7 - LightGray
     8 - DarkGray      9 - LightBlue
    10 - LightGreen   11 - LightCyan
    12 - LightRed     13 - LightMagenta
    14 - Yellow       15 - White

-----------------------------------------------------------}
```

```
procedure Palette (PALETTE_ID: integer);
{
DESCRIPTION:
    This procedure sets the palette for 320x200 pixel
    mode color graphics. See the description of palettes
    given here.
```

```
PARAMETERS:
    PALETTE_ID (in): the desired palette

SAMPLE CALL:
    Palette (1);

NOTES:
    There are 4 available palettes.  Each palette has 4
    possible colors:

    palette 0 - background   green          red            brown
    palette 1 - background   cyan           magenta        light gray
    palette 2 - background   light green    light red      yellow
    palette 3 - background   light cyan     light magenta  white

    After a palette is selected, the graphics routines will
    choose the desired color from the palette.

--------------------------------------------------------------}
```

```
procedure GraphBackground (COLOR: integer);
{
DESCRIPTION:
    This procedure sets the screen background color in
    320x200 color graphics mode.  See the constants
    listed here.

PARAMETERS:
    COLOR (in): the desired background color

SAMPLE CALL:
    GraphBackground (BLUE);

    Turbo defines the following constants
     0 - Black        1 - Blue
     2 - Green        3 - Cyan
     4 - Red          5 - Magenta
     6 - Brown        7 - LightGray
     8 - DarkGray     9 - LightBlue
    10 - LightGreen  11 - LightCyan
    12 - LightRed    13 - LightMagenta
    14 - Yellow      15 - White

--------------------------------------------------------------}
```

Window Procedures

```
procedure Window (LCOL, UROW, RCOL, LROW: integer);
{
DESCRIPTION:
    This procedure creates a window in text mode with the
    coordinates specified.
```

```
PARAMETERS:
    LCOL (in): the leftmost column of the window
    UROW (in): the top line of the window
    RCOL (in): the rightmost column of the window
    LROW (in): the bottom line of the window

SAMPLE CALL:
    Window (10, 5, 70, 20);

---------------------------------------------------------------}
```

```
procedure GraphWindow (X1, Y1, X2, Y2: integer);
{
DESCRIPTION:
    This procedure creates a window in graphics mode with the
    coordinates specified.

PARAMETERS:
    X1 (in): the leftmost column of the window (pixel coordinates)
    Y1 (in): the upper row of the window (pixel coordinates)
    X2 (in): the rightmost column of the window (pixel coordinates)
    Y2 (in): the lower row of the window (pixel coordinates)

SAMPLE CALL:
    GraphWindow (100, 50, 300, 250);

NOTES:
    In low-resolution graphics, the pixel coordinates are
    0 to 319 x 0 to 199.
    In high-resolution graphics, the pixel coordinates are
    0 to 639 x 0 to 199.

---------------------------------------------------------------}
```

Overlay Procedure

```
procedure OvrPath (PATH: string [1..255]);
{
DESCRIPTION:
    This procedure specifies the path to the overlay files.
    If the .COM file does not reside in the same subdirectory
    as the overlay files, OvrPath specifies the path to be
    used to obtain the overlays.

PARAMETERS:
    PATH (in): the DOS path to the overlay subdirectory
SAMPLE CALL:
    OvrPath ('\TURBO\OVR');

---------------------------------------------------------------}
```

DOS File Procedures

```
function LongFileSize (FILE_VAR: file of record): real;
{
DESCRIPTION:
    This function returns the number of records in a file.

PARAMETERS:
    FILE_VAR (in): the file variable returned by Assign, which
                    references the file to manipulate

SAMPLE CALL:
    NUM_RECORDS := LongFileSize (FP);

NOTES:
    The value returned is type real to support files of
    more than 32,767 records.

-------------------------------------------------------------}
```

```
function LongFilePosition (FILE_VAR: file of record): real;
{
DESCRIPTION:
    This function returns the current position of the file pointer
    (record number) within a file.

PARAMETERS:
    FILE_VAR: the file variable returned by Assign, which
              references the file to manipulate

SAMPLE CALL:
    CURRENT_POS := LongFilePosition (FP);

NOTES:
    The value returned is type real to support files of
    more than 32,767 records.

-------------------------------------------------------------}
```

```
procedure LongSeek (FILE_VAR: file of record;
               RECORD_NUMBER: integer;);
{
DESCRIPTION:
    This procedure moves the file pointer to the record
    number specified.
```

```
PARAMETERS:
    FILE_VAR (in): the file variable returned by Assign, which
                   references the file to manipulate
    RECORD_NUMBER (in): the record number desired

SAMPLE CALL:
    LongSeek (FP, 43000.0);

NOTES:
    The record number is type real to support files of
    more than 32,767 records.

------------------------------------------------------------}
```

```
procedure Truncate (FILE_VAR: file of record);
{
DESCRIPTION:
    This procedure truncates a file from the current file
    pointer position to the end of the file.

PARAMETERS:
    FILE_VAR (in): the file variable returned by Assign, which
                   references the file to manipulate

SAMPLE CALL:
    Truncate (FP);

------------------------------------------------------------}
```

```
procedure Append (FILE_VAR: file of record);
{
DESCRIPTION:
    This procedure opens a file in append mode.  If the file
    already exists, the file pointer is advanced to the end
    of the file.

PARAMETERS:
    FILE_VAR (in): the file variable returned by Assign, which
                   references the file to manipulate

SAMPLE CALL:
    Append (FP);

------------------------------------------------------------}
```

Absolute Address Functions

The functions in this section apply to those machines that use the 8086 or the 8088 family of processors.

```
function Addr (VARIABLE: any type): MEM_PTR;
{
DESCRIPTION:
    This function returns a 32-bit pointer to the first byte
    in memory that contain the variable specified.

PARAMETERS:
    VARIABLE (in): the variable to return the address of

SAMPLE CALL:
    MY_PTR := Addr (NAME_STRING);

------------------------------------------------------------}
```

```
function Ofs (VARIABLE: any type): integer;
{
DESCRIPTION:
    This function returns the offset address of the variable
    specified within the segment of memory that contains
    the variable.

PARAMETERS:
    VARIABLE (in): the variable to return the offset
                   address of

SAMPLE CALL:
    OFS_PTR := Ofs (NAME_STRING);

------------------------------------------------------------}
```

```
function Seg (VARIABLE: any type): integer;
{
DESCRIPTION:
    This function returns the segment address of the variable
    specified.

PARAMETERS:
    VARIABLE (in): the variable to return the segment
                   address of

SAMPLE CALL:
    SEG_PTR := Seg (NAME_STRING);

------------------------------------------------------------}
```

```
function Cseg: integer;
{
DESCRIPTION:
    This function returns the base address of the code
    segment.

SAMPLE CALL:
    writeln ('The program begins at ', Cseg);

------------------------------------------------------------}
```

```
function Dseg: integer;
{
DESCRIPTION:
    This function returns the base address of the data
    segment.

SAMPLE CALL:
    writeln ('The data segment begins at ', Dseg);

------------------------------------------------------------}
```

```
function Sseg: integer;
{
DESCRIPTION:
    This function returns the base address of the stack
    segment.

SAMPLE CALL:
    writeln ('The stack segment begins at ', Sseg);

------------------------------------------------------------}
```

DOS and ROM-BIOS Procedures

```
procedure MsDos (REGISTERS: record AX, BX, CX, DX, BP, SI,
                         DI, DS, ES, FLAGS: integer);
{
DESCRIPTION:
    This procedure provides an interface to the DOS services
    available through interrupt 21H.

PARAMETERS:
    REGISTERS (in): a record that represents the 8088 registers

SAMPLE CALL:
    MsDos(REGISTERS);

------------------------------------------------------------}
```

```
procedure Intr (INTERRUPT: integer;
                REGISTERS: register AX, BX, CX, DX, BP, SI,
                           DI, DS, ES, FLAGS: integer);
{
DESCRIPTION:
    This procedure provides an interface to the ROM-BIOS
    services.

PARAMETERS:
    INTERRUPT (in): the desired ROM-BIOS interrupt number
    REGISTERS (in): a record that represents the 8088 registers

SAMPLE CALL:
    Intr(10, REGISTERS);

-------------------------------------------------------------}
```

Chain and Execute Procedures

```
procedure Chain (FILE_VAR: file);
{
DESCRIPTION:
    This procedure allows a Turbo program to execute a
    .CHN file that has been compiled with the chn-file
    compiler option.

PARAMETERS:
    FILE_VAR (in): the file variable returned by Assign, which
                   references the file to manipulate

SAMPLE CALL:
    Chain (FP);
```

```
procedure Execute (FILE_VAR: file);
{
DESCRIPTION:
    This procedure allows a Turbo program to execute a TURBO
    .COM file.

PARAMETERS:
    FILE_VAR (in): the file variable returned by Assign, which
                   references the file to manipulate

SAMPLE CALL:
    Execute (FP);

-------------------------------------------------------------}
```

Basic Graphics Procedures

```
procedure Plot (XPOS, YPOS, COLOR: integer);
{
DESCRIPTION:
    This procedure plots a point at X- and Y-coordinates
    specified.  The color is selected from the current
    palette.

PARAMETERS:
    XPOS (in): the X-coordinate
    YPOS (in): the Y-coordinate
    COLOR (in): the desired pixel color

SAMPLE CALL:
    Plot (100, 150, 3);

NOTES:
    See the routine Palette for pixel colors.
    If -1 is specified for the color, the color
    translation table (see ColorTable) is used
    to select the color.

    ---------------------------------------------------------}
```

```
procedure Draw (X1, Y1, X2, Y2, COLOR: integer);
{
DESCRIPTION:
    This procedure draws a line from X1,Y1 to X2,Y2 in the
    color specified.

PARAMETERS:
    X1 (in): the starting X-coordinate of the line
    Y1 (in): the starting Y-coordinate of the line
    X2 (in): the ending X-coordinate of the line
    Y2 (in): the ending Y-coordinate of the line
    COLOR (in): the desired line color

SAMPLE CALL:
    Line (100, 150, 200, 150, 3);

NOTES:
    See the routine Palette for pixel colors.
    If -1 is specified for the color, the color
    translation table (see ColorTable) is used
    to select the color.

    ---------------------------------------------------------}
```

Extended Graphics Procedures

```
procedure ColorTable (CLR1, CLR2, CLR3, CLR4: integer);
{
DESCRIPTION:
    This procedure supplements Palette by defining a color
    translation table.  The table is useful in animation
    or similar applications.  Before the graphics routines
    draw a pixel, they examine the current color of the pixel
    on the screen.  The current color is then mapped (via
    the color translation table) to a new color.  For example,

        ColorTable (0, 1, 2, 3)

    is the default color translation table.  If a pixel is
    currently color 0, the table says draw it in color 0.
    If instead, the table is

        ColorTable (3, 1, 2, 3);

    A pixel that is currently color 0 will be drawn in
    color 3.

PARAMETERS:
    C1..C4 (in): the color table entries

SAMPLE CALL:
    ColorTable (3, 2, 1, 0);    (reverse colors of all pixels)

NOTES:
    The routine PutPic uses the color translation table.
    If the other graphics routines specify -1 in the
    color argument, the color translation table is used
    in place of the palette.

------------------------------------------------------------}
```

```
procedure Arc (XPOS, YPOS, DEGREES, RADIUS, COLOR: integer);
{
DESCRIPTION:
    This procedure draws an arc starting at XPOS, YPOS
    with the degrees and radius specified.

PARAMETERS:
    XPOS (in): the starting X-coordinate position
    YPOS (in): the starting Y-coordinate position
    DEGREES (in): the number of degrees in the arc
    RADIUS (in): the radius of the arc
    COLOR (in): the color of the arc

SAMPLE CALL:
    Arc (50, 50, 360, 20, -1); (draws a circle with a radius of
                                10 pixels.  The color is from
                                the color translation table)

------------------------------------------------------------}
```

```
procedure Circle (XPOS, YPOS, RADIUS, COLOR: integer);
{
DESCRIPTION:
    This procedure draws a circle whose center is at XPOS,YPOS
    with the radius specified.

PARAMETERS:
    XPOS, YPOS (in): the center of the circle in pixel coordinates
    RADIUS (in): the radius of the circle
    COLOR (in): the color of the circle

SAMPLE CALL:
    Circle (100, 100, 100, 3);

--------------------------------------------------------------}
```

```
procedure GetPic (var PIXEL_BUFFER: array of integer;
                  X1, Y1, X2, Y2: integer);
{
DESCRIPTION:
    This procedure copies a rectangular portion of the
    screen into PIXEL_BUFFER.  This procedure is used
    with PutPic to achieve animation.

PARAMETERS:
    PIXEL_BUFFER (out): the buffer to place the screen image into
    X1,Y1 (in): the upper-left coordinates of the rectangle
    X2,Y2 (in): the lower-right coordinates of the rectangle

SAMPLE CALL:
    GetPic (PIXEL_BUFFER, 10, 10, 100, 100);

NOTES:
    The routine places header information at the
    beginning of PIXEL_BUFFER which is used by
    PutPic.  Adequate space for this information is
    guaranteed by using the following equations to
    determine the buffer size:

    320x200 mode graphics

   BUFFER_SIZE := (((X2-X1) + 3) div 4) * (Y2-Y1) * 2 + 6

    640x200 mode graphics

   BUFFER_SIZE := (((X2-X1) + 7) div 8) * (Y2-Y1) + 6

--------------------------------------------------------------}
```

```
procedure PutPic (PIXEL_BUFFER: array of integer;
                  XPOS, YPOS: integer);
```

```
{
DESCRIPTION:
    This procedure places a rectangular image to the
    screen.  The image is created by GetPic. This procedure
    is used with GetPic to achieve animation.

PARAMETERS:
    PIXEL_BUFFER (in): the buffer to place on the screen
    XPOS,YPOS (in): the upper-left coordinates of the rectangle

SAMPLE CALL:
    PutPic (PIXEL_BUFFER, 10, 20);

------------------------------------------------------------}
```

```
function GetDotColor (XPOS, YPOS: integer): integer;
{
DESCRIPTION:
    This function returns the pixel color at XPOS, YPOS.
    In 320x200 graphics mode the color can range from 0 to 3.
    In 640x200 graphics mode the color ranges from 0 to 1.  If
    XPOS,YPOS is out of the window coordinates, -1 is returned.

PARAMETERS:
    XPOS,YPOS (in): the coordinates of the pixel of interest

SAMPLE CALL:
    PIX_COLOR := GetDotColor (10, 20);

------------------------------------------------------------}
```

```
procedure FillScreen (COLOR: integer);
{
DESCRIPTION:
    This procedure fills the active window with the color
    specified.  In 320x200 graphics mode, the color can be
    0 to 3.  If -1 is specified, the color translation
    table is used.

PARAMETERS:
    COLOR (in): the desired window color

SAMPLE CALL:
    FillScreen (-1);

------------------------------------------------------------}
```

```
procedure FillShape (XPOS, YPOS, BORDER_COLOR, COLOR: integer);
{
DESCRIPTION:
    This procedure fills a shape enclosed by BORDER_COLOR
    with the color specified.  The coordinates XPOS, YPOS
    must be inside the region to be filled.

PARAMETERS:
    XPOS,YPOS (in): coordinates within the image to fill
    BORDER_COLOR (in): the color of the border that surrounds
                        the image to fill
    COLOR (in): the desired window color

SAMPLE CALL:
    FillShape (10, 20, 3, 2);

NOTES:
    FillShape does not support the color translation table.

-----------------------------------------------------------}
```

```
procedure FillPattern (X1, Y1, X2, Y2, COLOR: integer);
{
DESCRIPTION:
    This procedure fills a rectangular area with the active
    pattern specified by the routine Pattern.

PARAMETERS:
    X1,Y1 (in): the upper-left coordinates of the region to fill
    X2,Y2 (in): the lower-right coordinates of the region to fill
    COLOR (in): the desired color of the pattern

SAMPLE CALL:
    FillPattern (10, 20, 100, 200, 3);

-----------------------------------------------------------}
```

```
procedure Pattern (FILL_PATTERN: array [0..7] of byte);
{
DESCRIPTION:
    This procedure defines the fill pattern to be used by
    the routine FillPattern.

PARAMETERS:
    FILL_PATTERN: the array containing the pattern to display

SAMPLE CALL:
    Pattern (FILL_PATTERN);

-----------------------------------------------------------}
```

Sound Procedures

```
procedure Sound (FREQUENCY: integer);
{
DESCRIPTION:
    This procedure uses the PC's speaker to produce a sound
    with the frequency specified until the routine NoSound
    is invoked.

PARAMETERS:
    FREQUENCY (in): the frequency of the sound to produce

SAMPLE CALL:
    Sound (800);

----------------------------------------------------------}
```

```
procedure NoSound;
{
DESCRIPTION:
    This procedure turns off the PC's speaker.

SAMPLE CALL:
    NoSound;

----------------------------------------------------------}
```

Directory-Related Routines

```
procedure ChDir (DIRECTORY: string [1..255]);
{
DESCRIPTION:
    This procedure changes the default directory as specified.

PARAMETERS:
    DIRECTORY (in): the desired default directory

SAMPLE CALL:
    ChDir ('TURBO');

----------------------------------------------------------}
```

```
procedure MkDir (DIRECTORY: string [1..255]);
{
DESCRIPTION:
    This procedure makes the directory specified.

PARAMETERS:
    DIRECTORY (in): the directory to made

SAMPLE CALL:
    Mkdir ('RLH');

---------------------------------------------------------}
```

```
procedure RmDir (DIRECTORY: string [1..255]);
{
DESCRIPTION:
    This procedure removes the directory specified.

PARAMETERS:
    DIRECTORY (in): the directory to remove

SAMPLE CALL:
    Rmdir ('FORTRAN');

---------------------------------------------------------}
```

```
procedure GetDir (DRIVE: integer;
          var DIRECTORY: string [1..255]);
{
DESCRIPTION:
    This procedure returns the current directory in the drive
    specified.  The global variable IOstatus is set if an
    error occurs.

PARAMETERS:
    DRIVE (in): the disk drive to return the directory for
    DIRECTORY (out): the current directory

SAMPLE CALL:
    GetDir (1, DIRECTORY);

NOTES:
    Drives are specified as 0 = default
                            1 = A
                            2 = B
                            3 = C

---------------------------------------------------------}
```

A P P E N D I X

B

ASCII Codes

Table B-1 lists the ASCII codes for characters.

Table B-1. ASCII Character Codes

DEC	OCTAL	HEX	ASCII	DEC	OCTAL	HEX	ASCII
0	000	00	NUL	10	012	0A	LF
1	001	01	SOH	11	013	0B	VT
2	002	02	STX	12	014	0C	FF
3	003	03	ETX	13	015	0D	CR
4	004	04	EOT	14	016	0E	SO
5	005	05	ENQ	15	017	0F	SI
6	006	06	ACK	16	020	10	DLE
7	007	07	BEL	17	021	11	DC1
8	010	08	BS	18	022	12	DC2
9	011	09	HT	19	023	13	DC3

Table B-1. ASCII Character Codes (*continued*)

DEC	OCTAL	HEX	ASCII	DEC	OCTAL	HEX	ASCII
20	024	14	DC4	64	100	40	@
21	025	15	NAK	65	101	41	A
22	026	16	SYN	66	102	42	B
23	027	17	ETB	67	103	43	C
24	030	18	CAN	68	104	44	D
25	031	19	EM	69	105	45	E
26	032	1A	SUB	70	106	46	F
27	033	1B	ESC	71	107	47	G
28	034	1C	FS	72	110	48	H
29	035	1D	GS	73	111	49	I
30	036	1E	RS	74	112	4A	J
31	037	1F	US	75	113	4B	K
32	040	20	SPACE	76	114	4C	L
33	041	21	!	77	115	4D	M
34	042	22	"	78	116	4E	N
35	043	23	#	79	117	4F	O
36	044	24	$	80	120	50	P
37	045	25	%	81	121	51	Q
38	046	26	&	82	122	52	R
39	047	27	'	83	123	53	S
40	050	28	(	84	124	54	T
41	051	29	)	85	125	55	U
42	052	2A	*	86	126	56	V
43	053	2B	+	87	127	57	W
44	054	2C	,	88	130	58	X
45	055	2D	—	89	131	59	Y
46	056	2E	.	90	132	5A	Z
47	057	2F	/	91	133	5B	[
48	060	30	0	92	134	5C	\
49	061	31	1	93	135	5D	]
50	062	32	2	94	136	5E	^
51	063	33	3	95	137	5F	—
52	064	34	4	96	140	60	`
53	065	35	5	97	141	61	a
54	066	36	6	98	142	62	b
55	067	37	7	99	143	63	c
56	070	38	8	100	144	64	d
57	071	39	9	101	145	65	e
58	072	3A	:	102	146	66	f
59	073	3B	;	103	147	67	g
60	074	3C	<	104	150	68	h
61	075	3D	=	105	151	69	i
62	076	3E	>	106	152	6A	j
63	077	3F	?	107	153	6B	k

Table B-1. ASCII Character Codes (*continued*)

DEC	OCTAL	HEX	ASCII		DEC	OCTAL	HEX	ASCII
108	154	6C	l		118	166	76	v
109	155	6D	m		119	167	77	w
110	156	6E	n		120	170	78	x
111	157	6F	o		121	171	79	y
112	160	70	p		122	172	7A	z
113	161	71	q		123	173	7B	{
114	162	72	r		124	174	7C	|
115	163	73	s		125	175	7D	}
116	164	74	t		126	176	7E	~
117	165	75	u		127	177	7F	DEL

Bibliography

Davies, Russ. *Computes! Mapping the IBM PC and PCjr*. Greensboro, N.C.: Compute Publications, 1985.

Horowitz, Ellis, and Sartaj Sahni. *Fundamentals of Data Structures in Pascal*. Rockville, Md.: Computer Science Press, 1984.

Jamsa, Kris. *The C Library*. Berkeley, Calif.: Osborne/McGraw-Hill, 1985.

King, Richard Allen. *The IBM PC-DOS Handbook*. Berkeley, Calif.: SYBEX, Inc., 1983.

Koffman, Elliot B. *Pascal: A Problem Solving Approach*. Philippines: Addison-Wesley Publishing Co., 1982.

Norton, Peter. *Programmer's Guide to the IBM PC*. Bellevue, Wash.: Microsoft Press, 1985.

Purdum, Jack, et al. *C Programmer's Library*. Indianapolis, Ind.: Que Corp., 1984.

Turbo Graphix Toolbox Reference Manual. Scotts Valley, Calif.: Borland International, 1985.

Turbo Pascal Reference Manual. Scotts Valley, Calif.: Borland International, 1985.

Turbo Toolbox Reference Manual. Scotts Valley, Calif.: Borland International, 1985.

Wirth, Niklaus. *Algorithms + Data Structures = Programs*. Englewood Cliffs, N.J.: Prentice-Hall, 1976.

Trademarks

IBM®	International Business Machines, Inc.
MS-DOS®	Microsoft Corporation
Turbo Pascal®	Borland International, Inc.
Turbo Graphix Toolbox™	Borland International, Inc.
UNIX™	AT&T Bell Laboratories

Additional trademarks, pages 497-500:

Apple®	Apple Computer, Inc.
COMPAQ®	Compaq Computer Corporation
Lotus®	Lotus Development Corporation
Macintosh™	Macintosh is a trademark of McIntosh Laboratory, Inc., and is used with express permission of its owner
MBASIC®	Microsoft Corporation
Microsoft™	Microsoft Corporation
1-2-3®	Lotus Development Corporation
Tandy 6000®	Radio Shack, a division of Tandy Corporation
WordStar®	MicroPro
Z80®	Zilog

Index

Other related Osborne/McGraw-Hill titles include:

Using Turbo Pascal™
by Steve Wood

Maximize your advanced programming skills with *Using Turbo Pascal™* by Steve Wood. Wood, a programmer for Precision Logic Systems, thoroughly covers Turbo Pascal, including version 3.0, for the experienced programmer. The book discusses program design and Pascal's syntax requirements, develops a useful application of the program, and gives an overview of some of the advanced utilities and features available with Turbo Pascal.

$19.95p
0-07-881148-1, 350 pp., 6½ x 9¼

Advanced Turbo Pascal®: Programming & Techniques
by Herbert Schildt

For instruction and reference, *Advanced Turbo Pascal®* is an invaluable resource. This guide benefits experienced Turbo Pascal® users who want to build their programming skills. Every stand-alone chapter presents a complete programming topic: sorting and searching; stacks, queues, linked lists, and binary trees; dynamic allocation using pointers; and operating-system interfacing. You'll also examine statistics, encryption and compressed data formats, random numbers and simulations, expression parsers, converting C and BASIC to Pascal, efficiency, porting and debugging.

$18.95p
0-07-881220-8, 350 pp., 7⅜ x 9¼

Advanced Pascal Programming Techniques
by Paul A. Sand

"...this is an excellent book....If you're interested in doing a good job as a systems analyst or programmer, you owe it to yourself to read this book, whether you're interested in Pascal or not. And I'm not just talking to beginners; there's a lot in this book for computer workers at all levels."
(Microcomputing)

$21.95p
0-07-881105-8, 350 pp., 6½ x 9¼

The First Book of Macintosh™ Pascal
by Paul A. Sand

This discussion of Macintosh™ Pascal fundamentals shows you how to write Pascal programs that utilize the special capabilities of the Macintosh. Through the use of hands-on exercises and numerous examples, you'll write and edit your own useful programs. Build your programming skills as you learn about variables and loops, library functions and procedures, data types, arrays, records, sets, and more. Sand's coverage of debugging techniques is especially helpful and provides you with tools you'll need throughout your programming career. For a solid foundation in the essentials of Macintosh Pascal, *The First Book* is the best book.

$17.95p
0-07-881165-1, 272 pp., 7⅜ x 9¼

Modula-2 Made Easy
by Herbert Schildt

Herbert Schildt, author of *C Made Easy,* has written a new "Made Easy" tutorial on the Modula-2 programming language. Modula-2's modular structure allows teams of programmers to write segments that can be easily linked together. In many ways, Modula-2 is more suited to today's competitive programming environment than are C and Pascal. With *Modula-2 Made Easy,* beginning programmers can quickly learn Modula-2 techniques through step-by-step, hands-on exercises. Start with the fundamentals—basic structure, variables, constants, and program control statements—and you'll soon be handling more advanced procedures—pointers, arrays, modules, and co-routines. By the time you finish *Modula-2 Made Easy,* you'll be writing and debugging effective, full-scale applications programs.

$18.95p
0-07-881241-0, 375 pp., 7⅜ x 9¼

C Made Easy
by Herbert Schildt

With Osborne/McGraw-Hill's popular "Made Easy" format, you can learn C programming in no time. Start with the fundamentals and work through the text at your own speed. Schildt begins with general concepts, then introduces functions, libraries, and disk input/output, and finally advanced concepts affecting the C programming environment and UNIX™ operating system. Each chapter covers commands that you can learn to use immediately in the hands-on exercises that follow. If you already know BASIC, you'll find that Schildt's C equivalents will shorten your learning time. *C Made Easy* is a step-by-step tutorial for all beginning C programmers.

$18.95p
0-07-881178-3, 350 pp., 7³/₈ x 9¹/₄

Advanced C
by Herbert Schildt

Herbert Schildt, author of *C Made Easy*, now shows experienced C programmers how to develop advanced skills. You'll find thorough coverage of important C programming topics including operating system interfacing, compressed data formats, dynamic allocation, linked lists, binary trees, and porting. Schildt also discusses sorting and searching, stacks, queues, encryption, simulations, debugging techniques, and converting Pascal and BASIC programs for use with C. A complete handbook, *Advanced C* is both a teaching guide and a lasting resource.

$19.95p
0-07-881208-9, 350 pp., 7³/₈ x 9¹/₄

The C Library
by Kris Jamsa

Design and implement more effective programs with the wealth of programming tools that are offered in *The C Library*. Experienced C programmers will find over 125 carefully structured routines ranging from macros to actual UNIX™ utilities. There are tools for string manipulation, pointers, input/output, array manipulation, recursion, sorting algorithms, and file manipulation. In addition, Jamsa provides several C routines that have previously been available only through expensive software packages. Build your skills by taking routines introduced in early chapters and using them to develop advanced programs covered later in the text.

$18.95p
0-07-881110-4, 220 pp., 7³/₈ x 9¹/₄

Z80® Assembly Language Subroutines
by Lance A. Leventhal and Winthrop Saville

An overview of assembly language programming for the Z80® this book provides over 50 useful subroutines which will save you valuable programming time. It includes array, bit and string manipulation, code conversion, arithmetic operations, sorting and searching techniques, and much more. All routines have been thoroughly tested and debugged.

$19.95p
0-07-931091-5, 497 pp., 7³/₈ x 9¹/₄

Available at fine bookstores and computer stores everywhere.

For a complimentary catalog of all our current publications contact: Osborne/McGraw-Hill, 2600 Tenth Street, Berkeley, CA 94710

Phone inquiries may be made using our toll-free number. Call 800-227-0900 or 800-772-2531 (in California). TWX 910-366-7277.

Prices subject to change without notice.